Clay Clemens

Reluctant Realists

The Christian Democrats and
West German Ostpolitik

Duke University Press
Durham and London   1989

© 1989 Duke University Press
All rights reserved
Printed in the United States of America
on acid-free paper ∞
Library of Congress Cataloging-in-Publication Data
Clemens, Clay, 1958–
Reluctant realists: the CDU/CSU and West German Ostpolitik,
1969–1982 / by Clay Clemens.
p.   cm.
Bibliography: p.
Includes index.
ISBN 0-8223-0900-9
1. Europe, Eastern—Foreign relations—Germany (West) 2. Germany
(West)—Foreign relations—Europe, Eastern. 3. Christlich-
Demokratische Union Deutschlands (Germany: West) 4. Christlich-
Soziale Union.   I. Title.
DJK45.G3C58 1989
327.47043—dc19   88-29340

To my Mother and Father

Contents

Abbreviations   vii
Foreword by William E. Griffith   ix
Acknowledgments   xi
Introduction   1

Part I The Origins of CDU/CSU Foreign Policy
1 Union Ostpolitik from Adenauer to the Grand Coalition   13

Part II Debate over the Eastern Treaties
2 The Initial Agreements, 1969–1971   55
3 From the Ratification Debates to Karlsruhe, 1972–1973   89

Part III Beyond the Eastern Treaties
4 Interpolation: Beyond the Eastern Treaties   127
5 Finding the Limits of Ostpolitik, 1973–1976   145
6 The Changing Ostpolitik Debate, 1977–1979   172
7 Crisis and Consensus, 1980–1982   193

Part IV Conclusion
8 The Union's Ambivalent Adaptation   235
Postscript: The Union in Government, 1982–1988   277

Appendix: CDU/CSU Leadership Factions on
Ostpolitik Party and Government Positions,
1969–1982   315
Notes   320
Selected Bibliography   345
Index   356

Abbreviations

CDU	Christian Democratic Union
CMEA	Council on Mutual Economic Assistance (Soviet bloc)
CoCom	Coordinating Committee for Multilateral Export Controls
CSCE	Conference on Security and Cooperation in Europe
CSU	Christian Social Union
DGB	German Trade Union Federation
EAK	Evangelical Working Circle (CDU Protestants)
EC	European Community
ERW	Enhanced Radiation (Neutron) Weapons
FDP	Free Democratic Party
FRG	Federal Republic of Germany
GDR	German Democratic Republic
INF	Intermediate-Range Nuclear Forces
JU	Young Union (CDU/CSU youth group)
Jusos	Young Socialists (SPD youth group)
MBFR	Mutual and Balanced Force Reductions
NPD	National Democratic Party of Germany
NPT	Nuclear Non-Proliferation Treaty
SALT	Strategic Arms Limitation Talks
SED	Socialist Unity Party (East German Communist party)
SPD	Social Democratic Party of Germany
UN	United Nations

Foreword

That "the German question" is with us again is a realization which, however promising or painful, is likely to become more, not less, the case. Objective analysis has never distinguished most studies on this subject; passion, prejudice, and propaganda have bedeviled them. Moreover, there have been more studies in English on the West German left, which has been in opposition for the greater part of the Federal Republic's history, than on the Christian Democrats, now again the principal governing party.

Therefore many Western observers were surprised by the continuity in West German policy toward the East when Helmut Kohl replaced Helmut Schmidt as chancellor in 1982. Professor Clemen's book provides us with the first, most objective, authoritative, and complete analysis of how, when, and through whom and what influences the CDU shifted from its opposition to the Social Democrats' eastern policy in the early 1970s to its continuation, in fact, in the 1980s.

Clemens carefully balances the domestic and international factors which explain how the CDU gradually learned to live with, and even love, what it had once so denounced. He thus demonstrates clearly that the CDU has proved itself ready to deal effectively with East Berlin on these issues, to downplay but not to abandon its aim of German reunification, and, until now, its persistent, albeit waning, refusal to link eastern policy with security issues.

This may now be changing. If it does, how far it might and what the consequences might be, especially for American policy, are issues that make this book required reading for anyone who wants to understand the present and future policies of the most important, and militarily, economically, and technologically the most powerful, ally of the United States in Europe.

William E. Griffith
Ford Professor of Political Science
Massachusetts Institute of Technology

Acknowledgments

The assistance of many different organizations and individuals made this project possible. I would like to thank the German Academic Exchange Service, which provided me with a grant to cover the costs of my year in Germany (1983–84). In addition, I would like to acknowledge the Fletcher School International Security Studies Program, which provided me with supplemental assistance for my research.

My gratitude also goes to the German Society for Foreign Affairs in Bonn for making its extensive research facilities available to me. The kind, helpful, and infinitely patient employees of the Dokumentationsstelle were invaluable in the research stage of this project.

Several other organizations made their facilities and/or resources available: the Gesamtdeutsches Institut (Bonn), the Konrad Adenauer Stiftung (Bonn), the Bundespresse- und Informationsamt (Bonn), the Rheinische-Friedrich-Wilhelms-Universität (Bonn), the Exil-CDU (Berlin), the Stiftung Wissenschaft und Politik (Ebenhausen), the CSU (Munich), the Institute for Foreign Policy Analysis (Cambridge and Washington), and the Government Department of the College of William and Mary.

Much of the background material for this study was gained from interviews in 1984 with several dozen West German government officials, party politicians, journalists, and academics, all of whom generously made time to aid the research effort of an American doctoral student. They include Burckhard Dobiey, Siegfried Kupper, Eduard Lintner, Hans Klein, Günther Hindrichs, Dieter Schmidt, Reinhardt Rummel, Christoph Royen, Bernard von Plate, Hans-Jürgen Kaack, Wilfried Rupprecht, Elizabeth Pond, Arnulf Baring, Manfred Görtemaker, Friedbert Pflüger, Harald Rüddenklau, Werner Kaltefleiter, Michael Naumann, Hans Merkel, Olaf von Wrangel, Hans Joachim Veen, Norbert Schäfer, Günther Schmid, Hans-Adolf Jacobsen, Wolfgang Dexheimer, Herbert Hupka, Walther Leisler Kiep, Werner Marx, Alois Mertes, Kurt Sontheimer, Wolf Schönbohm, Karl-Heinz Niclauss, Hans Graf Huyn, Dettmar Cramer, Hans-Peter Schwarz, Wolfgang Bergsdorf, and Wolfgang Pfeiler.

In subsequent years I was able to hear the views of a number of German politicians, government officials, and academics, thanks to the German-American Travelling Workshop, organized by Wolfgang-Uwe Friedrich of the Hochschule Hildesheim and Wilfried Bock of the Kuratorium Unteilbares Deutschland (Niedersachsen).

I would also like to thank Susan Souder and especially Sharon Clarke for typing this heavy document and putting up with the illegible handwritten manuscript. During the revision stage Mike Tierney, Alan Calandro, Delta Helmer, Barbara Wright, and Eric Bansleben put in hours of work, for which I am again grateful. My gratitude also goes to the editorial staff of Duke University Press for its careful reading of the original manuscript. Dick Rowson, Valerie Millholland, Bob Mirandon, Dan Ross, Mary Mendell, and Enid Hickingbotham all helped to improve the final product substantially.

A whole host of friends and colleagues are owed thanks for offering their support, their encouragement, and their generally constructive criticism. My thanks even, or especially, goes to those who warned against undertaking this project and consistently expressed their cynical suspicion that it would never be completed; in an odd sort of way, their input gave me my greatest incentive to finish it. At the risk of omitting important names, those to be thanked include first my family, especially my parents; undergraduate instructors during my student days at the College of William and Mary who first gave me an interest in international affairs; graduate instructors at the Fletcher School, including Uri Ra'anan and especially Robert Pfaltzgraff; Fletcher School classmates; my hosts for a year in Bonn, the Kreiss family; friends and colleagues who made my stay in West Germany so enjoyable, including Bill and Elspeth Zuckerman, Alice Cooper, Joachim and Cathy Fesefeldt, and Karl and Patricia Wimberger; and last my friends and colleagues at the College of William and Mary who helped me through the final stages of this project, including Sharon Clarke, Andrew Walpole, Ron Rapoport—whose help with the word processor was invaluable—and my other colleagues in the Department of Government.

Foremost among those whom I would like to thank is my friend —and since completion of this project, colleague—Bill Griffith, whose insight, good sense, and encouragement were indispensable.

All of the people named above provided valuable assistance in this project, though needless to say none bears any responsibility for remaining flaws in the book or for my personal judgments.

Introduction

Shortly after the West German federal election of October 1980, a cartoon poked fun at the badly beaten Christian Democratic Union/Christian Social Union (CDU/CSU). It depicted two despondent Union politicians, their heads swollen and covered with bandages from an unsuccessful attempt to ram through a brick wall. In frustration, one remarks, "The third try, and still no luck; there must be an easier way through." Both are plainly disregarding a large door just to one side boldly marked "Ostpolitik."

This cartoon captures the essence of the CDU/CSU opposition's struggle to deal with West German foreign policy after 1969. Throughout thirteen long years out of power, the Union faced numerous difficulties responding, and later adjusting, to the Eastern policies introduced and conducted by the Social Democratic–Free Democratic (SPD-FDP) coalition government. As the cartoon suggests, the Union could not easily bring itself to follow the SPD-FDP path to a new Ostpolitik, whatever the rewards it might have offered.

Instead, throughout its opposition period the CDU/CSU remained largely hostile to the new policy toward the Soviet bloc. This hostility took different forms at different times and varied in intensity from group to group within the party. There was both unyielding resistance and more conditional opposition. Yet almost all party leaders shared suspicions of what underlay and what might follow from the Ostpolitik introduced by Chancellor Willy Brandt's SPD-FDP governing coalition after 1969. This made for a bitter dispute over Brandt's initiatives, which dominated German politics in the early 1970s. For another decade the debate simmered, as the CDU/CSU remained largely suspicious and critical of, at times virulently opposed to, the way its rivals conducted relations with the East. Even as the Union prepared to re-enter government in 1982, it still harbored numerous reservations about SPD-FDP Ostpolitik.

Yet paradoxically there were many indications during its opposition period that the CDU/CSU had resigned itself to taking over and continuing this policy. Even in the early 1970s, and certainly thereafter, signs pointed to the conclusion that Union leaders were adapting to the new relationships established with the East bloc, including the German Democratic Republic (GDR). When it regained a dominant role in government in 1982, the Union was widely expected to ensure continuity in foreign policy. Indeed, the new CDU/CSU chancellor, Helmut Kohl, gave his first formal statement on foreign policy on 13 October 1982 and pledged that his government would change the tone but not significantly alter the substance of Bonn's relations with all Soviet bloc states.

In practice this meant that the CDU/CSU would honor the treaties negotiated a decade earlier by the SPD-FDP. It also meant that the Union aimed to continue political, administrative, commercial, and humanitarian arrangements reached with Bonn's Eastern neighbors, including the GDR. Moreover, the party pledged to seek ways of expanding this interaction with the Soviet bloc states. In so doing, moreover, it was promising to preserve and promote an Ostpolitik based on Bonn's de facto acceptance of the European territorial and political status quo—that is, the continent's postwar division, Germany's partition into two sovereign states, and the existence of the GDR.

Yet it was the implications of just such a policy that had long troubled so many in the CDU/CSU, and even after accepting continuity in policy as all but inevitable, they could not banish their own reservations. Much of this same ambivalence, and as a result some frequent internal debate, carried over into the Kohl government's years in office since 1982. On one day the party takes steps toward cooperation with the Soviet bloc that arouse accusations of appeasement or national neutralism from some; on the next it makes declarations prompting charges of aggressive revanchism from others.

What follows is an attempt to understand the reluctant, yet at times seemingly preordained, CDU/CSU acceptance of Bonn's new relationship with the Soviet bloc. A full explanation requires a look back at the history of postwar German foreign policy and frequent excursions into the territory of domestic politics; it demands as well an introduction to several key personalities who have shaped West German politics and a number of complex, even at times arcane, policy issues.

Before we go further, this point offers a logical place to pause and examine two terms of obvious significance that are nonetheless not easy to define. In its simplest sense "Ostpolitik" means "Eastern policy"—Germany's conduct of relations with Eastern Europe, including Russia. Every German leader from Bismarck to Helmut Kohl has pursued *an* Ostpolitik, but for many the term became almost inseparable from a specific policy of normalization and negotiation introduced in the late 1960s and pursued in some measure by every West German government since. In the first chapter of this study, which deals with historical background, the term will be used in its generic sense—an eastern policy; after that, unless otherwise specified, "Ostpolitik" refers to a policy of dialogue with the East bloc based on acceptance of the continent's postwar division.

Given that relations with Moscow (as well as Eastern Europe) and the problem of national division since 1945 are inseparable, Ostpolitik is generally taken to encompass "Deutschlandpolitik" —which simply means "German policy" or, more accurately, policy toward Germany's national division. Although it is a subset of Ostpolitik, "Deutschlandpolitik" is also used by itself at times to describe issues involving Germany alone. Changes in policy have brought changes in terminology: before 1969 "Deutschlandpolitik" meant primarily reunification policy; since 1969 it has generally referred to relations between East and West Germany.

The CDU/CSU's Ambivalent Adaptation

The CDU/CSU adapted to the SPD-FDP Ostpolitik because party leaders felt they could no longer ignore the changes Ostpolitik represented, and no longer necessarily needed to fear that it would produce the dangers of which they had long warned. If by 1982 the CDU/CSU's approach to Ostpolitik was far more in harmony with a broad consensus in the Federal Republic than it had been a decade earlier, it was not only because the Union's attitudes had changed, but also because the policy itself had been partly rechanneled into what the Union considered a less potentially dangerous direction. The argument of the book runs this way:

—CDU/CSU criticism of SPD-FDP Ostpolitik stemmed from the party's traditional beliefs about the question of German unity and East-West relations, beliefs that sustained deep concern that the possible long-term impact of the new Eastern relationships would be permanent national division, political neutralism, diplomatic isolation, and even the triumph of socialism. In many respects the CDU/CSU's internal balance of power, which long favored its most conservative wing, ensured that party policy would forcefully, at times virulently, voice these concerns.

—At the same time, a combination of international constraints and domestic influences upon West German foreign policy compelled the party to accept the operational dimension of the new Eastern policies, especially after 1972. A CDU/CSU government could not suspend, let alone reverse, Bonn's relations with the Soviet bloc and return to a policy aimed at national reunification unless it were ready to lead the Federal Republic into a lonely struggle against the consolidation of postwar Europe's state system, alienate its Western allies, create doubts about Bonn's reliability as a treaty partner, and expose West Berlin to possible counterpressure. As if those risks were not enough to sober even the most convinced critic, the party would also have had to take on the risks of alienating a public largely comfortable with the normalization brought by Ostpolitik, making itself an unpopular coalition partner and disrupting established trade patterns important to certain sectors of the German economy. Developments within the CDU/CSU, such as the increasing influence of the CDU party apparat and a gradual shift in the Union's strategy for regaining power—toward greater programmatic clarity and an emphasis on bipartisanship—only made eventual adaptation to the new policies all the more complete.

—Yet just as the CDU/CSU could not take the Ostpolitik backward, the Social Democratic Party could not take it further forward

—which in part enabled the Union to live with lingering doubts about the possible long-term impact. Some of the same external and domestic factors that necessitated CDU/CSU acceptance of a policy of dialogue—the exigencies of the European state system, subtle pressure from Bonn's allies, public desire for a normal and uncontroversial foreign policy, the moderating influence of coalition politics—also in effect slowed the pace and showed the limits of SPD-FDP Ostpolitik. Consequently the CDU/CSU sensed that accepting the status quo and bargaining with the East need not be the first steps on a slippery slope toward permanent partition and neutralism.

—By 1982 the result was an evolving, dualistic CDU/CSU approach to Ostpolitik combining, but not fully synthesizing, the party's traditional assumptions and objectives (which created a mistrust of dialogue with the East) with a willingness to continue the day-to-day operation of its predecessor's policy. The party acclimated itself to the practices and instrumentalities of SPD-FDP Ostpolitik, as well as to the circumstances that policy created, but retained its own basic beliefs about the long-term prospects and risks of cooperation with the East. In effect, CDU/CSU leaders came to pursue two policies: one aimed at continuity in the everyday process of negotiation, the other designed to allay their own concerns about the potential long-term implications of that dialogue.

—This CDU/CSU adaptation contributed to the reestablishment of a domestic consensus on the short-term conduct of Ostpolitik, namely the commitment to negotiation. Yet the consensus rested on widespread recognition of the above-mentioned international constraints and societal influences affecting Bonn's foreign policy, and on a corresponding willingness to divorce the operational dimension of policy from theories and concepts of its long-term purpose. For whatever else it endorsed, the Union never came to share the original Brandt policy's central premise—that acceptance of Europe's status quo as a point of departure for policy could actually advance hopes for a form of German unity and enhance West German security—and thus never assimilated the SPD's long-term goals in relations with the East. In this respect the CDU/CSU's experience leading up to 1982 suggests that West Germany's consensus came to rest not so much upon shared visions of Bonn's future relationship with the Soviet bloc, but instead upon a combination of factors that narrowed the number of policy options any West German government could follow.

West German Foreign Policy: Constrained Choices

Understanding the CDU/CSU's response to the post-1969 Ostpolitik, then, requires understanding the key role of constraints in West German foreign policy. For ultimately it was these constraints that made it necessary *and* made it possible for the Union to accept a policy about which so many of its leaders still had reservations.

It is by no means an original contribution of this author to suggest that constraints are a decisive factor in foreign policy generally and in the case of West Germany specifically. In past decades much of international relations theory has moved away from the traditional idea that the policymaker devises rational strategies in the light of national interests, and toward a concept of policy formulation determined by systemic or domestic forces. In trying to establish a framework for the comparative study of foreign policies, Wolfram Hanrieder argues that all states must strive to act in a way compatible with their external environment—the obstacles and challenges of the international system—and in a manner designed to win a domestic consensus. How well a country's decisions meet these two simple measures of feasibility shapes policy and determines the difference between success and failure. Hanrieder suggests, moreover, a link between compatibility and consensus: choices that are compatible with the international system reinforce consensus; those that are not force a domestic change to bring about a greater degree of consensus.[1]

Significantly, one of the prime examples Hanrieder employs is the adaptation by West German Social Democrats to the pro-Western policies of the CDU/CSU's Konrad Adenauer in the late 1950s.

More recently Gebhard Schweigler argues that formal external constraints upon the conduct of West German foreign policy after 1945 have gradually been relaxed, yet points out that many of these constraints—limits on the use of force, ties to the West—have been internalized in the attitudes that shape domestic politics. The result is both political stability and firm attachment to the Western community of states.[2]

It is not the aim of this study to develop Hanrieder's conceptual framework further or to test Schweigler's thesis about the domestic setting of West German foreign policy. In essence what follows is a piece of political history, a story about politics and foreign policy in the Federal Republic. But it is worth bearing the concept of constrained choices in mind while examining the CDU/CSU's reluctant adaptation to Ostpolitik, for this adaptation illustrates some of the particular, even unique, forces that have shaped and will continue to shape the foreign policy of the most important state in Europe. Such forces include:

—The Federal Republic's responsiveness to its external environment, manifested in sensitivity to developments in interbloc relations, the policies of its allies, the policies of its Communist neighbors, and Berlin's unique situation, as well as its inclination toward "predictability" in its own conduct of foreign affairs.

—West German society's preoccupation with a return to normalcy, reflected in a desire for a more routine foreign policy, a more practical and tangible (as opposed to idealistic or legalistic) approach to the nation's division, and the imperatives of centrist, coalition politics and bipartisanship.

Past, Present, and Future

Originally this study dealt only with the CDU/CSU's period in opposition between 1969 and 1982, and it still focuses primarily on those critical years. Many if not all of the important developments that ensured that the CDU/CSU would pursue a dualistic policy took place before it regained power; the factors making for adaptation to the SPD-FDP Ostpolitik are most easily seen by examining that policy's formative years and the then-opposition CDU/CSU's response to it. The official policies of the CDU/CSU-led government since 1982 can be seen most clearly only in light of the CDU/CSU opposition's experience before 1982.

After part 1's summary overview of how CDU/CSU Ostpolitik evolved in the two decades prior to 1969, this book focuses on the critical years of the 1970s and early 1980s. Part 2 covers the debate over the Eastern treaties negotiated and ratified between 1969 and 1973. It explores the origins and range of CDU/CSU reactions to those agreements, as well as the party's decision on ratification. Part 3 treats the period following ratification of the major treaties, that is

1973 to 1982, when the Union first grappled with the consequences of its defeat on both the policy and political fronts, and then, from the late 1970s onward, began evolving a more credible approach to Ostpolitik as the SPD-FDP encountered increasing difficulties with its foreign policy. Part 4 draws upon the preceding chapters in attempting to support the hypotheses outlined above and thus in accounting for the CDU/CSU's adaptation to SPD-FDP Ostpolitik, as well as for the origins and persistence of its resistance. It also offers some generalizations about the domestic context of West German foreign policy.

A review of CDU/CSU policy since the party regained a major role in government in 1982 is useful for more than one reason. Clearly it offers the best way to see how the conclusions drawn from the party's opposition years stand up. More important, any adaptation to the new Ostpolitik was greatly accelerated after the transition from an SPD-FDP government back to a Union-led coalition in October 1982. For these reasons a postscript has been added discussing the official Eastern policies of the Kohl government from 1982 to 1988.

Studying both the Union's opposition years and its period in government can also yield insight into issues the importance of which transcend any particular decade. Perplexed foreign observers, including American policymakers, have tried to divine the guiding impulse of the conservative, Western-oriented Union's continuing interest in Ostpolitik. Alternatives suggested by some include a lingering desire for national reunification, a persistent Russophile tendency on the German right, a vestigial interest in the idea of *Mitteleuropa*, or "central Europe," an inclination toward appeasement, and a susceptibility to pressure from export-dependent corporations.

Yet the CDU/CSU never consciously or willingly chose to pursue the policy it inherited. Nor did party leaders sit down together and conceive a comprehensive, long-term strategy of which dialogue was the means and unity or peace or security the end. Observers who believe they have discerned such far-reaching goals—reunification, "common security," restoration of Mitteleuropa—look well beyond the more complex reality of an uncertain and divided party reacting in large part to circumstances beyond its control and content to make do in the short run with incremental progress while postponing deliberation over long-term consequences.

At the same time, analyzing the CDU/CSU's struggle with Ostpolitik in opposition as well as in government also helps illuminate, if not resolve, one of the persistent debates in West German politics since 1982. Many critics of the Union, above all in the SPD, have insisted that its conversion to Ostpolitik was disingenuous, strictly opportunistic, and unlikely to last—and thus a danger to real continuity in FRG foreign policy. This book provides important indications about the actual depth and potential durability of the Union's commitment to cooperative relations with the East bloc in the 1990s and beyond.[3]

The Origins of CDU/CSU Foreign Policy

1

Union Ostpolitik from Adenauer to the Grand Coalition

The postwar German politicians who chose to label themselves Christian Democrats emerged from diverse political, religious, and geographic backgrounds. But this ideological "patchwork" had several strong common threads—above all a desire to expunge the legacy of Nazism by creating new political and economic structures infused with traditional Christian values. Though most early movement leaders and supporters were drawn from the old pre-1933 Catholic Center party, they appealed successfully for cooperation between Germany's two long-divided Christian communities.[1]

Early on, however, tension developed between those who wanted to let the Christian Democratic Union's initial burst of idealism propel it to political success and those with a more pragmatic bent. Many of the former, led by Jakob Kaiser, Ernst Lemmer, and Karl Arnold—men from the Catholic trade union movement in the Rhineland and Berlin—advocated a Christian "third way" between capitalism and communism, making Germany, socially and politically, a "bridge" between East and West. The CDU's Aahlen program of 1947 partly reflected this stream of thought. But the "Christian socialists" were handicapped because much of their grass-roots strength was in the Soviet-occupied zone, which quickly underwent Stalinization.

Moreover, they were outmaneuvered by Catholic Cologne's former mayor, Konrad Adenauer, who—though a cofounder of the new Christian Democratic Union—was skeptical of the Christian third way and aimed to transform Germany into a bastion of anticommunism. A master of sharp polemics and the ironic witticism, a tireless campaigner and stubbornly patient bargainer, this aging Rhinelander allied with south German conservatives against the trade union and Berlin wings of his party, and quickly rose to the top of the CDU. He also became chairman of the council established by the Western-occupying authorities to draw up a constitution for the new West German state. At the same time Adenauer brought into the CDU a man whose economic policies had already proven popular and successful—Ludwig Erhard, father of the so-called social market economy: free enterprise rather than central planning, yet with some constraints on monopolies and social welfare programs to protect against the excesses of capitalism. In 1949 Adenauer was named the party's candidate for chancellor in the first federal elections following the establishment of the new state.[2]

After the CDU eked out a narrow victory over his archrival, Social Democratic chief Kurt Schumacher, Adenauer formed a center-right majority coalition (including the nationalistic, conservative-liberal Free Democrats) and set about building the Federal Republic. First and foremost the chancellor wanted to make his country a paragon of stability and respectability, thereby erasing the legacy of Adolf Hitler. At the same time he was determined to mold West Germany into a bulwark against Soviet communism. These goals impelled him to purge the country of those extremist viruses on the left and right that he considered potentially fatal. The chancellor also aimed at undercutting Social Democracy, which he suspected was inherently vulnerable to subversion from the far left.

To achieve these goals, Adenauer took personal command of the new federal government, which he maintained against challengers from his party or coalition partners for at least the first ten of his nearly fifteen years as chancellor. Under his paternalistic guidance the FRG became a "chancellor democracy." With supreme self-confidence, this elderly pragmatist regarded the survival of political stability in West Germany as dependent upon his continuing ability to shape its domestic and foreign policies.

Adenauer transformed the CDU into his personal political vehicle. Its express purpose became to assure the chancellor's reelection and facilitate his governance of the country. Only the party's top elected officials in the FRG's ten separate states maintained some influence over Adenauer; thanks to the country's federalist system they retained independent power bases, and decision-making in the party to some extent remained decentralized. Yet in general the regional "barons" shared Adenauer's basic goals. Consequently, year by year the Union's original ideological momentum slowed as it took on the character of a broad electoral coalition reaching out to all classes, confessions, regions, and interest groups of the center-right. As the Union co-opted and absorbed the smaller political rivals that had represented those diverse groups, its early idealism waned and was replaced by pragmatic political objectives. Intraconfessionalism remained a major leitmotif of the CDU, but more because of its desire to attract Protestant votes in the 1950s than because of any lingering idealistic Christian impetus.[3] In spirit the Union abandoned its search for a "Christian path" between capitalism and socialism; enough of the party's initial progressivism on social issues survived to sustain at best a modest trade union–supported Christian socialist wing.[4]

Under Adenauer's tutelage—and thereafter—the Union was thus formally a broad church that included some social and liberal groups but was dominated by conservatives and pragmatists. This was largely due to Adenauer's success as chancellor and Erhard's as economics minister. As the Union received ever-greater credit for a flourishing social market economy, waxing world influence, and respectability, its willingness to tamper with the status quo waned. The party's famous 1957 election slogan—"No experiments!"—expressed its growing identification with the emerging West German social and political establishment. Industrialists as well as small-scale, independent businessmen and farmers became ready adherents of the chancellor's party. Eventually the CDU established auxiliary organizations to institutionalize the representation of large corporations and smaller private firms within the party (Germany's well-organized farm lobby also maintained close ties to the CDU). With Erhard as their chief spokesman, leaders of business and industry became a dominant force in shaping CDU economic and social policy, generally—if not always—prevailing over the Christian trade unionists.

Reinforcing the CDU/CSU's conservatism was the impact of the expellees. During the early 1950s a small, independent political party represented those thirteen million ethnic Germans who had been forced to leave territories lost to Russia, Poland, and Czechoslovakia in 1945. Adenauer gradually co-opted and absorbed this party's supporters. Silesians, Upper Silesians, Pomeranians, East Prussians, Sudetens and the nearly twenty other expellee groups continued to maintain their own individual leagues, as well as an umbrella organization, but they increasingly made the Union, and to some extent the SPD, their political home. Although younger expellees over time identified less with their *Heimat* or "homeland," their political spokesmen, fearful of being written off politically and historically, remained active. These vociferously nationalist and anticommunist politicians received a hearing in the Union.

But no factor more clearly bolstered the Union's conservatism than its dual structure. From 1949 onward it was not one party but two—the Christian Democratic Union throughout all of West Germany except the state of Bavaria, and the Christian Social Union (CSU) in Bavaria alone. Like the CDU, the CSU traced its political lineage back to a pre-1933 Catholic party, one that had fervently espoused Bavarian Catholic interests and resisted Protestant-Prussian domination of Germany. After 1945 there was an identity crisis among founders of the CSU, ultimately resolved by a decision to break with its pre-1933 predecessor's particularism and form a close partnership on the federal level with the CDU. The two branches of the Union agreed not to compete in each others' territory, and created a joint delegation in the lower house of the federal parliament, the Bundestag. The CSU constituted from one-fifth to one-fourth of the Union group and maximized its influence by caucusing separately before each vote and confronting its sister party with a united bloc.

This unique relationship gave the CSU an opportunity to push its sister party in a more conservative direction. For though the CSU claimed to be a genuine catch-all party, its constituency remained predominantly Catholic, middle class, and conservative. More important, the CSU overcame all competitors to identify itself successfully during the 1950s and thereafter with the fierce sense of Bavarian regional pride, a pride arising from that kingdom's centuries of existence as a distinct, cohesive political unit. In the words of one CDU official, "[For the CSU] national policy is always a bit of provincial politics."[5] This sense of tradition, continuity, order, and affinity for the Heimat (CSU politicians often closed speeches proclaiming "God be with you, land of the Bavarians!"), as well as the region's agrarian and middle-class social composition, made the CSU—as Bavaria's leading party—fervently anticommunist and antisocialist.

Enhancing the CSU's growing influence over its northern sister party was the shrewdness of Franz Josef Strauss, a top boss from the mid-1950s onward. His caustic oratory and autocratic style made Strauss the natural, at times brilliant, champion of hard-line Bavarian conservatism. Yet his fierce desire for a personal role in major issues of the day also made him acutely sensitive to shifting political winds, giving the stocky Bavarian the skills of an adept trimmer. As one Strauss advisor remarked, "There is no label for him; there are [merely] attributes."[6] Admirers insisted that he maintained a clear set of guiding principles, but critics generally regarded him as totally lacking in consistency, a talented populist, or—less flattering, but more widely believed—a shrewd, if at times demagogic opportunist. But friends and adversaries alike agreed that the CSU boss by his very nature polarized opinion, often by vitriolic conservative rhetoric, often by unexpected shows of pragmatism.

From the 1950s onward, Strauss capitalized on the CSU's role as a Bavarian "bastion in Bonn" and its decisive importance in providing the Union a parliamentary plurality to influence overall CDU/CSU policy in a conservative direction. Because there was considerable, if not total, congruence between the views of Adenauer, Erhard, and Strauss, relations between CDU and CSU remained stable during the 1950s, though the CSU leader's ambitions and style then and later created tensions.[7]

Economic prosperity and political stability, so closely identified with the figure of Adenauer (and to a considerable extent with Erhard), made the Union a successful establishment party. Adenauer's impressive longevity deferred the question of succession until the early 1960s, when he finally, reluctantly shared his power and then stepped down. Despite over a decade of political power, Adenauer's legacy included his party's organizational weakness;

it continued to prosper during the 1960s largely on the merits of past achievement, an entrenched position within the halls of governmental power, and the still-popular appeal of luminaries like Erhard, who initially succeeded Adenauer but lacked the latter's skill. A strong, coherent, centralized party structure and a clear, identifiable political program open to new ideas were missing. This contributed to a drop in support for the Union. From a high point of 50.7 percent of the vote in 1957, it slipped to 46.6 percent in 1965 and 46.1 percent by 1969, an erosion of support large enough eventually to cost the party its control of the government.

Elements of Adenauer's Foreign Policy

CDU/CSU Westpolitik and German Unity

From its first day in power to its last, from September 1949 to September 1969, the CDU/CSU viewed itself as guardian of a revolution in German foreign policy—a revolution launched by that most unlikely of radicals, Konrad Adenauer. As part of his effort to sweep away the legacy of Adolf Hitler—totalitarian fascism and aggressive, racist expansionism—and to establish an entirely new order in what remained of Germany, Bonn's first chancellor fundamentally changed the country's relationship with its neighbors. Though Adenauer's Westpolitik in part simply reflected his cool calculation that the Western allies were in a position to shape postwar Germany's fate, he had more far-reaching aims. Adenauer hoped to end centuries of suspicious uncertainty about Germany's geopolitical orientation—Was it part of Eastern Europe, Western Europe, or a balancer between the two?—by turning the Federal Republic unequivocally Westward. He and his political heirs in the CDU/CSU believed that only harmonious relations with the West and commitment to Western values would restore Germany to a constructive role in world politics. Making Germany feel part of the Western community of nations would also reinforce the transformation Adenauer hoped to achieve at home, namely the conversion of West Germany into a stable, durable democracy, free from the temptation of fascism, communism, or socialism. Close cooperation with the West and above all Europe's "guarantor," the United States—made tangible by a controversial decision in 1950 to contribute forces to the Western Alliance—also assured West Germany security against a perpetual threat to its long, exposed eastern border. Finally, Westpolitik guaranteed against a "return to Potsdam," that is, a return to the days of complete national impotence, when the country's fate was settled entirely by external powers in the absence of German representatives. For Adenauer, the complete integration of the Federal Republic into an evolving West European federation allied to the United States, which had to be kept in Europe to counter Soviet power, was the optimal goal of this Westpolitik.[8]

For Adenauer and his successors, Westpolitik took precedence over another aim—national unity. Before 1949 Germany lay partitioned into four zones of occupation (with Poland and the Soviet Union in control of the Eastern provinces); after 1949 the occupation zones became two states that would gain full sovereignty in 1955. As the party saw it, any attempt to reunify the nation should not interfere with the effort to regain respectability, rebuild democracy, provide for its security, and assure sovereignty—interests best served by Westpolitik and (at least until the mid-1950s) specifically West European integration. Binding the country's Western half to the Western camp in the Cold War was, given Soviet control over East Germany, bound to delay or complicate national unity, but Adenauer was ready to pay the price.[9] He did not want to press German reunification at the expense of relations with the West or at the cost of democracy, for he believed that the only form of unified Germany the Kremlin would permit was a Sovietized or at least strictly neutralized state, as a large Germany armed and aligned with the West would be Moscow's worst nightmare. As the chancellor observed, neutralization of Germany would heighten the risks for all of Europe, creating a vacuum in Central Europe, effectively inviting some form of Soviet hegemonial effort. For that reason he remained eternally vigilant, suspicious that every Soviet hint of flexibility on the unity question represented an effort to play upon national sentiment and detach Germany from its newfound Western partners.[10]

This order of priorities raises the question of whether CDU/CSU leaders were in essence ready to write off those parts of the old empire under communist control. Some historians maintain that Adenauer not only accepted but welcomed the loss of largely Protestant Prussia, which had occupied and attempted to "Prussianize" his own overwhelmingly Catholic Rhineland during the nineteenth century. Moreover, Adenauer and many of his supporters partly blamed Prussian militarism for Germany's catastrophic war efforts. Given these views, his Weimar-era proposals for an autonomous Rhineland and his enthusiasm for complete integration of the FRG into a unified Western Europe, Adenauer was often considered a Rhineland separatist or a Carolingian—that is, someone inclined to regard Germany's Western regions and France as what they were in Charlemagne's time, part of a Western world not yet divided by nationality, and held together by the Church.

On a less lofty plane, Germany's division was also said to serve the purely political interests of any party that—like the CDU/CSU—initially drew most of its support from Catholics. Those areas of Germany under Communist rule were predominantly Protestant, ensuring that the ratio of Catholics to Protestants in the Federal Republic was far more favorable to Adenauer's party than it would have been in Germany as a whole.

The Bavarian character of the CSU could be said to have given it an equally small stake in German unity. Many early CSU leaders even found the FRG's creation a threat to their region's autonomy. This residual particularism reflected how well the CSU embodied Bavaria's antipathy for anything north of the River Main. Rival CSU concepts of Bavaria as a Christian bulwark against or a Christian missionary to the rest of Germany were both fundamentally anti-Prussian and anti–north German visions. For the CSU, the nation's dividing lines ran both north-south and east-west.

Yet there is good reason to qualify such a characterization. After all, resistance to Prussian-Protestant domination did not mean opposition to all forms of German unification. Moreover, Adenauer and his allies did not race to sever Western Germany from the old empire but accepted creation of the Federal Republic as the second-best solution only after they—unlike their more optimistic Christian socialist party colleagues—sensed that the Four Powers were unlikely to agree quickly upon a plan for German unity. Indeed, far from embracing close ties with France, Adenauer remained distrustful of French efforts to humble and weaken postwar Germany. It was only when more conciliatory tones came from

Paris in 1948–49 that he saw reason to hope that Germany could indeed find its future as a part of a new united Europe.[11]

Nationalism and Reunification

Not only were Union leaders from Adenauer onward not separatists; they had good reason to endorse and pursue reunification in some form. Important as it was for them to subordinate this goal to the requirements of democracy, security, and sovereignty, the CDU/CSU feared letting the banner of German unity fall, for it could easily be picked up or captured by unsavory right-wing, even neo-Nazi elements. As it had in the Weimar era, the nationalistic right could attempt to generate revanchist sentiments and this time direct them against the Union and Bonn's Westpolitik by claiming that the latter came at the price of permanent national division. For some in the CDU/CSU, this concern was reinforced by a simple fear of being outflanked on the right and losing votes.

Similarly, the Union had no desire to see a left-wing monopoly of the national issue, for during the 1950s the rival Social Democrats vigorously sounded the theme of unity. The Union foresaw long-term problems if more and more Germans came to accept the SPD argument that CDU/CSU Westpolitik, by binding the Federal Republic to a military bloc, had made Germany's division permanent without securing in exchange a genuine, lasting peace in Central Europe. This assumption, it was feared, might generate sympathy for a left-wing policy of accommodation toward the Soviet bloc, even theoretically a variation of neutralism—with or without reunification. That in turn would erode the domestic consensus for Westpolitik, while damaging the CDU/CSU politically.

After relating an incident in which Adenauer shocked allied officials by having the German national anthem sung, biographer Hans-Peter Schwarz concluded that the chancellor sought "to occupy and transform [umfunktionieren]" national emotions: occupying them so to prevent others from doing so, while converting them to a form consistent with a democratic state.[12]

But it was not merely that the Union could ill afford the political image of a party resigned to national division. For different reasons, and with varying degrees of intensity, almost all CDU/CSU leaders throughout the 1950s and 1960s genuinely believed in the desirability of reunification.

By and large this support for national unity was not a revival of the ethnocentric chauvinism of right-wing groups of the Wilhelmine empire or the Weimar republic, let alone the racist expansionism of Nazism. Such extremism had been somewhat less widespread in the areas where the Union's appeal after 1945 was strongest.[13] Many Catholic Rhinelanders and Bavarians had shied away from zealous German nationalism. Their sense of being a discrete community within the nation, plus the "clear set of coordinates" provided by their hierarchical and dogmatic faith, made Catholics somewhat less prone to (though by no means immune from) the absolutist claims and messianic appeal of racist German nationalism. Moreover, the Rhineland and especially Bavaria had never developed a great attachment to the 1871 empire; these regions had long since evolved traditions and identities of their own. For that reason the Rhineland CDU and especially the CSU were not emotionally *gesamtdeutsch*, or "all-German," in outlook.

Genuine and more emotional gesamtdeutsch attitudes did exist among Protestants in the CDU, especially in northern and central Germany. Because these areas had been splintered into many tiny feuding principalities they developed a weaker sense of regional identity than did the south German provinces and consequently maintained a greater sense of identification with the post-1871 empire. Perhaps more important still was the fact that northern and central Germans, predominantly Protestant, were more at home in the larger Protestant-dominated empire. Thus the CDU's gesamtdeutsch outlook was best exemplified by politicians from these regions, as well as West Berliners, East German refugees (like Johann Baptist Gradl) and prominent Protestants.

Whether gesamtdeutsch or not, moreover, Union leaders all shared a belief that Germany's division was historically unnatural and intolerable from a humanitarian standpoint. They agreed that the 1871 Bismarckian empire, whatever its many faults as a system of government, embodied the nation's will to live within the same political community. For them the nation's sense of identity was shaped by 1871; it gave tangible form to more vague characteristics that the people of the German-speaking world held in common —language, culture, and history. All that had passed since that time, however catastrophic, had in Union eyes not destroyed this consciousness of a common national identity. To most CDU leaders, pre-1933 nationalism and Hitler's racist totalitarian imperialism marked a perversion of German national aspirations and could not justify a permanent, involuntary division of Germany forever. As one contemporary observed, Adenauer had grown up when a larger Germany, whatever its drawbacks for Catholic Rhinelanders, formed "the natural order of things," and during his time as chancellor he became ever more conscious of his duty as a *German* statesman.[14]

Union leaders believed as well that Germans on both sides of the dividing line—especially in the East—continued to feel part of one nation. Like most SPD leaders, they felt a sense of empathy and fraternal obligation to work toward ending the partition so that friends, family, and fellow countrymen "over there" could live in the hope of someday enjoying a better life.

Moreover, gesamtdeutsch sentiments often had a more annexationist and irredentist tone. Personal experience made most politically active ethnic Germans who had fled territories lost in 1944–45 bitterly resentful of Germany's dismemberment. Spokesmen for the roughly six million people from those traditional provinces east of the Oder-Neisse line now "under Polish administration"—Silesia, Upper Silesia, Pomerania—regarded their Heimat as coequal parts of the nation, like East and West Germany. Even Sudeten Germans —whose Heimat was annexed by Germany only in 1938, restored to Czechoslovakia after 1945 and therefore *not* coequal—also often espoused a virulent gesamtdeutsch outlook.

Most expellees knew the Eastern territories most likely would not be included in a reunited Germany, but they feared that if Bonn ever stopped pushing for a revision of the status quo in Central Europe they would lose all hope of gaining a say in the final disposition of their Heimat. They also argued that the FRG should continue reminding the world of the often brutal postwar expulsion of Germans from Eastern Europe. In part this fervor arose from a desire to demonstrate solidarity with those ethnic Germans left behind in Eastern Europe, and in part because the expellees did not want to be written off historically and politically. Often the torch was kept alight with volatile political fuel—resentful, even revanchist, rhetoric.

For reasons of political expediency—there were after all thirteen million expellees—and genuine ideological affinity, many nonexpellees in the Union expressed support for the right to Heimat. Though CSU leaders conceded that restoring the status quo ante seemed improbable, fierce loyalty to their own region, along with their often-instinctive anticommunism, created a bond between the Bavarians and the expellees. Sudetens came to enjoy a special influence in the CSU, as Bavaria was a "protectorate" for these fellow Germans from Habsburg Europe who spoke a dialect similar to Bavarian.

Realpolitik, Ideology, and CDU/CSU Deutschlandpolitik

Yet gesamtdeutsch sentiment, whether of the mild or the virulent variety, was not the only driving force behind traditional CDU/CSU Deutschlandpolitik. Most Union politicians did espouse reunification as a duty to the nation, but this sentiment was accompanied, perhaps even subsumed, by other powerful concerns. As observed at the outset, respectability and political influence, along with military and political security from the threat of Soviet communism, were the objectives of CDU/CSU Westpolitik; these same goals also shaped the party's (and especially the CSU's) approach to reunification.

Adenauer and many other Union leaders like Strauss feared that the collapse of Hitler's empire in 1945 would reduce Germany's role in international politics to that of a passive object whose fate would be decided by others. This "Potsdam complex" reinforced Adenauer's Westpolitik, leading him eventually to purchase sovereignty for the Federal Republic as a way of preventing total political emasculation. Yet in the long run the FRG by itself constituted too small a vehicle to influence world events or even control its own destiny. This sense of relative powerlessness grew as West Germany's economic miracle highlighted the disparity between the country's wealth and Bonn's still-modest political influence: it was an "economic giant but a political pygmy," said Strauss.[15] Adenauer, Strauss, and many colleagues, especially in the CSU, increasingly showed their frustration whenever the FRG was treated like a second-class ally, especially by the United States. This frustration, coupled with the party's self-denying ordinance with respect to traditional nationalism, made the national division seem a source of relative impotence.

More important still, Adenauer's party persisted in seeing Germany's partition as a potential threat to the stability and peace of Europe. Adenauer believed true security could come only with reunification: "With the current condition, the equilibrium of Europe was considerably disturbed. This disruption of the European equilibrium concealed great dangers for the other European states and for the geopolitical situation. I had to continually direct the attention of leading Western statesmen [to this fact]."[16]

Last, both Union sister parties' conservatism already made them almost instinctively anticommunist in outlook. The national partition, repression in East Germany, the Red Army's physical presence across an exposed border, and, for the expellees, personal experience intensified these sentiments. For largely similar reasons, the rival SPD at this time was even more virulently anti-Soviet.

Clearly, then, all Union leaders in the Adenauer era shared a commitment to reunification in some form. Yet just as plainly the source and intensity of that commitment varied. What Hans-Peter Schwarz labels "the national camp," those with the strongest, emotional gesamtdeutsch orientation—Berliners, North Germans, expellees—remained wary of Adenauer and the Union's southern, Catholic leaders who in turn saw overt nationalism in Union ranks as a danger to their Western policy. Yet the chancellor realized that he needed both groups, and used every resource at his disposal to win "the national camp" over.[17]

Adenauer's Concept

How did Adenauer hope to pursue reunification in a way that served all of these varied concerns and yet remained consistent with his overriding objective—Western unity?

Adenauer's policy began by dismissing any hope of rebuilding a new nation-state configured like the old empire. He felt that such an entity would reawaken fearful memories of recent German expansionism in neighboring states, or at the very least destabilize the European balance of power in a way favorable to Soviet communism. His policy also excluded from the outset any manner of neutral Gesamtdeutschland, arguing that it would constitute neither a bridge nor a buffer between East and West, but a power vacuum inviting Soviet hegemony; a state in Germany's geopolitical situation could hardly be neutral like Switzerland without rapidly becoming neutralized like Finland.

Yet "reunification" as proposed by party leaders from Adenauer onward did envision all Germans once again living within the same state—the notion of state unity. There was some ambivalence in this regard because certain Union politicians increasingly emphasized "self-determination" as Bonn's real goal, and a nation could experience self-determination even if it was divided into two states. But by and large, the CDU/CSU treated "reunification" and "self-determination" as entirely compatible, if not literally synonymous. A majority in the party believed that any process of true self-determination—such as an all-German plebiscite—would certainly lead to a "yes" vote for reunification within one state. Even many who stressed self-determination generally agreed that if the nation chose to remain divided, the division would be only for a transition period preceding total reunification. And all Union leaders vigorously argued that Germany had the *right* to seek state unity.

This still left the question of specifically what form state unity could take if restoration of the pre-1945 German nation-state were excluded. Union leaders proposed as their alternative the inclusion of all Germans, East and West, in a broad, united, democratic West European federation of nations, to which East Germans could eventually accede. In this way, the Union tried to synthesize the ultimate goals of its Westpolitik and its Deutschlandpolitik: European integration or unification *and* reunification of Germany. Such a federated (or confederal) Europe would abolish internal political and economic divisions but permit each constituent nation to preserve its distinct identity. Such a political framework would thus heal the nation's historically unnatural partition and restore liberty to East Germans. Because a federated Europe might eventually, peacefully draw Eastern Europe into its orbit, it held out some hope for satisfying the expellees and realizing their right to Heimat.

Adenauer believed the safest route to fully equal status lay in reuniting Germany within the framework of a new Europe, even a European superpower. If the continent were once again a center of global influence, not a mere chessboard for external powers, the largest constituent unit of such a Europe—reunited Germany—would be in a position to determine its own fate.[18]

For the Union from Adenauer's time onward, pushing the cause of German reunification within a West European state was also a concrete way to keep Soviet communism on the defensive; actual achievement of unity would be a major step in rolling back the communist threat to Western civilization and its basic values.

What the Union presented as a sophisticated synthesis of Westpolitik and Deutschlandpolitik was dismissed from the outset by critics as a mere hodgepodge of irreconcilable elements. Political rivals and many impartial commentators saw German reunification and European unity as largely incompatible, indeed mutually exclusive goals; they contended that the CDU/CSU offered this elaborate scheme merely to placate nationalistic voters.

Did CDU/CSU leaders believe that reunification via European unity was possible? Certainly they believed it should not be *impossible*. In their view, bringing all Germans together within the same broad federation should not necessarily arouse fears of German economic and political hegemony over Europe. After all, this European state would be an entirely new political construct in which such rivalries were subsumed or outmoded. As the CDU/CSU saw it, theirs was a national policy without nationalism, ideally suited to overcoming the wary, cynical mood toward Germany's national problem typified by François Mauriac's pointed quip, "I like Germany so much I am glad there are two of them."

In short, many Union leaders from Adenauer on might simply have convinced themselves that because their goal should be achieved, it would be achieved. A more plausible explanation is that Union leaders considered any *other* form of reunification either less likely or completely unacceptable because it compromised on democracy and a Western orientation. As Adenauer observed, "In Germany, opinions were represented according to which we could only have either a policy for Europe or a policy for German unity. I considered this 'either-or' a fatal error. No one could explain how German unity in freedom could be realized without a strong and united Europe."[19] In any event, as Waldemar Besson concluded, Adenauer's faith in this scheme for reunification, well-founded or not, was genuine during the early 1950s.[20] Moreover, despite their wariness, his more gesamtdeutsch party colleagues endorsed government policy and effectively legitimized it as "national"—partly persuaded by Adenauer and his anticommunism, partly out of resignation in the face of the lack of alternatives. Years later, his successors in the party continued to regard the Adenauer model for German unity as sound in principle and no more implausible than any other acceptable option.

The Policy of Strength and the Holding Policy

What Union leaders from Adenauer's time on *did* openly concede was that realization of German unity through European unity hinged upon events in part beyond Bonn's control. Most important, "reunification in a West European framework" was contingent upon a broad shift in Europe's balance of power. Quite simply, Moscow must no longer be in a position to resist it.

CDU/CSU leaders generally regarded Soviet control over Eastern Europe as belated fulfillment of czarist Russian expansionist ambitions and the first stage in communist world revolution. In the party's view, this synthesis of equally dangerous designs meant that Moscow had a powerful stake in preserving its control of Eastern Europe. As the Union read Moscow's motives, the GDR remained a valuable economic and military component of the Soviet bloc. Moreover, the Kremlin could never permit democratic reunification of Germany, for that might well spawn a contagious virus of liberalization, ultimately fatal to Kremlin hegemony and Soviet ideology. In this view, the most Moscow could freely tolerate was a strictly neutralized, emasculated gesamtdeutsch state, pliable in the face of pressure and cut off from the West.

Given this perception of a basic conflict between long-term Soviet and German aims, reunification—through European unity or in any other conceivable democratic framework—could be realized only when the Soviet Union was no longer in the position to resist it. A shift in the correlation of forces against the Soviet Union could ultimately make its hegemony in Eastern Europe untenable and force Moscow to ease or relinquish its grip, thereby prompting Kremlin leaders to reconsider their position on German unity. By throwing its own economic, political, and military weight onto the Western side of the scales, Bonn could help tip the balance of accumulated power decisively against Moscow, eliminating the Kremlin as an obstacle to reunification.

This was the classic definition of a "policy of strength" from Adenauer's time onward, for some a German version of "rollback," an approach to the national problem promising reunification as a result of Westpolitik. But neither Adenauer nor his successors saw mobilizing military pressure against Moscow as decisive in overcoming Soviet resistance to German unity. Hans-Peter Schwarz makes the case that CDU/CSU confidence in a "policy of strength" arose from hopes for a form of early East-West detente.[21] Schwarz points out that Adenauer became firmly convinced the Kremlin would seek East-West cooperation out of frustration at an unending arms race, some impending domestic crises (primarily economic), the looming threat of China, the thwarting of Moscow's postwar goals in Europe by the resolute unity of West Europeans and the irrepressible nationalism of East Europeans. Given this mixture of factors, Adenauer and his successors anticipated an increasingly conciliatory Soviet stance on the division of Europe: "I have always been of the view that the Russians, when they come to see that the methods of Cold War against a stronger Europe promise no more results, would then—in view of their internal economic difficulties—be more inclined to negotiate with the West. . . . My hope was that the Soviet Union would one day see: 'we can not achieve everything together.' My hope was that it would concentrate its power on dealing with China and leave Europe in peace. [We would have] to wait for this decision."[22]

This very appeal for patience on the premise of a major change in Soviet policy, however, indicates that the party saw actual achievement of unity in some form as a long-term, maximal goal. Indeed, Adenauer's first statement as chancellor indicated that reunification would at best come as the result of other policies or other events; its achievement would not be the actual guiding goal of day-to-day policy. This too remained his party's assumption for the ensuing two decades. Most critics—even many sympathetic observers—have interpreted this to mean that all CDU/CSU talk of unity was disingenuous. Such a conclusion is unwarranted. Adenauer and his successors regarded unification as the most desirable, long-term objective, but were preoccupied with the short-term, minimal goal of Deutschlandpolitik—namely preventing an unacceptable resolution of the German problem that favored Moscow. This CDU/CSU "holding policy," as William Griffith has termed it, originated with Adenauer, but dominated much party behavior regarding the national question up to 1969 and beyond.[23] Well before Western counterpressure or other internal and external forces could cause the Soviet tide in Eastern Europe to retreat, Union leaders felt Bonn faced the more immediate task of shoring up its own position against what appeared to be the Kremlin's persistent efforts to undermine Germany's Western foundations. This meant rejecting unacceptable schemes for resolving Germany's division and leaving the controversial Eastern border question open: Adenauer was vague on whether the Eastern territories would belong to a reunited Germany, yet was by no means ready to write them off.

In other words, during the 1950s especially, the primary immediate purpose of CDU/CSU policy on the national problem was in substance defensive: thwarting Soviet hopes of absorbing, neutralizing or permanently dividing Germany. Vigorous rhetorical support for reunification on West German terms helped to blunt Soviet policy; believing the best defense to be a good offense, Union leaders from Adenauer onward continued to speak as if German unity were their immediate objective. In part, they hoped that keeping it on the agenda might compel the Kremlin ultimately to compromise.

Adenauer's Ostpolitik and Deutschlandpolitik in Practice

Adenauer's Policy at the Outset: 1949–1954

During the late 1940s and early 1950s, Adenauer pursued West European integration while preventing the creation of a unified but neutralized Germany, which to him appeared to be Moscow's primary goal at the time. The war-time Four Powers had deferred a final peace settlement with defeated Germany, but retained the right to do so at a future date. So long as such a treaty was outstanding, the Four Powers technically retained rights in a *single* Germany, made up of territories that became the Federal Republic, the GDR, and Poland's western regions: formerly Silesia, Pomerania, Brandenburg, East Prussia, and Posen–West Prussia (what many Germans continued to call the eastern territories). In this respect, all developments since 1945, including the establishment of two German states and the Oder-Neisse border between the GDR and Poland (which put the above-mentioned territories "under Polish administration," as the Union phrased it), thus remained, strictly speaking, provisional, to be regarded as such by the Four Powers until they signed a final treaty. Until a treaty was signed they retained in effect a veto over changes in the actual territorial and political configuration of the country.

Although Adenauer continually agreed that resolution of the German question could come about only through a Four Power accord, his "Potsdam complex" convinced him that Moscow would use Four Power conferences to pressure the Western allies into creating and signing a formal treaty with a neutralized Gesamtdeutschland. As he observed candidly, "A Four Power Conference was a risk. It had to be the task of German policy to limit this risk in a reasonable way."[24] To prevent what for him was a worst-case scenario, Adenauer sought to exploit Bonn's waxing influence with the Western allies by urging them to reject any resolution of the German problem that fell short of a fully unified, democratic, and sovereign Gesamtdeutschland. In other words, Adenauer insisted on all or nothing, and because he hardly expected the former, was really assuring the latter: no settlement of Germany's fate by the Four Powers that in any way resembled neutralization.

Accordingly, from 1949 to 1955, during the last phases of occupation and years of limited sovereignty, Adenauer pressed Washington, Paris, and London in their multilateral talks with Moscow to insist upon a major precondition for any German formula: free, internationally monitored elections in both halves of the country before any interim "coalition" government, which he feared the communists would manipulate and dominate as they had throughout Eastern Europe. Adenauer's critics correctly pointed out that this condition precluded any conceivable compromise settlement, such as a phased-in democratic reunification. Yet Adenauer had few qualms about resisting such schemes, which he suspected would merely be Soviet bargaining ploys to create an impression that Bonn would sacrifice ties with the West to gain unity, thereby sow dissension in the West, and stave off the future restoration of a genuinely democratic, sovereign Germany.

There was a legalistic basis for Adenauer's holding policy. The Federal Republic's 1949 constitution classified the country not as a new state or even a successor state, but as a rump of the prewar empire that—as a legal entity—had survived World War II. Under CDU/CSU governments, the FRG maintained that it was entitled to represent this undivided nation or Gesamtdeutschland until a final peace treaty. The Four Powers might be regarded as trustees of the nation's inherent rights of self-determination, but that did not mean Germans were without legal competence. Bonn argued instead that the country as a whole merely lacked the ability to act for itself because it remained in part under foreign, namely Soviet, occupation. As Bonn under CDU/CSU leadership saw it, until East Germans were free to exercise the inherent, internationally recognized right of self-determination, that right must be protected and preserved for them by the Federal Republic. As implied in its 1949 constitution, West Germany, as a democracy, could (and indeed must) speak for the nation as a whole in the interim and do everything it could to promote conditions under which all Germans could together determine their future. Adenauer sought and won Western endorsement of this stand and ensured that Bonn did nothing to compromise it—such as deal with and thereby legitimize the "so-called GDR." Moreover the party argued that it was vital to keep alive the legal claim to represent territories west of the Oder-Neisse line: to give up on those regions would compromise Bonn's right to represent an undivided nation. Only a sovereign reunited Germany could dispose of—or as the expellees hoped—regain those lands.

At the same time, the early 1950s, Adenauer—in pursuit of his combined Westpolitik and Deutschlandpolitik—took a step that critics, many more gesamtdeutsch members of his own party included, regarded as heresy. In exchange for West German rearmament, he reached an accord with Paris, London, and Washington that dissolved the Western occupation authority (pending a final peace treaty among the war-time Powers), granted state sovereignty to the Federal Republic, and established full diplomatic ties between Bonn and the Western powers. The opposition SPD and members of the FDP, one of the Union's coalition partners, condemned rearmament as a step certain to make peaceful reunification impossible; Adenauer responded that only through a strong Western bloc could unity ever be attained. National-minded critics in the Union argued that the accord prejudiced Bonn's legal rights to regard the nation's division as provisional and work for reunification. The chancellor dismissed these fears by pointing to a clause of this new Germany Treaty that obliged all parties to "cooperate in the effort to realize through peaceful means their common goal: a reunified Germany that possesses a free, democratic constitution similar to the Federal Republic's, and that is integrated into the European community."[25]

Historian Arnulf Baring contends that Adenauer regarded this pledge of solidarity from his new allies merely as a way to placate critics. In this view, the chancellor's "Potsdam complex" made him concerned solely with gaining a greater say for Bonn in events affecting German interests. So long as West Germany was occupied (1945–49), or subject to the authority of the High Commission (1949–55), its fate could be sealed by external powers. But after the Federal Republic gained sovereignty, it would have leverage, enabling it to prevent the West from resolving the German question "over Bonn's head." Baring sees this, and not the pledge of allied support for German reunification, as the Germany Treaty's main purpose, even if FRG rearmament dimmed the prospects for winning Soviet acceptance of reunification, and sovereignty compromised Bonn's claim to represent a legally undivided nation.[26]

But the formal declaration of allied support did have some role in the holding policy; neither Adenauer nor his party regarded Bonn's legal positions as useful if treated strictly as unilateral claims. A demonstration of Western solidarity for democratic reunification reinforced the apparent credibility of his maximal goal—national unity within the West European framework—which in turn guarded against Western willingness to settle for an unsatisfactory resolution of the German problem. Similarly Adenauer insisted upon a clause leaving the border question open until a final peace treaty—which meant no acceptance of Poland's eastern border in the meantime. Reluctantly the allies agreed.

So great was Adenauer's commitment to this course that he rebuffed all alternatives. For that reason he refused even to consider East German offers to discuss reunification, a refusal broadly supported by his coalition, save for the CDU's gesamtdeutsch wing.

Similarly, the chancellor urged the Western allies to reject a series of Soviet proposals in early 1952 that seemed to call for reunification without demilitarization. Adenauer was convinced that this sudden Soviet willingness to permit a German army was designed to stir up nationalists, and thus create Western mistrust. In any case he argued that even an armed neutral Germany would be unable by itself to resist Soviet hegemony. As for Soviet pledges to hold free elections in this German state, Adenauer found the precedent in East European states far from promising. He saw the entire Soviet offensive simply as an effort to sow mistrust in the West at a critical time in negotiations over a Western defense community. Despite pressure from some gesamtdeutsch nationalists in the CDU to consider Stalin's initiatives, he urged the allies to counter with the West's traditional proposals based on Western-style elections. He need not have worried: Bonn's allies were no more anxious than Adenauer to see either Western unity cracked by Soviet tactics or Germany actually neutralized.[27]

Adenauer's Holding Policy Stalemated: 1955–1958

In 1954 the cornerstone of Adenauer's Western unity policy, an integrated European Defense Community, collapsed. In 1955 West Germany instead joined the NATO alliance, at which point it regained full sovereignty under the Germany Treaty. Facing unrest in its own camp, the Soviet Union's post-Stalin leadership resigned itself to the FRG's existence and began pursuing a new strategy aimed less at creating a neutralized, united Germany than at formalizing Europe's new configuration as the basis for an "all-European" collective security system.

Adenauer feared that such a strategy, if successful, could first formalize Germany's division and then neutralize most of Europe by undermining the Western alliance. Under these circumstances, his holding policy took on a new task: in the mid to late 1950s its emphasis on pursuing unity took on the substantive purpose of preventing a new European security system based on the status quo, and with it, international recognition of the GDR. After years of urging the allies to stave off the wrong kind of reunification, Adenauer now worried that they might settle for no reunification at all: "For us Germans the highest commandment had to be to clear away any notion that Germany could grow accustomed to the existence of two German states."[28]

Adenauer and his Union colleagues sought to thwart Moscow's goal of deferring all talk of reunification and winning recognition for the GDR. The CDU/CSU argued that reunification must remain atop the agenda and insisted that regarding the GDR in any way as a state, rather than an occupation zone, would infringe upon Four Power authority—the authority over a final peace settlement with, and thus the final configuration of, Gesamtdeutschland. Since these Four Power rights kept all postwar developments provisional, infringing upon them in any way (by recognizing borders, for example, including the Oder-Neisse) would cast doubt on the prospect of reunification. Adenauer reminded his allies of their pledge to accept Bonn's claim that it alone represented the undivided nation.

As always, then, Adenauer and his party argued vigorously for their maximal goal, reunification, in large part to prevent Moscow from achieving its own aim—which, at this stage, was status for the GDR and acceptance of borders. In practice Bonn under the CDU/CSU adopted a strict policy of nonrecognition, indeed ostentatious aloofness, in regard to "the Soviet-occupied zone," and it hoped to prevent third countries from accepting the GDR and the overall territorial and political configuration of Central Europe. Accordingly, it established the Hallstein Doctrine (named for Walter Hallstein, state secretary in the Foreign Ministry), according to which West Germany would and did break diplomatic relations with any third state that recognized the GDR—except Moscow, which, as one of the Four Powers, was a "unique" exception. The Hallstein Doctrine reminded Bonn's potential diplomatic and commercial partners that if they wanted a harmonious relationship with the Federal Republic, they must agree not to treat the existence of two states in Germany as normal. The Hallstein Doctrine was largely successful; even as late as 1969, only a handful of countries—primarily from the Soviet bloc—recognized the GDR.

As a *Realpolitiker*, however, Adenauer by no means abstained from diplomatic maneuvers that might have conceivably reinforced and supplemented his holding policy. Soon after the Federal Republic gained formal sovereignty in 1955, he journeyed to Moscow and officially established relations with the Soviet Union. Some of the chancellor's own followers were confused by this direct contact with the Kremlin, which apparently flew in the face of Bonn's strict refusal to accept the status quo Moscow had created. Adenauer responded by noting that Moscow was exempt from the Hallstein Doctrine because the Soviet Union retained special rights over a final German peace settlement. Bonn thus had to deal formally with the Kremlin in order to assert West Germany's special interests on the question of state unity. Adenauer conceded that Moscow's offer to open relations could not be ignored lest Germans feel a great opportunity to discuss state unity—which he insisted be on the agenda—were being passed up. Mindful of Western suspicions, however, Adenauer insisted with equal vigor that Bonn was not arranging reunification; that remained a matter for the Four Powers. As he saw it, his task was to satisfy Germans of his commitment to unity and the allies of his unwillingness to act unilaterally.[29] Dialogue with the Kremlin in fact thus had an aim largely consistent in substance with the holding policy: it headed off domestic and external pressure (implicit in renewed Four Power talks, which revived his Potsdam complex) for a more far-reaching detente that might have compromised CDU/CSU insistence upon democratic reunification.[30] Adenauer's trip had another aim. By normalizing Bonn's relations with the Kremlin, he won the release in 1955 of ten thousand war prisoners still held by Moscow.

Bonn's Hallstein Doctrine was partly successful in internationalizing the German question and isolating the GDR because many underdeveloped countries needed trade ties with and aid from the FRG. But the party's primary concern remained the attitude and policy of its Western allies: their signatures under the Potsdam accord kept Germany's division provisional, and their signatures under some future pact would make it final. There was reason for West German doubt about the extent of its allies' actual commitment to the maximal goal of German unity. Quips such as "The West only wants German reunification so long as it is impossible" conveyed a meaning that was not lost on CDU/CSU leaders. But if Bonn's partners could hardly be expected to share West German enthusiasm for reunification, Adenauer believed that all Western states shared a common, long-term interest in a "policy of strength" designed to tip the global power balance against Moscow. This belief, rather than the Germany Treaty or the Hallstein Doctrine (which in any case Bonn could hardly brandish against its friends), gave Adenauer confidence that the Western allies would back his unwillingness to recognize the status quo.

But Adenauer erred in estimating the extent of his partners' patience. In a variety of ways, the West began signaling its desire for a detente that effectively accepted Europe's political division. A return to East-West summitry in 1955, the shift in NATO's force structure from conventional to nuclear arms (a more defensive posture), discussion of mutual East-West disengagement, and various other plans for arms limitation all indicated a growing willingness in Western capitals to treat Europe's division as a fact of life. Any credibility a policy of rollback might once have had was waning by the mid-1950s. Bonn's allies were tiring of a seemingly endless confrontation and in part encouraged by the post-Stalin leadership's flexibility on such issues as Austria. The gradual erosion of America's nuclear monopoly argued strongly for arms control, and thus for an East-West modus vivendi based on the status quo—that is, post-Potsdam Europe's configuration.

Bonn's chancellor feared that if the West could be enticed by Moscow into categorizing post-Potsdam Europe as stable and thus as the point of departure for East-West rapprochement, Western willingness to challenge or even question Soviet hegemony over half of Europe would quickly wane. The German question would thus be effectively closed, as Moscow could subsequently depict even the most passive efforts to keep the issue alive as a destabilizing, revanchist threat to peace. Clearly Adenauer feared for the credibility of his claim that reunification remained a real possibility, and thus for his short-term holding policy and any long-term hope of achieving unity.

The party sensed that the Soviet policy of detente also had a dangerous offensive dimension. In Union eyes, Soviet "peace offensives" were designed to incite dissension in the Western camp by holding out a publicized olive branch, persuading elements of U.S. and European public opinion that their own governments were responsible for persistent East-West hostility. In Union eyes, "*divide et impera*" also underlay Soviet efforts to deal with Washington separately from Europe: if the Kremlin could lure the United States into a strictly bilateral detente, the Americans might be persuaded to disregard their allies' interests—thus making the Atlantic a political as well as a physical dividing line within the

West, jeopardizing FRG security *and* the holding policy.

In part as reassurance, the chancellor and Defense Minister Strauss advocated deployment of U.S. nuclear weapons on German soil. Union leaders distrusted the American "New Look"— which emphasized massive nuclear retaliation at the expense of conventional forces—on security grounds alone. Moreover, they saw it as a reactive posture that undercut any notion of rollback and thereby appeared to undermine Bonn's claim that a Western "policy of strength" would gradually pressure Moscow into accepting reunification. But they also felt that as long as Washington was shifting its emphasis to nuclear weapons, deployment of some such systems in Germany would maximize the FRG's importance in American eyes, and thus give it leverage to resist any further U.S. drift toward detente on the basis of the status quo.

Adenauer also tried adapting his holding policy to the apparent stabilization of East-West relations. First he joined the chorus of those calling for detente, but he insisted that East-West rapprochement be premised on "progress toward reunification." When there was movement toward renewing U.S.-Soviet negotiations and mounting pressure for arms control in the mid-1950s, Bonn took up the theme of disarmament. But Adenauer's preconditions were again designed to protect West Germany's holding policy, its resistance to the European status quo: he called for comprehensive worldwide disarmament, arguing that this was vital to create the necessary atmosphere for subsequent cooperation on political issues like reunification. Adenauer also used this linkage of *global* disarmament and the German issue to foil schemes for arms control and disengagement in Central Europe alone—proposals that he feared would kill the holding policy, cement the status quo, and strip the FRG of its security—in effect neutralizing the region.[31]

Similarly the chancellor continued his efforts to soften the burdens of German division. In the late 1950s he won expanded emigration of ethnic Germans from Poland, Russia, and the rest of Eastern Europe. To sustain this momentum, Adenauer in 1957 for the first time offered greater West German–Soviet trade (heretofore highly restricted, despite pressure from the business community).[32]

In secret he went much further. Adenauer approached the Soviet leadership three times between 1958 and 1962 with proposals to convert the GDR alone, at least for an interim period, into a separate, neutralized but entirely democratic state—a second Austria.[33] Historians still debate Adenauer's real motives for toying with a plan that seemingly accepted the status quo, indeed explicitly countenanced the existence of two Germanys, albeit provisionally and conditionally. Close associates of the chancellor insist that he was seeking any way possible to ease the plight of East Germans. They concede that for purposes of "internal deliberations," he indeed had to assume the actual existence of two states.[34] Yet there is little reason to believe that Adenauer considered "Austrianization" an acceptable, permanent solution for the German question. He also probably regarded his proposals a test of Soviet flexibility or—if Moscow actually went along—an interim measure preceding final reunification on West German terms. Although his back-channel, exploratory proposals still entailed no formal recognition of the GDR and kept the German question open, they remained largely confidential to avoid provoking the more virulently gesamtdeutsch members of the CDU/CSU, such as the expellees. The chancellor had in effect placed reunification on the back burner to deal with the more urgent issue of improving conditions in "the zone," but this shift in focus thus escaped public attention.

Berlin and the Collapse of the Holding Policy: 1958–1963

When Nikita Khrushchev launched the second Berlin crisis in 1958, it spelled, in Waldemar Besson's words, "the beginning of the end of the Adenauer era."[35] Moscow threatened to hand over its formal rights as an occupier of Berlin—still divided among the four victorious powers—to the GDR, a move that would call into question French, British, and American rights to travel to and remain in the still-occupied city. Since West Berlin's survival depended on the Western Powers' rights of access and their ability to station troops there, this threat was grave. The Soviet price for avoiding the crisis was conversion of West Berlin into a demilitarized, effectively neutral entity with no ties to the FRG—in short, a *third* Germany. This was Khrushchev's maximal goal, but he hoped in the short term to use Berlin's tenuous position as a way of pressuring the Western powers into distancing themselves from Adenauer's rhetorical goal of reunification and his substantive holding policy, and to secure worldwide recognition of the GDR. Another short-term aim was to seal off East Berlin, stopping a major threat to the communist regime's survival: the steady westward flow of that state's lifeblood —the technical, commercial, and professional elite.

So as not to jeopardize the momentum of East-West detente, Washington and London in particular began exploring ways of meeting Moscow halfway on the Berlin-access issue, rather than unequivocally rebuffing Moscow's efforts. The U.S. secretary of state expressed a readiness to meet GDR officials. The allies also continued seeking arms control and pressed Adenauer, cautiously, to soften Bonn's traditional stance on nonrecognition. Despite protests that Bonn remained in line with its allies, Adenauer faced what Hans-Peter Schwarz has called the pending collapse of his Deutschlandpolitik.[36] Bonn's Western partners were clearly severing any remaining link between rapprochement and reunification, showing their clear unwillingness to let hopes for the latter constrain chances of the former. During these last years of Adenauer's tenure, it became evident that no Four Power negotiations would bring unity to Germany.

Indeed, in those years it was all the chancellor could do to prevent his partners, in their desire for what he considered an unreal detente and false security for Berlin, from accepting a "status quo–minus"—namely an alteration in the status of Berlin and tacit, even full recognition of the GDR. He did so by reminding them of the FRG's importance to the NATO alliance, at times somewhat bluntly. But claiming success in this rearguard action only exposed Adenauer to increasingly heavy criticism from those who argued that CDU/CSU Deutschlandpolitik could now clearly never reach its stated goal, unity—which thus cast doubt on the value of Adenauer's holding policy.[37]

Adenauer tried one last gambit in hopes of salvaging his strategy: a Franco-German entente. Throughout the Berlin crisis, while London and Washington seemed bent on compromise, Charles de Gaulle stood behind Bonn's insistence that the West maintain its full rights in Berlin. Adenauer hoped a new, even stronger, Franco-German entente in the 1960s could shield his holding policy from Anglo-American pressure for detente. For his part, de Gaulle increasingly aimed to challenge *both* superpowers, so the general was interested in luring Bonn away from its close ties to the United

States and creating a European "third force within the Alliance." Adenauer knew that Bonn, with its dependence on the United States, could not go nearly so far, and he also sensed the general's relative lack of commitment to German unity. This clash of long-term goals, along with de Gaulle's scorn for West European integration, should have been enough to make the chancellor somewhat wary of his newfound friend in the Elysée Palace. Yet reconciliation with France long ranked high among Adenauer's hopes—and in the short term, he hoped a joint Bonn-Paris stand against Washington's implicit willingness to cement the status quo would be beneficial. Months of bilateral negotiation and regular meetings between the two men eventually led to a formal Bonn-Paris reconciliation treaty.[38]

Union Ostpolitik after Adenauer

But this flirtation with de Gaulle was Adenauer's last fling. His political stock, at an all-time high in the 1957 elections, had steadily slid since then due to his age and obstinacy, but also due to the perception that the chancellor's Deutschlandpolitik, with its promise of allied support for unification, had failed. Nothing manifested this failure more tangibly than the Berlin Wall, the construction of which in 1961 effectively sealed off East Berlin. Although the Wall violated the city's Four Power status, there was no allied response.

Shortly after the Wall's construction in 1961, the CDU/CSU suffered a stinging rebuke in federal elections, with the result that Adenauer was forced to share decision-making power with other Union and FDP leaders and agree to resign in 1963 in favor of Ludwig Erhard. By then, influence over Union foreign policy had devolved onto Foreign Minister Gerhard Schröder and Franz Josef Strauss, who represented contending schools of thought on which direction Bonn should take in the 1960s.

Gaullism, Atlanticism, and Schröder's Policy of Movement

Strauss, the Union's rising star since becoming defense minister in the mid-1950s, pictured himself as Adenauer's logical heir apparent (though conflicting ambitions and cabinet politics gradually poisoned their personal relations). As a Bavarian, his gesamtdeutsch sentiments were few, and reunification in itself held little appeal for him. But as a self-proclaimed devotee of Realpolitik, Strauss believed that a divided, vulnerable Germany could not protect its own security interests, let alone play an active role in world politics.

In the early 1960s Strauss advocated what would be in effect the creation of a West European union under West German and French directorship. Though he entitled his concept the Grand Design, it was, unlike John F. Kennedy's proposal of the same name, not a call for trans-Atlantic integration. Though speaking of a "two-pillar alliance," Strauss did not believe that Europe could long remain secure as a "welfare community" under the unreliable protection of the U.S. nuclear umbrella. Construction of the Berlin Wall and the U.S. enthusiasm for detente further weakened his faith in America as Europe's guarantor against Soviet pressure. Only a self-sufficient European confederation (albeit one allied with the United States), with its own multilateral nuclear deterrent, would be able to assure European security interests.[39]

Strauss portrayed this policy as the key to German unity. Under current conditions, all of Bonn's partners paid "pointless," if not hypocritical, "lip service" to the national problem because there was no real chance of revising Europe's political configuration. American intentions in particular might be "honorable" but could not be "particularly effective" in resolving the German question because the United States was far away and distracted by its many commitments. But a truly viable West European confederated state would constitute a new variable in the European power equation and a dynamic factor in the global equilibrium. Gradually and peacefully, but inevitably, this state would exert a pull on the countries of Eastern Europe through trade, close political relations, and diplomatic inducements, until the satellites—including the GDR —slipped out of Moscow's orbit.[40]

This new European union, having at its creation succeeded to West German legal claims for reunification—the right to represent an undivided German nation—would then see to it that reunification took place within the framework of the new confederation. In other words, the German problem would be "Europeanized," for a European confederation would logically come to view the German issue as "the nucleus of its own future organization and well-being." After all, continuing involuntary division of Germany by definition meant partition of Europe, which it would be in the confederated state's interest to overcome, and absorbing the vast potential of the entire German nation would also benefit the new Europe.[41]

Just as Strauss's Grand Design was in effect a more active "policy of strength," so too did it resemble Adenauer's policy in serving to rationalize a more realistic, near-term imperative: preventing what Strauss feared could be the finalization or legitimization of communist hegemony over Central Europe. In short, this vision of a new Europe justified an extended, even more rigid holding policy. Strauss argued that Bonn must commit itself totally to constructing a European state, which meant promoting a common economic and security policy but also required keeping the way toward a future confederation free from obstacles. In practice this meant no recognition of borders or political entities—namely the GDR— that might hinder the creation of the new state. Concretely, Strauss aimed at strict nonrecognition of a situation that he felt favored communism and abstention from any detente with the Soviet bloc premised on the continent's current political configuration.[42] This stance convinced Strauss and his "Gaullists" that they were in harmony with de Gaulle's hope of reversing Yalta and constructing a new Europe, even though the French leader was increasingly ready to accept the GDR and deal with Moscow.

The CSU's fundamental conservatism, anticommunism, and visions of Bavaria as a "Christian bulwark," as well as its relatively small core of foreign affairs experts and the awe in which Strauss was held by his party faithful ensured that he would have support for his Gaullist policy. Conservative Christian Democrats also endorsed the policy. Yet Strauss's Grand Design never had a chance of becoming Bonn's official policy: Strauss lost his cabinet post following the 1962 Spiegel affair, and in any case primary control over external policy lay in the hands of his antagonist, Foreign Minister Schröder.

Like Strauss, Schröder was a conservative with long experience in Adenauer's cabinet, but he was a more even-tempered, pragmatic politician. He typified those German politicians from the CDU, as well as the SPD, who represented "German Atlanticism," the label attached during the early 1960s to a second, all-embracing outlook on foreign policy that, unlike Gaullism, placed a premium on harmonious relations with the United States. Like the foreign minister, most Atlanticists were Protestant and from northern Germany. They felt Bonn could ill afford to ignore the Kennedy-Johnson administration's desire for detente and arms control, as well as its interest in trans-Atlantic integration (best symbolized by proposals for a multilateral nuclear force).[43]

Schröder believed that restoring trans-Atlantic harmony was vital to assure FRG security *and* to salvage Bonn's Deutschlandpolitik. He shared the CDU/CSU consensus view that a long-term shift in the global balance of power would be necessary to prompt eventual Soviet acceptance of reunification. But unlike Adenauer and Strauss, he thought a perpetual holding policy only weakened the prospects of such a shift because it damaged alliance cohesion by putting Bonn at odds with her Western partners. The latter were losing their interest in and patience with Bonn's insistence on a Four Power solution of the German question. Schröder also rejected the Gaullist scheme. He felt that any change in the global power balance would flow from changes in the U.S.-Soviet relationship; though strictly intra-European cooperation might strengthen the alliance in a supplementary way, a European superpower was an illusion. For Schröder's Atlanticists, Bonn's primary interest lay in demonstrating maximum solidarity with Washington, the key actor. In any case Schröder felt it was time for Bonn to "recognize itself," and no longer mortgage its foreign policy to that of a chimerical Europe.

Promoting trans-Atlantic cohesion meant, above all, no longer standing in the way of Western desires for detente. In place of a holding policy, Schröder opted for active West German participation in the effort to achieve East-West rapprochement. He considered detente inevitable and unlike Adenauer and Strauss did not believe it need necessarily come at the expense of Deutschlandpolitik. He assumed that there could be no reunification until a change occurred in Europe's postwar political structure, but felt rapprochement could be used to effect such a change gradually, peacefully, and in a way conducive to a satisfactory resolution of the German problem. In the interim, Bonn could find ways to avoid "cementing" the status quo.

In more concrete terms, Schröder hoped an active policy of trade and cooperation with Eastern Europe *except* the GDR could divide the Soviet bloc, drawing Bonn closer to the satellites while isolating East Germany from them. FRG help with modernization could expand West German influence in the East European states by making Moscow's satellites more dependent on Bonn, thus implicitly exploiting what many saw as a renationalization of East Europe and incipient diversity within the bloc. In this way, Schröder believed Bonn could maximize its own influence and weaken that of the GDR, thus isolating the nervous East German regime, depriving it of sympathy and support from its own bloc, and leaving it no choice but rapprochement on Bonn's terms—namely, *without* official recognition. In other words, Schröder believed that with a "policy of movement" Bonn could bypass East Berlin, making the GDR appear as the true holdout in Europe's detente unless it accepted West German calls for cooperation that did not first require closing the German question.

German Gaullists argued that Schröder's active Ostpolitik ruined the hopes of a common European policy on detente and the German question. At this point the differences between CDU and CSU, so long subsumed in Adenauer's popularity, erupted. The Bavarians (and their CDU allies) were less willing to compromise upon the basic positions of the old Adenauer policies by experimenting with new approaches to the East. Specifically, they protested that dealing with communist countries, even at a subdiplomatic level, implicitly violated Bonn's long-standing refusal to accept the status quo and invalidated the Hallstein Doctrine—unless those states severed diplomatic ties with the GDR.

Schröder himself wanted to avoid entirely abrogating the Hallstein Doctrine, but this pressure to stick rigidly by its letter and spirit struck him as counterproductive: in the name of protecting legal positions, his Union colleagues would deprive Bonn of all diplomatic flexibility. Nonetheless, the foreign minister was compelled to conduct his dealings with the states on the Soviet periphery on a lower level, avoiding all suggestion of formal diplomatic ties. Unless these states were willing to defy Moscow of their own volition and "de-recognize" the GDR, Bonn could not formalize its ties with them. Under these constraints, Schröder nonetheless managed to expand relations with Eastern Europe by setting up trade missions throughout the region, beginning with Poland and going on to include Rumania, Hungary and Bulgaria (Czechoslovakia proved too stubborn). By 1966 West Germany's influence among the satellites had grown considerably. In this way, much to the annoyance of many German Gaullists, Schröder circumvented the Hallstein Doctrine's restrictive effects on political cooperation without violating its formal intent: namely, to avoid full diplomatic ties with those states that recognized the GDR. He also worked out a formula according to which the satellite countries tacitly agreed to consider West Berlin part of the FRG for purposes of trade.

But at the same time Schröder sought to avoid antagonizing Moscow, which quickly sensed that Bonn's new Ostpolitik could in the long run erode Soviet control over Eastern Europe. Although such erosion of Soviet control was indeed part of the West German plan, Schröder felt that outright confrontation with the Kremlin could only be counterproductive. So in 1964 he attempted to arrange a summit between Khrushchev and Adenauer's successor as chancellor, Ludwig Erhard, and tried to expand Bonn-Moscow trade. These initiatives fell through, but toward the end of Erhard's brief tenure, Bonn delivered a detailed "peace note" to Moscow that in substance called for detente without the customary linkage to progress on the German question (though it reiterated Bonn's right to represent Germany within its 1937 borders).

Despite this improvement in the political atmosphere, there was an increasingly widespread perception that Schröder's Ostpolitik was destined to fail because it overestimated the amount of room that the satellites had to maneuver in dealing with the West. Moreover, the design of Schröder's policy would isolate the GDR, and that was something Moscow could not afford: the Kremlin had too great a stake in the stability and viability of its East German satellite to let Bonn achieve the fruits of detente without paying a price, namely, granting the GDR some status.

Outside of the CDU/CSU, there was a growing readiness for some manner of direct dealing, if by no means official relations, with the regime in East Berlin. The SPD, the FDP (now the Union's only coalition partner), Germany's church leaders, and an ever-larger share of public opinion wanted a more flexible policy toward East Germany. Polls showed dwindling confidence in the prospects for reunification. From the established Protestant and Catholic church hierarchies there was also pressure to accept, tacitly or outright, the Oder-Neisse border between East Germany and Poland so that West Germany might be reconciled with the latter. In other words, Schröder's Ostpolitik, seen as dangerously radical by so many Gaullist Union leaders, earned criticism elsewhere for not going far enough.

CDU/CSU Policy in the Grand Coalition

At the heart of this ever-greater readiness to deal with the Soviet bloc was an evolving concept of what Deutschlandpolitik should aim for. In the FDP, the SPD, the churches—and parts of the Union itself—it was increasingly argued that Bonn must concentrate less on overcoming the nation's division and more on overcoming the effects of that division: families and friends cut off from contact; limited tourism and emigration; disrupted internal networks of commerce; special problems for villages directly on the demarcation line; severed postal and telephone communications; and limited sports or cultural exchanges.

Many West German politicians and publicists felt that the nation as a whole would suffer if partition and the GDR's especially repressive character completely sealed off the FRG from East Germany. The German people's sense of a common heritage and a shared destiny would be undermined if the division's impermeable nature deprived them of any interrelationship. From this perspective, Bonn's main aim had to be to prevent Germans from becoming separated psychologically, as well as physically, by encouraging greater contact between both halves of the country.

During the 1960s this dimension of the national problem came to dominate FDP and SPD Deutschlandpolitik, and it increasingly affected even the Union, although trial balloons launched by maverick Union leaders like Rainer Barzel were quickly shot down.[44] But Chancellor Erhard's fall in late 1966 brought to power a new governing coalition that for largely domestic reasons consisted of the CDU/CSU and its main rival, the SPD (the FDP was excluded). Kurt Georg Kiesinger, a longtime member of Adenauer's cabinet and a conservative Catholic from the south, became chancellor; Willy Brandt, SPD leader, took over the Foreign Ministry.

As a much larger party than the Union's previous partners in government, the SPD could demand more influential cabinet posts and a commensurately greater say over official policy. In this Grand Coalition, the Union's policy toward the national problem set a new tone. In response to international events, public opinion, and the views of its new partner in government, the Union reluctantly agreed to put reunification on the back burner and expressed its willingness to seek a dialogue with the East bloc and, conditionally, East Germany. In his opening address to Parliament, Kiesinger talked of building bridges with the East, establishing relations with more neighboring states, advancing reconciliation with Poland—all signs of the government's commitment to detente. Kiesinger also pledged that Bonn would seek a conditional rapprochement between both halves of Germany: "We want . . . to prevent the two parts of our people from living apart from each other during this partition. . . . For that reason we want to promote human, economic and spiritual relations with our fellow countrymen in the other part of Germany with all our strength. Where the establishment of contacts between authorities of the Federal Republic and those in the other part of Germany is necessary for that goal, that does not mean recognition of a second German state."[45]

In a subsequent interview Kiesinger made clear that detente was a prerequisite for reunification: "It is correct that reunification of the divided parts of Germany would mean a change affecting the power and security interests of the Soviet Union. For that reason reunification cannot take place in an atmosphere of Cold War, but only in a process of climatic improvements that would achieve a weakening and overcoming of European antagonisms."[46] On other occasions, Kiesinger warned that a united Germany would constitute a "critical mass," too volatile for Europe unless a process of detente had first been achieved.

This apparent CDU/CSU readiness to regard detente as a necessary precondition for dealing with Germany's division took concrete form in 1967 and 1968. The Grand Coalition continued Schröder's policies toward Eastern Europe, actually establishing formal diplomatic ties with Rumania and Yugoslavia. Because neither Bucharest nor Belgrade severed its ties with East Berlin, this required a formula for circumventing the Hallstein Doctrine. The Federal Republic also proposed discussions on a "renunciation of force" accord with Moscow. Most significantly, Kiesinger's government advanced a series of proposals for practical agreements with the GDR, covering humanitarian, commercial, and cultural issues, as well as an inner-German agreement to renounce force. There was even an exchange of notes between the chancellor and the East German chief of government, Willi Stoph.

For the first time, CDU/CSU leaders—under SPD pressure—freed an active West German Ostpolitik from the condition that it must be accompanied by progress toward reunification. This was made easier because even Strauss—ever sensitive to shifting political winds—conceded that unity within the 1937 borders was unlikely. CSU programs very cautiously began to downplay unity as a goal.[47]

Bonn won praise from its Western partners, including the now detente-oriented de Gaulle, for taking the initiative, particularly with regard to the GDR. But the Grand Coalition "detente offensive" soon ran up against a wall of Soviet, Polish, and East German resistance. East bloc leaders sensed that the Federal Republic was out to destabilize their regimes, above all the one in East Berlin, by intensifying contacts across the board without formally accepting the status quo, namely communist control over the region. They thus kept the price for reconciliation high, insisting, among other conditions, upon full West German recognition of the GDR and the Oder-Neisse line, as well as classification of West Berlin as a separate political entity. Bonn would not meet these demands, and within months the detente offensive became stalemated. Talks on a Bonn-Moscow accord to renounce force bogged down over the question of whether such an agreement should recognize the status quo; the inner-German dialogue broke off when East Berlin insisted on elevating it to the diplomatic level.

Divisions within the Grand Coalition in part caused and in part reflected this stalemate on the Eastern front. SPD leaders wanted to explore formulas that might meet Moscow and East Berlin halfway by compromising on questions of status and borders; they even used the Italian Communist party as an intermediary to open a dialogue with the East German ruling party, the SED. CDU/CSU criticism of such a strategy compounded strains within the partnership. As the Union saw it, Bonn had already shown a readiness to negotiate without reunification as a precondition. For West Germany to go further and soften its stance—above all on nonrecognition and the right to represent an undivided Germany—would only reward communist intransigence by satisfying Soviet demands for Western legitimization of its hegemony over Eastern Europe. Until the Kremlin permitted a real process of liberalization that could ease the effects of the division, the CDU/CSU saw little point in interim measures that might appear to freeze the status quo by prejudicing West German legal positions. Concretely this meant continuing to isolate the GDR diplomatically and politically, denying it status. Any inter-German dealings to "soften the effects of national division" were subject to this strict condition. Union leaders feared that almost any method of bargaining with East Germany would imply tacit recognition of communist rule, and thus they did not follow up their rhetoric on inner-German rapprochement with concrete plans to bargain with the GDR. They increasingly returned in substance, if not rhetoric, to a policy of isolating the East German regime. Only an uninfluential minority continued to explore negotiating formulas for working around the problem.

In August 1968, following a year of defensive measures against the effect of East-West "bridge building" upon its sphere of influence, Moscow invaded Czechoslovakia, using as its pretext the charge of a German-inspired Czechoslovakian counterrevolution. For Union leaders in the Grand Coalition, if not the SPD, Moscow's move seemed to demolish the prospect for detente in Europe by vividly demonstrating how little room there was for liberalization and autonomy in the Soviet camp. More than that, Soviet tanks in Prague cleared the way for enunciation of the Brezhnev doctrine, which asserted Moscow's right to "protect" socialism from outside threats. Many Union leaders concluded that Moscow thereby hoped to win a detente-hungry world's acquiescence in Soviet hegemony over half the continent by depicting even indirect challenges to the status quo in Eastern Europe as destabilizing.

Moscow's invasion of Czechoslovakia and the Grand Coalition's foreign policy setbacks persuaded a majority of Union leaders to curtail any further Ostpolitik experiments. Further efforts to adapt party policy to international events were seen as fruitless and counterproductive. Only a minority of CDU leaders led by Schröder wanted to encourage the further evolution of CDU/CSU policy; most favored retrenchment. With an election looming at year's end, 1969 saw sharp debate over foreign policy. With ever-stronger rhetoric, CDU/CSU leaders hoped to undercut their rival and partner, the SPD, send it to a defeat at the polls, and thereby end the Grand Coalition. Union leaders charged that if SPD chief and current foreign minister, Willy Brandt, had his way, Bonn would recognize the GDR, ending all hope of eventual reunification. Kiesinger, Strauss, and others overruled SPD calls for more modifications in the Hallstein Doctrine, despite ever-greater difficulty in preventing countries from attempting to recognize the GDR, and attacked Brandt's interest in the Soviet idea of an all-European conference on security issues, which they said would merely be used to legitimize the division of Europe. Voters thus confronted a choice between, on the one hand, backing slowly away from the Grand Coalition's initial policies and on the other, with the SPD, carrying those policies further than originally promised.

CDU/CSU Ostpolitik changed relatively little during the two decades between 1949 and 1969. At least in public, the Union stayed with a holding policy that rejected even tacit acceptance of the Soviet sphere of influence in the East, let alone of the GDR. Schröder's experiments and official Union policy in the Grand Coalition accepted that the onset of East-West detente invalidated the policy of strength and made it necessary to develop a more adaptive Ostpolitik. But Gaullists rejected that argument, and the party largely held to its defensive position: complete rejection of the status quo. Its leaders claimed that though this stance had produced few positive results, it had averted what they considered the real risks posed by any and all alternatives.

II

**Debate over
the Eastern Treaties**

The Initial Agreements, 1969–1971

After the September 1969 elections the CDU/CSU —though still the FRG's largest party—formally became a parliamentary opposition for the first time, banished from the government benches by the somewhat surprising formation of a new coalition between the SPD and FDP (or Liberals). This exile from political power resulted in part from the unpopularity of Union prescriptions for the economy, but also from the party's apparent inability to reconcile its Deutschlandpolitik and Ostpolitik with changing public attitudes and the movement toward East-West rapprochement. CDU/CSU policies had cost the party votes and created a common bond between its rivals in the realm of foreign policy.

Brandt's Ostpolitik Concept and the Union Response

Three men would shape the new SPD-FDP government's policy: Chancellor Willy Brandt, former Berlin mayor, foreign minister in the Grand Coalition, longtime SPD chairman, and an advocate of reconciliation with the East; Herbert Wehner, the SPD's gruff parliamentary leader who devised its strategy for winning a place in government during the 1960s by endorsing Adenauer's Westpolitik, yet felt a deep commitment to easing the plight of East Germans; and Egon Bahr, a former journalist, and all-purpose aide to Brandt who had pleaded since 1963 for a new approach to Germany's national division.

SPD thinking on the German question had undergone a transformation in the late 1950s and early 1960s. The party had gradually reconciled itself to West German membership in NATO and the European Community (made formal in a 1960 parliamentary address by Wehner), abandoned its long-held hopes for a reunified independent *Gesamtdeutschland*, and—especially after construction of the Berlin Wall—became increasingly convinced that national partition was a fact of life. The SPD saw reunification or the achievement of self-determination in any form as such remote possibilities that they could no longer realistically be the guiding goals of Bonn's foreign policy. Brandt and the chief architect of his policy, Egon Bahr, felt that the Federal Republic's policy had heightened the insecurity of the communist regime in East Berlin, which responded by sealing off its subjects from any contact with the West, causing the nation's two halves to drift apart.

As Brandt and Bahr saw it, if Bonn instead agreed to grant the SED state status, agreements could be reached to "soften" the impact of Germany's division. Specifically, this softening could include greater contacts between citizens of the two states: West Germans visiting relatives in the East, and vice versa; expanded tourism; sport and cultural exchanges; more trade; and regular discussion of political, administrative, transportation and environmental problems created or complicated by the division. In the short term, Brandt and Bahr believed these contacts could alleviate practical problems and ease tensions; in the medium-range future, they could foster "cultural unity" and "a sense of togetherness," permitting Germans in both halves of the country to feel part of one nation, if not one state, thus preserving "the substance of the nation." SPD strategists talked of "accepting the status quo in order to change it."

Brandt and Bahr did not expect East Berlin's stubbornly Stalinist SED party boss, Walter Ulbricht, to welcome such a scheme. "Transformation (in East German policy) through accommodation (with Bonn)" could in the long run prove more destabilizing to the SED regime than confrontation. But West German SPD leaders also banked heavily on what they considered Moscow's strong, near-term desire for overall East-West detente. Given a changing Soviet Westpolitik, reinforced by heightened anxiety about China, the time seemed ripe for a good bargain. Even relatively modest concessions by Bonn at this stage would, they hoped, result in Soviet pressure on East Germany to negotiate about practical and humanitarian problems. Not only could detente between the superpowers be exploited to facilitate a German-German compromise, but, in a mutually reinforcing process, Bonn would contribute to easing world tensions by removing the burdensome German problem as an obstacle to rapprochement.

In accelerating rather than braking movement toward East-West accommodation, Bonn would also stay in step with its allies, for 1969 was the beginning of the Nixon-Kissinger policy of detente.

Social-Liberal leaders knew that political and constitutional barriers prevented them from granting the GDR full-scale diplomatic recognition. Treating the GDR as a foreign state like any other, moreover, would make it hard to justify the quest for measures "preserving the substance of the nation." Nonetheless, Brandt still saw room for flexibility: Bonn could accept the existence of "two states in one nation," agree to treat the GDR as a fully equal negotiating partner, and pledge to respect its territorial integrity. Bonn could formalize, if not normalize, relations between the two states. Moreover the FRG could abandon its Hallstein Doctrine. All of these measures would signal West German willingness to stop challenging the SED regime's legitimacy and stability in the near term at least, thus, it was hoped, satisfying Moscow and clearing the way to negotiations over human, cultural, and commercial contacts.[1]

When it came to short- and medium-term objectives as well as general approach, the SPD had considerable support from its new coalition partner. Once a virulently *gesamtdeutsch* party, the FDP had come to reject the CDU/CSU's near-term, defensive policy toward the East. Many Liberal leaders like Foreign Minister Walter Scheel saw it as a largely impractical policy that entailed clinging to unrealistic claims at the expense of a *modus vivendi* that might help to ease the effects of national division. The FDP also felt that CDU/CSU policy created unnecessary strains with both East and West.

To be sure, there were differences over tactics within the new coalition even in 1969 and, more important still, uncertainty as to the compatibility of long-term SPD and FDP visions. Though Liberal leaders were happy to throw overboard the "excess baggage" of traditional CDU/CSU policy, which they felt slowed the momentum of FRG Ostpolitik, few were entirely comfortable with SPD talk of a "new European peace structure," Bahr's concepts for an eventual East-West collective security framework, and left-wing talk of a neutral confederation or even convergence between the two German states. Many more conservative Free Democrats were quite uncomfortable with the accommodationist tones of their new partners. Yet for the immediate future there was a congruence of aims, and because Scheel trusted Brandt implicitly, the two parties deliberately left the question of ultimate goals ambiguous.[2]

A similar ambivalence marked the relationship between the SDP and Bonn's major ally. Richard Nixon and Henry Kissinger were content that West Germany would no longer isolate itself by allowing a "near obsession with continuity [and] . . . unfulfilled national aims" to block an East-West rapprochement that would stabilize the situation in Europe. Yet the very aim of U.S. policy was to stop Moscow from capitalizing on the emerging European desire for detente, luring the Western allies into special arrangements that would divide NATO. Kissinger worried in particular that Bonn's Ostpolitik "could create a momentum that may . . . unhinge [Germany's] international position." He considered Bahr a German nationalist who might exploit Bonn's central position to bargain with both East and West, a man who "believed that Germany could realize its national destiny only by friendship with the East." For this reason Washington would seek "to channel Bonn's Ostpolitik in a constructive direction by working closely with Brandt and his colleagues." Washington would link all East-West and European issues, including a settlement over Berlin and the idea of a security conference (Moscow's cherished aim), thus ensuring that Ostpolitik was "embedded in a matrix of negotiations." This matrix would enhance Bonn's bargaining position yet also set limits "beyond which it could not go without allied consensus."[3]

Bonn's European neighbors showed even greater enthusiasm for German efforts to remove the national question from the international agenda and promote stable East-West relations. Yet like the United States, they worried about Bonn becoming more independent and preoccupied with its new Eastern and national policies at the expense of its Western commitments. Paris also sensed that Bonn's Ostpolitik could eclipse France's own detente policies and thus its leadership role in the West.

The Union Response

Social-Liberal Ostpolitik—an Eastern policy based on acceptance of the status quo and negotiations—directly challenged assumptions that had long shaped CDU/CSU policy on the national question and East-West relations.

Union orthodoxy held, first, that the SED could have no interest in rapprochement because, as a democratic German state, the FRG intrinsically threatened the GDR's legitimacy and thus its survival. Moreover, as events in Prague vividly demonstrated, Kremlin leaders would continue to isolate their bloc from any meaningful contact with the West; Ulbricht had no interest in copying Alexander Dubček's ill-fated experiment.

From the CDU/CSU standpoint, moreover, long-term SPD goals were contradictory and likely to prove counterproductive. The Ostpolitik would, in substance, strengthen Soviet and East German communism's hegemony by formally accepting Europe's division, yet tacitly promote a loosening of the Soviet empire's internal structures. In the Union's view, this could raise false hopes in the East's population and lead to brutal reapplication of the Brezhnev Doctrine. An offensive detente could not succeed.

Even if the Social-Liberal method could make it possible to alleviate problems caused by Germany's division by practical and humanitarian measures, in the Union's view, such measures were an inadequate goal of Deutschlandpolitik. Though the Social-Liberal method might well foster a sense of national fraternal solidarity, as Bahr and Brandt hoped, for the Union, this did not in itself constitute German unity. "Preserving the substance of the nation" was no substitute for Bonn's traditional goal: *true* national unity. Real unity could be achieved only by ending the physical, involuntary separation of the German people into two states, and it was precisely this goal that the Union suspected Brandt and Bahr were ready to abandon. By speaking primarily of the nation's "substance," by downplaying reunification, by refusing to aim for state unity (unity within a single state), by soft-pedaling the goal of national self-determination, Social-Liberal Ostpolitik, as the Union saw it, would cement or "deepen" Germany's division.

In Union eyes, moreover, by placing a premium on humanitarian and practical concessions from the Soviet bloc, Brandt and

Bahr opened themselves to Moscow's blackmail: the Kremlin would seduce Bonn with tempting concessions, such as the promise of expanded human contacts within Germany, in exchange for treaty terms that in effect would compromise Germany's claim against the status quo even further. Reinforced by what seemed to be lessons of the Grand Coalition's experience, Union orthodoxy feared the loss of Bonn's legal claims. If the Social-Liberal quest for practical and humanitarian gains led to more official and unofficial contact with and implicit acknowledgment of the GDR, this flexibility would be translated into a new set of legal norms, thus undermining Bonn's exclusive right to represent an undivided nation. Union orthodoxy argued that Brandt should leave issues that might affect the status of inner-German relations to the Four Powers. Detente should be and could be facilitated without compromising the German question, but if that proved impossible, then there must be no rapprochement.[4]

From the standpoint of Union orthodoxy, the new SPD-FDP policy threatened more than the case for German unity. The Union also saw West German accommodation of the Soviet bloc as certain to create doubts abroad about Bonn's long-term orientation, raising the specter of neutralism, sowing disunity in the alliance, and risking FRG security. In the Union's eyes, detente and above all treatment of the SED as an equal negotiating partner, would also weaken the FRG public's sense of the basic divergence between East and West. SPD-FDP policy could undermine the will to resist Soviet expansionist pressure and further alienate West Germany from its Western allies. Ostpolitik and long-range SPD visions of convergence between East and West would, it feared, also strengthen radical left-wing opposition to the FRG's democratic, capitalist institutions.

What explains the strength of this emerging CDU/CSU critique of SPD-FDP policy, especially concerning the German question? As noted above, CDU/CSU orthodoxy regarding Ostpolitik and Deutschlandpolitik had survived largely intact since the days of Adenauer. It was still dominated by rhetoric and behavior designed to promote the case for reunification on Western terms, which implied disappearance of the GDR and thus effectively excluded explicit, provisional acceptance of the SED state. Neither Adenauer nor his successors had revised or expanded the goals of CDU/CSU policy in a way that might have permitted the party to develop a new stance toward the GDR; the rhetoric of reunification remained dominant in party policy. (Adenauer's various initiatives, such as the Austrian solution, had been completely covert—even his foreign minister was kept largely in the dark—and during the Grand Coalition, the party had proposed some form of negotiations only under conditions unacceptable to the Soviet bloc.)

Yet, to be sure, the party in 1969 did not believe or try to argue that the day of unity was close at hand. It conceded that German reunification could occur only in the context of a united Europe, and after a peaceful change in the bloc structure of Europe as a whole. Even CSU leaders admitted that, short of a catastrophic war, no change in Europe leading to reunification in the foreseeable future was likely.

The Union nonetheless insisted that an opportunity to overcome the division would never arise if Germans quit asserting their rights as a nation. Reunification and self-determination might seem only declaratory goals, but from the standpoint of Union orthodoxy, rights and rhetoric mattered. Like Poles in an earlier era, the Union proclaimed, Germans must patiently promote their cause if a new European order was to evolve, and if it was to give them a say in their own future; unless they asserted their will and right to live together, Germans would be implicitly forfeiting any claim against the status quo.

Union orthodoxy argued that in this respect assertion of the right of state unity was especially important. Germany's sense of identity had been largely shaped by the Bismarckian empire, and any disavowal of the legal and political validity of the right to restore that state in its full form meant undermining the foundations of German nationhood. Such a Bismarckian state should, the party said, never reemerge, but it was as impossible to disregard the logical relationship between state and nation as that between form and content. In this respect, the case for state unity remained instrumentally, rather than intrinsically, important for the CDU/CSU. The case for state unity kept alive the sense of German nationhood and helped to keep Europe's structures provisional until a political change allowed all Germans to exercise their right of self-determination. For this reason, from the standpoint of Union orthodoxy, it was vital to preserve the case for state unity, rather than expressly lower Bonn's sights and aim for mere "cultural unity."

From this line of thought came the Union's concern about treating the FRG's legal positions as negotiable. The CDU/CSU rejected SPD arguments that the juridical basis for pursuing reunification was unimportant or unpolitical. It insisted that legal norms codified political intentions, which explained why the communist bloc was preoccupied with altering the juridical labels in Europe: Moscow hoped thereby to undermine the FRG's entire case for challenging the status quo, and thus for challenging Soviet hegemony.

Fundamentalists

Yet as the Ostpolitik debate commenced, there were varying degrees of commitment to Union orthodoxy. The party was not of one mind on how far it should be guided by its traditional views when responding to SPD-FDP innovations in official West German policy. A majority espoused a strictly fundamentalist interpretation of party beliefs, and thus stiff resistance to SPD-FDP policy. Most virulent in this group were the expellee leaders, who saw the SPD policy as a threat to their movement and its cause. They feared that treating the German question as closed would deprive them of any eventual hope of having a say in the disposition of their *Heimat*. And a loss of importance of the national issue would also undermine their movement's domestic political influence.

Opposition was not limited to the expellees. SPD-FDP proposals also ran up against the gesamtdeutsch sensitivities of many north German and Protestant conservatives in the CDU. But the most numerous and influential in the fundamentalist majority were, as always, CDU and CSU conservatives from relatively homogeneous, middle-class, Catholic, and southern regions, or nonurban parts of the Rhineland. Though these politicians were not necessarily possessed of strong German national attitudes, SPD-FDP Ostpolitik as it emerged conflicted with their long-held feeling that Germany's unjust and ahistorical division must be resisted and overcome.

More important, however, both those with and those without strong gesamtdeutsch sentiments, including above all the CSU, saw the SPD-FDP formulas for accepting the division as a dangerous concession to Soviet political and ideological hegemony in Europe. For staunch conservatives and anticommunists, keeping the German question open was one part of a comprehensive policy to prevent complete consolidation of the Soviet sphere of influence and thus also to stave off perceived Soviet pressure on Western Europe —including the FRG. Fundamentalists feared above all that SPD-FDP Ostpolitik, by effectively closing the German question and weakening the alliance, would permit West Germany to be sucked into neutralist currents. Many of these fundamentalists were political descendants of the old Union Gaullist faction; they saw Bonn as leader of an assertive, anticommunist Western Europe, and though pro-NATO, they distrusted the U.S. proclivity for detente.

This resistance to accommodation was also generated by domestic politics. Fundamentalists pointed out that the Union had fallen short of an absolute majority in 1969 partly because many of its right-wing supporters, disenchanted with the Grand Coalition of conservatism and socialism, had voted for the small radical National Democratic Party (NPD). They believed a sharp right-hand turn on the national issue could regain this 4 percent of the electorate and attract and maintain the support of expellees.

Thus even those Union conservatives without a genuine gesamtdeutsch perspective spoke more and more of resisting compromise on the German question as a matter of national duty. They also increasingly echoed the expellee argument that Bonn's policy toward the East must take into account not merely German crimes, but also crimes against Germans. This argument pleased the expellees but also exploited hostility toward reconciliation, especially with Poland.

These motives, reinforced by expellee—especially Sudeten —presence, were also at work in the CSU, lending the Bavarian party's hostility to the new Ostpolitik a somewhat uncharacteristic gesamtdeutsch tone. The CSU was especially preoccupied with "reorienting" and winning the backers of the NPD. The latter's virulently nationalistic, antisocialist appeal had been especially strong in the Protestant regions of northern Bavaria, namely Franconia. In co-opting this movement, the CSU took on an even more gesamtdeutsch, nationalistic tone, while vigorously denying any similarities with the NPD.

Finally, Strauss, the CSU, and most prominent CDU leaders such as Kiesinger (a majority in the parliamentary delegation) were still stunned by the formation of an SPD-FDP coalition; they saw the

Union as the rightful government "in exile." They were not interested in wooing the FDP away from the SDP with a display of bipartisanship and centrism; rather they aimed to drive the Liberals out of state parliaments and eventually out of the federal parliament. They pursued a relentless assault upon Brandt, above all over foreign policy, in hopes of undermining the new chancellor's razor-thin parliamentary majority and restoring the CDU/CSU to power.

Reformists

A minority viewpoint in the Union, however, eschewed strict CDU/CSU orthodoxy in favor of a new approach. This approach acknowledged Bonn's juridical claim to represent an undivided nation, but showed relatively little confidence in "the automatic healing power of a policy of holding onto rights," since in this view legal positions and "the content of policy" were not synonymous.[5] Repeatedly asserting unilateral legal claims was morally satisfying, but it was a defensive tactic and unlikely to effect a positive change in the political structure of Europe. Thus, this minority advised using some of Bonn's rights as bargaining chips—neither clinging to them at all costs, nor freely giving them up—to gain concessions in other areas, namely in the humanitarian, technical, or administrative spheres. From this point of view, a certain, limited degree of status for the GDR (if not full recognition as a separate state), and some formal acknowledgment of the Oder-Neisse line were at least negotiable in the search for a "useful compromise." This minority strategy was distinguished from the Social-Liberal Ostpolitik because it supplemented Bonn's traditional effort to keep reunification and self-determination alive as a political (if not legal) cause, instead of supplanting it.

Exponents of flexibility were found exclusively in the CDU, mainly among several small subgroups. Some older, gesamtdeutsch-oriented politicians, especially from Berlin and northern Germany, belonged to this "reformist" minority, as did many exiles from the GDR (led by former CDU chairman of the GDR, Johann Baptist Gradl) and prominent spokesmen for the Union's Protestant minority.

Also among this loose minority as the party entered opposition were a host of rising stars in the CDU. One was Helmut Kohl, the minister president, or governor, of Rhineland-Palatinate, and an advocate of reform and renewal of party policy as well as party organization. More important was Richard von Weizsäcker, the son of prominent German diplomat Ernst von Weizsäcker, who had ties to the resistance against Hitler, yet was imprisoned by the Allies. Himself a soldier on the Eastern front, and afterward an active layman in the Protestant church, the younger von Weizsäcker looked on his role in German foreign policy as "an act of personal restitution." His Berlin background gave him a personal tie to that city, and his time abroad as a youth made him sensitive to foreign attitudes toward Germany.[6]

Yet the reformists also included younger politicians without gesamtdeutsch roots, mainly from urban-industrial areas, Protestant northern Germany, or the Rhineland, where trade-union influence was strong. These younger figures had sympathies for the Union's original Christian-socialist tendencies and were more reformist on domestic and foreign affairs issues. They emerged from and interacted with a voter milieu similar to that which most strongly supported the SPD and thus were more exposed to (and in sympathy with) the ideas of the SPD than were their fundamentalist colleagues.

Thus CDU reformists shared above all the growing sense that ordinary Germans were ready for a greater degree of normalcy in FRG foreign policy. They believed the public was wearying of an emphasis on reunification that came at the expense of tangible measures to ameliorate the division's effects. Many also wanted reconciliation with Germany's former enemies in the East, above all Poland, in order to earn international respectability for the FRG. Above all, as heirs to the Atlanticist tradition (oriented more toward Britain and America than toward Europe and France), these reformists did not want the German issue to alienate Bonn's allies. Though less sanguine about the prospects for East-West detente than the Social Democrats, they did not want Bonn to risk its Western credentials by appearing to obstruct movement toward a modus vivendi.

Purely political motives were also at work among those CDU politicians with reformist inclinations. As noted above, they often came from regions where the SPD was strong—Protestant north Germany and urban-industrial areas, above all the Rhine-Ruhr region. Unlike colleagues from Union strongholds, they keenly felt the need to compete with (rather than merely confront) the SPD to attract voters, including trade unionists. This gave them a stake in a more flexible interpretation of party orthodoxy, including Ostpolitik. Reinforcing this incentive for moderation was the desire of reformists like Kohl to woo the FDP away from the SPD and reestablish a Christian-Liberal coalition.

Two key figures sympathized with the reformists but tried to remain somewhat independent. One was former foreign minister, Gerhard Schröder, author of the "policy of movement." The other was Rainer Barzel, CDU/CSU parliamentary party chief and, now in opposition, the Union's most visible leader. A Catholic with experience in the CDU's trade-union wing, Barzel had made waves in 1966 by proposing a relatively radical model for German democratic reunification that accommodated Soviet military and economic concerns. Despite equally strong anticommunist credentials, this inclination to experiment and a flexible political temperament made Barzel an advocate of some change in FRG Ostpolitik (his many reservations about the Bahr-Brandt approach notwithstanding).

But Barzel was poorly positioned to enforce unity within the joint CDU/CSU parliamentary delegation when it came to Ostpolitik or any similarly contentious issues: in a group of powerful party "barons," he was at most *primus inter pares*. Since the decline of Adenauer, no single Union leader had consolidated power over the party. Barzel hoped to do so by holding on to his title as CDU/CSU parliamentary chief, replacing Kiesinger as CDU party chairman, and eventually becoming the Union's candidate for chancellor—the three most prized positions. But it would be an achievement for him simply to outduel rivals like Schröder and Kiesinger, who aimed at replacing him as parliamentary leader themselves before seizing the ultimate title: CDU/CSU chancellor candidate for the next election. Barzel had support from many younger party colleagues and the CDU's trade unionists, but other important constituencies within the Union were divided. Moreover, like Kiesinger and Schröder, he was tempted to offer the government constructive opposition, but faced pressure from the hard-liners—above all Strauss's CSU—to attack the SPD and FDP. During the critical years ahead, Barzel would be forced to balance his constructive criticism of Social-Liberal Ostpolitik with harsh rhetorical attacks.[7]

The Initial Negotiations

Debate over the Inner-German Dialogue

Brandt introduced the major elements of Bonn's new Ostpolitik in an address to Parliament on 28 October 1969. The chancellor stopped short of formally recognizing the GDR but tacitly acknowledged that there were "two states in Germany." This formula for de facto, if not de jure, acceptance of East Germany, coupled with official modification of the Hallstein Doctrine, launched a predictably fierce domestic debate.

For the CDU reformists, Brandt's move seemed risky in large part because it left Bonn no room to maneuver. Such a concession as granting the GDR status as a state ought to have come at the end, not the outset, of negotiations; this "politically constitutive" unilateral concession committed Bonn to dealing with a second German state regardless of whether East Berlin reciprocated with concessions. This would hardly convince the world that West Germany remained genuinely committed to keeping the national question "open." As Gradl warned, the world would conclude that "the Germans have adapted to their country's division by force."[8]

Union fundamentalists agreed but were even more alarmed by the *legal* impact of Brandt's initiative. They feared that subtle distinctions between de facto and de jure recognition would become meaningless. In their view, accepting the GDR as a state and effectively terminating the Hallstein Doctrine would inevitably enhance East Germany's status, damaging Bonn's traditional juridical claim to represent an undivided nation. This made Brandt's first step not merely imprudent, but irreparably harmful. Worse still, de facto recognition of East Germany implicitly infringed upon the rights of the Four Powers to determine the final configuration of Germany in a future peace treaty. At the very least, they argued, Bonn's Western allies would see Brandt's opening move as the Federal Republic's tacit termination of the 1952–54 Germany Treaty, under which they were obliged to promote German unity. Such a termination would be due ultimately to Brandt's Ostpolitik, not Western ill will. How, Union leaders asked, could the allies be expected to insist on working toward German unity when the Federal Republic itself did not; why should the allies be "more German than the Germans themselves"?

There were, then, some differences in substance between the CDU reformists and the Union's more orthodox majority in criticizing the first stage of Social-Liberal Ostpolitik. But the party's response sounded even more cacophonous because of conflicting political temperaments and intraparty rivalries. Strauss fulminated against Brandt's "sellout," while the more mild-mannered Schröder cautioned his party against too much discordant "background music" during the opening act of the new Ostpolitik.[9] Already Barzel simply lacked the power to enforce agreement.

After Brandt's opening address to Parliament in October 1969, Bonn awaited some sort of East German reaction. In early winter, under apparently heavy Soviet pressure, East Berlin proposed a meeting between leaders of the two German states to discuss "normalizing" relations. Bonn accepted, providing there were no preconditions—namely the establishment of formal diplomatic ties. The early months of 1970 were taken up with preparations for a historic summit between Brandt and East German Premier Willi Stoph.

Since Barzel had pressed Brandt as early as December to seize the initiative on intra-German talks, he and the CDU/CSU parliamentary group endorsed the upcoming summit. But their full approval was contingent upon assurances that Bonn would vigorously reject persistent East German demands for diplomatic ties and avoid enhancing the GDR's status.[10] East German demands for a treaty "binding under the norms of international law" would put Bonn on a "slippery slope" leading to full-scale diplomatic relations. Like some members of the governing parties, opposition spokesmen also insisted that the summit benefit Germans on both sides but did not specify how Stoph could be convinced to make the necessary concessions. CSU spokesmen even declared that the summit would be considered a success only if Brandt demanded that the Berlin Wall and East Germany's "order to shoot" on the demarcation line be done away with. Other CDU leaders had more modest hopes. Indeed, Schröder continually warned against weighing Brandt down with the "heavy baggage" of over-optimistic demands or over-pessimistic expectations, and Barzel refused to "complicate" the summit with his prognoses. Shortly before Brandt's departure for Erfurt, Barzel assured the chancellor that he should feel free from pressure for quick results in the talks with Stoph.[11]

Brandt returned from his highly symbolic, if inconclusive, meeting with Stoph to a volley of general and specific criticism. Erfurt had enhanced the GDR's political and diplomatic standing without securing gains for Germans on either side, the Union charged. Strauss and Kiesinger said the meeting, the handshakes, the communiqué, would all be seen by the world as tacit recognition of the SED regime. As proof they cited the foreign-press reaction.

One episode in Erfurt, however, tempered the Union's criticism. Several thousand East German citizens had gathered at Brandt's hotel, applauding, chanting his name and breaking through police lines in their enthusiasm. This spontaneous demonstration left the CDU/CSU both moved and uncertain. Barzel observed that the applause of Erfurt "speaks for itself," but what was the message? It clearly indicated in a dramatic way the strength of the bonds of nationhood even after decades of division. But did it also—as Barzel claimed to much ridicule from critics—demonstrate a desire for self-determination among the GDR's subjects? Or was it, rather, a show of support by ordinary East Germans for Brandt's policy of practical and humanitarian measures?[12]

The CDU/CSU challenged this latter claim on the grounds of insufficiently clear evidence, but there was no ignoring the fact that Social-Liberal Ostpolitik had captured the public imagination in both parts of Germany. Proof of its popularity in the Federal Republic was confirmed in scientific sampling: opinion polls showed large majorities favoring detente in general and backing Brandt.[13]

Next on the diplomatic agenda came a second Brandt-Stoph meeting, set for May. As with Erfurt, the CDU/CSU formally endorsed the summit, but urged Brandt to *insist* on East German concessions that would ease the human effects of the division; if the prospects for such concessions appeared bleak, the meeting ought to be cancelled. When the Kassel summit did in fact prove largely fruitless, the CDU/CSU saw its skepticism justified: Stoph's all-or-nothing approach—"more precisely said, all for him, nothing for us"—showed that East Berlin would insist on full recognition before even discussing practical matters. This cast doubt on prospects for progress; the GDR did not want coexistence.[14]

CDU reformists at first attempted to concentrate their criticism largely on East Berlin and stressed that Brandt's government was guilty primarily of raising unfulfillable expectations. Even newspapers sympathetic to Brandt considered the Union's tone "reasonable" and "moderate." But Strauss denounced Kassel as proof that Bonn's new Ostpolitik was a "failure," "bankrupt," "a disgrace"; under such CSU pressure, the Union position hardened. A declaration of the joint parliamentary group said Kassel had failed to meet the minimum requirements of improving political relations and human conditions, and rejected Brandt's policy, which would lead "in practical terms to recognition." This sharper CDU/CSU criticism focused specifically on one of the "20 Points" Brandt had proposed at Kassel as the basis of a potential treaty, namely a commitment by each side "to respect the independence and autonomy of the other state" in affairs relating to its internal jurisdiction.[15]

This issue made for one of the more dramatic and symbolically significant moments in the Ostpolitik debate. Visibly suffering the effects of an illness that would soon kill him, the CSU's premier foreign policy spokesman, Baron Karl Theodor zu Guttenberg, made a compelling speech to the Parliament. At times weeping from the physical effort, he passionately pleaded against legitimizing the GDR by enhancing its status: "We, the CDU/CSU, are not ready to acknowledge, respect, let alone recognize realities that bear the name 'injustice.'" Comparing Ulbricht's regime with Hitler's, he asked if injustice becomes justice simply because it has endured: "Would anyone here be ready to make his peace with Adolf Hitler if the man had succeeded in holding out for thirty-seven years?" Blurring the distinction between democratic and totalitarian states had once before led Germany to disaster; it must not happen again, lest Bonn prove unworthy of the Federal Republic's very raison d'être—the destruction of Hitler's legacy through the restoration of German democracy. Friend and foe alike were moved by this *cri de coeur*, but it revealed how far apart government and opposition (especially fundamentalists) were on the desirability of an ambitious Ostpolitik and their willingness to bargain with East Berlin.[16]

An event several days later won fewer tributes but was equally illustrative of deep interparty differences. With Union support, various expellee groups rallied in Bonn, Essen, and Munich, virulently attacking Social-Liberal Ostpolitik. Placards in the Bonn marketplace accused Brandt of "capitulation," and "treason"; some even read "Hang him." Expellee spokesmen called for legal "resistance." Although most of the fire was directed at the German-Polish talks, the inner-German summits were scathingly denounced.[17]

Negotiating with Moscow and Warsaw

Two largely fruitless sessions with GDR Premier Stoph at Erfurt and Kassel confirmed Social-Liberal leaders in their original belief that the GDR's obstinacy could be circumvented only if West Germany first achieved an accord with the Kremlin. They hoped Bonn-Moscow rapprochement would ultimately compel the SED to accept an agreement improving the situation in divided Germany.[18] Early in his term, Brandt had proposed a West German–Soviet renunciation-of-force accord that would explicitly respect the territorial integrity of existing European states. This offer won a positive Soviet response, and exploratory talks on the idea were already underway. They were conducted initially by Bonn's ambassador in Moscow, but soon thereafter Egon Bahr took over direct responsibility.

Bahr kept with the tradition of past West German governments by insisting that both countries renounce the use of force without abandoning their respective positions on contentious issues. Specifically, any accord should be a modus vivendi, leaving open the legal option of an eventual, peaceful alteration of the status quo. But Bahr also conveyed a new, more accommodating message—Bonn's willingness to "acknowledge" (if not formally recognize) the status quo, and accept "existing realities" (without fully confirming their legitimacy). The significance of these fine semantic distinctions was not lost upon any of the participants: to clear the way for a broader detente, Bonn would sign an accord tacitly accepting the current territorial and political configuration of Europe—explicitly including the GDR—so long as the Federal Republic could formally reserve the right to work for German unity at some future date.

Parallel to the talks in Moscow, Brandt had negotiators in Warsaw attempting to establish diplomatic ties with the Polish regime and thereby reconcile West Germany with a country ravaged during World War II. As early as the mid-1960s, Brandt's SPD had experimented with formulas for overcoming the major obstacle to normalization: Polish insistence that Bonn fully and formally recognize the Oder-Neisse line as the border between Poland and East

Germany. Brandt hoped a compromise agreement tacitly accepting the border would satisfy Warsaw.

These formal negotiations with Moscow and Warsaw drew an ambivalent response from the CDU/CSU. In principle the Union had endorsed a German-Soviet renunciation-of-force accord ever since Adenauer's time. Despite reservations, most party leaders saw it as a potentially useful way of both winning Soviet-bloc concessions on the German issue and demonstrating Bonn's desire for rapprochement.

Dealing with Poland aroused more intense feelings. Formally the party endorsed Bonn-Warsaw talks as a way to bring about reconciliation and improve the lot of those ethnic Germans still living "under Polish administration." Some CDU reformists echoed Brandt's arguments and those of many West German church leaders that these negotiations were a moral duty and would help close an unhappy chapter in European history, and that Bonn-Warsaw rapprochement would discredit the image of a revanchist West Germany that Moscow used to hold all its satellites in close orbit. But a considerable majority of Union leaders dismissed the second point, insisting that few East Europeans were truly frightened into submission by Soviet propaganda about aggressive German nationalism. Expellee leaders added that a poorly negotiated accord with Warsaw would retroactively legitimize their own expulsion from that country. Fundamentally anticommunist conservatives added that a pact with Poland's communist regime hardly served the purpose of reconciliation with the oppressed Polish people.

But Union support for negotiating with both Moscow and Warsaw was tepid primarily because of CDU/CSU orthodoxy on the German question. For a broad majority of party leaders, any accord with the Kremlin had to uphold explicitly the German right of self-determination—or at least must not be seen as labeling peaceful efforts at reunification as a threat to peace. Thus as in the 1960s they insisted on agreements that could not be construed as recognizing, ratifying, or formalizing Europe's present political and territorial status quo. It should be the purest possible form of modus vivendi—an entirely provisional compromise between Bonn and Moscow, declaring peaceful intentions, but leaving every disputed issue, above all borders, unmentioned, and thus legally unprejudiced, to be permanently settled at a later date. As Guttenberg observed, "a renunciation of force accord is seen as necessary precisely because unresolved disputes exist."[19]

As for the Polish talks, almost all CDU/CSU leaders, except some expellees, agreed with the CSU's newspaper, the *Bayernkurier*, in its assertion that belief in the actual restoration of Germany in its 1937 borders was an "illusion."[20] Nonetheless, only the reformist minority was ready to tolerate FRG acceptance of the Oder-Neisse line as part of a Bonn-Warsaw agreement (and even that minority cloaked its willingness in careful ambiguity). Formalizing a border within the territory of the old German empire would threaten the legal foundation of state unity. Expellee opposition was fierce, and the Union urged Brandt to downplay the border issue.

Most details of the exploratory talks in Moscow and Warsaw remained confidential until mid-1970, leaving the Union to concentrate its fire on the manner, rather than the merits, of this new Ostpolitik. Opposition leaders were irked by the secrecy and by what they called a tendency to inform opposition leaders after decisions were made rather than consult them beforehand. Making matters worse was the rebuff of bipartisanship delivered by SPD floor leader Herbert Wehner, who scoffed, "I don't need the opposition." Union leaders also deplored the choice of Bahr as a negotiator: they described him as an amateur, likely to be coerced into concessions by the crafty Soviet veteran Andrei Gromyko. Finally, Bonn seemed to be in haste to reach an accord, arousing CDU/CSU charges of sloppy, unprofessional, overly anxious and thus overly accommodating diplomacy.

Union leaders also charged that Bonn's Eastern negotiations were a dangerous solo venture. The Union asserted that Bonn did not consult sufficiently with its allies and was making unilateral offers that called into question decades-old Western policy on the German question. Worse still, in its zeal for detente, the Social-Liberal coalition was said to be allocating relatively less attention to European cooperation, downplaying the goal of eventual West European integration (Brandt had said it was "a goal for later generations"), transforming Bonn into Moscow's proxy in pushing for an "all European" security conference, and speaking of a pan-European (East and West) peace order as more vital than West European unity. In these and other respects, the Union said, Brandt was not only weakening the sense of solidarity in Western Europe, but reviving the image of Germany balancing between East and West. CDU/CSU politicians charged that overblown expectations of permanent detente would undermine an appreciation of the need for defense efforts, fueling fears of neutralism and reinforcing neoisolationism in America, thus eroding the very military equilibrium that even Brandt said made any East-West detente tenable.

The Bahr Paper

As the gulf between government and opposition widened, so did the Union's proposed range of options for thwarting Brandt. Party leaders claimed that by compromising the case for reunification, any SPD-FDP treaties would in effect alter the FRG's constitution — and would thus require a two-thirds majority in Parliament for ratification. Bolstered by a string of victories in state elections, the Union also hinted that it would soon have the strength to bring Brandt down on a vote of no confidence over Ostpolitik. The government defiantly pointed to favorable public opinion–poll ratings and claimed that were new federal elections constitutionally permissible, the SPD-FDP would win convincingly. During the May parliamentary debates and expellee rallies against Ostpolitik, political threats were accompanied by harsh rhetoric—accusations of "sellout" by the Union and "Weimar-era revanchism" by the SPD. Observers found the scene reminiscent of the 1950s debate over rearmament, with the common ground steadily crumbling.[21]

Mild tones from the Union were not entirely absent. Schröder, von Weizsäcker, and most reformists echoed their party colleagues' criticism of Social-Liberal Ostpolitik—too little consultation and too much haste—while urging that Brandt nonetheless be given the benefit of the doubt. Schröder cautioned Brandt to avoid Moscow's "capitulationist" conditions on the German question, yet he also expressed "astonishment" that Bahr had apparently given away little in Moscow.[22] This comparatively constructive tone persuaded Foreign Minister Scheel to try rekindling a spirit of bipartisanship with Schröder's help. In June he invited the ex–foreign minister to accompany him to Moscow for the last, formal stages of the talks.

As this offer was being debated inside the Union leadership (not surprisingly it exacerbated differences between fundamentalists and reformists), the cloud of secrecy surrounding Bahr's negotiations in Moscow lifted rather unexpectedly. Government officials hostile to the new Ostpolitik leaked copies of a ten-point Bahr-Gromyko working paper, labeled "Elements" of an agreement, to two organs of the stridently conservative Springer publishing house, *Bild* and *Quick*. Union leaders charged that Bahr had committed Bonn to these terms before his nominal superior, Scheel, had even begun formal negotiations in Moscow. Social-Liberal denials notwithstanding, the CDU/CSU insisted that this paper was in essence the treaty, a claim reinforced by Soviet press reports. Party leaders lamented that the Federal Republic was thus in a no-win position: if it tried to alter this "draft," Moscow would break off the talks—a setback for detente, but a formal treaty on this basis would put fundamental national interests at risk.

For in the "Bahr paper" many Union leaders saw their worst suspicions confirmed. They believed that Bahr, in his zeal for accommodation, had simply accepted Soviet code words or ambiguous wording that Moscow would interpret in its own favor for the legitimization of Kremlin hegemony over Eastern Europe. As by far the weaker treaty partner, Bonn would have little choice but to acquiesce. By formally agreeing to treat all Ostpolitik-related issues —from the Oder-Neisse line to Bonn–East Berlin relations—as a "uniform whole," and by discussing arrangements relating to all European borders, Bahr had, they said, recognized Moscow as "guarantor" of Europe's current political configuration. Moreover, the Bahr paper called for entry of two German states into the United Nations, explicitly referred to a "second German state," "accepted" the Oder-Neisse line as Poland's western border, and designated the intra-German demarcation line as a "border" that Bonn and Moscow would regard as "inviolable" (the Kremlin had wanted the word "unchangeable"). In this latter point, and in agreeing to renounce "territorial claims," to observe "the territorial integrity" of European states, and to "respect" all European borders, Bahr had, the Union critics charged, played into Soviet hands: the Kremlin would interpret these clauses as forswearing any change in Europe's territorial configuration (not simply "forceful" changes as Bahr claimed), and would thus castigate West German efforts to hold out for reunification as a violation of the agreement. Furthermore, Bahr and Gromyko had agreed to work on the basis of "the real situation in Europe," to accept "existing realities" and seek "normalization"—which the Union fundamentalists again regarded as Soviet terms for recognition of the political status quo, and thus of Moscow's hegemony.

The Union demanded renunciation of the Bahr paper as a condition for sending Schröder along with Scheel on the last stage of formal treaty talks. Though the government rejected this out of hand, an uneasy "truce" was called in the summer while the foreign minister was negotiating.

The Moscow Treaty

In mid-August, Scheel's Moscow negotiations ended and the treaty was signed—with an understanding that Bonn would not vote to ratify it until the ongoing Four Power talks produced a settlement governing conditions in Berlin. Washington had urged this linkage so as to win some leverage over Moscow in the Berlin discussions and also in part to exert some restraining influence on the FRG Ostpolitik; Brandt, sensing the importance of a Berlin accord to his entire policy, had agreed.

The final German-Soviet accord did indeed contain the Bahr paper's most controversial points. But in his last round of talks the foreign minister had also won Soviet acceptance of several formulations, some in the treaty text, others in accompanying documents, designed to protect the legal basis of Bonn's case for pursuing German unity. Government spokesmen and most leading newspapers declared that the way was now paved to detente with little risk of fully foreclosing any future prospect of German self-determination and a formal peace treaty. Scheel's improvements were seen as offsetting the allegedly negative impact of Bahr's concessions, thus depriving the CDU/CSU of any valid reason for opposing the agreement. Polls showed broad public approval of the accord as a step toward detente.[23]

Compounding this pressure on the Union to accept the treaty was a strikingly favorable foreign reaction. Although Peking denounced it as a pact between "German militarists" and "Soviet social-imperialists," Washington spoke of "a first real step forward" to detente, and Paris called the accord "an important contribution to the restoration of genuine security." Britain, NATO, the West European Union, Scandinavian governments, the Vatican, Italian leaders (including the Christian Democrats), and, of course, Soviet bloc countries endorsed the treaty.[24] Press reaction abroad was even more enthusiastic.[25]

Under this kind of pressure, Barzel had to tread carefully. At first he won party backing for a cautious, noncommittal letter to Brandt calling the treaty incomplete (it contained no practical concessions on Germany) and premature (it was signed before a Four Power Berlin accord was reached), but offering CDU/CSU support for a bipartisan policy on Berlin in the coming months. Struck by this relatively limited criticism and mild tone, and by the fact that Barzel did not even exclude eventual CDU/CSU support for the accord, press observers and government officials at first believed that the party had found Scheel's final version a vast improvement over Bahr's draft.

But it rapidly became apparent that the opposition's fundamentalist majority was unimpressed by the final treaty; to them it was the Bahr paper with "cosmetic changes." For example, Scheel had hoped to defuse criticism by stressing the new preamble, which reiterated Bonn and Moscow's commitment to "previous bilateral agreements." He argued that the language of the preamble could be interpreted as Soviet endorsement of a 1955 Bonn-Moscow letter exchange affirming the goal of German unity. For the Union, this was far too vague a way of protecting Bonn's rights in the national question. Scheel had also written a new diplomatic letter stating Bonn's intention to reserve the "German option" of pursuing unity, and Moscow had accepted this communication without comment. Union leaders saw the letter as a strictly unilateral interpretive document; it described unity merely as a "political goal," rather than a constitutional obligation and legal right. Finally, though a clause in the new accord stated that the "previous agreements" with third states would remain unaffected, most Union leaders doubted Scheel's claims that this constituted tacit Soviet acceptance of the old Germany Treaty between Bonn and its allies (which pledged support for reunification). According to Union critics, the Moscow Treaty—given its repetition of all the earlier Bahr paper formulations—in fact compromised the Germany Treaty by appearing to settle the German question politically and legally before a final peace, long a Soviet goal. By "previous agreements"

Moscow instead meant the Potsdam accord, which it wished to transform from a provisional into a final settlement.

In short, most CDU fundamentalists, as well as the entire CSU and the expellee groups, argued that it was pointless to shore up the legal framework of the German question with Scheel's ambiguous, entirely formalistic reservations, when the *substance* of the treaty —containing Bahr's formulas—had signed those rights away. This fundamentalist majority considered law to be Bonn's primary leverage in pursuing self-determination, and they saw the Moscow Treaty as irremediably damaging and even a form of appeasement. Expellee leaders condemned the treaty bitterly for appearing to ratify Soviet annexation of Eastern Europe and the division of Germany, and thus for legitimizing their past mistreatment at Moscow's hand. Kiesinger declared that the Union would "naturally" seek to block the treaty in Parliament, and others mentioned possible recourse to action in Germany's constitutional court.

This same majority in the Union dismissed much of the "applause" in allied capitals, above all in the press, as deceptive. They said it did not reflect sympathy for "German interests," but came instead from the ranks of those who—with "hidden smiles" —welcomed the treaty as an end to the bothersome German question.[26] If Scheel's improvements were serious, Bonn should emphasize to its friends abroad that the treaty did not foreclose the national question. As for the formal endorsements Brandt received from friendly governments, CDU/CSU leaders claimed that the allies considered the Ostpolitik a largely West German affair and could hardly be expected to interfere with it publicly. In any case, the Union argued, French and U.S. support was in fact tepid.

The reformist minority of Union leaders treated the treaty more cautiously, viewing it as hastily and sloppily negotiated, but not irreversibly damaging. Kohl, von Weizsäcker, Schröder, and Barzel were worried that unrestrained CDU/CSU criticism would isolate their party at home and abroad. They agreed that Washington and Paris harbored some doubts about the accord, but believed that killing it completely would disrupt the timetable for overall East-West detente.

In a difficult position, Barzel played for time, hoping to restore an image of unity in the Union ranks. Bitter bargaining inside the CDU itself yielded a compromise between hard-line treaty foes and reformists. Given even more intense CSU hostility, Barzel bought additional time by insisting that the Union could fully evaluate the accord only when the broader picture was clear. More specifically, because Ostpolitik, in Bahr's own words, constituted a "uniform whole," the Union could judge Scheel's Moscow Treaty only when it was clear that the Kremlin would accept a Four Power settlement making Berlin more secure. Barzel thus gave himself a reprieve of at least several months while the United States, France, Britain, and the Soviet Union negotiated over Berlin.[27]

Despite the agreement to withhold final, formal judgment until after a Berlin settlement, most opposition spokesmen freely gave their opinions on the treaty and on Barzel's leadership. Expellee leaders and CSU politicians roundly condemned the accord, and some said Barzel's tactics created an impression that the Union would retreat from its opposition to Brandt's appeasement. At the same time, CDU reformists were speculating about how to cooperate with Brandt and improve the treaty so that the CDU/CSU could support it. Interested observers, like SPD parliamentary chief Herbert Wehner, noted with satisfaction that Barzel was gradually backing his party away from a "rigid no" to Social-Liberal Ostpolitik, but it remained to be seen whether the attempt would succeed.[28] Barzel himself made a heavily publicized tour of major Western capitals in late 1970 to demonstrate that the Union was in harmony with Bonn's allies.

The Polish Treaty

By early autumn attention was shifting to the ongoing Polish talks, on which the Union also appeared split. Fundamentalists could not support a policy recognizing the Oder-Neisse line. Yet, despite the furor aroused by the Bahr paper on this issue, the Union's reformist youth wing explicitly called for recognition of Poland's western border, some maverick CDU/CSU parliamentary deputies advocated a treaty that explicitly dealt with the issue, and Union reformists like Helmut Kohl and von Weizsäcker seemed inclined to accept some form of compromise (they and several others had traveled to Warsaw for talks).

For reformists, nonrecognition of the Oder-Neisse line had never been dogma. In their view the Oder-Neisse line already formed a de facto border that was qualitatively different from the dividing line within Germany, and any theoretically damaging legal impact of such a conciliatory gesture to Poland could be offset by a statement noting that the German question remained unsettled and reaffirming Four Power responsibility for its ultimate resolution.[29] Even some Union leaders who explicitly opposed a formula accepting the border spoke increasingly of the need for a "consensus" policy regarding Poland. Barzel too could ill afford more confrontation, and Brandt was willing to meet him halfway. The government invited a CDU/CSU leader to accompany Scheel to Warsaw for the final round of negotiations. Journalists speculated that the Union would back a treaty that allowed members of Poland's German minority greater rights to emigrate west.

In October a CDU/CSU position paper opposed political "cementing" of demarcation lines before a peace treaty. Although Warsaw angrily declared that "revanchists" had won out in the Union, this declaration was in fact a difficult compromise, a modest change expressed through clenched teeth: "Poland can rely, as far as the Federal Republic is concerned, on being secure in its current configuration until a freely agreed upon, enduring settlement."[30] This contrasted with the tone of expellee warnings against approving the "annexationist" policies of a "Polish Superpower." Nonetheless in the last weeks of negotiations expellee and fundamentalist pressure mounted, and the CDU/CSU eventually decided against sending a representative to the talks.

In short, the party leadership was ambivalent, an attitude made still more obvious by its caution after Scheel in November initialed the Warsaw Treaty, which accepted the Oder-Neisse line as constituting Poland's Western border, and Brandt signed it in December. As with the Moscow Treaty, Barzel played for time. Although the CSU had already attacked the accord harshly, the combined CDU/CSU parliamentary group worked out a compromise insisting that the government must strengthen humanitarian measures helping members of Poland's German minority to come west, and must prove that its treaty would not prejudice an eventual peace settlement. Above all, Bonn was called upon to refute Polish claims that West German acceptance of the Oder-Neisse line cemented that border for all time.

Barzel thus again avoided outright Union rejection of a treaty that the German and foreign press had already greeted warmly. U.S. and British newspapers had praised Brandt's efforts at reconciliation (symbolized by his dramatic gesture of kneeling before a monument to victims of the Warsaw ghetto massacre), and called his treaty a "long step" toward peace, "an important moment in the history of Europe."[31]

Some CDU reformists openly endorsed the treaty and certain leaders like von Weizsäcker seemed inclined to back it. They accepted government claims that the treaty wording did not commit a future German state legally to support the Oder-Neisse line in any future peace talks and were increasingly anxious not to be seen as blocking the chance for reconciliation.

But powerful arguments against giving in to this temptation were advanced by fundamentalists who saw Brandt's treaty as an unmitigated disaster. Guttenberg, Strauss, and other defenders of CDU/CSU orthodoxy dismissed Brandt's claim that this recognition was phrased so as not to bind a prospective, sovereign united German state. As they saw it, Germany's commitment to recognize the Oder-Neisse line might or might not be formal, but it was material. Otherwise, they argued, Moscow and Warsaw would neither have held out so long to obtain this treaty nor celebrated it as an end to the contentious border issue. These Union leaders held that the "normative power of facts" ensured that the world would come to regard Bonn's right to represent all of prewar Germany as nullified by this treaty—the formal reservation of that right in an accompanying letter notwithstanding. CSU leaders thus spoke of Brandt's "sellout," and were even considering court action against the accord. Both the CSU and the expellees also found the treaty's measures allowing emigration of Poland's German minority inadequate. They pledged to fight the accord.

Ultimately, the CDU/CSU parliamentary group, in another difficult compromise, proposed a *new* treaty explicitly accepting the Oder-Neisse line until a final Four Power–German peace accord and agreed to reject the current treaty if it came to Parliament before the "broader context" of Ostpolitik was clear. In other words, Union leaders lumped the Warsaw Treaty with the Moscow Treaty, temporarily linking their decision on both to an eventual Berlin settlement, thus buying the party additional time to hammer out a more unified position.

Berlin

A Berlin settlement was indispensable to Brandt's Ostpolitik and detente in general from the outset. The divided city's geographical location and ambiguous legal status had made it an East-West flash point since World War II. The Western allies viewed *both* halves of Berlin as territory still formally under the sovereign administration of all four occupying powers: France, Britain, the United States, and the Soviet Union. But the Kremlin had transferred Soviet rights in *East* Berlin to the Ulbricht regime, which treated it as a constituent part of the GDR, and officially regarded West Berlin as an "independent entity." This claim provided Soviet and East German authorities with a pretext for controlling, hindering, or even blocking the access routes that linked the city with West Germany through nearly one hundred miles of East German territory. Such pressure was randomly applied in an effort to eliminate the West's "illegal" presence in Berlin altogether.[32]

As the Berlin Wall crisis of 1961 showed, the nuclear era's persuasive constraints made a forceful Western defense of the city unlikely. In any case, Soviet and East German intimidation of West Berlin usually fell far short of outright military measures. Most Western leaders thus hoped for a diplomatic formula for making the city more secure. Official clarification—and Soviet recognition—of Berlin's formal Four Power status would help ensure relatively unhindered access to its Western half by air, road, and rail through East Germany.

As the 1970s began, Richard Nixon and Henry Kissinger thought the time was ripe for such an accord. They believed that by tying formal confirmation of Berlin's occupation status to items Moscow desired—expanded trade and an all-European security conference—Washington could induce the Soviets to make Berlin less crisis prone. In Kissinger's words, Berlin was "living proof of our concept of linkage." America's pivotal role in guaranteeing the city's security and reaching a settlement also gave Washington "a major voice in the process" of Ostpolitik, allowing it to restrain the momentum of Brandt's policy and Bahr's impatience.[33] Talks among the Four Powers began in 1970.

During 1970 the Social-Liberal government had also broached the topic of Berlin—carefully, so as not to be charged with meddling in a Four Power affair. By convincing the Soviets that Berlin must enjoy detente in return for West Germany's various concessions in the Eastern treaties, Brandt hoped to soften Moscow's position in the Four Power talks. His goal, like Washington's, was to ensure guaranteed access to West Berlin—no more blockades, fewer East German delays and harassment of the traffic—along with increased visiting rights for West Berliners and West Germans to relatives across the Wall.

From the outset, CDU/CSU leaders agreed that Berlin should be a litmus test of Soviet desire for detente. Like almost all West German politicians, they declared that any infringement on the city's tenuous freedom must be resisted, not only for the residents' sake, but because Berlin symbolized overall Western determination to preserve democracy and pursue reunification. Overworked labels like "bastion of freedom" and "reminder of the unresolved German question" were applied to West Berlin. To give up on the city was to give up hope of reunification, the Union said, for it must by rights again be capital of a unified German state. More than that, the Wall, with its guard towers and graffiti, the trickle of legal emigrants, and the so-often ill-fated gamble taken to cross that Wall from East to West, demonstrated the "will to live in unity."

All of these homilies on Berlin were to be found in most West German politicians' political sermons. As for remedies, the CDU/CSU and its political rivals alike counted primarily on a Four Power settlement. Where the parties began to differ was in their emphasis on a *second* way to enhance Berlin's security and offer its people hope for the future: confirmation of the city's relationship with the FRG. It was the communist bloc's policy to regard West Berlin as a "separate entity," not part of West Germany, not (yet) part of the GDR, but an anomaly. Apparent Western acquiescence in this claim in the hope of promoting compromise would, the Union warned, be the step preceding and justifying massive Soviet pressure to absorb the entire city into its empire.

The Union thus considered it vital to reconfirm and where possible expand the de facto ties that had grown between West Berlin and the Federal Republic. Formalizing Four Power sovereignty alone would not suffice, for the city's residents must feel themselves part of a democratic state and the key to an overall German settlement. Though all parties agreed on this need to guard Berlin's links with the FRG, the CDU/CSU insisted that it be as strong and clear as possible, "a decisive component of the city's consciousness."[34]

But this goal was diplomatically delicate. The Western allies, fearing infringement on the Four Power occupation status and thus a stronger pretext for Moscow to deny them access to the isolated city, had never accepted the full extension of Bonn's constitutional authority to Berlin (in 1949 the allies suspended that clause of the Federal Republic's constitution calling West Berlin a West German state). CDU/CSU leaders contended that Bonn, with allied approval, had historically considered West Berlin "politically," if not legally, a constituent part of the FRG. It could and should thus do everything to underscore its presence in Berlin: highly publicized meetings of parliamentary committees, federal party conferences, visits by high-level government officials. In one CDU leader's words, the Federal Republic is only "in" Berlin when its "government organs and leading personalities can be visible."[35]

Here is where government and opposition differed most sharply. In their consultations with the Western allies, the Social-Liberal leaders, also anxious that Bonn and West Berlin not be entirely separated, sought to protect only what they considered the most important forms of "federal presence." For them, a Four Power pact should not be burdened with the obligation to preserve anything more than indispensable administrative and economic ties. Certain purely symbolic or "demonstrative" federal presence, such as parliamentary committee meetings, had been tolerated by the West merely to sustain the fiction that Berlin would someday become the capital again; thus, there was no legal basis for these forms of presence, and no need to insist they be continued. By thus more narrowly defining "presence," Brandt hoped he would be ensuring allied negotiators more flexibility, giving them the bargaining leverage necessary to entice Moscow into concessions on (1) rights to travel beyond the Wall and above all on (2) access to West Berlin, which he believed was more vital to the city's morale than federal presence.

Union leaders endorsed the other two objectives as highly desirable but gave priority to preserving presence (as did a minority in the FDP and some in the West Berlin SPD). What use, they asked, was guaranteed access to a city without a secure future, a city that felt abandoned by the rest of West Germany, a city that had been emptied of political purpose and had become merely an economic entity? Said the CDU's Franz Amrehn, himself once Berlin's mayor, "No material improvement of the access routes can outweigh the political-moral and psychological loss that would be bound up with a reduction of the actual federal presence."[36] The Union vigorously denied SPD-FDP claims that Bonn's rights in West Berlin were entirely baseless and disapproved even by the Western powers. In response they quoted Richard Nixon on the legitimacy of certain (unspecified) ties that had developed since the 1950s and asserted that the only allied concern was to ensure that Berlin was not represented by voting members of the Bundestag or occupied by Federal soldiers.

Debating the Berlin Agreements

During the initial phase of debate over Berlin, presence stood atop the Union's list of criteria for an acceptable accord: if the premise of Brandt's entire Ostpolitik were accepted—that realities were now truly being recognized so as to allow a modus vivendi and ease tensions—then West Berlin's long-standing ties to West Germany and the Federal Republic's official presence in the city must be accepted. Though backing the Western powers in their talks with Moscow, CDU/CSU leaders inferred from ambiguous statements and press reports that the Social-Liberal coalition was urging the allies to offer concessions on presence in exchange for secure access and visiting rights. The party complained about the mildness of Bonn's response to East German harassment of traffic on the access routes and to GDR attacks on meetings of the CDU/CSU federal parliamentary group in West Berlin and a visit to the city by the West German president.

But the Western allies were already in effect disavowing the CDU/CSU's position somewhat by agreeing to limit many forms of West German presence never before formally endorsed—such as the convening of an assembly to elect the federal president—in exchange for Soviet concessions. As word of this spread, the Union lamely responded that Bonn must persuade its allies to stand firm; the West could not be expected to be "more German" than the Germans themselves. Union leaders also sharply criticized Egon Bahr when telegrams were leaked to the press showing that, to accelerate progress, he had urged allied acceptance of Moscow's demand for a Soviet consulate in West Berlin. The CDU/CSU believed that such a consulate would be used to strengthen Soviet claims that West Berlin was an independent entity.

Yet these very concessions, along with Soviet reciprocation in the arms-control area, the Kremlin's unease about Sino-American rapprochement, and Moscow's elimination of Ulbricht as SED chief (the ailing, obstreperous leader was replaced by his initially more pliant deputy, Erich Honecker), were all clearing the way for a Four Power Berlin accord. In June 1971 a rough compromise was reached whereby Moscow grudgingly accepted responsibility for ensuring free access to West Berlin, followed in July by basic agreement to restrict but not eliminate West German presence. In August the accord was completed; Bonn approved, and it was signed on 3 September in the Allied Control Commission headquarters.

The West German press greeted the pact as a satisfactory *quid pro quo*, while major Western newspapers waxed more enthusiastic: "The Agreement that Europe has Awaited" pronounced the *Times* (London), and the *New York Times* declared Berlin an "Island of Peace."[37] Some members of the West Berlin SPD and the FDP voiced criticism, and opinion polls showed considerable uncertainty about the accord's impact, especially among West Berliners. Yet the reception was largely positive.[38]

This left the CDU/CSU in a dilemma. Although only half-satisfied with the accord, even fundamentalists did not want to blame Bonn's Western allies. The parliamentary group thus declared that some Union concerns had been eliminated, thanks to the three Western powers and despite the Brandt government's pressure for concessions, and did not condemn the pact outright. Yet it was clear that CDU/CSU fundamentalists believed desirable gains in "practical" areas, that is, ensuring access to and confirming Four Power sovereignty over the city, had been bought at the expense of concessions on "fundamental" issues, namely presence. The CSU's Guttenberg accused Bonn of "trading a garden of fruit for one apple." Strauss was hardest of all, declaring that the FRG's flag would have to be pulled down in West Berlin.[39]

Though the agreement stipulated that certain existing ties between Bonn and Berlin could be "maintained and developed," those ties were specifically enumerated and thus limited. Moreover, Union leaders were angered that the accord, with Bonn's acquiescence, made no mention of East Berlin but explicitly stated that West Berlin was not a state of the Federal Republic, a fact hitherto never put in binding form. Although the clause was diluted to imply confirmation of the status quo (it read Berlin shall "continue" not to be a state), Union leaders felt the damage had been done. Moscow now possessed a legal right to restrict federal presence, and with its new consulate, had an additional means of treating Berlin like a "third" state.

In another clause of the Berlin accord, Bonn won the right to represent West Berlin diplomatically. But CDU/CSU critics considered this Soviet concession to be so vaguely worded that it would allow Moscow's satellites (under Kremlin orders) to continue their past policy of concluding only those treaties with the Federal Republic that denied Bonn's right to represent West Berlin.[40]

In sum, critics charged that the accord offered no "quid" for the "quo" already given by Bonn in its two earlier treaties. For this they blamed not the allies, but the SPD-FDP's "sloppy negotiating" the previous year. The CSU thus pushed for outright denunciation of the pact. But even many CDU leaders who shared these critical views counseled caution, further study, and delay, wanting to avoid the noisome label "nay sayer." As for the reformists, Weizsäcker expressed pleasure with the pact, and Helmut Kohl found most parts of it "even better than he had wished for."[41] Moreover the party's Berlin wing gave a "conditional yes," welcoming the confirmation of Four Power responsibility for Berlin and Soviet responsibility for smooth access, while expressing concern about diminished federal presence.

Once again Barzel could do no better than to avoid committing the divided Union to a firm position on a major element of SPD-FDP Ostpolitik. He claimed the party would make its final judgment after the conclusion of talks between East and West Germany on the technical "follow-on" agreements to the Four Power pact, which were to cover precisely how the access routes would be administered. Once a compromise formula was reached allowing Bonn to negotiate for West Berlin, those talks commenced, and in late fall the accords emerged.

Union leaders found the final agreement, signed in December 1971, flawed in many specific areas. Small concessions "normalizing" transit had been obtained, but accommodation of the GDR's claim of sovereignty over the transit routes left a pretext for harassment. In particular they attacked the clause defining "misuse" of the access routes, saying it was formulated unclearly and gave East Germany too much latitude to search vehicles and persons. They said West Berliners were discriminated against by being permitted fewer visiting days and the right to use only a few crossing points when going into the city's eastern half. Opposition spokesmen said this problem and other clauses of the access accords, above all the one giving the GDR a right to issue visas to West Germans en route to Berlin, seemed to reinforce the claim that West Berlin was a separate entity. Polls showed dissatisfaction with the accord among West Berliners; a majority believed that Bonn ought to have held out longer in hope of obtaining a better agreement.[42]

Ultimately, however, the Union did not voice outright opposition to the Berlin settlement. Despite their reservations, CDU reformist leaders were convinced that the Four Power pact and, to a much lesser extent, the follow-on agreements together represented an acceptable, even beneficial, and unstoppable trade-off. In any case, one argument for the accord was unanswerable: the Union could hardly oppose an accord negotiated by the Four Powers and not subject to German ratification. Thus, even the most die-hard fundamentalists refrained from rejecting the Berlin accord completely.

Certainly this grudging acceptance had much to do with party strategy. But it also indicated an evolving awareness in the Union that the West as a whole was accepting detente on premises entirely different from its own, namely, on the assumption that sources of tension, including the German question and Berlin's peculiar status, could be left largely unchanged. Indeed, Washington seemed ready to accept a situation in which East and West acknowledged and even codified each other's maximal positions on disputed matters. Washington's sights were set largely on improved superpower relations, and the Social-Liberal short-term aim was the "narrower" objective of practical measures in Germany and Berlin. The CDU/CSU was the odd man out.

3

From the Ratification Debates to Karlsruhe, 1972–1973

With the Four Power pact and its follow-on accords signed, the focus of attention shifted from high-level diplomacy to parliamentary politics, from Berlin to Bonn. Brandt's thin majority in the Bundestag, the all-important lower chamber, had been crumbling since he first took office, as certain conservative SPD-FDP deputies were bolting to the CDU/CSU. Speculation grew that the Union could lure a few more deputies away from the majority, those either disaffected by *Ostpolitik*, such as the SPD expellee chief Herbert Hupka, or worried about their own political futures, primarily FDP members alarmed by the party's slipping popularity.

With a vote over ratification due in early spring, it was uncertain how Union leaders would exploit the situation—by trying to bring the entire structure of Ostpolitik tumbling down or by ultimately letting the accords survive to avoid any possible blame for undermining the Berlin agreement and complicating detente.

Divisions over Union Strategy

Most reformists within the CDU were unwilling to torpedo the treaties. Among those who constituted this minority were many younger CDU parliamentary deputies, those with ties to the party's labor wing, most north German politicians, prominent Protestants in the party, and those who had risen along with Barzel since 1969.

Although it could no longer look for leadership to Schröder, who was taking an increasingly hard-line position, this minority—best characterized by von Weizsäcker—continued to argue against killing the treaties. It dismissed as political propaganda many of the adverse consequences that Brandt's supporters warned would result from failure to ratify, but nonetheless felt that it was in West Germany's—and the CDU/CSU's—interests to let the accords survive.

But fundamentalists saw little reason to modify their longstanding objections to the treaties. This majority of CDU/CSU politicians believed that its reservations about the accords outweighed any fear of what might happen internationally if the treaties failed. Even Schröder, who had so long given Brandt the benefit of the doubt and still spoke of the need for an active Ostpolitik, increasingly saw his initial doubts about the Brandt accords hardening.

Indeed, their own tours of the West seemed to convince many Union leaders that there was considerable mistrust of the accords abroad.[1] At best they discerned widespread indifference to the treaties' fate and considerable criticism of Brandt—an attitude they said was voiced clearly behind closed doors but not in public so as to avoid embarrassing Bonn. Union fundamentalists, as well as Schröder, concluded from this tepid endorsement that a "no" vote would raise few Western objections and certainly not isolate Bonn or the party from the allies.[2] At worst they felt Bonn might anticipate some brief annoyance in the West if rejection of the accords provoked Soviet hostility and stalled overall detente, but the superpower dialogue would proceed regardless.

Strauss put it far more bluntly: it was "no affair" of the United States, Britain, and France to determine what "served the German interest," and Social-Liberal insistence that Bonn remain in step with the allies recalled "the worst of the occupation era." Indeed, he added, Western statesmen who actively supported Brandt's treaties were naive, intrusive ("If I am correctly informed, M. Schumann is the French, not the German, Foreign Minister!"), or false friends of Bonn who hoped Ostpolitik would close forever the burdensome German question and even emasculate the Federal Republic, thus preventing it from dominating Western Europe.[3]

This same CDU/CSU majority defied public opinion polls, which showed a strong majority favoring ratification. Half-anxious, half-belligerent, many Union fundamentalists claimed that by disregarding these surveys the party showed that it was not motivated by political expediency. Yet they also sought to minimize the importance of Brandt's popularity by arguing that most citizens who supported both Social-Liberal accords had "no clear idea of their contents"; the public naturally wanted peace and detente, and had simply proven "astonishingly susceptible" to Brandt's "blast of propaganda."[4] Fundamentalists worried as well that a positive stance on the treaties could prevent the Union from attracting the nationalist voters it had lost in the 1960s.

Barzel's *So Nicht* Strategy

Barzel desperately wanted to avoid a domestic political showdown over Ostpolitik, fearing that Brandt could use it to depict the Union as extremist and antidetente, thereby isolating it at home and abroad. But trying to persuade Union fundamentalists to support these treaties could split the party. Conviction and political calculation led him to conclude that the Union must neither kill the treaties nor allow them to pass; instead, it must "capture" the Eastern accords, improve them, and convert them into agreements acceptable to a broad consensus.

Specifically, Barzel believed that his party must exploit the uncertain situation in Parliament to bring about a revision of the treaties and assuage Union concerns. For it seemed increasingly possible to him that Brandt's crumbling Bundestag margin could pave the way for a change in government, making Barzel chancellor. If the CDU/CSU attracted a few more wavering Social-Liberal deputies to its banner, Barzel could unseat Brandt as head of government through a constructive vote of no confidence—that is, by winning a mathematical majority of his own in the lower house.[5] As chancellor, the CDU chief would woo more supporters from the FDP to bolster his majority and renegotiate his predecessor's treaties. In this way, he could separate the SPD-FDP from its most successful issue—and the main issue on which an otherwise incompatible pair of coalition partners could agree.

Above all, international factors shaped Barzel's determination to revise rather than reject the accords. Admittedly, several visits to the United States had confirmed for him the lack of American enthusiasm over Social-Liberal Ostpolitik and Washington's unwillingness to intervene overtly in a domestic German decision. At the same time, however, it seemed increasingly clear to Barzel that Washington would hardly welcome collapse of the treaties, as it did want to avoid a sharp break in German-Soviet relations that could complicate detente by, for example, undermining the Berlin settlement. Proratification sentiment appeared stronger in Europe; government officials and even conservative politicians in Paris, London, Rome, and elsewhere were on record favoring the accords. In Barzel's private talks, French leaders expressed their commitment to detente and concern about the consequences (especially in Berlin) of failure to ratify. President Georges Pompidou warned Barzel not to be left behind by detente: "The train is departing."[6] A CDU emissary, Kurt Birrenbach, heard similar warnings in several allied capitals, as well as a concern that the Union not resist the accords with arguments that might isolate it from the West or reawaken fear of German nationalism.[7]

If his Western tour convinced Barzel that the Union must take over German Ostpolitik, travels in the East reinforced his belief that such a strategy could succeed. In December 1971 the Union chief accepted an invitation to visit Moscow and confer with Soviet leaders. Whatever goal the Kremlin had in mind, Barzel's own aim was to ascertain whether the Soviets would accept measures making the treaties palatable to more than one side of the West German Parliament. The mood of his visit was correct, even friendly, accompanied by much talk from both sides of peace and cooperation. Barzel's own gestures, such as a spontaneous visit to the Kremlin Wall graves, were matched by his hosts, who put him up in the same guest-house suite occupied by Adenauer during his 1955 visit. Atmospherics aside, however, both sides repeated their maximal demands. It quickly became clear that the Soviets would not openly concede an inch of ground to Barzel as opposition leader, but the CDU chief nonetheless sensed that possibilities for further compromise between Moscow and a future CDU/CSU government were by no means negligible. Thus, although he returned to Bonn declaring publicly that the Union's position on the existing treaties was hardening, the visit had confirmed his faith in his strategy.[8]

An equally persuasive factor shaping Barzel's approach was public opinion. At the height of uncertainty over the Berlin accords in early 1971 Brandt's public approval ratings had dipped, but by early autumn he was again riding high. As the first postwar German to receive the Nobel Peace Prize, the chancellor had brought the country honor and prestige with his Ostpolitik; the policy was increasingly seen as synonymous with detente and reconciliation, and West Germans clearly wanted both. By year's end, polls showed a solid majority favoring Brandt's approach and opposing an "energetic" policy against the Soviet bloc.[9]

There was in these figures a dilemma for the CDU/CSU. A majority of its own supporters scorned Social-Liberal Ostpolitik, but a substantial minority (one poll said even a majority) of Union sympathizers, even many rank-and-file expellees, shared the prevailing, positive perception.[10] Facing these facts, Barzel saw his strategy as the only way to placate most Union sympathizers without totally alienating the reformist minority and isolating the party domestically.

Barzel's aims were to avoid a domestic showdown over foreign policy, prevent the total collapse of German Ostpolitik, and help his party escape the odium for such a collapse by demonstrating that a CDU/CSU government would take over rather than kill the Eastern treaties. In the short term this meant the CDU/CSU had to phrase its criticism of the present treaties in a convincing, but concrete, conditional, and constructive manner: an all-out, unrestrained attack on the Ostpolitik would destroy the very impression that Barzel hoped to create—that of an opposition ready to conduct its own detente. Barzel accordingly began to assail the existing Moscow and Warsaw agreements as an unsound basis for rapprochement, stressing not fundamental, irremediable flaws, but rather areas where they could be corrected and improved.

Not coincidentally this strategy also seemed best suited to preserve Barzel's position atop the party. By appearing both flexible and critical he could hold together his coalition of younger activists and trade unionists, without entirely alienating the larger bloc of conservative fundamentalists. Consequently in late 1971 the Union parliamentary leader positioned himself to snatch the two other titles he cherished: CDU party chairman and chancellor-designate of the CDU/CSU. Even many of his critics favored the idea of centralizing party leadership in this fashion.

Barzel launched his Ostpolitik strategy in late 1971. He promised that rejection of Brandt's accords as they stood meant not an end to reconciliation and detente, but the onset of a new Union government's policy. "With patience and persistence" the Union would negotiate agreements that didn't "stop where the problem begins, but bring real settlements, detente and peace."[11] He outlined specific conditions, the fulfillment of which would make the treaties supportable: (1) Moscow must formally accept the European Community as a first step toward eventual West European integration; (2) the German right to seek self-determination must be expressly recognized in the treaty; (3) there must be concrete guarantees of freer movement of people between the two halves of Germany. In this way Barzel combined a full-scale assault on the treaties as they stood with an appeal for specific improvements. He thus tried to keep his party on the offensive, while concentrating his attack on specific, remediable flaws. The strategy was labeled "*so nicht*," that is, the treaties as they are will be rejected, clearly leaving the CDU/CSU an option; as many Union politicians observed, "so nicht" was in effect "yes, if."

So Nicht and Party Unity

But Barzel's "so nicht" strategy presupposed his ability to maintain a united CDU/CSU front. There was some reason to believe he could keep the CDU in line, for after September 1971 his position in the party—parliamentary chief, CDU party chairman, and chancellor candidate—seemed relatively if not permanently secure. But there were still many uncompromising CDU critics of Ostpolitik, now including even the formidable Gerhard Schröder, the expellees, and above all the CSU. Strauss was alarmed by Barzel's moderation on Berlin and now by his mild tone toward the treaties. Although the Bavarian boss also liked to keep his options open, and frequently spoke of finding "a better, more clean and clear Ostpolitik," he pledged "total confrontation" against Brandt's treaties: they were "falsely constructed," with flaws that could not be ameliorated by interpretive devices or "gestures of [Soviet] good will."[12]

A tenuously united front could thus be preserved behind Barzel's leadership only if the party placed far more emphasis on the "nicht" than upon his conditions for possible acceptance of the accords. Strauss and the other longtime fundamentalists, as well as Schröder, ultimately tolerated the Barzel "so nicht" strategy only because its ambiguity permitted them to keep on attacking the Ostpolitik. A chorus of CDU/CSU criticism thus just barely concealed discord between those who saw the treaties' defects as remediable and the majority that did not.

Fundamentalists continued to argue, as they had for two years, that the letter of both accords effectively (or even explicitly) recognized borders and formally legitimized the political status quo, thereby infringing upon West Germany's claim to represent an undivided nation. They belittled Scheel's various safeguards against that interpretation (including his letter on German unity) as inadequate. Fundamentalists, and now even Schröder—so long undecided—thus saw little hope of salvaging a useful policy from the treaties: Moscow had what it wanted and the strength to ensure that Bonn would acquiesce in the claim that the German question was closed.

Even reformists agreed that Brandt's policy created—in von Weizsäcker's words—"dangerous uncertainty" by trying to keep the German question open formally while compromising it substantively.[13] But the reformists posed their criticisms as a challenge to the government: Could Brandt somehow bolster his long-standing claim that these accords did indeed constitute a strict modus vivendi by which both sides would agree to leave disputed questions open "in substance" until a final peace treaty? Could the government somehow reinforce its assertion that West Germany, Poland, and Russia did *not* regard these borders as final and the current configuration of Central Europe as permanent? Thus one of Barzel's three conditions for making the accords acceptable: Brandt must include an explicit affirmation in the treaty package of Germany's right to self-determination such as Adenauer had won from Moscow in the 1955 exchange of letters.

All CDU/CSU leaders argued that while Social-Liberal Ostpolitik undermined Bonn's traditional stance on the German question, the policy had won in exchange few reciprocal concessions that would truly preserve the substance of the nation. Rather than converting the GDR into "a status quo power," Brandt's policy of unilateral concessions since 1969 had strengthened communist hard-liners: East Berlin's new ruler Erich Honecker, with Soviet approval, had felt free to practice "delimitation," restricting what few inner-German contacts there were in a conscious effort to isolate his subjects from the inherent threat of Western influence and to emphasize the GDR's sovereign separateness.

Schröder attributed this flaw largely to Bonn's sloppy, hasty negotiating, which he said only emboldened the communist bloc; Strauss saw it as the inevitable consequence of believing that one could "buy concessions" from a dictatorship.[14] For most Union fundamentalists, this failure to obtain counterconcessions irreparably weakened the treaties. Reformists argued, in subtle distinction, that the present accords should be set aside until a satisfactory inner-German accord had been reached, or at least—another of Barzel's conditions for ratification—until East Berlin eased restrictions on travel across the dividing line.

As Union leaders saw it, the treaties could also help in luring Bonn into the role of Soviet proxy within the West. Gaining Bonn's support for an "all-European peace conference" was a major step toward formalizing Soviet hegemony over the continent: such an institutionalized framework for cooperation among all individual European states would directly undermine West European efforts at integration and leave those states "Finlandized." Not all party politicians went so far as to charge, as one fundamentalist did, that Ostpolitik "has opened the gates of the West to bolshevism."[15] But they nonetheless feared that the FRG would be loosened from its Western moorings and drift into neutral currents, thus risking its security and any hope of achieving self-determination.

Again, although fundamentalists saw the risks as imminent, the reformist minority implicitly believed that they could be averted if Brandt convinced the Kremlin to accept the European Community as one of those "realities" upon which detente rested, perhaps even granting it full diplomatic status as a multilateral organization.

On one other point there was less difference of emphasis in the party. Union leaders charged Ostpolitik with encouraging and abetting domestic left-wing extremism, a trend they said was already appearing in universities and factories. By raising unfulfillable expectations of detente and by speaking about cooperation between communism and capitalism, Bonn's coalition seemed to blur the fundamental distinctions between East and West: communism was no longer openly depicted as a totalitarian form of government, they complained, but merely as a rival social system with bad habits. In their view, this contributed to an upsurge of leftist radicalism and a weakening consensus for the FRG's postwar structures (signaled by an increase in draft avoidance), which could play into the GDR's hands. Thus Union spokesman urged the government not merely to distance itself from extremists, but also to "name the dangers of communism by name." In its characteristically colorful political vocabulary, the CSU went further and warned Brandt against legitimizing "red fascism" abroad and at home.

The Process of Ratification

As the actual process of ratification got underway in January 1972, the variety of ways in which Barzel's strategy could be applied became immediately apparent.

Both treaties had to be reviewed initially by the upper legislative chamber, the Bundesrat, a body elected by the various state governments. The CDU/CSU had a one-vote majority in this house of Parliament, and could thus have the treaties "rejected." But because the chamber's legal affairs committee determined that the accords did not touch upon the states' constitutional authority, the upper house's "rejection" could be overridden by a Bundestag majority.[16]

Although it thus could not block the accords, the CDU/CSU nonetheless had to choose its argumentation. CSU and fundamentalist CDU leaders urged the Union to seize and exploit the *constitutional* case against Brandt's treaties (any law or treaty changing the constitution required a two-thirds majority); they also laid the groundwork for possible action in Germany's Supreme Court in Karlsruhe. Most CDU leaders, however, preferred to downplay the constitutional option. A constitutional battle would make the party appear committed to total obstruction, an unpleasing prospect for Barzel and those anxious to end the Ostpolitik debate as painlessly as possible. Moreover, even many older fundamentalists in the party recalled that they had themselves argued strongly against judicial interference with foreign policy when the SPD tried to block Adenauer's Western treaties on constitutional grounds.

For purposes of the Bundesrat deliberations in January and February, the Union hammered out an internal compromise, expressing "legal reservations" about the treaties but deferring a final decision on going to court until after the entire Parliament finished its review in several months' time. When it came to a Bundesrat vote on February 9, the Union majority thus rejected both treaties as unclear, incomplete, and in need of revision, but not necessarily unconstitutional. In the accompanying debate, Bavaria (that is, the CSU) did raise constitutional arguments, but the CDU-governed states, led by Helmut Kohl's Rhineland-Palatinate, argued largely on political grounds, adding only that the treaties' impact on West German legal rights to work for self-determination should be "clarified."

The fate of both treaties thereafter lay in the hands of Bonn's more powerful political body, the Bundestag. A final vote was not due there until May, but the first reading came in late February. For several days the modernistic plenary hall rang with by-now familiar arguments for and against ratification. Barzel made it appear that the Union would agree to work with the new Ostpolitik on a bipartisan basis if returned to power, modifying but not undercutting it, which won him praise from even his normally hostile critics. Schröder, however, gave what Egon Bahr called "the very best speech I have ever heard against the Eastern treaties," indicating that opponents of the accords were not giving in to Barzel.[17]

At the same time, Herbert Hupka, the SPD expellee spokesman, abandoned Brandt's coalition and joined the CDU. With his switch, Brandt's lower-house majority slipped to 250–246, a tenuous edge given that at least one FDP deputy had made his intention to vote against the treaties known. The prospect of a very close vote loomed, with an ever-better chance that Union "no" votes would prevail—something Barzel had hoped to avoid. Unless he could persuade government leaders to modify the treaties or topple Brandt through a no-confidence vote before the treaties' fate was decided, he feared the Union would suffer the onus of killing the Ostpolitik altogether. Barzel continued to maintain publicly that the West considered ratification a strictly domestic German matter, but he saw ever-clearer signs that blocking the accords would disrupt the East-West detente timetable. In his annual foreign policy report to Congress, Richard Nixon had praised the Berlin accord and expressed his hope for East-West cooperation in Europe. Failure to ratify would complicate these aims and—if Soviet threats were to be believed—jeopardize Nixon's planned visit to Moscow. FRG officials showed Barzel a telegram from Bonn's ambassador in Washington that predicted that failure of the accords would set

U.S.-German relations back. Paris declared ratification "desirable," and London and Copenhagen predicted problems for detente if the accords fell through.[18] As Barzel observed after meeting the French president, "If the treaties are rejected, I don't believe Georges Pompidou will send me a thank you card."[19]

Ever-sensitive to events in Germany, the Kremlin began practicing a carrot-and-stick strategy. Foretelling grave consequences for German-Soviet relations if the treaties failed, Moscow nonetheless started addressing Union objections to them. The Soviet ambassador sought discreet meetings with moderate CDU leaders, including Kohl. Moreover, to demonstrate that Bonn-Moscow rapprochement would improve the lot of ordinary Germans, the Kremlin temporarily enacted provisions of the still-unimplemented Berlin settlement, lifting restrictions on visits between East and West Berlin for Easter and Pentecost Sundays; West Berliners flooded across the Wall on those two days. Moscow also enacted a bilateral trade treaty that had lain dormant.

In addition, the Kremlin agreed that in its own "ratification" process in the Supreme Soviet, it would "take note" of Walter Scheel's unilateral letter reserving Germany's right to seek unity. Barzel and his closest allies tried to depict this as an accommodation of the CDU/CSU insistence on safeguards for self-determination. But Schröder and Strauss dismissed the gesture as legally meaningless: the "unity letter's" contents would not be published or even disclosed by the Soviet government, and would therefore not become part of the "treaty complex." Similarly, when Brezhnev called the EC, like the East bloc's own Council on Mutual Economic Assistance, a "reality," Barzel saw the comment as a sign of a Soviet movement toward recognizing the European Community —another of his conditions for supporting the treaties. Schröder and the fundamentalists, however, disagreed: Brezhnev's comparison of the two very differently constituted organizations in their view only confirmed the Kremlin's hostility to real West European integration. As Werner Marx observed, "There is nothing which could change our position on the treaties."[20] Despite the apparent signs of bipartisan cooperation, Barzel's "so nicht" approach seemed to be losing its appeal for much of the party.[21]

In late April the FDP lost ground in a critical state election, prompting one of the party's Bundestag deputies to bolt. A few other dissident Liberals had already assured Barzel in private that they would support him in a parliamentary confidence motion against Brandt. Suddenly the Union leader was in a position and under pressure—partly from rivals who hoped he would fail—to take the unprecedented step of nominating himself for the chancellory. Despite some reservations—Could he govern effectively with a mere one-vote majority?—the CDU chief consented. This was his chance to seize power, modify much of Social-Liberal domestic policy, and over time renegotiate the Eastern treaties, thus preventing a domestic showdown directly over Ostpolitik, which could only hurt the Union. Although in public Soviet leaders unconditionally refused to reopen talks with *any* Bonn government, they too could count votes: Barzel might very soon be chancellor, so the Kremlin thus sent out more feelers to the CDU/CSU. Barzel grew increasingly confident of his chances both of pulling off the no-confidence vote and of renegotiating the treaties. He issued a statement that sounded very much like a government declaration. Three of its four paragraphs dealt with foreign policy: one appealed for bipartisanship, and the other two contained conciliatory words for Moscow and "our inner-German partner, namely those responsible in the GDR," with whom a Chancellor Barzel would hope to negotiate measures making the impact of national division "more bearable." He charged Schröder, foreign minister–designate in a new cabinet, with preparing a draft Bonn-Moscow declaration that would contain language satisfying CDU/CSU concerns about the treaties, and even booked a flight to Moscow for two days after the no-confidence vote.[22] He hoped that after he had renegotiated the treaties, the Union would be spared the onus of rejecting them and even the party's harshest critics would be satisfied. As one newspaper close to the Union put it, "the constructive no-confidence vote was in the end nothing more than the dramatic attempt [by Barzel] to divert pressure to reject the treaties."[23]

From the No-Confidence Vote to May 17

With world attention focused on Bonn, conflicting rumors and speculation in the press, widespread pessimism in the SPD-FDP, and even the threat of a general strike in protest of any change of government, the secret ballot of confidence was held on 27 April 1972. Barzel lost by one vote. Three of his own deputies had voted against him.[24] It was a bitter blow to the CDU chief and the beginning of the end of his tenure as Union leader. But only one day later, in another vote, Brandt also failed to receive a majority. In short, the Bundestag had reached absolute deadlock. Barzel saw one last chance to salvage his Ostpolitik strategy in the stalemate. The Union was still at least able to deny Brandt a majority for the treaties. Barzel could promise Brandt to let the accords survive *providing* that the government first ameliorated major CDU/CSU concerns about their impact. With little choice, Chancellor Brandt obliged by delaying a vote on the treaties for several weeks and launching new, confidential consultations with Barzel and other CDU/CSU leaders. Under discussion were a diplomatic note to Moscow and a joint parliamentary resolution laying out a bipartisan interpretation of the treaties, acceptable to government and opposition alike.

Expellee spokesmen viewed the last-minute bipartisanship with hostility; already some of their supporters were threatening to abandon the Union. The CSU showed clear skepticism toward Barzel's strategy, as did several prominent CDU spokesmen, including Schröder, who was proving to be as hard-nosed a foe of the treaties as Strauss. As always, to be sure, an internal power struggle was raging, with Strauss aiming at Barzel from one side and Kohl from another. As a popular quip had it, of the CDU/CSU's Bundestag members, one-third hoped to topple Brezhnev, one-third wanted to topple Brandt, and one-third aimed to topple Barzel.

But many Union leaders simply had genuine doubts that a unilateral note or declaration would ameliorate the treaties' impact. Schröder argued that at the very least Moscow must formally recognize any West German interpretive declarations as part of the "treaty complex"; the CSU argued that the treaties posed a threat to domestic and foreign peace, unity, and legal rights—a threat that could not be ameliorated by any unilateral resolution or declaration that would "not in the least alter the content of the treaties."[25]

For two weeks after the failed no-confidence vote, then, an unusual atmosphere reigned in Bonn, with confidential talks between government and opposition leaders late into the night, Barzel and Brandt discussing policy over a beer, and bitter bargaining inside the Union itself. An initial SPD draft resolution on the treaties was rejected by Barzel as too weak, but work continued. Several bipartisan committees were established, and Barzel made certain that his chief critics—Strauss and CDU fundamentalist Werner Marx—were deeply involved. Brandt also authorized Bahr to brief another Union representative on the contents of the minutes of the 1970 German-Soviet negotiations. Moscow announced that it would "acknowledge" a Bundestag declaration as reflecting the official West German interpretation of the treaties. Soviet ambassador Valentin Falin even participated as "umpire" in some of the government-opposition meetings, notifying the Germans whether any phrases of the declaration would conflict with Moscow's own reading of the accords. This lent a bizarre touch to an already-confusing scene.

Most perplexing was precisely what objective Strauss had in mind by participating in this bipartisan effort to formulate a joint resolution. According to one theory, he saw in this his chance to reshape the Ostpolitik and (the explicit skepticism of CSU colleagues notwithstanding) came to believe that Moscow would accept a new interpretation of the accords. A more cynical view suggests that the Bavarian, on the contrary, pressed for a resolution worded intentionally to elicit Soviet rejection, thus justifying a CDU/CSU "no" vote and making the treaties a political issue for the next campaign.

According to this latter theory of his motives, Strauss duplicitously insisted that the resolution read "these treaties create no basis at law for the existing borders" and was startled when the SPD actually accepted just such a clause during the negotiations. By design or not, the CSU chairman had helped to hammer out a joint resolution that met with widespread acclaim. Barzel and the Union were delighted, and Strauss himself had to concede that it was "optimal," as did his primary CDU ally Marx, who spoke of ever-narrowing differences between government and opposition.[26] It began to appear that longtime critics of the treaties might support them, or would at least tolerate enough "yes" votes from the Union—namely von Weizsäcker and company—to permit passage. Some newspapers spoke of a "certain majority" for the treaties, and congratulated Brandt and Barzel for successfully pulling off their "highwire act."

But CSU politicians quickly began expressing second thoughts about tolerating "yes" votes by their CDU colleagues. It would not do, they argued, to have the Union divided on such a critical issue; there were also the expellees to think of. Just as Barzel was trying to allay the renewed doubts of his Bavarian allies, Moscow upset the delicate equilibrium (or, alternatively, rescued Strauss) by announcing its reservations on precisely that controversial phrase of the resolution that Strauss had insisted upon—the one that declared the treaties a legal modus vivendi. Worse still, on the same day SPD parliamentary chief Wehner, speaking for many in his party and for reasons of his own, downplayed the joint resolution as a strictly unilateral German measure with no international legal relevance. Fundamentalists like Strauss immediately cried that these statements made a farce of the resolution.[27]

It was as though events conspired against a bone-weary Barzel, who met with the Soviet ambassador to discuss Moscow's new objections, and—when that failed to satisfy Union fears of Soviet resistance to the resolution—won a delay of the ratification vote. If forced to decide now, he said, his party would reject the treaties unanimously.

With a few more days of bargaining between government and opposition and a letter exchange between Barzel and Scheel on the outstanding issues a compromise once again seemed near: Bonn agreed to classify the resolution, which still referred to the treaties as a modus vivendi, as an interpretive document (presenting it to the Soviets along with the treaties), and Moscow announced that the resolution would be formally acknowledged during the Soviet Union's "ratification" process. An elated Barzel, his fluctuating stock apparently once again on the rise, notified the CDU party executive board that in his view the treaties now left the legal instruments for eventual restoration of German self-determination unprejudiced. Consequently thirty of the board's thirty-two members voted their approval of a statement reading in part, "The Bundestag resolution on the treaties is in its contents unambiguous. We will act in harmony with the treaties if we base our policy on this resolution."[28] In what would be Barzel's last major political victory, the CDU board also freed its members from any pressure to reject the accords and urged them to vote as their consciences dictated. This cleared the way for a substantial faction of reformists, perhaps ninety out of some two hundred CDU deputies, to support the treaties and thus give Brandt a clear-cut majority. Newspapers went to the presses that evening announcing that the CDU/CSU had finally backed down from its "no," and that the treaties would pass with votes to spare.

Within hours after winning this impressive endorsement from the CDU executive board, Barzel confidently addressed the combined CDU/CSU Bundestag delegation. He hoped now to win even CSU support for the treaties, or at the very least CSU abstention and acquiescence in some ninety CDU "yes" votes—including his own. Repeating his earlier arguments, he assured his colleagues that the CDU/CSU had won respect for helping to modify the treaty complex, which it could now "live with"; indeed, he said, there was now "no reason to assume" that Moscow would renegotiate better treaties if these were rejected.[29]

But Barzel immediately discovered how unready the Union was for this tactical shift. Although most CDU colleagues endorsed the joint resolution itself as wholly satisfactory, they remained suspicious of Brandt's government. They argued that the Social-Liberals could simply use the resolution to win ratification of the treaties, after which it would be ignored. Many claimed that even Foreign Minister Scheel was declaring how tired he had become of the phrase "keeping the German question open."[30]

Strauss played the decisive role. According to some accounts, the Bavarian boss had received a rude shock on a visit to his political base the previous weekend. At a Munich party meeting he was upbraided by CSU activists and expellees for "caving in" on the treaties. What Barzel later called "local influence" had begun stiffening resistance among Union leaders "above all in the south."[31] In the more cynical, and more plausible, interpretation of Strauss's objectives, his party's reaction merely convinced him to go ahead with what he intended to do all along—prevent Union support for the key elements of Social-Liberal Ostpolitik. Referring to Soviet statements and Wehner's comments, Strauss charged that the resolution was too little, too late truly to alter the treaties' impact; Brandt's government had already acquiesced in the Soviet view that the treaties formally confirmed Germany's division. Strauss and like-minded skeptics in the CDU argued *for* the joint resolution but *against* the treaties. What is more, they insisted that it would be politically fatal for the Union to divide its forces, some voting "yes," some "no" on the accords: How could the Union face voters as a common front when its division so plainly showed?[32] Echoing this argument, the CSU deputies caucused and decided that they would vote "no" as a bloc unless the Union acted unanimously. Schröder and even Kohl agreed that "yes" votes should not be permitted.

Suddenly Barzel's hope of winning over the fundamentalists, or at least convincing them not to reject the treaties, vanished. It was no longer possible to let Union deputies "vote their conscience" without splitting the party, perhaps irrevocably. Under this pressure, and at the advice of his closest advisors, Barzel agreed that the CDU/CSU should unanimously abstain. As he later recorded, it would have been defensible to vote "yes" on the "improved treaty complex," but not at the risk of destroying party unity; nor could he face an election as leader of only part of his party. At least abstaining meant that the party could not be blamed for killing the treaties, nor would it be identified with them. At any rate, Barzel felt it was a greater concession for the treaties' die-hard foes to abstain than for him and his minority to do so. With these arguments as his consolation for a humiliating political defeat, Barzel joined those Union colleagues arguing for abstention on the treaties—and acceptance of the Joint Resolution.[33]

Critics vainly protested that the whole notion of abstaining in so critical a vote damaged the Union's image. Indeed it did; within hours there were references to the "debacle of May 17"— the day of the Bundestag's final decision, when the Union unanimously accepted the now-official Joint Resolution, but neither the Moscow Treaty (238 CDU/CSU deputies abstained, 10 voted "no") nor the Warsaw Treaty (231 CDU/CSU abstentions, 17 negative ballots). Not only had Barzel urged reformists to abstain, he then proved unable to prevent a handful of fundamentalists from voting "no."

The decision to abstain revealed that the "so nicht" approach of conditional opposition to Brandt's accords never had the Union's full support. For as Union leaders themselves conceded, Barzel's three criteria had essentially been satisfied by the Joint Resolution, yet the party still could not muster a majority on the accords' behalf. Clearly the majority of Union leaders were more hostile to the Social-Liberal treaties than Barzel's short official list of conditions for a CDU/CSU "yes" vote suggested: the Joint Resolution's improvements made it easier for them to abstain than vote "no," but it could not lead them to cast favorable votes.[34]

The Basic Treaty

Ratification of the Eastern treaties was but the prelude to Brandt's main goal and another controversial step—rapprochement with the GDR.

For months, Egon Bahr had been negotiating with an East German representative about "traffic [Verkehr]" between the two states. In May 1972 they signed an accord that left the special legal status of FRG-GDR relations unchanged, but was nonetheless the first agreement in divided Germany not concluded solely under the auspices of the Four Powers. It was instead an interstate treaty that permitted West Germans to visit relatives in the GDR if invited, and visits by sports, business, religious, or cultural groups if they were invited by a corresponding organization in the GDR. Travel from East to West was restricted to those with urgent family reasons, a criterion left undefined. Negotiations then began on a broader "basic treaty" formalizing overall relations between the FRG and GDR.

Divisions over Union Strategy

Demoralized by its division and defeat during the May ratification debate, the Union struggled to regroup for a new round in the domestic battle over Ostpolitik. Internal wrangling between fundamentalists and reformists continued on the issue of who was responsible for forcing the party to lose face by abstaining. Both sides, however, agreed that the Union must avoid further open divisions over Ostpolitik, especially because Bahr's most recent flurry of diplomatic activity came as West Germany was preparing for an unprecedented early election in November 1972. Earlier in the year the opposition had boldly called for new elections.[35] Game rhetoric to the contrary notwithstanding, the CDU/CSU now faced this campaign with little optimism. Brandt's popularity was hitting new highs with each opinion poll, and the Union's conduct during the May treaty debate had hurt its image.

While Strauss successfully persuaded other party leaders to wage a confrontational campaign on domestic issues, Ostpolitik was downplayed. Consequently Union leaders approached Bahr's FRG-GDR Traffic Treaty regulating travel between the two states cautiously. They contended that it was too restrictive: East German citizens could invite West German visitors only with government permission and could themselves go West only if the authorities found that "urgent" family circumstances obtained. CSU leaders charged that the accord marked another juridical seal on the German division. Yet as the election approached, Union leaders grew wary of appearing opposed to even the most modest humanitarian gains. Publicly they began conceding that there was no purpose in blocking this accord, and in late September the Union voted for the Traffic Treaty's implementing legislation in both houses (nine members abstained in the Bundestag). The Union justified this decision by contending that parliamentary approval of this law did not constitute formal ratification of a treaty. More important, government and opposition agreed that the treaty did not explicitly touch upon status questions, and thus left the German question legally unaffected. Yet the SPD and Union critics could now point out that the opposition *had* in effect approved a treaty with the GDR that was as legally binding as one with any third state (even if the agreement did not formally label the GDR a "foreign" state or officially establish any diplomatic relationship).[36]

Union leaders also raised no "fundamental" objection to a comprehensive or "basic treaty" with East Berlin, and let it be known that a new CDU/CSU government would continue negotiating for such a treaty. At the same time the party outlined strict conditions: Bonn–East Berlin relations must retain their "special," that is subdiplomatic, character (and accordingly no exchange of ambassadors was permissible); moreover, the text must clearly indicate that the German question remained open and must mention the right of unity and self-determination. Even reformists like von Weizsäcker insisted that Germans be able to read somewhere in the new treaty that they belonged to one nation. Moreover, the treaty must leave Bonn's juridical claims, and the West's Four Power rights, untouched.

Von Weizsäcker, Gradl, and CDU reformists viewed these points as conditions for supporting an accord to which they had, in principle, no objections; so long as it did not foreclose national unity, a basic treaty and, especially UN membership, were desirable. Strauss and fundamentalists, on the other hand, unable to countenance the idea of normalized FRG-GDR relations and two German states in the UN, again viewed CDU/CSU demands as objections, not criteria for approval.

In part because Bahr sensed that a signed accord offered Brandt an enormous bonus at the polls, he hurried the final phase of his talks with East Berlin. On 6 November 1972, despite FDP reservations (raised above all by Interior Minister Hans-Dietrich Genscher), Brandt's cabinet approved the treaty on "the basis of relations" between the FRG and the GDR, or the "Basic Treaty." It contained many familiar phrases. "Both German states" renounced force, and pledged to "respect" the "inviolability" of their existing border; they upheld the principles of "independence," "territorial integrity," the "equality of all states," "non-discrimination" in bilateral dealings, and—for Bonn's benefit—"self-determination" and "human rights." New were the promises that neither state would act for the other in foreign affairs (Article 4) and that each would respect the other's legal jurisdiction within its own territory. Bonn and East Berlin agreed to exchange "permanent representatives," thus establishing relations below the ambassadorial plane. Mutual willingness to regulate humanitarian, post, traffic, cultural, and sports relations was declared, yet most of the specifics were left for a series of follow-on agreements. Shortly after the treaty was initialed, the Four Powers published a statement declaring that following ratification, both German states would be welcome in the UN.[37]

CDU/CSU leaders could read in the foreign-press reaction precisely what they had feared: that the treaty would be seen as formalizing national division.[38] But CDU strategists warned that the SPD-FDP would gleefully seize upon a hasty, negative judgment by the opposition and convert it into political capital for use in the campaign. Barzel thus warned that so hastily done an accord would have to be studied in detail—his proven technique for buying time in order to devise a unified CDU/CSU position. Most CDU leaders heeded Barzel's advice in part, deferring final judgment, but declaring that a new CDU/CSU government could overhaul the treaty. Not surprisingly, the CSU's tone was more sharply critical, with the party's *Bayernkurier* declaring that this treaty "seals Germany's division" and "destroys the Germany Treaty."[39]

Barzel's effort to downplay Ostpolitik as an issue was ineffective and, in any case, futile: it had overtaken inflation and social reform as the campaign's dominant theme. By initialing the Basic Treaty and postponing formal signing of it until after the election, Brandt shrewdly turned Germany's vote into a referendum on his foreign policy. The SPD-FDP clinched a massive victory on 19 November, garnering 54.2 percent of the vote, with both coalition parties gaining votes. Brandt now possessed a comfortable margin for ratifying his Basic Treaty.

Reeling from its worst performance in nearly two decades (44.9 percent of the vote and major losses among most voter groups, especially the young), the Union was all but committed to opposing a treaty that had just apparently received a popular mandate. CDU/CSU objections to the Basic Treaty had been expressed already and were too strong for most party members to consider voting "yes." Political considerations entered in as well. The CSU, which actually gained at the polls in Bavaria, was far less demoralized than its northern sister party. Strauss in effect insisted that the joint parliamentary delegation could be reconstituted only if the Union voted against the Basic Treaty.[40] When the Union deputies were polled in December they all but unanimously voiced opposition (of nearly two hundred deputies, only five, led by reformist Walther Leisler Kiep, said they would vote "yes").[41] Yet since the election gave Brandt a comfortable Bundestag majority, the Union could not block his treaty in that body, and to repeat the debacle of May 1972 by abstaining was unthinkable.

Barzel and the reformist minority drew from this predicament the conclusion that the Union should simply classify the treaty as an "inadequate" way of regulating Bonn–East Berlin relations, cast a "no" vote in the Bundestag, and close the whole unhappy chapter as painlessly as possible. They were resigned to vote "no" *once* in a losing cause but felt it would be senseless to carry the fight further by seeking to delay Brandt's treaty in the Bundesrat, or to kill it in West Germany's courts on constitutional grounds. These leaders justified their resignation by pointing out that the treaty had already created facts—Western approval of GDR membership in the UN, worldwide recognition of East Germany—that would not be reversed by blocking formal ratification or implementation. Moreover, they also knew that if the party were to succeed in such all-out obstruction, it would be blamed for isolating Bonn, and itself, from Germany's Western allies, while also jeopardizing humanitarian gains that the public wanted. Polls showed that over 60 percent of all West Germans, including one in four Union voters, favored ratification. Whether or not the Basic Treaty contained actual humanitarian gains, it was clearly identified with them.[42]

But stout defenders of the CDU/CSU orthodoxy still favored just such a concerted effort to block the treaty. As they saw it, another display of indecisiveness would be particularly damaging at a time when in their view Soviet, Polish, and East German manipulation of Social-Liberal Ostpolitik only vindicated long-standing CDU/CSU skepticism. Fundamentalists thus held that the Union must torpedo the treaty on constitutional grounds if necessary. They maintained that there would be no backlash from public opinion after the Union exposed the treaty's lack of real humanitarian gains to a hitherto underinformed or deliberately misinformed FRG public. As for the risk of alienating Bonn's allies, these CDU/CSU hard-liners displayed their increasing irritation with "false friends": German decisions, they declared, must be made in the German interest. Clearly the national issue had become "burdensome" for Bonn's partners, some said, but that was no reason to approve a treaty that let them escape from their obligations to promote unity (contained in the old Germany Treaty).[43]

Once again, the party appeared ready to play Hamlet, plunging into an historic decision on West German foreign policy with mixed emotions, conflicting intentions, and a lack of discipline. A crippling election defeat had handicapped Barzel more severely than ever in his efforts to enforce a common CDU/CSU position. There was widespread agreement in condemning his "sheer pragmatism" and "weak guidance." Given the party's traditionally merciless treatment of election losers, his days of primacy in the Union were plainly numbered.

CDU/CSU Objections

CDU/CSU criticism of the Basic Treaty throughout early 1973 actually reflected little new thinking on Ostpolitik; much party argumentation instead represented almost the apotheosis of long-standing opinions.

Union characterizations of SPD-FDP Ostpolitik's underlying assumptions and long-term approach to reunification differed. According to one view government strategists considered state unity of any form so unlikely that they were content instead with preserving cultural unity, that is, a sense of national identity among Germans in two separate states, strengthened through increasing human and cultural contacts. Conversely, those contacts and the resulting sense of togetherness were sometimes seen to be aimed at sustaining, even intensifying, national sentiment, thus generating pressure for joining the two states, perhaps in confederal form —even if that meant a form of neutralization.

In any event Union politicians classified *both* of these concepts as flawed: the first because it all but explicitly gave up on state unity; the second because it could be seen as compromising on sovereignty and democracy. They held that a form of national unity that "mechanistically" fused two systems, one democratic and one totalitarian, or forced them to converge, only deprived Germans of a say over the political conditions under which they lived. As for neutralization, it "could only lead to unfreedom" by splitting Germany politically and morally from the democratic West.

Union leaders readily agreed that a treaty was in principle desirable, and need not necessarily damage German unity. But the present accord, predicated on either of the above concepts, could undermine hopes for democratic state unity. It committed Bonn to respect the GDR's "equal rights" as a state, its "sovereign equality," and its "independence in internal and external affairs"—thus, as the Union saw it, granting East Germany the attributes of an equal state. Yet it failed to assert unambiguously the continued existence of one nation or the cause of unity: the word "Germany" did not even appear in the text (save for references to the FRG or GDR individually). Indeed, Union leaders pointed out that Brandt's original formula for "two states in Germany" was becoming "two German states."

At best, the party said, the treaty contained a formulation shrouded in Bahr's semantic fog: it vaguely referred to "differing views on the unresolved national question," which struck the Union as a hazy expression of Bonn's position and made national unity seem more like a disputed issue than an accepted goal. In any case, the clause surely did not oblige East Berlin to respect the idea of reunification that GDR leaders so openly denounced. Indeed, Honecker's regime was actively engaged in ideological delimitation, stressing that East Germany constituted a separate "socialist nation"—which, many Union leaders fumed, Bonn tolerated. Thus the CDU/CSU claimed that Brandt had failed to fulfill even his own original goal, which the opposition now vouchsafed: to make unity of the nation, given the existence of two states in Germany, the foundation of the Treaty.

A unilateral West German letter upholding national unity was attached to the treaty. But Union leaders downplayed the document as likely to have even less of a "corrective effect" than similar letters accompanying the Moscow and Warsaw accords: this strictly unilateral note was addressed in this case not to a third country, but to a German recipient, the GDR, which manifestly rejected its contents and resisted true national unity.

From the Union's view, moreover, while Brandt was undermining Bonn's own latitude with regard to unity, he was attempting to compensate by stressing the Four Powers' reservation of the right to settle Germany's final configuration in a peace treaty. Most Union leaders claimed that even if this trade-off at the expense of West German unilateral legal leverage were acceptable, it was poorly managed: the Four Power rights received explicit mention only in a supplementary set of diplomatic letters. As for the Western allies' commitment in the Germany Treaty to promote German unity, this found at best oblique coverage in the familiar clause that declared that the Basic Treaty left all current agreements between the signatories and third parties "untouched." Again, the CDU/CSU complained, Brandt hoped to support with formalistic constructs a legal structure he had substantially gutted.

As the CDU/CSU saw it, there was little in the accord upholding the bond of nationhood or even the "special nature" of Bonn–East Berlin relations. Consequently, the treaty, East German UN membership, and worldwide diplomatic recognition of the GDR (even by Bonn's allies), would be greeted as German acceptance of permanent partition: "two German states," not even merely "two states in Germany," would be welcomed into the world body. The Union lamented the fact that foreign commentators already welcomed the final collapse of the Bismarckian state and a definitive end to "the burdensome German problem."

These essential concerns were widely shared within the Union. Indeed, when it came to the Basic Treaty's impact upon German unity, party leaders were more unified in their substantive criticism than they had been during debate over Brandt's initial Eastern accords a year earlier. But a dispute arose over whether the party should act as if it could not live with this treaty. Reformists, as well as Barzel and—once again—Schröder, argued that the treaty and its consequences, including greater status for East Germany, were irreversible. They urged that after casting a protest vote against the treaty's "inadequate regulation of Bonn–East Berlin relations," the party must agree to work on the basis of new circumstances and do what could be done to preserve national unity. Accordingly, Gradl declared, the Basic Treaty should not be condemned as a partition agreement: "The treaty and its accompanying declarations and interpretations by the [Bonn] government are insufficient, but they leave room for the interpretation . . . that the German question and the claim to national self-determination are open."[44] Fundamentalist hard-liners, however, again regarded CDU/CSU objections as grounds for *total*, not token, resistance to the treaty (which they derided as a partition pact) and UN entry.

It was the Basic Treaty's impact upon hopes for reunification that promoted opposition from the fundamentalists, but reformists devoted greater attention to humanitarian measures. They acknowledged that Bonn–East Berlin negotiations (primarily the Berlin regulations and the Traffic Treaty) had improved opportunities for travel to the GDR, expanded visiting privileges within Berlin, and "considerably" reduced harassment on the transit routes to the divided city. But these "valuable" gains notwithstanding, they said, Ostpolitik and the Basic Treaty failed to meet artificially raised expectations for freer mobility: Bonn made irreversible concessions on fundamental questions of status in return for only a "declaration of intent" to ease the many harsh effects of national division; the treaty left concrete commitments in this area partly to supplementary, nonbinding protocols and largely to *future* follow-on agreements covering humanitarian, cultural, sport, ecological, and economic relations. As the Union saw it, the absence of a genuine quid pro quo permitted opportunities for East German delay, manipulation, and delimitation. East German authorities were already blatantly exploiting loopholes in previous agreements.

Union leaders also believed that Brandt's government now had little leverage left to soften GDR policy: with greater status, including UN membership, East Berlin had what it wanted and would have no reason to moderate its behavior (except for West German cash inducements). Given SED insecurity, they argued, it did little good to "routinize" or "de-ideologize" relations between the two states in hope of "humanizing" relations because inhumanity was systemic in the GDR in practice and ideology.

Furthermore, in CDU/CSU eyes the approach embodied in the Basic Treaty was not merely futile but could backfire. Party leaders reiterated their argument that Bahr's "transformation through accommodation" was transforming the FRG. By working for a detente based on a "de-ideologized" competition between systems in East and West, by acknowledging the GDR as a state, by depicting German-German relations as routine, by downplaying East German repression, and by allowing the sense of political nationhood to wane, Social-Liberal Ostpolitik was weakening the appreciation of the basic distinctions between a totalitarian state and a liberal democracy. Campus radicalism and draft avoidance were the first signs of growing self-neutralization. This neutralization would favor the communist version of reunification: conversion, or worse still, convergence of the "bourgeois" Federal Republic into a socialist state. Fundamentalists again converted criticisms into reasons for unequivocal rejection of the treaty; reformists were more reserved.

CDU/CSU leaders also depicted the treaty as the "capstone" of an overall policy that if unchecked could result in a neutralist foreign policy. As the Union saw it, Brandt's policy helped Moscow to stabilize its position in Europe and gave it new opportunities to destabilize the West. The Kremlin could achieve this by combining intimidation, the reason behind an unceasing Soviet arms buildup, with demands for further steps toward detente in the "spirit" of existing agreements. Above all, the Soviets would seek arms-control, "trust-building," or even disengagement measures that would dilute the consensus behind close, active security cooperation in the West. Moscow also hoped to thwart further European integration. In Union eyes, given Bonn's anxiety to justify its Ostpolitik through more human contacts, the Bonn coalition would succumb to such tactics. CDU/CSU fundamentalists went further: citing various journal articles that ostensibly outlined Egon Bahr's concept of Ostpolitik as the first step toward dissolution of the military blocs in Europe, they said members of the Brandt government secretly intended to withdraw West Germany from NATO. They accused the SPD's left-wing youth group of furthering this goal by fostering anti-Americanism and of promoting neutralism by painting a rosy picture of Soviet motives.[45]

The Treaty Debate

Whether the Union would ultimately opt for total or token opposition depended as in the past largely upon Strauss's CSU. The Bavarian boss initially appeared willing to accentuate or at least tolerate CDU/CSU pragmatism. Parliamentary deliberation over the Basic Treaty began, unofficially, after Brandt's 1973 government declaration in January. Union leaders roundly denounced the accord, but it was the CSU chief's proclamation of his party's respect for the principle of *pacta sunt servanda* that struck observers. This phrase —"treaties are binding"—seemed to be a major signal of pragmatism, or at least resignation, on the part of a leading Union fundamentalist.

During January and February Bundesrat debates all of the CDU/CSU-governed states, including Bavaria, cast a ritualistic "no" vote on the Basic Treaty, but only after unanimously determining that it did not in any case require Bundesrat approval. Simultaneously, the Union's delegation endorsed a law formally proposing West German UN membership while insisting that its approval should not be taken as implied endorsement of East German entry into that body. During a plenary session Kohl explained these decisions, outlining the CDU/CSU's objections to Social-Liberal policy, lamenting the absence of a genuine quid pro quo, but conceding that Brandt had created facts that could not be reversed by blocking the agreements.[46]

Despite the signs of some flexibility, however, events were whetting the fundamentalists' appetite for confrontation. East German measures aimed at isolating West Berlin, an outburst of anti-Americanism, and the apparent neutralism within the SPD left increasingly discredited the strategy of token opposition and bipartisanship in Ostpolitik. More decisive still was Barzel's pending downfall. In mid-January, Helmut Kohl formally opened his bid to strip the latter of his second title, chairman of the CDU. Almost immediately, party activists flocked to the challenger's banner. Sensing Barzel's ever-greater vulnerability, Strauss decided to bring him down in the parliamentary group as well.

As part of his effort to undercut Barzel, the CSU chief dropped all reserve toward the Basic Treaty. Once ambivalent about fighting the treaty on constitutional grounds, Strauss in mid-February joined those supporting a court battle, arguing that only such a step could make the CDU/CSU appear serious about its objections. Barzel still preferred to raise only political opposition, and even many hardliners sensed that the odds of a court actually ruling against Brandt were negligible. Worse still, judicial deliberations could drag out, forcing the Union to continue an old battle that would presumably yield a decision that set guidelines for interpreting the treaty —something another joint resolution of Parliament could do. Even newspapers unsympathetic to Brandt observed that Barzel's strategy must prevail or the Union would once again be stuck "in the nay-sayers' corner."[47]

On 13 February the CDU executive board voted fifty to ten against "the trip to Karlsruhe." A day later CDU/CSU parliamentary members in a caucus split: 102 voted against a court suit, 83—with the entire CSU delegation—voted for such a step. They approved the UN membership bill, but under strict conditions, including a stipulation that membership for both German states not be taken as diplomatic recognition of the GDR. Only Kiep and a few others objected to these conditions.

Once again the Union parliamentary delegation appeared openly ambivalent. Amidst promises like *pacta sunt servanda* and "cooperation on the basis of existing agreements," nearly one half of its members were nonetheless arguing for a court ruling against the Basic Treaty. To compound the image of confusion, even those who preferred to avoid the Karlsruhe option wanted to cast a protest vote against the treaty in the Bundestag, yet continued to argue for conditional approval of the UN bill that was a direct result of that treaty.

Nothing became clearer in subsequent months. There was more CDU/CSU talk of renegotiating the treaty to make the follow-on accords part of a binding package; of delaying ratification until the follow-on agreements were done to ensure East German concessions; or at the very least, of laying out a bipartisan interpretation of the treaty in a new parliamentary joint resolution. On substantive issues, reformists continued to treat episodes of GDR repression and delimitation as proof of the need for closely monitoring East German conduct and for negotiating unambiguous follow-on agreements. Party fundamentalists condemned the Basic Treaty itself for failing to prevent East German crackdowns.

Finally, in May, came formal Bundestag ratification proceedings. Caucusing beforehand, the Union deputies voted almost unanimously to reject the Basic Treaty; of two hundred members, only a tiny four-man minority led by Walther Leisler Kiep favored passage. A slim majority, 101–93, also opted to turn down the UN membership bill, arguing that consistency and credibility demanded it.

This split decision against his recommendation did not necessarily represent a vote of no-confidence in Barzel; some of his bitter personal rivals sided with him, and certain close supporters did not. But he accurately regarded it as a clear reflection of his inability to control the parliamentary party, and he resigned as its chief.

During the subsequent debate before a half-empty Bundestag chamber, both parties went through the motions—rehashing familiar arguments for and against the Basic Treaty and voting on ratification. Although the outcome lacked the suspense aroused by a similar vote one year earlier, it revealed similar CDU/CSU confusion and ambivalence. Strauss launched an especially furious assault on the treaty, blaming it for GDR delimitation (its assertion of sovereign separateness and restrictions on contacts) and incipient neutralism. The CDU reformist minority merely labeled the Basic Treaty inequitable, saying it failed to fulfill expectations and formed a poor basis for regulating Bonn–East Berlin relations. Those reformists who spoke for UN entry stressed that they shared their colleagues' suspicions: in light of the Basic Treaty's flaws, UN membership might reinforce the impression of a permanent German partition. But they also insisted that this could be offset so long as Bonn used the world body to assert the national question's provisionality, to bring international pressure to bear upon GDR violations of human rights, and to proclaim West German representation of West Berlin. Moreover, they conceded that West German rejection of the UN would be misinterpreted abroad.

In the vote's immediate aftermath, CDU/CSU disorientation became still more apparent. Strauss's *Bayernkurier* editorials still openly condemned Barzel for having accommodated SPD-FDP Ostpolitik, and scorned the "crocodile tears" being shed on the fallen leader's behalf.[48] Although the CDU's Karl Carstens had voted in favor of the UN bill, he was Strauss's favorite to succeed Barzel as parliamentary leader. On 17 May the Union delegation did overwhelmingly elect Carstens, a former state minister in the Foreign Ministry, as its leader; he defeated von Weizsäcker and trounced Gerhard Schröder, a clear sign that new faces were desired. Further proof came in June, when a special party gathering elected Kohl—more reformist and younger than Carstens, yet also a newcomer—to replace Barzel as CDU party chief.

Karlsruhe

For fundamentalists still unwilling to close the book on Brandt's Basic Treaty, there remained two last ways of affecting, or even completely obstructing, its implementation. After Bundestag approval, the accord had to undergo a second and final review in the Bundesrat, and the Union-governed states could delay its passage there for some time. More significant, the party could still seek a court ruling that the treaty violated West Germany's constitution. Yet even many fundamentalists were beginning to concede that Bonn's negotiators had insisted upon treaty terms that might *technically* conform to the constitution's various provisions on national unity. At most, then, the CDU/CSU could presumably hope to win judicial guidelines for ensuring that the SPD-FDP coalition held to a strict, constitutionally consistent implementation of the agreement.

For most reformists, a brief delay and a judicial interpretation of the treaty—which might even bolster Brandt—hardly seemed worthwhile reasons to prolong the fight. It could only further damage the party's credibility, especially since the Union now claimed to be looking ahead rather than back. Moreover, many CDU politicians genuinely opposed extensive involvement in foreign policy by the Bundesrat or the federal courts.

Consequently there was an almost unavoidable rift between the sister parties, for Strauss was determined to continue resisting. He said that fighting Brandt's treaty in the Bundesrat and, above all, in court was the logical extension of long-standing Union concerns and thus necessary to Union credibility. Yet early on, Strauss had all but conceded that the treaty could not be stopped. Aside from giving the CDU a lesson in resolute leadership Bavarian style, what were his motives? The *Times* (London), finding it "difficult to believe that the Bavarians are really serious," wondered if the whole exercise was not a shrewd attempt by Strauss "to get the party off the hook on which it has been systematically hanging itself" by finally clearing away all doubts about the treaty's constitutionality. Recalling that Strauss had been among the first to concede the unlikelihood of ever actually restoring state unity, *Die Zeit* suggested that the Bavarian now actually wanted Karlsruhe effectively to reinterpret out of existence what he considered the bothersome emphasis on unity in the constitution.[49]

Neither theory is supportable. Strauss, like many Union fundamentalists, considered the actual attainment of state unity under any foreseeable circumstances unfeasible. But downplaying, let alone forswearing, that goal was in his mind still an intolerable concession to Soviet Westpolitik. It would permit consolidation of the GDR, and allow Moscow to move toward what he considered its next aim: neutralization of the Federal Republic itself. Though by no means a gesamtdeutsch nationalist, Strauss the anti-Soviet Realpolitiker saw considerable danger in weakening the case for reunification. Thus he wanted at least a Karlsruhe verdict forcing Brandt's SPD to stand by the Basic Treaty's literal reading: that the legal basis of state unity remained alive.

After Strauss decided on this course, *Bayernkurier* editorials dutifully proclaimed that Bavaria was acting out of responsibility for the nation: "As so often in German history, the south thus again has a key position." A court fight was depicted as no mere legalistic squabble, but an effort to resist Soviet expansion, to preserve German unity, and to aid East Germans. Bavarians should have "no fear of being the 'last Prussians'" if history demanded it.[50] Strauss encountered some unexpected reluctance in Bavaria itself, one of the few occasions on which he overestimated his influence. Some CSU Bavarian state officials questioned the court appeal's "suitableness." After a split vote in the Bavarian cabinet, Strauss ultimately prevailed upon a reluctant minister-president to endorse the action. Despite some similar annoyance with his heavy-handed tactics in a few local branches of the CSU party organization as well, all but four of the CSU's forty-four Bundestag delegates eventually went along. *Bayernkurier* editorials reassured the party faithful that Bavaria should not be afraid to act alone on "Germany's behalf," for this course was the logical conclusion of CDU/CSU reservations about the treaty, even if "short range tactical considerations" prevented the CDU from going along.[51]

Bavaria's challenge rested on five arguments, the first two carrying the most weight. A clause in the preamble of Bonn's 1949 constitution obliged West Germany to act for all Germans, even those who could not freely join in the nation's postwar "reorganization" —that is, East Germans. Past court decisions used the preamble to rule that the FRG thus legally constituted a reorganized part of prewar Germany, *not* a new state. Bavaria now held that the Basic Treaty violated this "legal identity" of the FRG and the pre-1945 German empire because it failed to mention Gesamtdeutschland and accepted two sovereign states on German soil, implying that Bonn could now no longer act for the entire nation.

In a second, discrete argument, Bavaria held that the treaty violated another part of the constitution's preamble: that which (as past court decisions interpreted it) obligated all West German government organs to "complete German unity" and avoid any steps deepening the division. Bavaria held that an internationally valid treaty accepting two fully equal, sovereign states on German soil, without affirming the legal continuation of Gesamtdeutschland, would ratify the nation's legal division, regardless of whether fully normal diplomatic relations were established. Third, and for much the same reason, Bavaria argued that the treaty violated a constitutional provision obliging Bonn to create conditions making East Germany's accession to the Federal Republic possible.

Fourth, Bavaria maintained that the treaty seemed to permit even fewer ties between Bonn and West Berlin than the allies had historically considered consistent with their sovereign rights there; this undermined the constitution's applicability in the divided city. Finally, Bavaria held that although a treaty protocol did uphold the Federal Republic's right to grant its citizenship to all Germans, the protocol also seemed to countenance East German citizenship.

In making its first two points, the Bavarian brief delicately distinguished between accepting the GDR as a state, which the Union now did (by supporting the Traffic Treaty, for example), and accepting the GDR as a second, fully sovereign *German* state, which it said seemed to compromise the right to work for state unity. Only if hitherto weak, strictly formal Social-Liberal reservations of the right to seek unity were strengthened and GDR interpretations of the treaty vigorously refuted, would it be considered constitutional. Strauss said that he would be satisfied if the court mandated such a strict reading of the treaty.

In late May, after raising these constitutional reservations, Bavaria urged the Bundesrat to delay passage of the treaty and summon an interparliamentary mediation committee to review it. CDU-governed states declared that Bavaria's concerns were entirely valid, but declined to support the resolution: the enterprise had no hope of success because the chamber truly responsible for foreign policy —the Bundestag—had acted, thereby "creating irreversible facts." Consequently, with CDU states abstaining, Bavaria's motion failed and the treaty survived, as did the law governing UN membership. Undeterred, Bavaria submitted the above list of constitutional points to the court of Karlsruhe.

The Ruling

In mid-summer 1973 the court twice rejected Bavarian requests for an injunction to block the treaty's implementation (thus allowing it to go into effect after Bonn and East Berlin exchanged diplomatic documents), and in July it ruled on the substance of Bavaria's appeal. To Brandt's relief the judges upheld the treaty's constitutionality. Yet simultaneously they laid down strict guidelines for interpreting it. All eight judges concurred that the accord did not violate and must be interpreted so as not to violate or call into question

1. the Federal Republic's legal identity with the prewar empire;
2. the obligation to resolve the "national question" by pursuing "state unity" (and not merely unity);
3. the proscription against renouncing or compromising Bonn's own constitutional positions on reunification (and thus also against reducing the legal basis of Gesamtdeutschland to Four Power rights);

4. the goal of reunification within an integrated democratic Europe;
5. the ban on diplomatic ties with East Berlin;
6. the classification of the "inner-German" border as one similar to the borders between two states, not two countries;
7. the existence of one German citizenship;
8. Bonn's duty to give all Germans legal help;
9. the obligation to uphold West Berlin's inclusion under the constitution and its other legal and political ties to the Federal Republic; and, among other points,
10. the need to work toward eliminating "inhuman conditions" on the border between the two states.[52]

In holding that the treaty as it stood did not infringe upon these principles, the decision favored Brandt; but in ruling that it must be interpreted strictly so not to compromise them, the decision favored Strauss. Remaining within constitutional bounds would henceforth restrict Bonn's room for concessions on practical policy matters such as citizenship, the inner-German border, and political relations. Even mail going to the GDR would have to be classified differently from that with a foreign destination. More generally, the decision also obligated West German government bodies to work for reunification, which included "the demand to keep alive the reunification claim domestically and persistently convey it externally."[53] Moreover, the court ruled that Bonn must strive to clear up conflicts in interpreting the treaty. West Berlin would also have to be explicitly covered in future accords. These conditions narrowed West German flexibility and latitude.

Strauss declared that he would have preferred outright rejection of the treaty but never expected it given the carefully worded text; he thus labeled the decision a victory for Bavaria. In a dig at his sister party, he regretted that "fear of being a 'loser'" had prevented the CDU from helping to make this a victory for the Union as a whole.[54]

In part because Strauss confronted them with an implicit challenge, in part from genuine pleasure with the verdict, CDU leaders embraced Karlsruhe's decision. Parliamentary leader Carstens openly thanked Strauss for Bavaria's effort, and party colleagues welcomed the court's "binding limits and guidelines." Even those who customarily cautioned against a strictly legal approach expressed gratification: Karlsruhe, they said, had made it clear that Deutschlandpolitik's continuity in legal and political principle outweighed the "plebiscitary" basis of SPD-FDP policy. Karlsruhe gave the party an almost unchallengeable, neutral standard against which to match SPD-FDP policy—a standard very similar to their own orthodox positions. To be sure, this left much room for partisan debate, above all, over how forcefully and narrowly Bonn had to read the verdict. Karlsruhe's verdict was to be the centerpiece of Union argumentation now that its effort to block the treaties themselves had failed completely. Yet, somewhat paradoxically, by defining the treaties so restrictively the ruling in effect made it easier for the CDU/CSU to live with the new Ostpolitik. From that point on, only a policy that treated legal issues cautiously would be seen as clearly constitutional. As one CDU leader remarked in retrospect—and with some slight exaggeration—"Thank God the Bavarians went to Karlsruhe; after that the debate was over."[55]

Beyond the Eastern Treaties

4

Interpolation: Beyond the Eastern Treaties

Throughout the ratification debates CDU/CSU leaders, directly or indirectly, were grappling with a long-range issue: how the Union, in opposition or in government, would approach Ostpolitik after the treaties took effect. Early in 1973 Strauss had proclaimed "*pacta sunt servanda*," a term he and others continually invoked in attesting to their respect for legally binding treaties. But a pledge to abide by the letter of accords that they lacked the power to alter begged the real question. Would the party's approach to relations with the East remain unchanged in all respects, except where strict, literal adherence to new treaty law demanded certain modifications? To what extent would CDU/CSU decision makers accept not only the letter, but also the spirit of the accords, as well as the new circumstances reflected by and created by the Social-Liberal policy? How could the Union leaders deal with a detente process that was gradually taking on a multilateral form, with bloc-to-bloc negotiating fora?

Even fundamentalists conceded, in the words of the CSU's Claus von Stauffenberg, that although the "essential goals and foundations" of party policy remained the same, the conditions under which it now had to operate were changed by Brandt's fait accompli.[1] Yet as von Weizsäcker delicately observed, it was difficult for the party (especially fundamentalists) to "accept the irreversibility of these developments."[2] Would there be changes in

Union attitudes and behavior bringing the party more into line with SPD-FDP policy or would the Union aim to take over the new Ostpolitik largely in order to reverse it?

The following chapters in part 3 analyze in depth how the party tried to deal with the new circumstances after 1973 and what form its response took. The motivations and arguments of the Union's different wings will be partly addressed, but a more systematic analysis of the underlying, objective factors at work in CDU/CSU policy is reserved for part 4.

The Substance of Adaptation

Even after the treaty debates, fundamentalists, interpreting orthodox CDU/CSU positions strictly, continued to argue that SPD-FDP policy was bringing no gain and would pose ever-new dangers. Whether *gesamtdeutsch* in background, like the expellees, or gesamtdeutsch in argumentation only, like the much larger conservative majority in the Union (including above all the CSU), the fundamentalists insisted that Bonn was accepting an ahistorical and inhumane division of the German nation. They also contended that accepting the division in effect helped to consolidate Soviet hegemony over Central Europe. These same anticommunist and *Realpolitik* instincts also underlay lingering fundamentalist fear that SPD-FDP Ostpolitik would weaken the FRG's ties with the alliance and fortify neutralist, anti-Western forces at home.

Their persistent fears of the risks of Ostpolitik made Union fundamentalists wary about the posttreaty phase. More specifically, they were concerned about further concessions that might, as they saw it, weaken the case for state unity and reduce the entire German question to a matter of mere inchoate fraternal solidarity. Fundamentalists felt that only as long as Bonn upheld the continuing legal existence of the German state in its 1937 borders (which also meant the Eastern territories, the expellees emphasized) would the nation's right to unity survive and be recognized. Only if there were still a German state could there be a German citizenry to exercise the right of self-determination.

Never convinced that the various clauses of the SPD-FDP treaties adequately protected these various legal positions, the Union's fundamentalists stressed that Bonn's conduct of policy after ratification must be all the more cautious on questions affecting status and title. Although resigned to dealing with the GDR after 1973, they feared that acceding to any more SED demands, even treating the regime as an equal partner, was dangerous to the legal basis of Deutschlandpolitik. The wrong kind of government-to-government contacts, even the wrong kind of semantics on the part of FRG officials, could in their view undermine the last legal constructs of state unity. Meeting with SED parliamentarians, for example, was deemed a dangerous elevation of the GDR Parliament's status to that of a fully equal state. In the fundamentalist view, speaking of "two German states" or speaking only of the "German nation" also undercut the constitution's emphasis on "the national and state unity of Germany."

A similar wariness pervaded fundamentalist attitudes toward Ostpolitik on another level. Fundamentalists stressed that detente had not ended the cold war and that Moscow would count upon the new euphoria about peaceful relations to weaken Bonn's Western ties and lure it into a Finlandized status. In this context, Union orthodoxy bred suspicion of SPD enthusiasm for a Kremlin-supported all-European Conference on Security and Cooperation in Europe (CSCE) and multilateral troop reduction talks known as Mutual and Balanced Force Reduction (MBFR) negotiations. Fundamentalists feared that the former would split Europe from the United States and slow West European integration, and the latter would weaken Western defenses and isolate the FRG still further from its alliance partners. All of these risks were, from the standpoint of Union orthodoxy, compounded by detente's corrosive impact on West German public opinion, which could weaken support for defense spending and create indifference toward European unity.

Taken in this way, *pacta sunt servanda* hardly implied broad adaptation to the SPD-FDP policy. Rather, fundamentalists at most argued for "saving what can be saved" by constraining Ostpolitik. Even now, or especially now, they believed further Western concessions in the name of compromise would only further bolster the Soviet bloc's position. Moscow would now seek to consolidate its gains and gradually transform Bonn into its proxy; this it could achieve by insisting on behavior consistent with the spirit of recent treaties. As defined in Moscow, this meant coercion reinforced with waxing Soviet military might. With the claim of a right to national self-determination and Bonn's alliance ties thus at stake, fundamentalists argued, now was hardly the time for the Union to join Brandt in assuring more chances for a "coffee klatsch with Aunt Minna" in East Berlin.[3]

In any case, CDU/CSU orthodoxy sustained fundamentalist pessimism—a pessimism unchanged by Brandt's treaties—that dialogue could not yield further humanitarian gains. In their view, communist rulers generally, and above all those in the GDR, had to limit their populations' exposure to contact with the West in order to prevent a growth of sentiment for liberalization and reunification: "Every encounter with freedom represents a deadly danger for repression."[4] There was little point in seeking to play off GDR doves against GDR hawks, as the communist clique shared a clear hostility to the West and wanted only to make the partition of Germany permanent. At best there could be what even Egon Bahr called an "abnormal normalization," something Union fundamentalists scorned as akin to a "dying convalescent." At any rate, they contended, even if "routinizing" relations with the GDR could facilitate cooperation, Bonn had already given East Berlin what it most wanted—international status. This left the GDR free to restrict contacts completely, offering only phony concessions as a form of blackmail. Bonn simply had no useful leverage.[5]

Fundamentalists also continued to belittle Ostpolitik's value as atonement for Nazi crimes. They dismissed such reconciliation as an "artificial issue," a "theological" rather than political matter: Soviet-bloc subjects despised not West Germany, but their repressors; and Bonn's deals with communist authorities hardly benefited the average person.

CDU Reformists and Helmut Kohl

A sizable CDU reformist minority shared the traditionally pessimistic Union view of Soviet ambitions, and thus also continued to see risks in detente. But it interpreted Union orthodoxy more flexibly, reflecting a conviction that failure to reconcile the realities of ongoing East-West conflict with the "imperatives of coexistence" would magnify those very dangers. This minority, composed of younger CDU leaders, trade unionists, and some conservatives, generally emerged from and interacted with the same milieu that gave the SPD-FDP its support and had suffered losses in the 1972 election. Reformists were impressed by the desire of West Germany's public for a greater degree of tangible normalcy in relations with the East. Moreover, this CDU minority believed that the Western partners upon whom Bonn relied to blunt Soviet pressure also wanted the Federal Republic to downplay the national issue. Whatever their reservations about Ostpolitik, France, Italy, and Britan had no desire to see a resurrection of German emphasis on reunification. Moreover, if ever Bonn was seen by its partners to be slowing the momentum of East-West detente, those states might simply bypass the Federal Republic when making future policy. Bonn had an important stake in all areas of its allies' policies, especially those regarding security, and obstructionism might exacerbate the risks of detente by weakening West German influence. Finally, these Union reformists believed that detente, and Ostpolitik itself, was certain to continue. Despite some U.S.-Soviet tension in 1973 and 1974, rapprochement between the blocs was considered a function of the bloc system's stabilization, and thus unstoppable.

From the reformist perspective, just as it was vital for Bonn to pursue coexistence, it was critical for the Union to have a hand in the process. Although not so vehemently critical of the SPD as their fundamentalist colleagues, reformists still viewed that party's proclivity for concessions with unease, fearing that the SPD underrated detente's potential hazards and was preparing for an even more unilateral, comprehensive Ostpolitik in the name of greater West German diplomatic latitude. Yet CDU reformists argued that the Union could not head off the danger this posed by obstructing Social-Liberal detente altogether. It must participate in, not abstain from, formulation of West German policy, particularly with regard to multilateral East-West talks on arms control and security; traditional national interests and the foundations of Westpolitik must be protected. The same applied with regard to Berlin: the Union must actively guard that city's ties to West Germany and keep its sense of purpose alive. Such codetermination on the Union's part required abandoning old battles and all-out resistance; it called for adaptation to new circumstances.

In contrast to their colleagues, moreover, CDU reformists saw some possible benefits and not merely risks in detente. They praised

Bonn's Western allies for defusing the cold war. Detente could bring about, if not formally normalized relations, perhaps less abnormal conditions; if not Bahr's sense of national solidarity, at least marginally less estrangement between people in the nation's two halves. In addition, many CDU leaders, particularly active Protestant laity, shared von Weizsäcker's view that rapprochement with the East (especially Poland) was an act of atonement for Nazi crimes. And many Berlin politicians like Gradl saw reason for increasing optimism about the divided city's future.

The Politics of Adaptation

How much the Union would ultimately adapt to the new shape of West German foreign policy was to depend in large part on the CDU/CSU's internal politics and balance of power. A continuing frontal assault on Ostpolitik would, fundamentalists argued, lead the Union to political victory; past indecisiveness had cost votes, and total opposition would regain support. Thus they saw no political incentive to adapt to Ostpolitik, to again fall into the trap of "disingenuous bipartisanship."

Fundamentalists still made up a numerical majority in the CDU/CSU parliamentary leadership and commanded disproportionate influence over the party's foreign policy. This was due in large part to the CSU's special leverage in the parliamentary group and the still considerable, if waning, influence of expellee spokesmen, whom Union leaders would not risk alienating, even when some appeared to be engaged in an often-pathetic rearguard action in defense of their interests. Fundamentalists thoroughly dominated those organs primarily responsible for foreign policy: the overall parliamentary group and CDU/CSU representation on various parliamentary committees (Deutschlandpolitik, Foreign Affairs, Defense). Barzel's successor atop the parliamentary group was the more conservative ex–foreign ministry official Karl Carstens, who, given his political inclinations and lack of parliamentary experience, allowed fundamentalist domination during his tenure.

Strauss remained this group's standard bearer, and combined his hard-line stance on Ostpolitik with a characteristically no-holds-barred effort to bring down the Social-Liberal coalition and replace it with a CDU/CSU-only government, led ideally by a Bavarian chancellor. He wanted no coalition with the FDP, long his personal and political nemesis. He enunciated this strategy of all-out confrontation in 1974 at a secret session of the CSU leadership at Sonthofen in the Bavarian Alps. A leaked copy generated considerable adverse publicity, for Strauss had stressed the utility of strictly negative campaigning and of avoiding constructive CDU/CSU alternatives:

> We must not shy away from confrontation.... We must always identify the others with socialism and the opposite of freedom, with the idea that ... their policies will eventually result in the hegemony of the Soviet Union over Western Europe.... We must say that the SPD and FDP are handing this state over to criminal and political gangsters. There is not the slightest difference between criminal and political gangsters—they are all criminals. If we come and clean up, none of these bandits will dare to open their mouths in Germany again, even if we can't exactly keep our promise.... And now to the tactics: just accuse and warn but don't offer concrete solutions.[6]

This preference for a confrontational approach was also forcefully proclaimed before large gatherings of the CSU faithful, such as in his traditional Ash Wednesday speeches. Party regulars, often having waited for hours (and having thoroughly quenched their thirst), would sit through Strauss philippics that could last up to three hours, pounding the wooden plank tables and roaring their approval—or, where appropriate, whistling in derision at the mention of Brandt or Bahr.

But an active CDU/CSU detente, an "active *pacta sunt servanda*" approach, was seen by the reformist minority as politically indispensable. This minority believed that Brandt had correctly sensed the *Zeitgeist* and that the Union would jeopardize its future electoral hopes by appearing in any way antidetente. In the near term, reformists felt the Union must press the government to achieve humanitarian measures with vocal support and constructive criticism, and encourage it to help keep the national question open by resisting communist delimitation and endorsing Bonn's interpretation of the treaties. This meant forswearing "Weimar-style" rhetoric that could only polarize political opinion. Advocates of this less uncompromising CDU/CSU Ostpolitik came mainly from subgroups such as the youth and labor wings, which until now had often been divided and generally ineffectual, above all when it came to foreign policy. Ever since the 1972 election, these groups had been appealing for programmatic and structural renewal of the party. They blamed its disastrous setbacks on an overly reactive, negative approach to many policy issues and on a lack of active proselytizing among new voter groups. CDU trade unionists urged a more positive stance, for example, toward greater labor "codetermination" of management decisions in industry, and the youth groups urged a dialogue with university students. This reformist coalition also wanted the CDU party organization to develop as a counterweight to the influential joint parliamentary group with the CSU. This meant establishing independent research, publicity, and policymaking organs, and recruiting large numbers of new dues-paying members to finance the transformation.

The hope for renewal depended on Helmut Kohl, who received overwhelming endorsement as Barzel's successor atop the CDU at a June 1973 conference. Though a provincial politician with no federal experience, Kohl had risen as a reformer and an advocate of a stronger CDU party structure; he quickly overshadowed Carstens and thereby helped the party organization to overshadow the more conservative parliamentary delegation.

Younger than most of his peers, Kohl was a teenager during World War II; he "grew up" politically in the era of his idol, Adenauer. Adenauer's view of Germany was shaped by the Wilhelmine, Weimar, and Hitler periods; Kohl's by the Adenauer era and its foreign and domestic triumphs. Consequently Kohl felt relatively free from many burdens of Germany's past and preferred to dwell instead on the Federal Republic's achievements: mass democratic parties, the social-market economy, and reconciliation with the West. Moreover, his sense of national consciousness and commitment to German unity was shaped less by a personal, family, or regional attachment to the gesamtdeutsch tradition than by a somewhat more vague, often sentimental notion of Germany's prewar past, pride in Bonn's efforts at reconciliation since 1949, and faith in the merits of democratic nationalism. As a second-generation FRG politician, he felt less constrained by the past and espoused what he considered a "natural, healthy" German national pride.

If in these respects Kohl resembled Strauss, he lacked the Bavarian's ambition to see reunited Germany at the helm of a European superpower. Although a fervent proponent of European integration and unity, Kohl was among those latter-day Atlanticists who implicitly believed that the Old World should remain a helpful junior partner, not aspire to be a coequal, of the United States. To talk of a second Western superpower, he argued, overlooked Europe's inability to unite politically, and its thickly populated, small landmass, which made an independent European nuclear force inherently noncredible.[7] Moreover, Kohl's sense of dependence on the United States was strengthened by the deep pro-Americanism of someone who constantly recalled that as a boy he had lived on U.S. CARE packages.

Kohl was thus viewed not only as an advocate of reforming the CDU's structure and domestic-policy positions, but as a pragmatist in foreign affairs. For years he had urged the party to adapt to irreversible circumstances, arguing that much had changed since 1969: the Union must get off the defensive and shape a new Ostpolitik rather than merely count on the collapse of Social-Liberal policy. For years Kohl had also attempted to underscore the bond between commitment to unity and commitment to democracy, reinforcing traditional party principles while insulating the Union from the charge of nationalism. All of these tests were, for Kohl, vital in ending the polarization of the treaty debates and permitting greater bipartisanship in the pursuit of Bonn's consensus interests—national unity and Westpolitik—and in the defense of the FRG's sociopolitical structures against communist manipulation, encroachment, and pressure.[8]

This approach also conveniently suited Kohl's persistent desire to woo the FDP away from the SPD and form a new Christian-Liberal governing coalition. Kohl believed that German voters disliked one-party governments and would be most comfortable with a bloc composed of nonsocialists, as in the Adenauer era. In any future coalition he also wanted the Liberals to counterbalance the virulently conservative CSU, thus putting the CDU at the center.

Yet even as Kohl consolidated power and the CDU party apparatus under his appointee as general-secretary, Kurt Biedenkopf, waxed at the expense of the joint CDU/CSU parliamentary delegation, Kohl did not automatically bolster the cause of a different CDU/CSU approach to Ostpolitik. For the new chairman, anxious like Strauss to be chancellor, also placed a premium on party unity and feared that a major shift in policy would split the Union into different factions, similar to its Italian sister party's *correnti*. Above all he was careful not to antagonize his main rival, the CSU chief. Thus Kohl proceeded cautiously and incrementally, always careful to preserve intra-Union harmony. Like the primate of a church badly divided on questions of doctrinal interpretation and application, Kohl rhetorically encouraged openness and experimentation, but only until it explicitly called orthodoxy into question. Then he brought the reformers he had initially encouraged back into line by benignly counseling unity in defense of first principles. This was to become his style in most matters and it sustained him in power for much longer than many critics expected. Though it left leading reformers feeling misled, most other party leaders found Kohl's solicitousness of party opinion reassuring.

In short, Kohl and Strauss approached foreign policy the way they approached domestic politics. The CDU leader placed a premium on harmony, consensus, and trust—within the Union and within the West—while the Bavarian eagerly seized options and exploited openings to defeat his adversaries. But neither approach favored a rapid adaptation by the CDU/CSU to new circumstances in the 1970s.

CDU/CSU Conditions: Limiting Detente's Risks

As in the past, after the treaty debates Union leaders continued to paper over their ambivalence on Ostpolitik with a strategy of "conditional support" for continuing dialogue with the East. Fundamentalists treated the conditions as demands for broad change in SPD-FDP policy, while CDU reformers regarded the conditions as guidelines or limits beyond which Bonn should not venture.

Given CDU/CSU orthodoxy, Union leaders unanimously declared that the German question must above all remain open. Accordingly, they stipulated that further dialogue with the East should involve no new steps that would weaken the legal, political, and moral case for state unity or undermine West Germans' national consciousness. Though pressing the SPD-FDP to discuss the national question and openly asserting the valid right to self-determination, the Union warned against further infringement upon the legal provisionality of Germany's division. The treaty provisions on borders and political relations were, according to the Joint Resolution, a modus vivendi; they and all future Bonn–East Berlin dealings had to remain within the limits set out by the Karlsruhe verdict. For Union leaders this applied to three specific issues that dominated the agenda after the Basic Treaty's ratification.

First, the party held that Bonn must never be seen as compromising upon its long-standing extension of citizenship to all East Germans; this undergirded the legal basis of state unity. Second, Bonn and East Berlin in 1973 had agreed to exchange "permanent representatives," rather than ambassadors (as the GDR demanded). CDU/CSU leaders continually insisted that this arrangement avoid even the least appearance of full diplomatic ties.

Third, in accordance with the Basic Treaty, Bonn and East Berlin had also set up a commission to define the "border" between their states. West Germany was careful to emphasize that such a demarcation would have safeguards to avoid infringing upon Four Power sovereignty. At one brief stretch, the Elbe River formed the border, and here there was considerable disagreement. Referring to Four Power documents, Bonn claimed that the victors clearly gave the entire river to the West, meaning the border ran along its northern bank. East Berlin insisted that the river's middle must constitute the border, consistent with international practice and—it held—Four Power intentions. Great Britain, occupier of the area, had left a complicated legal legacy; it claimed to control the entire river, but permitted East German ships to use it freely. Periodic reports beginning in the mid-1970s suggested that SPD-FDP officials might treat Bonn's traditional claims as negotiable. Union leaders vigorously resisted any readiness to accommodate East German demands for an "internationally valid" border demarcation that backed away from the original zonal boundaries. Such a compromise would compromise Four Power legal rights, the rights of a future gesamtdeutsch sovereign, and thus the whole basis of state unity.

Beyond their agreement on these basic points, however, Union leaders split over how much the open national question should constrict Bonn's room for political and diplomatic maneuver. From a fundamentalist perspective, keeping the German question open required a narrow, restrictive interpretation of the treaties because their actual content and the attached letters on German unity left the basis of state unity unprotected. Accordingly, Bonn had to uphold the "official," "binding" 1972 Joint Resolution, with its classification of the treaties as a "modus vivendi," and even proclaim the resolution's legal significance as a unilateral declaration under the Vienna diplomatic convention. All efforts by communist leaders and left-wing Social Democrats to devalue the Joint Resolution as "unofficial" must be vigorously denounced. Fundamentalists also insisted that Karlsruhe's restrictive reading of the accords become guidelines for FRG foreign policy; they assailed government claims that the ruling's ramifications were strictly domestic in nature and urged that its terms be formally conveyed to foreign governments—even at the risk of diplomatic contretemps.[9]

Such demonstrative emphasis on legal positions at home and abroad mirrored the Union fundamentalists' suspicious attention to any hint of compromise on the citizenship question, the Elbe border, or the status of East Berlin's representative in Bonn. They demanded, for example, that the latter deal only with Bonn's Chancellory and not the Foreign Ministry, and that he not receive his credentials or any formal recognition from the federal president, as was the case with ordinary diplomats.

By contrast, without disavowing their own colleagues, the CDU's reformist minority contended that the German question could and should be kept open *with* the treaties, not despite them, and *with* the Social-Liberal government, not against it. Thus they pointed out that the accords, however faulty, left some hope of keeping the national issue alive. In their view, Brandt's letters on unity and the clauses formally reserving Four Power rights, though of limited utility, should not be denigrated; that would only reinforce communist claims that the German question was indeed formally closed. The reformist minority treated the Joint Resolution and Karlsruhe's verdict as valuable interpretive devices, but not, as the Union majority argued, the sole barriers to closing the national issue. Moreover, such CDU leaders as Gradl, Barzel, and Weizsäcker could often be mistaken for Brandt, as they argued repeatedly that preserving the "substance of the nation" (through human contacts) would help to make self-determinations more achievable. In general, the reformist minority seemed to imply that because Bonn's effort to keep the German question legally open was in fact defensive, it should be treated as such, and the party should avoid rhetoric that suggested that the East was expected to accept Bonn's position on the national division. As Gradl noted, no Union government had ever achieved that.[10]

With regard to Bonn–East Berlin dealings under the new treaties, all Union leaders insisted that the FRG must negotiate firmly. It should, they said, reject GDR statements that distorted the accords' treatment of legal and status issues; it must hold out for a genuine quid pro quo with concrete and binding East German reciprocation on travel and emigration; Soviet-bloc treaty violations, restrictions on contacts, and isolation of Berlin must all be met with criticism and countermeasures. In this respect reformists wanted the Union to appear as a nonpartisan monitoring agency: the opposition would help the government by publicly holding communist governments accountable to standards laid down by SPD-FDP Ostpolitik. Union fundamentalists, however, aimed their fire at both the Eastern states and the coalition in Bonn; they were intent on using violations of the treaties to argue against further development of relations with the Soviet bloc.

As part of their conditional support for more dialogue with the East, Union leaders also insisted that Bonn pay greater attention to reputedly neglected issues and interests. They argued with conviction that "shoring up" other areas of West German foreign policy would limit what the party considered Ostpolitik's damage and future risks (though, to be sure, changing the subject also focused attention on issues where the Union's own record was more coherent). But although fundamentalists clearly hoped thereby to restrict relations with the East altogether, their more flexible colleagues sought to make Bonn "balance" its Ostpolitik with more activity in other areas.

One way to limit the risks of detente and simultaneously get off the political defensive lay in a campaign to highlight Soviet-bloc repression. After the treaty debates the Union increasingly stressed the need for "clear language" when addressing conditions in the East. Soviet-bloc, and above all GDR, repression must be "called by its proper name," without ambiguity or euphemism. Detente should entail no limit on the competition of ideas, and thus such candor—in the media, academia, or political circles—should not be defined as "cold war rhetoric." With regard to the GDR, the CDU/CSU pressed for official criticism of both internal conditions and the shooting of would-be escapees. Bonn should press its claim that East Germans were covered by the West German constitution, or at least by the UN charter, and thus had basic rights. Union politicians also urged Bonn to condemn Soviet crackdowns on dissent.

Quite clearly the Union saw little hope of actually altering conditions in the communist bloc. Indeed, Strauss—ever the Realpolitiker—freely conceded that human rights issues should not necessarily be a main issue on the official agenda of talks with the East.[11] For Union leaders, underscoring repression in the Soviet bloc was more a way "to meet the ideological challenge of Soviet communism offensively."[12]

Although all Union leaders agreed on this theme, Union fundamentalists contended that SPD-FDP Ostpolitik had already conceded major advantages in the ideological confrontation to the East. By contrast, the CDU reformists often tried to stress bipartisanship, acknowledging even that Social-Liberal Ostpolitik laid the foundations for "a political and moral competition" with the East, above all, the GDR. As Kohl observed, moreover, detente and a campaign for human rights were mutually reinforcing: "We must successfully make clear to the citizens of our country the dialectical unity of detente and ideological class struggle between East and West. We cannot permit the necessary discussion of the real, controllable detente of which we so deeply approve, to lead to a softening of the readiness for contending [Auseinandersetzung] with the communist ideology."[13]

Sustaining an ideological offensive against Soviet communism and thereby offsetting or ameliorating SPD-FDP Ostpolitik had, in Union eyes, other components. Union spokesmen persistently demanded that their Social-Liberal rivals give Westpolitik absolute priority over Ostpolitik. Western cohesion and strength were, in the Union view, vital both to FRG security and to avoiding Finlandization through detente. Accordingly, the Union challenged the Bonn government to give Westpolitik more than lip service by accelerating West European integration, pressing for greater West German defense spending, promoting West European military collaboration, working for a change in basic French security policy, constructing a common MBFR European position that was closely linked to America's, and encouraging European backing for U.S. efforts to halt Soviet expansion outside of Europe.[14]

Differences of emphasis surfaced again. Union fundamentalists argued that it would be impossible to meet the above demands and satisfy Soviet conditions for further detente: the two were mutually exclusive. They implied that Bonn's government must not merely subordinate Ostpolitik and detente to Westpolitik but must choose between them (and choose the latter).[15] For them, then, CDU/CSU emphasis upon alliance solidarity and effectiveness was another phase in the fight against Ostpolitik specifically and East-West detente in general. Bolstering Westpolitik with political and financial capital would obviate the need to seek compromises through concessions and make "peace through strength" credible. Implicit in this was fundamentalist skepticism about multilateral detente and an indifference toward MBFR and CSCE, negotiations that were not seen as consistent with the real purpose of Bonn's Western relationships because they would turn the alliances into "detente societies."

For von Weizsäcker, Kiep, Biedenkopf, and other reformists, the CDU/CSU effort to shore up Westpolitik did not offset, but complemented the process of detente. Far from mutually exclusive, "an intensive Westpolitik is also simultaneously an intensive Ostpolitik, and vice versa."[16] More specifically, the argument ran, bolstering Western strength and cohesion would enhance Western credibility in multilateral negotiations with Moscow. It would deny Kremlin leaders the luxury of practicing divide and rule, thus helping to prevent disproportionately large U.S. troop reductions in MBFR and thwarting Soviet efforts to undermine West European integration in exchange for "pan-European" cooperation at CSCE. Unlike their fundamentalist colleagues, then, they espoused CDU/CSU support for and participation in multilateral detente: the party could play an important, highly credible role in making detente work by countering SPD-FDP efforts at an independent FRG detente.

Government and Opposition after the Treaty Debates

A critical variable in the CDU/CSU's adaptation to Social-Liberal Ostpolitik was the character and pace of that policy after 1973.

How the Social-Liberal coalition proceeded after its initial treaties were in force would partly determine whether CDU/CSU ambivalence—and thus fundamentalist resistance—increased or moderated. Discord was emerging in the SPD-FDP, however, precisely on the question of Ostpolitik's next phase.

Until this point Brandt had sustained the momentum of his foreign policy by focusing on the short-term aim of a modus vivendi with the East (in exchange for softening traditionally rigid West German legal positions). This objective had broad support within his own coalition. At the same time, during its first four years the Social-Liberal team had been content to leave longer-range goals somewhat hazy because here there was less agreement. But with ratification (and after tying up a few loose ends, such as treaties normalizing relations with Czechoslovakia, Bulgaria, and Hungary), the government attained its one clear goal; it had scaled the first summit and was now looking into the foggy high ground beyond. What should follow from the modus vivendi, now formally codified in a set of accords? As William Griffith has observed, the "Brandt-Scheel Ostpolitik was always intended to be long range and the treaties its beginning, not its end." But there was little consensus on the long-term objectives or how to achieve them.[17]

It was clear which direction the allies wished Bonn to take. French and British leaders remained somewhat wary of German Ostpolitik, and the United States harbored even deeper doubts about the direction of this policy. Now that the national question no longer blocked East-West rapprochement, Bonn's partners wanted to channel Ostpolitik into a controlled, multilateral set of negotiations. Washington wanted even more: a renewed emphasis on and tighter integration of the Western community.[18]

Some Social Democrats and the FDP as a whole were indeed satisfied that their efforts had resulted in an historic reconciliation, removed the German question as an impediment to East-West detente, and cleared the way for humanitarian measures; more should not be expected of a purely bilateral Ostpolitik. As SPD strategist Richard Löwenthal warned, SPD-FDP Ostpolitik, having substantially ameliorated the "special German problem," should not be developed further in the hope of creating a special German-German relationship. Instead, German-German relations should become stable and routine and the GDR's compliance with existing agreements carefully monitored.[19] Although Karlsruhe's decision was treated by this group as strictly domestic in its effect, its members nonetheless wanted to ensure that the East respected Bonn's official interpretation of the treaties. Further initiatives toward East-West detente should henceforth come on the multilateral level—at MBFR and CSCE. Liberals such as Interior Minister Hans-Dietrich Genscher were especially cautious about the next stage.

But a substantial portion of the SPD, primarily its left wing and younger members, but including the aging parliamentary leader Herbert Wehner, had more far-reaching aims. For them, this was no time to routinize German-German relations, to treat progress in Deutschlandpolitik like "bookkeepers or accountants," or to pressure East Germany into good behavior. Rather than conducting "old policy with new treaties," Bonn must demonstrate more flexibility and readiness for compromise on fundamental issues, so as to soften the SED's insecurity and thus its hard-line stance. This was the route to more humanitarian measures (Wehner's primary goal) and a new "peace order" in Europe (a cherished aim of most younger SPD leftists). Many party members wanted to set about constructing that order of which Bahr and Brandt so often spoke. It would be based on detente, arms control and German-German cooperation, and thus help to overcome all the sources of Europe's bloc division. For some, this pan-European future was intrinsically desirable, for others, like Bahr, it opened the way to a form of national unity. In either case, many Social Democrats felt that rather than subordinating its interests in detente to the West, Bonn should exploit the greater national independence Ostpolitik created; its burgeoning relationships with the East constituted West Germany's *force de frappe*, a means of greater autonomy in foreign affairs, which should be used to facilitate detente.[20]

Coalition and opposition leaders alike, each in their own way, were grappling with the basic dilemma that confronted West Germany's Eastern policies after 1973. The removal of long-standing barriers to relatively routine relations with the Soviet bloc cleared the way for greater political, economic, and personal contact. But as many commentators at the time pointed out, greater interaction and the expectations it created inevitably imposed certain limitations upon further cooperation. West and East alike were bound to fear the effects that expanded interaction could have on their political cohesion and ideological legitimacy. In the Eastern bloc, such contacts threatened to raise expectations of change and liberalization, which could endanger the legitimacy of communist rule. For the insecure SED, it was especially vital to restrict further contacts and refute the thesis that one German nation still existed; and this required a heavy dose of ideology, "delimiting" the worker's state from the bourgeois FRG. The West too had reason for caution. Detente could weaken Western public opinion's readiness to sustain the military equilibrium that made it possible to bargain credibly with the East. Bonn and its allies had reason to fear that the spirit of accommodation would even weaken appreciation for the fundamental differences between East and West.

What form of cooperation with the East could break down the barriers put up by an uneasy GDR (and its Soviet patron), yet keep the FRG within the mainstream of Western policy on security issues? Even critics of the Union conceded that it had sensed the delicacy of this task, but they added that the fundamentalist solution—curtailing East-West relations—only created new risks. For their part, left-wing Social Democrats either pretended to ignore the probability of stalemate, or were willing to overcome it by displaying greater sensitivity to Eastern insecurity and reducing the importance of military questions in East-West relations. As for the SPD-FDP center and the CDU's reformist minority, both sought ways to reconcile further interbloc dialogue with the demands of intrabloc cohesion. That common effort was ultimately to restore a broad domestic consensus on Bonn's Ostpolitik, but only after nearly a decade of further debate.[21]

5

Finding the Limits of Ostpolitik, 1973–1976

The Last Phase of Brandt-Scheel Ostpolitik

After the Eastern treaties were ratified, Willy Brandt's Ostpolitik agenda called for tying up several loose ends—normalization of relations with three East European states—and negotiating the follow-on accords with the GDR. Bonn also planned to play an active role in the new multilateral Conferences on Security and Cooperation in Europe (CSCE) and Mutual and Balanced Force Reductions (MBFR).

But Brandt's policy ran up against East-bloc efforts to isolate West Berlin. East Germany refused to include West Berlin in German-German agreements on sports and youth exchanges, and declared that the 1971 Four Power accord permitted merely "ties," not "bonds," between West Germany and the divided city.[1] Moreover, after the Karlsruhe ruling Prague and Budapest declared that in normalizing relations with Bonn they would recognize the Federal Republic's right to represent ordinary West Berliners ("natural persons"), but not West Berlin official organs ("juridical persons"). This challenged West Germany's reading of the Four Power agreement and heightened fear of West Berlin's diplomatic isolation even among Brandt's SPD colleagues in the divided city. Throughout 1973 SED officials cracked down on illegal "misuse" of the transit routes to West Berlin by West Germans helping would-be East German escapees, and they demanded that Bonn stop tolerating these violations of the 1971 Berlin agreements. The GDR also continued imposing measures to restrict human contacts, culminating in a drastic increase in the amount of money Western visitors were compelled to exchange for Eastern currency when crossing into East Berlin and East Germany—a move designed to reduce contacts without losing badly needed Western currency. East Berlin also heightened ideological delimitation, refuting Bonn's claim that the Basic Treaty, by mentioning the national question, implied the existence of a German nation. A revised version of the GDR constitution eliminated all remaining references, explicit or implicit, to *Gesamtdeutschland*.

In a reflection of underlying differences within the coalition over the long-range aims of Ostpolitik, Bonn's reaction to these moves was divided. The FDP and conservative Social Democrats, above all in Berlin, insisted that Bonn stand by its own reading of the accords and resist this delimitation and East German restrictions on humanitarian measures. Led by FDP interior minister, Hans-Dietrich Genscher, who was always more suspicious of the GDR than party chief Scheel, they argued for the construction of a federal environmental agency in West Berlin to test the GDR's respect for the Four Power accord's ambiguous approval of FRG presence. Herbert Wehner and SPD leftists countered that this stance would only compound East German insecurities and thus prove counterproductive. Wehner publicly remarked on a visit to the Soviet Union that Bonn had "pulled a bit too hard" on the Berlin issue. In characteristically outspoken style, he went further, assuring his hosts that opponents of the Eastern treaties—by which most presumed he meant the CDU/CSU and Social-Liberal hard-liners —would not determine how they were implemented.

Despite his convincing personal election triumph, Brandt vacillated and proved unable to enforce coalition unity. Fearful of further GDR restrictions on travel, he promised to uphold Bonn's obligations under the Berlin accords and crack down on those who took money for helping escapees on the transit ways. At the same time, however, Brandt pledged *not* to interfere with the basic human right of people to flee the GDR. On Berlin, the chancellor reacted firmly at first, holding up further negotiations on a treaty with Czechoslovakia until Prague accepted Bonn's legal right to represent all West Berliners; he demonstratively canceled his planned trip to Prague in the summer of 1973, prompting Wehner's criticism. Nonetheless, in December 1973 Brandt signed the normalization treaty with Prague, although Bonn had won at best a vague compromise on its right to represent West Berlin "juridical persons," that is, institutions. Even longtime sympathizers in the German press and abroad were critical.

Government spokesmen could point to many areas where Ostpolitik had delivered on its promises: travel, emigration, access-route security. Yet even *Die Zeit* and *Der Spiegel*, sympathetic to Brandt, agreed that his government appeared helpless to resist GDR restrictions and delimitation.[2] And public-opinion polls throughout 1973 and 1974 showed uneasiness about Brandt, his Ostpolitik and detente generally. Although nearly half of all West Germans in a 1973 survey expressed satisfaction with Bonn's Eastern policy, almost the same percentage did not—nearly double the share of a year earlier. In early 1974 another poll showed the percentage of West Germans who were optimistic about Ostpolitik had fallen from 61 percent in 1973 to 38 percent, with 45 percent pessimistic. West Berliners registered even stronger discontent, especially with regard to Bonn's defense of their own interests, and voiced growing pessimism about their city's future. In early 1974 one poll (by Allensbach, an institute sympathetic to the Union) showed that most West Germans would have greater confidence in a CDU/CSU Ostpolitik than Brandt's; a majority even agreed that "it is being shown ever more clearly, that CDU/CSU warnings about [Social-Liberal] Ostpolitik were correct."[3]

The Union Response

Not surprisingly these events in late 1973 and early 1974 fueled the fires of CDU/CSU fundamentalism. To be sure, CDU reformists like Kiep and Gradl were also frustrated with what they considered Bonn's "exaggerated" caution about East German sensitivities, but they still argued for a milder tone toward SPD-FDP Ostpolitik. Behind closed doors they urged Union colleagues to refrain from overly harsh criticism and obstructionism.

But fundamentalists saw this GDR delimitation and restrictiveness as confirmation of their skepticism. They mocked Brandt for "playing the hard-liner," contending that if he were serious, the chancellor would confront East Berlin openly, for example, on its "show trials" of those West Germans caught helping escapees on the Berlin transit routes. They castigated him for failing to disavow Bahr's apparent sensitivity to the GDR on this issue and for failing to denounce Wehner and the SPD left's effort to accommodate East Berlin. Above all, fundamentalists condemned Wehner's "outrageous" and "scandalous" attempts to undermine Bonn–West Berlin ties. They urged the federal government to honor Karlsruhe's verdict by expanding its "presence" in West Berlin on the assumption that anything not explicitly prohibited by the Four Power pact was permissible—more official visits by "federal" politicians, for example. After the GDR raised the minimum mandatory exchange, Union fundamentalists demanded a hard response, and when it was not forthcoming they accused the government of weakness and even "complicity" in East German attacks on detente.

CDU/CSU fundamentalist vehemence was also fueled by what seemed to them fresh evidence in 1973 and 1974 of neutralist tendencies in the SPD. Resolutions passed by the party's youth wing (the Jusos) called for dissolving the alliance system and gave "class solidarity" precedence over Western democratic solidarity. More ambiguous and more controversial was disclosure of a five-year-old paper by Bahr that seemed to indicate his preference for disbanding the military blocs, U.S.–Soviet troop withdrawals, and a new Central European collective security system made up of communist and Western states. Publication of this document, coupled with interviews in which Bahr described the alliances as an "obstacle" to detente, and therefore negotiable in the not-so-distant future, intensified CDU/CSU criticism.

At the same time the opposition seized upon signs of what it called SPD-FDP neglect of West Germany's Westpolitik. Bonn's alleged failure to promote West European cooperation, especially on military affairs, its apparent preference for "the Europe of [Austria's Bruno] Kreisky and [Sweden's Olof] Palme"—that is, a neutral Europe—meant that the Europeans were united only by their weakness. Ostpolitik was thus blamed for the "sluggish" and "clumsy" response of West Germany and Western Europe as a whole to the October 1973 Mideast war, which so alienated Washington. Unless Bonn took the lead in shaping a cohesive, assertive Europe, capable of answering Henry Kissinger's appeal for "a new Atlantic Charter," Europe would never be taken seriously by Washington as a partner, and would "fall between two stools," East and West.[4]

The 1973–1974 Accords

The fundamentalist revival manifested itself clearly in the Union's treatment of the last "loose ends" to Brandt's Ostpolitik—three accords that were discussed throughout 1973 and 1974 and formally voted upon in 1974. Union leaders had warily followed GDR-FRG talks on the idea of exchanging "permanent representatives." They watched for any hint that this would lead to formal recognition or otherwise undermine the division's legal provisionality. When Bonn and East Berlin finally released their joint protocol in March 1974, the Union was pleased that it permitted Bonn's emissary to represent West Berlin as well. Against this considerable advantage, however, was the fact that the GDR representative would receive his credentials from the federal president. Fundamentalists immediately voiced constitutional reservations based on the Karlsruhe ruling; there were suggestions that the party would block this protocol in the Bundesrat or take it to court. Union reformists like von Weizsäcker persuaded the party that it had little to gain and much to lose from appearing responsible for blocking the establishment of missions. To save face, the party requested formal clarification of the protocol's constitutionality from the government and urged that steps be taken to avoid any hint of diplomatic relations. Although this compromise won praise for pragmatism, Bavaria did abstain on the Bundesrat vote, and CDU/CSU spokesmen criticized the protocol as another "unilateral concession" by Bonn.[5]

Further evidence that Union fundamentalism remained dominant in 1973 and 1974 came during parliamentary deliberation over the treaty normalizing relations with Czechoslovakia. For months it was unclear whether the party would reject the accord's main, controversial substantive clause: classification of the 1938 Munich agreements as "void" (the German-Italian-British-French document had turned the Sudetenland over to Germany). Prague had made normalization contingent upon acceptance of this point. Since the 1960s the Union had been in principle willing to nullify the Munich agreement, thus forswearing any claim to the Sudetenland. But Union expellees, above all Sudetens, insisted that Czechoslovakia's communist regime could interpret "void" to mean that Munich was a legal nullity from the outset. This, they said, made all Sudeten expellees Czech citizens during World War II, and legally liable for reparations or even criminal prosecution. Bonn's negotiators had won additional wording in the text to guard against such a possibility, but the Union again insisted that the two treaty partners could interpret this formula differently. There was also sharp protest from Union fundamentalist ranks that the preamble explicitly condemned Nazi crimes in Czechoslovakia without specifically mentioning the postwar expulsion of the Sudetens, which involved violence and considerable loss of property.

These points alone made CDU/CSU support for the Bonn-Prague treaty unlikely. Opposition to ratification stiffened further, however, when Prague in 1973 rejected a clause allowing Bonn to represent West Berlin and Brandt settled for a compromise on the issue. During parliamentary deliberations in early 1974, Union speakers reiterated the above objections, voted against the accord unanimously, and used their Bundesrat majority to delay formal ratification.

Final deliberations over FRG ratification of the now nearly decade-old Nuclear Non-Proliferation Treaty (NPT) also demonstrated Union divisions and fundamentalist persistence. Fundamentalists, with their Gaullist inclinations, contended that the NPT was a function of superpower bilateralism and discriminated against Europe; they argued as well that the NPT could be used to prevent a future West European state from developing its own nuclear deterrent, or at least might give the Kremlin a right to intervene in NATO's decisionmaking on nuclear weapons, compounding the "hidden security risks of Ostpolitik." They depicted all of these dangers against the backdrop of a continuing Soviet nuclear buildup.

Reformists shared these last reservations to some degree. But with their largely Atlanticist inclinations, they viewed the NPT above all in terms of its effect upon intraalliance unity. All NATO partners except France had signed it, and Union reformists believed Bonn's alliance credentials would suffer if the NPT were blocked. They generally accepted U.S. assurances that no future European state could be bound by this accord. Most observers agreed that the CDU (if not the CSU) was resigned to the NPT's passage, and simply wished to avoid further isolating the party at home and abroad by waging another fruitless rearguard action.[6]

In an initial straw vote, a bare majority of the parliamentary group rejected the accord, but in the Bundestag in February 1974 these proportions were reversed. A minority of ninety rejected it, echoing Strauss's argument that on all the main points it was unclear and that the Kremlin rejected Bonn and Washington's interpretations. Some fundamentalists, however, accepted government reassurances and joined the CDU reformists to vote "yes."

Given such ample time for deliberation on this vote, the Union at least averted the mutual recriminations that followed earlier ratification debates. Yet two years after the initial Eastern treaties had passed, the party's divisions and ambivalence persisted.

Schmidt-Genscher Pragmatism

In late April 1974 Bonn's intelligence service unmasked an East German spy in the Chancellory, touching off a series of events that led to an already weakened and weary Brandt's resignation.[7] His successor, the brilliant and multitalented, if ambitious and abrasive, Helmut Schmidt, had enjoyed success as an SPD deputy, mayor of Hamburg, parliamentary chief, and—after 1969—minister of defense, economics and finance. An expert in security policy and trade, he placed a premium on Bonn's Western ties. Partly for this reason, and because of his thinly disguised disdain for Brandt, his comparatively modest enthusiasm for Social-Liberal Ostpolitik was well known. From the start, he gave Westpolitik greater attention than relations with the East and made it clear that Bonn would approach detente in a pragmatic, businesslike manner, offering economic incentives but few substantive concessions to the East.[8]

This new emphasis became even more pronounced when Scheel stepped up to the presidency and was replaced as foreign minister by fellow Free Democrat Hans-Dietrich Genscher. In his earlier post as interior minister, Genscher was known as "the brakesman," given his frequent efforts to slow Brandt's Ostpolitik, an attitude related in part to his background: as a very young man he had emigrated from the GDR. Genscher also displayed a shrewd sense of political strategy; unlike Scheel he was not deeply committed to a coalition with the SPD and had often flirted with the Union.

At the same time, French elections produced a new president, Valéry Giscard d'Estaing, a friend of Schmidt's from the time when both were finance ministers. The two leaders soon began pursuing a number of joint policy ventures, especially within the European Community (EC), further reducing Schmidt's willingness to become embroiled in old or new controversies over Ostpolitik. As the chancellor saw it, following Union fundamentalists back to a renewed emphasis on German reunification or following the SPD strategists forward to closer cooperation with the East might arouse French concerns that could jeopardize this new Bonn-Paris partnership.

Clearly Schmidt and Genscher could not break with their predecessors' policy in substance, but their administration represented a change in priorities and approach. In fact, Schmidt-Genscher pragmatism in many respects seemed to be what the opposition had prescribed for years as an antidote to Brandt's "naive moralism." The new team began pursuing Ostpolitik without downplaying Bonn's traditional stance on the national question. In his 1975 state-of-the-nation address, for example, the chancellor upheld national unity and called for an honest appraisal of German history, but counseled realism in relations with the communist bloc. An editorial observed that "Union speakers had nothing to add." This pragmatic approach earned wide approval, even from bastions of conservative caution.[9]

Yet at the same time Schmidt and Genscher won some political concessions, largely with economic leverage. At a 1974 summit meeting in Moscow they engineered a compromise on Berlin's status in an agreement to construct a nuclear power plant. A few weeks later the chancellor purchased another concession by agreeing to extend the "swing," the interest-free overdraft in inner-German trade, in exchange for a substantial cut in East Berlin's mandatory exchange for Western visitors.

Opinion polls bore out this renewed, or at least stabilized, confidence in Bonn's Ostpolitik among West Germans and, importantly, West Berliners. In early 1975 the Allensbach institute concluded that "optimism is trump": the sense of shock and crisis and the initial disappointment with the results of Brandt-Scheel policy had passed. Even Union voters were again becoming less dissatisfied with Ostpolitik under Schmidt.[10]

By emphasizing the need for a balance of power and by closely coordinating policy on security and energy with the allies, Schmidt and Genscher also at least temporarily allayed U.S. concern that Bonn might subordinate its Western commitments to the pursuit of detente. For Henry Kissinger it was "great solace to have such an absolutely trustworthy" man in Bonn.[11]

The Union and Helmut Schmidt

Schmidt and Genscher's success put the Union in a quandary. Opposition leaders praised the new chancellor's firmness on the Berlin issue and relations with the GDR, but fundamentalists downplayed the results of his policy and simultaneously raised the ante, arguing that Bonn should be winning more concessions. Fundamentalists insisted that the Union had and would offer economic concessions only in turn for concrete, binding reciprocation —not in return for "retractable promises." Fundamentalists argued that the chancellor ought to make cooperation contingent upon expanded emigration of ethnic Germans from the Soviet Union; they approvingly cited the Jackson-Vanik amendment linking U.S.-Soviet trade to Jewish emigration. Union spokesmen also roundly criticized Schmidt for extending the swing *before* East Berlin cut the mandatory exchange level: they said it appeared that Bonn was paying for the privilege of seeing East Berlin honor a *prior* commitment to ease inner-German travel. As Barzel put it, in at best restoring the status quo ante, Bonn had really "achieved" nothing; in any case, East Berlin might simply raise its fees again and demand more concessions.[12] Fundamentalists insisted that Schmidt should have won much more for extending the swing —release of political prisoners and an end to shootings at the border and the Berlin Wall.

Clearly Schmidt and Genscher's more pragmatic approach initially made it little easier for Union leaders to reconcile themselves to Bonn's relationship with the East bloc. Fundamentalists conceded that the new administration was ending the era of major substantive concessions and adopting more hard-headed policies. Yet they insisted that the SPD-FDP government had already crossed the Rubicon: acceptance of Germany's partition now formed the basis of relations with the East. Under these circumstances even minor status concessions and major financial incentives to the East might only stabilize the GDR further. Pointing to what they called the government's limited gains and the persistent influence of politicians like Bahr, they remained preoccupied with the risks of detente. Reformists shared some of these concerns, yet believed that the party could best ameliorate the risks by involving itself in detente. Yet suggesting nothing more concrete than cautious, constructive "monitoring" of SPD-FDP policy merely exposed the party's internal rift.[13]

Accentuating these differences in the CDU/CSU on the substance of Ostpolitik were disputes over domestic political strategy. Party fundamentalists led by Strauss saw a string of Union successes in state elections in 1974 and 1975 (the CSU achieved over 60 percent in Bavaria), along with more favorable opinion-poll ratings, as the Union's reward for unbending resistance to the governing coalition —Schmidt's popular pragmatism notwithstanding. By contrast, as CDU party chairman, Kohl generally agreed with reformist colleagues who believed that cultivating a new image for flexibility on Ostpolitik was more politically prudent. Under General-Secretary Kurt Biedenkopf the party was carrying through sweeping expansion in infrastructure as well as membership and was renewing its programs: the CDU was developing more innovative, moderate positions on most domestic issues. Reformists felt that voters would switch to the opposition because it pledged to conduct Eastern affairs more successfully, not because it might undo Social-Liberal policy.

But despite his reformist inclinations, Kohl was also the Union's increasingly obvious and, among voters, increasingly popular chancellor candidate for the 1976 election. He could ill afford openly to antagonize the parliamentary group—where policy was still determined and where fundamentalists prevailed—with initiatives to offset the Union's negative image on Ostpolitik. This issue, as history showed, was too divisive, and now more than ever, Kohl wanted a unified opposition.

So although Schmidt's pragmatism increasingly put his rivals on the defensive, Union leaders were still too uncertain on the substance of Ostpolitik and too divided on its political dimension to respond effectively. Kohl had to be content with papering over cracks in the CDU/CSU position, cultivating the impression of flexibility only to the point where it did not further weaken the party's cohesion.

Kohl's penchant for cautious consensus building showed through clearly in the CDU's deliberations over a new party program in 1975. His own reformist general-secretary, Kurt Biedenkopf, could rightly point out that the so-called Mannheim Declaration devoted greater attention to foreign policy than had previous CDU platform statements. But it did so by lumping together the familiar doctrines of Union orthodoxy on Ostpolitik with some modest hints of flexibility, and it did not reconcile them in a way that suggested a less reactive CDU approach. Admittedly the program gave a relatively high priority to Bonn–East Berlin relations, stressed that more human contacts would help to keep the national issue alive, and fended off charges of nationalism by underscoring the link between reunification and democratic freedoms. But anyone seeking CDU alternatives for the conduct of Ostpolitik was disappointed. An appeal to protect the past gains of West German foreign policy from "changing world conditions" suggested that concern about detente's dangers—and thus the need for a restricted Ostpolitik—still dominated CDU strategy.

The same mixture of different moods characterized the CDU party conference in June 1975. Kohl appealed for a prudent policy of cooperation with the Soviet bloc (and especially Poland) and urged his party colleagues to travel in the GDR, cultivating private contacts there in the process. At the same time, however, a CSU guest speaker declared that the Union's unequivocal criticism of the Social-Liberal approach was finding ever-greater resonance in public opinion. The latter won far more applause than did the reformist Kiep, who warned against "ideological restrictiveness," and asked "Do we have enough confidence to discuss foreign policy within our own ranks?"[14]

Part of the answer to that question came several weeks later. The parliamentary group pressured Kohl to convince CDU party officials in the Rhineland that they must disown an essay written by one of their members that challenged party orthodoxy by warning against efforts to put pressure on the GDR. Discussion of the case at a Rhineland CDU conference on Deutschlandpolitik shortly thereafter was so acrimonious that party leaders thought it unwise to record the proceedings.[15]

Kohl showed even more caution in promoting any modification of party policy when the CDU dealt jointly with its Bavarian sister party, as at an all-Union conference devoted to Deutschlandpolitik in November 1975 near Munich. Kiep, Biedenkopf, Barzel, von Weizsäcker, Schröder, and a delegation from the Rhineland CDU —and thus any hint of reformism—were absent. Instead, fundamentalists from the parliamentary delegation, including the chief expellee spokesmen, dominated the dais. They conceded that there were differences within so large a party as the Union, yet claimed to represent an overwhelming majority. Accordingly, long-standing party doctrines—and thus legal positions—won hearty endorsement. But no one made clear how this "permanent . . . living commitment" to unity could be reconciled with an Eastern dialogue: only ideas for containing the risks of Ostpolitik were discussed. Further underscoring their defensive approach, many CDU/CSU speakers declared that all the party's warnings had proven correct, often refused even to use the initials "GDR," and castigated the government's policy as a failure that endangered the West's resistance to a more assertive Soviet Union.[16] Though sharing many of their doubts and criticisms, the conservative *Frankfurter Allgemeine Zeitung* lamented the Union's "lack of a concept," a "sorry state" made evident at the conference. Another newspaper observed that this conference reflected the ideas and issues of 1965, not 1975, as current topics received no attention.[17]

The Completion of Ostpolitik

A major challenge for the Union came in midsummer 1975. After months of negotiating at the CSCE, statesmen from thirty-five nations were preparing to sign the Helsinki Final Act.

U.S. Secretary of State Henry Kissinger's long-standing skepticism about the Helsinki process increased as events in the Mideast and southern Africa led to a cooling in superpower relations. Nonetheless, he fought domestic pressure to change the agreement (by putting more emphasis on human rights) or abandon it; CSCE was after all one of the "carrots" he was using to establish detente. Bonn's European allies also harbored doubts about the value of an East-West statement of principles but hammered out a unified, consensus position supporting the Final Act.

Schmidt's government shared some of its allies' reservations yet saw CSCE as a critical contribution to detente. It thus endorsed the agreement. Although the document was not a treaty, and therefore not subject to ratification, Bonn's parliamentarians agreed to deliberate on it in a special session, forcing them to cut short their cherished summer vacation.[18]

Most Union leaders had at least some reservations about the Final Act, but not all were dead set against it. Fundamentalists nonetheless prevailed, and the parliamentary group decided to go on record as recommending that Schmidt not sign the document. To preserve an image of unity, the Union agreed to vote unanimously, but to foster the impression of flexibility, individual politicians were encouraged to explain their votes as they saw fit.

Most Union fundamentalists voiced their suspicion that Moscow had pursued the conference idea so doggedly for decades because it served the Kremlin's "offensive, expansive, aggressive" concept of peaceful coexistence. In their view Moscow aimed at gaining tacit Western acceptance of Soviet imperial holdings while conducting a peace offensive designed to divide Western opinion and distract it from the real security threat: Soviet hegemonialism. Union fundamentalists thus blamed Brandt and Bahr for promoting the conference, even prodding the otherwise skeptical or indifferent Americans to go along. They charged Schmidt with failing to make a final CSCE signature contingent upon progress at the Vienna troop reduction talks—the only forum where true cooperation could take concrete form. The pious declarations of the Final Act would, they argued, engender a false sense of detente and security at a time of Moscow's unrelenting arms buildup and Soviet involvement in Indochina, Angola, and even indirectly in the attempt to undermine the fledgling democracy of a NATO member, Portugal.

Viewing the conference as a Soviet gain, Union fundamentalists regarded the fact that Moscow did not get all it wanted in the Final Act as secondary. To them, this meant only that the document could have been worse, not that it was acceptable. Indeed, as the Union saw it, the provisions of "Basket I" on security contained formulations borrowed directly from the Eastern treaties, such as respect for the "sovereign equality of states," the "inviolability of borders," "territorial integrity," and "nonintervention" in another country's internal affairs. For Moscow, fundamentalists contended, these catchphrases meant Western political and legal acceptance of the status quo. At the same time, they added, the Brezhnev Doctrine could safely be said to have earned an exemption from the Final Act because Western negotiators failed even to raise the 1968 invasion of Czechoslovakia as a violation of the proscription against nonintervention. The Union argued that Bonn was yet again entering into an agreement that Moscow would read as it chose.[19]

On this point, even many reformists were concerned. An increasingly prominent CDU spokesman, ex-diplomat Alois Mertes, observed that CSCE was essentially, if not officially, a conference about Germany. These various, familiar formulations on territorial integrity and inviolable borders, for example, were "not designed with the French-Spanish or Swedish-Finnish borders in mind." Their evident purpose lay in gaining world recognition of Germany's division, which explained Soviet persistence on CSCE.[20] Union leaders did commend Schmidt for winning Soviet acceptance of a clause permitting peaceful border changes, but they disputed his claim that this left open the option of reunification: Moscow would insist upon giving precedence to the clause on "inviolability of borders." Moreover, the clause permitting peaceful border change was never explicitly linked to a subsequent section on self-determination, so it did not seem to allow reunification through the free choice of Germans. For the Union, this omission devalued Bonn's claim that the German people had a right at international law to be reunified; at best, Helsinki sanctioned a confederal arrangement between two existing sovereign states, which conformed to traditional Soviet concepts of "self-determination."

Union fundamentalists unanimously held that these drawbacks outweighed the possible gains from Helsinki's Basket III, its provisions covering freer movement of people and information. They noted that nothing about Basket III was binding, as it did not create legal obligations. In any case the document's wording was conditional and ambiguous, replete with phrases such as "according to the country's own modalities," or "taking security requirements into account." As for the use of Basket III to promote human rights, they predicted that Moscow would simply thwart it by citing the principle of nonintervention in the internal affairs of other sovereign states (also contained in the Final Act). In short,

Helsinki codified the rights of states, not individuals.

If most Union leaders generally shared in this substantive critique of CSCE and the Final Act, different politicians—in accordance with the parliamentary group's initial compromise—weighted and phrased their reasons for opposing Helsinki differently. Fundamentalists conceded only that the declaration had some "reasonable" points, but was characterized largely by gloss and illusions (or even the hint of SPD-communist collusion, as Strauss suggested). In sharp contrast, Kiep thanked Schmidt's negotiators, praised the Western states for their "excellent" cooperation and stout defense of German self-determination in CSCE. Although the Final Act proved unacceptable, he said, government and opposition could nonetheless "march separately and fight together" in the defense of German interests and a more humane Europe.[21]

But it was Schröder, Olaf von Wrangel, and Alois Mertes—not fundamentalists, yet not quite reformists—who best reconciled the Union's objections in substance with an effort to appear constructive. They acknowledged that detente and CSCE itself offered opportunities, and they praised Bonn's negotiatiors for attempting to exploit them and, indeed, actually achieving certain gains. Some Union concerns had been met, they added, but in the Final Act disadvantages outweighed advantages. Schröder summarized the basic difference between government and opposition on CSCE (and many issues since 1969) in concluding: "We view . . . the risks more strongly than the government; for you, the chances that you believe you see stand in the foreground. But who should point out the risks, the presence of which no one can dispute, who should raise their voices in warning, if not the opposition?"[22] Mertes added that as a constructive opposition, the Union would continue to defend Bonn's official reading of all Eastern agreements against communist-bloc interpretation. Beyond that, as von Wrangel observed a few weeks after the debate, the CDU/CSU would henceforth help Bonn "face up to the negative consequences and spiritedly use the positive opportunities" offered by the Final Act. Above all, it would press for greater humanitarian measures in Germany and thus help the ordinary citizens. Along the same lines, the CDU party executive board, without voting upon the Final Act, pledged "to use it offensively."[23]

The Union's "obstinate" defense of German interests and its cynicism about the "spirit of Helsinki" found some support in the press, and there was some praise of the party's more differentiated approach during the debate and thereafter. Nonetheless, the reaction was largely negative. As the SPD would be able to say for years, Albania's ruling communists and the CDU/CSU were the only parties in Europe to resist CSCE.[24] Years later, many party leaders would describe their opposition as a mistake.

The Polish Agreements

Despite some modest modifications in the CDU program and the "differentiated 'no'" to Helsinki, then, the party remained on the defensive concerning Ostpolitik. As the election of 1976 neared, its rivals could still accuse the Union of an "all-or-nothing approach." But almost immediately after Helsinki, several developments permitted the party to get off the defensive for the first time.

During the Helsinki summit Schmidt and Polish party chief Edward Gierek had broken a long deadlock in Bonn-Warsaw relations. For several years, Poland had exploited the vague, nonbinding character of the 1970 treaty protocol by which the two countries agreed to facilitate the emigration of ethnic Germans out of Poland. The communist regime had actually restricted exit visas and had disputed International Red Cross estimates of the number who wanted to leave. Now Warsaw agreed to permit 120,000 to emigrate in exchange for (1) a trade credit of 1 billion FRG marks on favorable terms, and (2) 1.3 billion FRG marks in compensation to Poles who, during Nazi occupation, had paid into Germany's social security system without receiving pensions. Both countries agreed that the three separate agreements on emigration, trade credits, and social security would close out "questions arising from the past."[25] It was another success for Schmidt-Genscher pragmatism.

Union politicians, including some top fundamentalists, had been cautiously building bridges with Poland for several years. Their expressions of goodwill and visits to Warsaw, where they were cordially received, had somewhat softened Polish hostility toward Union policy.[26] Yet though praising reconciliation with Poland in principle, CDU/CSU leaders now complained vigorously that Bonn was paying a high price for humanitarian concessions that Poland had previously promised and never delivered. Moreover, in their view the new emigration protocol lacked the binding nature of the credit and pension agreements, and it covered only half of the estimated 280,000 ethnic-German applicants for exit visas (if Red Cross figures were accurate, which Bonn officials doubted). The opposition also deplored Bonn's failure to win provisions ensuring linguistic and cultural rights for the German minority that remained in Poland. Moreover, they doubted that individual pensioners or victims would ever see the money being given in lump sum to Poland's government.[27]

In short, Union fundamentalists, not surprisingly, characterized the entire bargain as "blackmail": having fallen victim to the appeal of "pseudo-humanitarianism" and "pseudo-reconciliation," Bonn was paying twice for the same ground. Strauss insisted that CDU/CSU doubts about the value of Brandt's 1970 Warsaw Treaty and CSCE were thus confirmed. Bolstered by equally negative public-opinion polls, he and a Union majority wanted to reject the accords unless, as was unlikely, Schmidt renegotiated them.[28]

Kohl shared many of their misgivings and agreed that the Union parliamentary delegation should vote "no" as a protest in the Bundestag. But because the pension agreement—unlike most other treaties—directly affected state finances, it would also automatically require Bundesrat passage as well, which the Union, with its majority, could block. Kohl was unwilling to go this far: past "no" votes in the second chamber had at worst delayed Bonn's international agreements, but in this case that body could—if it chose—kill the accords. Kohl feared charges of irresponsibility for making foreign policy in a chamber that did not customarily have that prerogative, and he also feared accusations of obstructing reconciliation—both potentially damaging charges in an election year. Initially he and Strauss agreed that the CDU/CSU would vote "no" in the Bundestag, but permit Union-governed states to choose their own course in the second chamber. This would clearly lead to passage because the Saarland CDU could preserve its anomalous, shaky, tacit coalition with the FDP at the state level only by voting yes in the Bundesrat.[29]

But Kohl felt pressure from most prominent CDU leaders—Barzel, von Weizsäcker, Kiep, Schröder and others—who were not content merely to tolerate the survival of the agreements. Supported by the CDU's youth and labor groups, these "dissidents" considered it wise for the Union to be seen openly backing measures that, however flawed, would symbolize reconciliation with Poland and ensure some humanitarian improvements. They felt confirmed in this decision by meetings with West German church leaders and visits to Poland. Kohl clearly sympathized with these CDU reformists, refused openly to rebuke them, and even left his own decision on the accords vague.

Taking Kohl's actions as a violation of their understanding and a contradiction of Kohl's promise to oppose the agreement with no "ifs or buts," Strauss reciprocated by calling for an all-out fight against ratification in *both* chambers. He published an open letter to Union leaders—clearly aimed at Kohl—appealing for united action, warning against a repeat of past split votes and urging the party not to disavow long-standing criticism of Ostpolitik just as events were proving its objections to have been correct. Precisely those Union leaders who viewed the 1970 treaty with sympathy for its promise of reconciliation and humanitarian gains should, he argued, reject Poland's current use of these ideals as an "unlimited tool for political and financial blackmail." "Purchased freedom of movement, inequitable detente, and alleged popularity" of government policy were no reasons to vote "yes." Bavaria's government released a legal brief reinforcing Strauss's contention that the emigration protocol was not binding. It also reiterated his arguments that by indirectly meeting unfounded "reparation" demands before a final peace settlement Bonn was prejudicing such a treaty and undermining its own right to represent Gesamtdeutschland. Veiled threats surfaced, yet again, that if the CDU voted for these accords, the CSU would break away and form a fourth party.[30]

Fundamentalist pressure restricted further open support for the agreement within Union ranks, which prevented the parliamentary group from splitting into two roughly equal camps as in past instances, thus partly satisfying Strauss. But fundamentalist pressure did *not* force the small group of well-known dissidents back into line with the majority, and thus Kohl's aim of protecting the image of flexibility was satisfied. Consequently the two leaders again compromised and agreed that the Union must exercise its monitoring function and reject the agreements in the Bundestag. But Kohl made even this "no" vote vaguely conditional, leaving the door open for a possible change of course if his concerns were somehow ameliorated. More important, he continually insisted that CDU/CSU states like the Saarland must decide for themselves how to vote in the Bundesrat.

Events in early 1976 made Kohl's tactic—letting the accords survive the Bundesrat—appear more promising and thus a greater risk to party unity. Three anonymous FDP deputies in the Lower Saxony state parliament abandoned their SPD partners and surprisingly put a CDU minister-president in power—a young reformist, Ernst Albrecht. Albrecht could now bargain, at least implicitly, for a formal minority government tolerated by the FDP—a great coup for him and his party, especially in a federal election year. To entice the FDP he offered a pledge that Lower Saxony's Bundesrat delegation would ensure passage of the Polish accord, which had of course been negotiated by the Foreign Ministry under FDP chief Genscher.

Exasperated fundamentalists began vigorously pressuring Kohl to insist that CDU state leaders stop giving provincial politics priority over the Union's credibility in foreign affairs, an ironic demand coming from the CSU. But Kohl continued to allow both the Saarland and Lower Saxony state governments full latitude. He was even rumored to have assured both Schmidt and Protestant church leaders that his party would not stand athwart German-Polish reconciliation and humanitarian measures. Mertes met with a Polish official and later appeared to narrow the party's list of major conditions to a handful. Genscher began bargaining with the Union to see how its objections could be overcome.

Because Genscher's answers were not immediately satisfactory to the Union, and given counterpressure by fundamentalists, the party stayed with its original strategy in the Bundestag. Only the seventeen CDU reformist dissidents voted with the government.[31] Well over 200 Union parliamentarians voted "no." To preserve at least a surface unity, all Union leaders voiced their desire for reconciliation and humanitarian improvements *and* expressed doubts about government policy.

Almost immediately after the Bundestag vote, however, Albrecht declared that Lower Saxony's position could be seen as a "yes if." His conditions were that the accords must set no precedent for reparations and, more important, must clearly permit emigration beyond the 120,000 specifically agreed upon. Significantly, Albrecht agreed that new negotiations would not be necessary: in principle, Poland had already formally promised to facilitate emigration, and that promise must merely be reinforced in some "internationally valid way," not through "mere declarations."[32] Albrecht sent another clear signal by appointing reformist Walther Leisler Kiep as his finance minister and arranging to visit Poland.

These steps received Kohl's approval. In a pattern reminiscent of the 1972 "so nicht" strategy, while fundamentalists were treating the Union's reservations as irremediable objections to the agreement, Kohl and others increasingly talked as if they were implicitly fulfillable conditions. Alarmed fundamentalists, citing disputed opinion polls, contended that a solid majority of West Germans opposed the accord.[33] To slow the momentum of accommodation, they began lengthening the list of CDU/CSU conditions, insisting upon a bilateral commission to oversee the protection of ethnic German minority rights in Poland. But clearly the CDU leadership's list was rapidly being reduced to what Mertes called "the central question": further emigration beyond the agreed-upon 120,000 figure.[34]

To the dismay of many Social Democrats, Genscher seemed increasingly willing to satisfy the opposition. He solicited Polish approval of a letter of understanding, to be published in both East and West. Initially it merely stated that there would be no time or financial constraints upon processing exit visa "applications" beyond the 120,000 in four years noted in the text. The letter was later modified to read that "these emigration *approvals* [emphasis added] could also be distributed." When Warsaw's foreign minister agreed on the eve of the Bundesrat vote that the text should read "visa approvals *will* [emphasis added] be distributed," Genscher had his victory.[35]

Genscher's overall package, while "still flawed," now met Albrecht's and Kohl's approval. Late into the night before the second chamber's vote, they persuaded the last, reluctant Union state-level leaders that the party should not merely let it pass, but could and should now vote unanimous approval in the Bundesrat. Although the CSU leadership classified Genscher's letter exchange as "cosmetic," Kohl convinced Strauss in a two-hour long-distance phone conversation to go along. Strauss uncharacteristically gave in, and on 12 March the Polish-German package thus passed the Bundesrat without dissent.

Although Poland immediately challenged Bonn's now-bipartisan position on further emigration, the agreement's passage was greeted as a triumph for Kohl and Genscher. Kohl's mixture of "realism and firmness" had, said the *FAZ*, proven successful.[36] By isolating Strauss and persuading him to vote his half-hearted approval, Kohl had outmaneuvered his Bavarian rival and exercised some discipline over CDU/CSU fundamentalists, without totally undermining the always-vital united front. He had also allied with Genscher's FDP, exemplifying bipartisanship and taking a step toward patching up relations with the Liberals.

In sum, the Union for the first time appeared able to seize the initiative and endorse a major Eastern agreement without backing away entirely from its traditional stance on relations with the Soviet bloc. Avowed CDU/CSU orthodoxy and exploitation of the opportunities created by detente were made to seem compatible. As Mertes asked, "How much more could have been achieved before signing the treaty with tougher, more self-confident negotiating?"[37] One participant labeled the Polish accords "the major turning point [for the Union, because] the resonance was so positive."[38]

A second development—the stirring of dissent in Eastern Europe, including the GDR—had a similar effect. Shortly after the Helsinki conference, the CDU leadership urged a concerted effort to promote Basket III principles, especially in the GDR. Subsequently, in early 1976 the party submitted Bundestag resolutions calling upon the Social-Liberal government to include an assessment of East German human-rights violations in the annual state-of-the-nation report. They demanded that the government protest GDR repression more vehemently, use all possible economic and political leverage to stop it, and raise the issue before a world forum like the UN.

Certainly this theme was not new for the Union. But championing the cause of basic liberties in Eastern Europe took on a new dimension with the Final Act. Monitoring communist compliance with internationally accepted human-rights standards East-bloc states had signed would be the natural role of a "constructive opposition" that wanted to exploit the "positive opportunities" of detente and not merely guard against the risks.

In truth, CDU/CSU orthodoxy gave little reason to hope that external pressure for human rights could seriously affect communist behavior. As Karl Carstens observed, "We do not assume that the general course of GDR policy, which is largely identical with that of the Soviet Union, can be influenced." Most party fundamentalists saw proof of this in continuing, indeed heightened, Soviet-bloc crackdowns on dissent. The Final Act was thus declared "a clear setback" as late as the summer of 1976 by Kohl himself; party fundamentalists were still more vehement.[39]

But the gradual stirring of dissent in Eastern Europe and the GDR in 1976 nonetheless compelled even many fundamentalists to acknowledge tacitly that detente, even as conceived by the Social-Liberal coalition, *could* bring pressure upon the Soviet bloc. The number of visa applicants in the GDR and throughout Eastern Europe increased markedly as a result of the Final Act, and several "Helsinki" monitoring groups emerged. This encouraged Union spokesmen to concede more openly that dialogue need not pose risks only for the West, and indeed offered certain benefits. Party leaders consequently began incorporating Helsinki into their statements and urged that it be fully implemented. As one participant noted, it gradually became almost routine for the CDU/CSU to act as if it had written, and not resisted, the Final Act.[40]

The 1976 Campaign

As the 1976 election approached, the Union seemed to be regaining much of its traditional constituency. Despite Schmidt's popularity, the SPD's image was tarnished by economic problems and internal strife. Meanwhile the Union, having recovered its composure somewhat under Kohl, seemed less openly divided than in 1972, and could campaign on "CDU/CSU issues" such as the economy, and law and order. In contrast to 1972, even Union foreign policy was not out of the mainstream. On one hand, Union spokesmen promised a more realistic approach to the East bloc, pointing out that the U.S. president, in response to Soviet activities in the third world, had ostentatiously dropped the term "detente." Yet its role in passing the Polish accords and the resonance of its views on human rights permitted the CDU/CSU to campaign with somewhat greater confidence in the credibility of its own "illusion-free" yet increasingly flexible Ostpolitik.

Union strategy corresponded closely to the public mood, which passed no "generally negative judgments" on Ostpolitik, but voiced disappointment with the results to date.[41] Accordingly, the party no longer pledged merely to respect the treaties if returned to power, but promised to honor their "letter and spirit," operate on the basis of their "complete content," and "fill them with life." CDU/CSU leaders also pledged that there would be no "ice age" in relations with the East if their party won.[42] To polish up his own Ostpolitik credentials, Kohl arranged visits to East-bloc capitals. There was fresh talk of bipartisanship, not merely on Westpolitik and security policy, but throughout the conduct of foreign affairs. One foreign correspondent noted the "remarkable" fact that much of Kohl's standard campaign speech—"almost the whole of the foreign policy and military security sections"—could have been "copied verbatim from the SPD election manifesto." Union leaders stressed in particular their agreement with the FDP on major issues.[43]

Indirect confirmation of the apparently narrowing gap between government and opposition policy appeared in their similar responses to a direct Soviet intervention in the election campaign. In June 1976 Moscow published a philippic condemning "certain circles" in the FRG "to whom a sober view of the world is alien"; it described the German election as a choice between war and peace.[44] Even party critics noted that certain phrases of the Union's quick response "could be drawn from government statements"—such as those pledging an Ostpolitik based on "equal rights and mutual respect, as well as a constructive spirit" that would result in real normalization.[45]

Indeed, Moscow's sudden attack on the Union, coupled with comments by Polish and East German officials, testified in part to Soviet-bloc concern that the Union had neutralized Ostpolitik as a campaign issue. In the view of some, Moscow was tacitly acknowledging that the Union could gain power and would "respect the treaties," without reversing Social-Liberal policy or "seeking revenge" (as East-bloc propaganda charged), yet would nonetheless be a less "easy-going" negotiating partner than the SPD.[46]

Union efforts to continue neutralizing Ostpolitik as an issue also survived a spate of incidents at the inner-German border during the tense summer of 1976. Several West Germans were seized or shot at, and there was one fatality: an Italian communist truckdriver returning upon request to the GDR checkpoint to retrieve his papers. With German-German relations suddenly at their lowest point since the Basic Treaty, Schmidt reacted cautiously, and the government warned against exacerbating the situation. Union leaders urged tougher action but remained vague. They hastily disavowed the comments of a CSU politician that were widely construed—and condemned—as an appeal for West German "protective fire" during violent border incidents. Instead, Union leaders urged Schmidt to recall Bonn's representative in East Berlin, make an appeal at the UN, request Four Power adjudication, and suspend talks on demarcation of the border, though many privately agreed with Schmidt that existing agreements should not be abrogated. But most CDU/CSU appeals for retaliation, such as Kohl's, proposed primarily economic measures, including restricting economic cooperation, scaling back on trade, reducing the swing credit, or even applying sanctions. Von Wrangel proposed a "good behavior" clause in all future accords with the East, entitling Bonn to suspend financial transfers. A Union government would, it was said, make economic relations, above all trade credits, contingent upon cancellation of East Germany's "order to shoot" at would-be escapees and others at border crossings.[47]

Social Democrats and their supporters warned that any explicit economic leverage would heighten SED insecurity, resulting in further crackdowns and delimitation. The FDP pointed out that economic sanctions could jeopardize perhaps 350,000 West German jobs and roughly 3,000 small firms—the CDU/CSU's natural constituency—which depended upon trade with the GDR for more than half of their contracts. FDP spokesmen also warned of the impact that economic measures would have on the international commercial image of the Federal Republic, a country dependent on world trade.[48]

Union leaders retorted that the GDR depended heavily on inner-German trade, especially since its high-technology component furthered economic modernization. These benefits came to the SED state on especially favorable terms through the swing, and this commercial relationship with Bonn also eased East Berlin's access to trade and trade credits with other Western countries. At the same time, they pointed out, Bonn's direct payments to the GDR under various agreements—to improve roads or telephone communications—amounted to several billion marks, a considerable contribution to the East German treasury if no strings were attached. The Union claimed to find it intolerable that the GDR should receive such benefits without granting concessions in return and without abiding by formal commitments or a humane code of conduct. Union campaign literature showed how many schools and hospitals could be built in the FRG with the resources flowing into communist coffers.

But Union leaders became cautious or vague when describing precisely how they thought leverage should be used. To begin with, CDU finance experts like Gerhard Stoltenberg openly criticized trade sanctions or trade limitation as "inappropriate." Bonn should avoid one-sided credits and perhaps use subtle economic leverage when first negotiating an accord to win East German concessions, Stoltenberg declared. But Bonn's basic interest in its image as a reliable trading partner and in continuing a "regulated, balanced economic relationship" with East Berlin argued against sanctions as a political lever. Only a further dangerous "escalation of political differences"—threatening West Berlin or cutting off traffic—warranted such retaliation. For this caution, Stoltenberg won FDP praise.[49]

Most other Union leaders vaguely maintained that Bonn must explicitly link all practical and humanitarian issues with economic cooperation, treating the relationship with East Berlin as a "comprehensive whole" so that SED authorities "would not be encouraged to continue their inhuman practices." As Kohl pledged, a Union government would take economic measures "under consideration." Such vague ideas of linkage, rather than explicit demands for sanctions, suggested that although Union leaders professed to believe a harder stance would not undermine dialogue with East Berlin, they nonetheless harbored doubts about directly pressuring the SED regime. Shortly before the election Kohl thus began downplaying the prospect of sanctions, stressing instead that a Union government would seek a negotiated improvement in relations. He also spoke more of reconciliation with the East.[50]

With the border incidents, Ostpolitik became a campaign topic, but it played little decisive role in the election's outcome. Most

West Germans thought the government's response too weak (61 percent), and wanted a more energetic reaction (73 percent), including an appeal before the UN (78 percent). But fewer wanted countermeasures (52 percent), and almost none favored "protective fire." Consequently neither the Union's call for tougher action nor its ambivalence on specifically how to respond were out of keeping with the public mood. One German in four thought the Union could handle such border problems better than the SPD, another 25 percent trusted Schmidt's party more, and 27 percent thought no party could handle the issue effectively.[51]

Schmidt still fully exploited the "protective fire" controversy to heighten fear that a CDU/CSU government would overreact and prompt near–civil war. His standard campaign speech contained a dramatic passage quoted and described here by a British correspondent: "'They shoot, then we shoot back. . . . Where will it all lead?' Here comes the blockbuster. His face suffused, his hair disarranged, his hands almost joined and throbbing with intensity, he uses the full power of the electronics to cry 'We Germans have lived through two world wars.' Then a short step back from the microphone to give him room to raise his hands, fingertip to fingertip, to his chin for the punchline. 'We Germans have had shooting up to here!' It brings the house down."[52]

In the midst of these events, a Chancellory study was leaked to the weekly *Stern*. Like Schmidt's campaign oratory, the study warned against overreaction to the border incidents, arguing that an aggressive policy could alienate the GDR population and push it into the arms of the SED. The study held that further human contacts were possible only if FRG leaders treated the GDR system as a given; otherwise those in East Berlin backing cooperation would be undercut by hard-liners. It also stressed that only a few prudent Union politicians could be counted on to accept these facts. The CDU/CSU dismissed this "secret" study as a transparent SPD effort to distract attention from GDR behavior, make the Ostpolitik work for it as in 1972, and split the Union.[53]

Despite Schmidt's histrionics and his aides' leaked study, the Union successfully neutralized Ostpolitik as a voting issue, even if the party gained little with its response to the border incidents. Whereas in 1972 the Union's image suffered from the bitter treaty debates, in 1976 its approach was credible enough that the electorate split evenly when asked which party could best handle relations with the East.[54] Kohl thus focused on other issues more favorable to the Union's cause. Consequently, on election night, the Union received its largest share of the vote in two decades: 49 percent. It fell just 1 percent short of duplicating a feat that only Adenauer had achieved, a single-party absolute majority. Although that one point made all the difference, leaving Schmidt's SPD-FDP coalition with a majority of seats in the Bundestag, 1976 seemed to indicate that avoiding an all-out attack on Ostpolitik reaped rewards at the polls.

The Changing Ostpolitik Debate, 1977–1979

In the late 1970s Bonn's relationship with the East bloc continued to lose some of the momentum it had enjoyed earlier in the decade. One reason was the increasingly inauspicious international climate, marked by the stagnation of East-West detente. Domestic politics also played a part.

Given that the chancellor ranked well ahead of his own party in public-popularity ratings and that the FDP had gained votes, the 1976 election was interpreted as a personal victory for Schmidt and Genscher and an endorsement of their centrist policies. With regard to Ostpolitik, this meant continuation of a businesslike dialogue with the East. Both men believed that Bonn's initial opening to the East had already yielded its major gains by deemphasizing reunification as an objective, and by accepting the status quo as a basis for effectively (if not formally) normalized relations. In their view, further major initiatives, let alone concessions, were to be approached warily, above all if they impinged upon Bonn's Westpolitik. Emphasis would be upon the "everyday business" of practical negotiations, punctuated by summit meetings with Soviet-bloc leaders.

A Status Quo Party

Toward Constructive Opposition

The Union's showing at the polls in October 1976 testified to its political recovery during the previous legislative period. Kohl had moderated party rhetoric and his more reformist general-secretary, Kurt Biedenkopf, had rapidly constructed a CDU party machinery (complete with a staff of advisors and based on increased numbers of dues-paying members) that helped act as a counterweight to the fundamentalist-dominated parliamentary group. But Kohl remained susceptible to pressure from Union fundamentalists led by Strauss, who scorned the CDU chief and his centrism. Indeed, at a top-level CSU conference in the Bavarian spa of Kreuth shortly after the election, Strauss's party (at his instigation) voted to end the joint parliamentary group and transform the CSU into a fourth nationwide party. Strauss contended that a separate CSU could become the conservative party of the entire FRG, absorbing all right-wing voters, thus "permitting" the CDU to shift to the center and lure away FDP voters. His stated aim was to assure the two former sister parties a permanent majority, his unstated aim to maximize CSU leverage. Immediate CDU threats to establish a Bavarian wing and polls showing that it would seize half of the CSU electorate alarmed Strauss's colleagues. CSU party activists and Bundestag delegates (only thirty of fifty had approved the plan to begin with) saw their influence over federal politics at risk. All but conceding a rare miscalculation of his party's interests, Strauss backed down.

Along with this victory, Kohl also earned the right to replace Carstens as chief of the joint parliamentary group. In a by-now familiar approach, he intended to promote a more flexible, constructive Union stance on dealing with the East—"Detente should not push us on the defensive"—while carefully guarding party unity. This strategy included a cautious, discreet effort to ease some fundamentalists out of powerful positions. They still dominated the overall parliamentary group as well as the CDU/CSU delegations to parliamentary committees on foreign affairs and Deutschlandpolitik, and their "stereotyped speeches" irritated Kohl.[1] He also encouraged more contact with Soviet and low-level GDR officials, as well as private trips to the GDR. In the CDU party organization, which he still headed, Kohl moved even more confidently, but again within limits. Between 1976 and 1978, half of the executive board visited East Germany privately, and politicians like Kiep, Stoltenberg, Biedenkopf, and von Weizsäcker expanded their regular contact with East Berlin's representative in Bonn and other East German officials.

More important, Kohl emphasized the need to continue narrowing partisan differences on Ostpolitik, and the primary agent of this effort was Bundestag deputy and former diplomat Alois Mertes. Mertes aimed first to present the Union as a constructive opposition by playing up areas of bipartisan agreement. He declared that a new "Union-led government" would "follow its predecessor's course" in areas such as trade, Berlin, Mutual and Balanced Force Reduction (MBFR) talks and the European Community. He argued that CDU/CSU policy had always aimed at peace and cooperation with the Soviet bloc, and it would remain "calculable and reliable" (if more "realistic, coherent, and balanced" than the current Ostpolitik). The various Eastern agreements—along with their interpretive documents—would thus form "an essential component of Union policy."[2]

To be sure, Mertes argued, "ending the old battles over Ostpolitik" need not mean renunciation of long-standing CDU/CSU objectives. It was merely "the legally and politically responsible consequence" of the treaties' implementation. Just as the SPD could base its policy upon Adenauer's Western treaties after having voted against them, Union leaders had the right and duty in opposition as well as in power to treat the Eastern accords similarly. Kohl backed Mertes up, acknowledging "the thoroughly necessary policy of recognizing realities" in the East (including explicitly the GDR) while reminding rivals and colleagues alike that binding treaties are not "the private property" of one party.[3]

Yet while pledging complete fidelity to the Eastern agreements and "their contents," Union leaders also tried to distinguish this moderation from the SPD conversion to Westpolitik, arguing that there need be no "revision" of traditional party policy, no "Wehner speech," "no Godesberg." Anyone inside or outside the party who suggested a parallel was quickly rebuked. Rather, Kohl and Mertes contended that without altering its basic premises, the Union could accept the treaties, at most clarifying and where possible narrowing its long-standing objections to them. As for the future, they contended that the government and opposition shared common aims but could divide the labor necessary to achieve them. Continued CDU/CSU monitoring and criticism of East German behavior was thus depicted as further confirmation that the party would make a constructive contribution to Ostpolitik.

This open effort to set the Union on a new course never gained real momentum. One reason was Kohl's own shaky position. Despite a good showing in 1976 and his double role as CDU chairman and opposition parliamentary chief, doubts persisted about his leadership. Kohl's efforts to accommodate the FDP fell afoul of party conservatives, and Union politicians across the spectrum increasingly felt a more dynamic opposition figure would be needed to unseat Schmidt as chancellor. Moreover, Kohl's modest effort to articulate a new Union Ostpolitik, understandably assailed by the SPD as a tactical maneuver, was not cautious enough to prevent grumbling in Union ranks. Often it was subtly contradicted. Though Mertes declared that opposition policy "rested" in part on the Eastern treaties, fundamentalist Werner Marx warned that "time does not heal all things"; the party could hardly embrace agreements when events had confirmed long-standing CDU/CSU reservations about them. Moreover, vitriolic anti-Ostpolitik rhetoric still prevailed in the parliamentary group, where, as Gradl saw it, there was still too much "insufficiently differentiated" thinking on the German issue.[4]

Even within the CDU party organization Kohl's effort to arouse discussion of Ostpolitik met with limited success. In early 1977 he sponsored a major CDU forum on Deutschlandpolitik in Düsseldorf to which he invited guest speakers with—for the Union—controversial and unorthodox views, including one who proposed recognizing GDR citizenship. Many observers anticipated, in effect, the CDU's own Godesberg conference. But although the guests were received cordially, many of their comments were firmly rebuffed. Gradl privately complained that party leaders avoided any real consideration of controversial themes.[5]

A final resolution did call for recognition "of the real power relationships" in Eastern Europe, readiness for "discussions, negotiations, and agreements with the GDR," expanding inner-German trade relations, and "realization" of existing "inner-German agreements." But although the resolution named interpretive documents such as the Karlsruhe verdict, the Warsaw, Moscow, and Basic treaties were not explicitly mentioned, and all the familiar elements of Union orthodoxy reappeared in what one newspaper termed a compromise between a treaty policy and ideological confrontation.[6]

Gradl noted with resignation that after Düsseldorf, Union fundamentalists showed even less enthusiasm for open discussion of party Ostpolitik, and subsequent programmatic statements appeared to signal little change or often even retrenchment.[7] Without consulting its sister party, for example, the CSU issued a declaration on Deutschlandpolitik in early 1978 that restated Union orthodoxy, mentioning the Basic Treaty only to attack it and advance a restrictive interpretation of its impact ("the treaty has not changed the basic political situation" in Germany). Where the GDR's name appeared, it was in quotation marks, and East Germany was frequently described as "Mitteldeutschland," "the Russian-occupied zone," or "a Soviet protectorate." When the CDU did not explicitly disavow the document, critics saw proof of a rightward slide by the whole Union and concluded that Kohl's modest effort to modify the party line had been abandoned.[8]

Throughout 1977 and 1978 a CDU commission under von Weizsäcker reworked the party's basic program, and it was approved overwhelmingly during a general conference at Ludwigshafen in Kohl's home district. But here too caution prevailed. Party spokesman boasted that thanks to "characteristic . . . unity and discipline" not one proposed revision from the convention floor "disturbed the broad stream of consensus."[9] Not surprisingly, Union delegates agreed that "none of the previous party program's statements on foreign policy needed revision." At Ludwigshafen the only major addition to Union orthodoxy on Eastern policy included a pledge to regard "treaties with foreign states and the GDR as binding," recognition of "the real power-political situation" in Europe, general approval of further negotiations with the East to ease the conditions of life, and emphasis on human rights.[10]

Indirect Signs of Adaptation: Deutschlandpolitik

There were, then, constraints on how far the Union could move toward a new Ostpolitik in formal programs and statements during the late 1970s. Given Union orthodoxy—and especially public fundamentalist adherence to it—the party could not bring itself to renounce past positions or embrace new ones openly. Yet during this same period the Union *did* nonetheless indicate increasing acceptance of SPD-FDP policy and a readiness in practice to temporize somewhat on Union orthodoxy. Evidence of this adaptation did not appear in bold programmatic declarations, but it nonetheless surfaced within and beneath the rhetoric in debates over government policy when party spokesmen tried to describe how traditional Union positions could be made compatible with the now-established Eastern dialogue.

Specifically, without ever explicitly downplaying the German question's legal dimension, party leaders began treating legal positions as less of an obstacle to dialogue. Not only reformists but even fundamentalists began to show greater caution.

To be sure, the Union continued to insist that the German question be kept legally and politically open, and thus monitored all negotiations possibly affecting the inner-German border, the citizenship issue, and other status questions. Most still refused to meet publicly with visiting GDR officials, shunting them off instead to lower-level party colleagues. They deplored SPD discussions with the East German foreign minister in Bonn's Foreign Ministry as designed to satisfy the GDR's desire for prestige.[11] Union fundamentalists in particular also continued to inveigh against any step that they feared would weaken *gesamtdeutsch* consciousness, especially among the young. This meant resisting an SPD initiative to make the country's main holiday the date of the Federal Republic's founding instead of the anniversary of the abortive East Berlin uprising, retaining the traditional national anthem, and stressing German history in school curricula.

Yet in public the party as a whole began to speak less about Bonn's legal positions and more about urging the GDR to meet a set of universal human-rights standards. Citing outbreaks of dissent in Eastern Europe since Helsinki and U.S. President Jimmy Carter's human-rights campaign, Union leaders stepped up their pressure on Bonn to "stop coddling" the GDR and to make human rights an issue in Deutschlandpolitik. This could be done, they said, by expressing solidarity with individual East European and, above all, East German dissidents; by deploring the Berlin Wall and Germany's division as barriers to human liberty; by pressing for an open, frank debate over human rights—rather than the less-controversial aspects of detente—at the Council on Security and Cooperation in Europe (CSCE) follow-on conferences; by publishing an official evaluation of East European and, again most important, East German compliance with Basket III provisions, which would expressly cite individual dissidents and describe their treatment; by urging the creation of UN and European human-rights' courts; and by linking economic relations with the Soviet bloc countries to the observance of civil liberties there. The Union proclaimed that in this effort, it was acting as a constructive opposition, offering specific ways to achieve goals that the government formally endorsed.

Although often still highly confrontational in tone, this argument nonetheless differed from an outright challenge to the GDR's legitimacy as an independent state. By the same token, the promotion of internationally accepted human-rights principles as part of Deutschlandpolitik seemed designed to win more understanding and sympathy among the FRG's neighbors than an emphasis on national unity. To be sure, CDU/CSU leaders maintained that promoting human rights and keeping the German question legally and politically open were both part of the same compassionate solidarity and commitment to winning freedom for all Germans. Nonetheless, as *Die Zeit* observed, in practice "just as the Union once shifted the accent a bit from the demand for reunification and self-determination to the protection of legal positions, now it is indisputable that it is beginning to shift the emphasis to something new: from legal positions to human rights." Indeed the *Frankfurter Allgemeine Zeitung* was worried that "the German question is being increasingly reduced to the human-rights issue," and argued that a lack of civil liberties in the GDR stemmed directly from the misery of national partition. Human rights were a "comfortable diversion": the more attention they received, the less Deutschlandpolitik "in the strict sense" would be practiced—even by the opposition, which the FAZ felt was having difficulty "thinking precisely" about the national issue.[12]

Similarly, the Union kept up its long-standing insistence upon a *quid pro quo* and tough bargaining with the GDR while simultaneously trying to show that this need not preclude dialogue. Party leaders still held that, rather than "opening its wallet" and receiving inadequate reciprocation in Bonn—East Berlin agreements, Bonn must treat its more than $10 billion dollars in economic dealings with East Berlin as part of a comprehensive negotiating package that would enable it to exert leverage on the DDR and win humanitarian concessions. Future accords must contain a clause permitting suspension of West German payments upon any violation of their letter and spirit. Fundamentalists went even further, implying the need for restrictions on trade and trade credits. Even the threat to meet an East German treaty violation by depriving it of a corresponding benefit from this trade—access to FRG (and even, indirectly EC) markets, Western technology, and credit —would, they said, engender caution in East Berlin.

Yet the Union also grew increasingly ambivalent and divided about pressing the GDR beyond certain limits in assuring a quid pro quo. Though they condemned Bonn's weakness in dealing with East Berlin, what most irked Union leaders was not the SPD-FDP's unwillingness to apply pressure, but its readiness to renounce such pressure. They contended that GDR leaders should never be encouraged to believe that delimitation was risk free. In parliamentarian Manfred Abelein's words, preemptive concessions would specifically undercut those SED "doves," above all, economic planners, who urged caution on their regime precisely in order to prevent West German retaliation. Accordingly, Union spokesman contended that Bonn must appear willing to employ strict measures —whether or not it did so—so as to sustain uncertainty and prudence in East Berlin. A CDU/CSU government, it was argued, would ensure that economic relations did not remain unaffected when the GDR acted belligerently, but would still honor agreements to pay East Berlin. Even doctrinaire fundamentalists forswore any intention to use "loud threats or reprisals against the GDR" or even to reduce trade.[13] Bonn's reaction, they said, should be neither placatory nor "demonstrative," but gradual and firm. Rather than calling it pressure, even the *Bayernkurier* often spoke of seeking a "rational cost-benefit relationship."[14]

Party leaders were also increasingly concerned in varying degrees with undercutting suspicions that CDU/CSU Deutschlandpolitik aimed openly to destabilize the GDR. Kohl denied any intention to "exert influence frivolously" over the GDR's internal affairs, as such an effort could prompt a crackdown and delimitation. Likewise,

Gradl urged "steady pressure" on East Berlin, but also "a certain caution" in instances where compromise seemed near; after all, the GDR's own interest in survival could not be ignored.[15] Acknowledgment of this came even from so vehement a fundamentalist as Abelein, who declared, "It is not our task to overthrow [SED chief] Honecker. . . . Naturally we need him. If we want to soften the German division and achieve relief for the people in Germany, naturally we need Honecker, who must also deal [with us]. . . . Herr Honecker has his set of interests, and we have ours. We have to bring these two things together."[16] Abelein argued that Bonn must use the SED need for Western capital to achieve what it wanted, but not take drastic steps to achieve maximal goals; rather it should settle for a good bargain. As one CDU study conceded, retaliation could result in an unwanted restriction of human contacts and more East German delimitation.[17]

To be sure, Union orthodoxy would by no means countenance the SPD left's theory that Bonn should consciously seek to stabilize the SED. Said Abelein, "It is not our task to overthrow Herr Honecker, but it is not our task to support him." Union leaders from von Weizsäcker to Abelein rejected the idea of openly promoting the survival of a particular regime, or the status quo as a whole in East Berlin; that would be a "reactionary approach" with no prospect of longterm success.[18]

Instead, the CDU/CSU was arguing for a tough style of negotiations largely in order to create an atmosphere that made East Berlin's leaders cautious and gave credibility to the arguments of GDR "doves" (whose existence it had long denied). Party leaders were becoming less committed to explicitly negative pressure on East Berlin than much of their strong rhetoric suggested, yet certainly they were not ready to accept SPD arguments that East Berlin be deliberately stabilized. Gradl openly characterized a view toward which, as described above, his colleagues were tacitly, gradually moving: "A crude policy of 'all or nothing' would make 'nothing' easier for the GDR leadership. One must always weigh the importance and the urgency of one's own goals against the other side's situation and interests. But one should not cripple oneself."[19]

The Union, Poland, and the Soviet Union

In its approach to relations with Poland during the late 1970s, the Union made an even more explicit effort to show that doing justice by its own traditional goals need not disrupt dialogue. This was apparent above all at a series of German-Polish conferences. Union participants, led by Mertes, von Weizsäcker and moderate expellee leader Philipp von Bismarck, stressed the Union's acceptance of the 1970 Bonn-Warsaw Treaty and a willingness to give it new life. They tried to persuade the Poles that this meant acceptance of the Oder-Neisse line. To be sure, keeping the German question open, they held, required keeping the border question legally open; the 1970 treaty could not bind a future gesamtdeutsch state. But they also insisted that this stance concealed no German claim on Polish territory; reunification need not come at Poland's expense. In short, Union spokesmen maintained that the basic elements of their Deutschlandpolitik were compatible with the 1970 accord.[20]

Although the *FAZ* observed that Polish participants seemed to believe their Union counterparts were sincere in hoping to improve relations, considerable skepticism persisted. For the CDU/CSU's careful phrasing of the issue was still accompanied by fundamentalist rhetoric outside the forum. Many Union conservatives and above all the expellees were pressing Schmidt to remind the Poles of Karlsruhe's ruling that the Eastern provinces were "under Polish administration," and to refute Warsaw's "territorial claims." Expellee leaders not so subtly reminded the CDU that its own "Basic Program" referred to Bonn's responsibilities for "Germany in all of its parts."[21]

There were additional complications. Even at the German-Polish forum, the Union irritated its Polish counterparts by cautiously reminding them of the postwar expulsion of Germans and of a "certain stagnation" in the lawful emigration of ethnic Germans from Poland. Fundamentalists were more blunt, insisting that a new, joint German-Polish history text use the word "expulsion" rather than "population transfer" to describe events in 1944 and 1945. They insisted as well that 150,000 people still wished to emigrate.

Nonetheless, what the *FAZ* called a "realistic, hard-hitting" dialogue was becoming a feature of German-Polish relations, and the

CDU/CSU was a participant in it. SPD spokesmen continued to insist that the Union's legalistic reading of the 1970 treaty violated its spirit, which in their view was acceptance of the Oder-Neisse border for all time. Polish spokesmen agreed, yet in practice seemed satisfied that even Union fundamentalists "could not bury certain facts" and return to the status quo ante before the treaty.[22] Poland continued to host Union leaders in Warsaw and invited the party's youth auxiliary to conferences.

Mertes began to espouse a similar approach to Bonn-Moscow relations—one that argued that frankness toward the adversary ultimately made for smoother cooperation than did efforts to blur deep differences. Moscow's "militant coexistence" policy set limits on detente, but as long as those limits were openly acknowledged, business could be done (above all Bonn-Moscow trade and, in return, humanitarian concessions in Germany). "There are common or parallel interests between the two countries," he declared, and a Union government conscious of the deep remaining differences would seek "mutually beneficial cooperation" in all possible areas.[23]

But it was also Strauss, not Mertes alone, who set the party's new tone. Nothing illustrated this better than Leonid Brezhnev's 1978 visit to Bonn. Aside from consultations with SPD-FDP leaders, the Soviet strongman expressed a desire to meet with Kohl and Strauss. The former's session went smoothly, but the conversation between Moscow's party boss and the Bavarian was even more harmonious. In a *tour d'horizon*, both men outlined their views of global politics, a discussion Strauss confidants proudly said had displayed how seriously Brezhnev regarded the opinions of their chief as a worthy *Realpolitiker*. The CSU chairman later reported that he had made Bonn's own interests, as well as his personal motive, clear: he told Brezhnev that "like Talleyrand" he aimed to "save what can be saved" for Germany after World War II, including national unity. Strauss contended that Brezhnev respected this blunt assessment of differences and extended the conversation by a quarter of an hour, impatiently waving off aides who were attentive to the schedule and making the gesture of accompanying Strauss personally to his car.[24]

Shortly afterward, before the Bundestag, Strauss called Brezhnev's visit a "milestone" in the history of Russian-German relations. Pointing to the recently signed Bonn-Moscow accord on economic cooperation, he declared that the "visionary phase of Ostpolitik," with its euphoria and overblown expectations, was giving way to growing pragmatism. So long as ideological differences were not glossed over, and provided that detente did not come at the expense of Bonn's Westpolitik commitments, a CDU/CSU government would welcome cooperation. The Eastern treaties would be honored "with no ifs and buts," with no "*reservatium mentalis*" (at this, SPD spokesmen cried, "Hear, hear!"). Consideration of the "possibilities, purposes, limits, chances, and risks" of cooperation should begin above all with Moscow's need for economic relations with West Germany. To Strauss, Brezhnev was "no warmonger," and the Russian people were "peace loving"; Russians and Germans were in truth "adversaries, not enemies." Indeed, Strauss expressed even greater hopes, noting that when relations in the past between Germany and Russia remained peaceful, such harmony had served both equally well. If Moscow could give up its ideological commitment to weakening and dividing Germany, the Kremlin would find the country a "thankful, fair, friendly . . . partner." If the interests and concerns of other European countries were taken into account, such a genuine partnership could mark a "new dawn" for the entire continent.[25]

In subsequent months Strauss constantly referred back to his session with Brezhnev, recalling how he had made clear to the Kremlin chief that the Union favored a "historic springtime" in German-Russian relations, but on the condition that "the great Russian people" respect the German nation's will to end its division. In short, Strauss claimed that he had been candid, which the Kremlin boss "in his own way respected and honored." Union leaders with more regular contacts in the East, like von Weizsäcker, reported that Moscow was reacting with "especially positive attentiveness" to Strauss's Ostpolitik.[26]

Developments within the party complemented Strauss's more active Ostpolitik. For two years CSU leaders had been winning sympathy in the CDU for the argument that only a more dynamic figure than Kohl could challenge Schmidt. Sensing his own unpopularity, Kohl tried to promote Ernst Albrecht as the Union's 1980 candidate for chancellor. But by this time the CSU had won over enough conservative CDU allies to make selection of Strauss unstoppable:

the Bavarian would get his chance at last to take on Schmidt. Strauss thus gained an added incentive to play the statesman on foreign policy.

The Union and Intracoalition Differences over Detente

In trying to show that Union orthodoxy was compatible with continuation of the Eastern dialogue, the Union was moving slowly toward the government's position on Ostpolitik. This movement was often shrouded in the fog of fundamentalist rhetoric, but the party's differences with Schmidt and Genscher's policy were narrowing.

Such congruence grew all the more apparent as tensions between the government and parts of the SPD over Ostpolitik became ever harder to disguise. Schmidt and Genscher held to a comparatively pragmatic, cautious policy that still formally reserved Bonn's rights regarding the question of unity. They thus had continually to resist pressure for a more active detente from a segment of the SPD leadership, including Wehner, Brandt, Bahr, and younger party leftists who impatiently grumbled that the policy of the chancellor and his foreign minister was "static," even "stagnant" and aimed merely to preserve what had already been gained. The SPD left believed that Bonn still read the treaties too narrowly, stressed the open German question too heavily, challenged East-bloc compliance with agreements too rigidly, and treated new NATO military measures too tolerantly. Most argued that this approach merely heightened SED insecurity, resulting in ideological delimitation and restricted human contacts, thus destroying hopes for a realistic amelioration of the national division. They urged Bonn to abandon the "juristic shadow world of reunification," accept the GDR "as it is," normalize relations, assuage communist insecurities, and even gradually stabilize the SED through political and economic concessions. Such an initiative to build mutual trust between the German states, coupled with phased-in demilitarization of Central Europe, would revive the spirit of 1969–73, end the estrangement of the nation's two halves, and help create a new "peace order"—which held out the only hope for some form of national unity.[27]

Whatever their own internal differences, Union leaders unanimously rejected this SPD vision of a new Ostpolitik. During the late 1970s a three-way debate consequently developed, with the Union insisting that the original Eastern agreements, as interpreted by Karlsruhe and by Schmidt's government, be protected from the SPD left's effort to reduce the national question to a matter of human contacts. Sometimes the opposition criticized Schmidt and Genscher for abandoning established policy by giving in to demands for a more ambitious detente, but often it praised them for standing firm. Mertes lauded the Foreign Ministry's "constitutional" reading of the Eastern treaties and suggested that Genscher might well remain foreign minister in a CDU/CSU coalition. Eventually even fundamentalists like Abelein began to speak of the FDP and Schmidt's more "differentiated" approach, and saw "nuances" of bipartisan agreement between those coalition moderates and the Union.

In specific, Union leaders shot down several SPD trial balloons meant to check whether Bonn's extension of citizenship to all Germans could be made less unpalatable to East Berlin through a compromise. They also called on Schmidt to disavow Social Democrats who implied that the national issue as traditionally conceived was dead because East German citizens both rejected the West's capitalist system and took pride in their state's economic achievements, which made them lose their national aspirations. A major episode in this later debate came after the 1978 publication by GDR dissident communists of a manifesto calling openly for "an offensive national policy" and "reunification" without the SED (albeit under democratic communism and socialism). Union leaders insisted that the manifesto showed how potent the idea of reunification remained within East Germany and charged that some SPD leaders like Wehner thus tried to belittle the manifesto or even call it "provocative." Even *Die Zeit* said these events called into question "the prevailing assumption in Bonn, that the national question would also fade in the GDR."[28]

The Union and Intracoalition Differences on Westpolitik

During the late 1970s members of the governing coalition were increasingly divided over the relationship between Ostpolitik and Westpolitik. Consequently it was on this aspect of detente that the Union came across as an increasingly credible constructive opposition.

Schmidt, Genscher, and Bonn's foreign-policy establishment recognized the need to guard the delicate balance between Bonn's security and detente policies, a perception strengthened by their growing uneasiness about the new U.S. administration. Contrasting personalities, political styles, and policy preferences created a deep animosity between Schmidt and Jimmy Carter. The chancellor doubted his new American counterpart's ability to lead the Western alliance, and continually reminded him of—or lectured him on—America's importance in assuring an equilibrium in Europe.

Yet Schmidt had to tread cautiously lest his emphasis on Washington's role as Europe's nuclear guarantor create an antidetente backlash in Washington. Despite Carter's personal commitment to harmonious East-West relations, many leading U.S. officials and legislators remained wary of Kremlin activities (especially in the third world) and saw Ostpolitik as evidence of diverging U.S. and German concepts of detente.[29]

For this reason, Schmidt's relationship with Giscard d'Estaing took on even greater importance. The French president shared the chancellor's doubts about U.S. leadership, his commitment to businesslike cooperation between East and West in Europe, and his emphasis on the need for a more assertive Western Europe. Close coordination between Bonn and Paris permitted Schmidt to present his case for both defense and detente as part of a broader, common West European policy, which was useful in dealing with Washington, the Union—and the SPD.

But many Social Democrats—led by Bahr, Brandt, and Wehner—wanted to blend rather than balance Bonn's security and detente policies. Stressing that since 1969 security had taken on a "new quality" and "ceased to be" mere defense policy, they hoped to move Bonn, and the West as a whole, toward a "security partnership" with the East. Alarmed by stagnating relations between the superpowers, they warned against overdramatizing Soviet military measures and suggested that Kremlin motives were basically "defensive." They urged the West to recognize Moscow's interest in peace as a step toward more cooperation and above all arms control.[30]

Alongside this faith in "political security," however, was the SPD tendency to treat East-West cooperation as the key prerequisite to any successful short-term amelioration or long-term resolution of Germany's national division. In Herbert Wehner's words, Deutschlandpolitik must "primarily concentrate upon rendering these borders less dangerous, instead of heightening the tensions between ... two military adversaries." Consequently, in his view, Bonn had a special interest in using its new weight within NATO to "push" for concrete arms control negotiations. Increasingly impatient with the cautious pragmatism of Schmidt and Genscher, Wehner, with considerable support in the SPD, argued that only a denuclearization of Central Europe (perhaps beginning with a Bonn–East Berlin arms-control dialogue) and creation of a German-German confederation could ensure peace and national unity.[31] Many in the party could fully agree that "the Eastern treaties and concrete results through arms control and disarmament policies are for us two phases of one political concept that we have been realizing since 1969."[32]

For the Union, arms control might help to reduce weapons and tension, but could never help resolve the central issues facing Bonn —security from Moscow and the national question. Because only Westpolitik could produce security and eventual unity, the party argued, arms control must remain completely subordinate to the demands of alliance policy. In this sense, the party stood closer to Schmidt's government than did Schmidt's own SPD, especially in the chancellor's effort to educate Washington on the need for a military equilibrium in Europe. As with the national issue, then, a three-way debate emerged on arms control and security, bringing the Union and the government closer together.[33]

Not surprisingly, the Union criticized SPD notions of political security that it said upheld peace as the absolute good and were exaggeratedly sensitive to Soviet security. CDU/CSU leaders depicted SPD talk of bolstering Ostpolitik by pursuing arms control, especially during years of cooler East-West relations, as certain to push Bonn in a dangerous direction—toward becoming NATO's special arms-control advocate, fulfilling a Soviet desire to have a "proxy" within the West. In playing this role, they argued, West Germany would be gradually decoupled from America, putting it "equal distance" between the superpowers or even eventually creating a de facto special Bonn–East-bloc relationship. Schmidt's own pro-Western credentials notwithstanding, then, the CDU/CSU charged that Ostpolitik's "second stage" would result in self-neutralization or Finlandization.

All of these differences surfaced in a running debate over proposals for giving the moribund East-West troop reduction talks new life. Wehner, Bahr, Brandt, and many Social Democrats, declaring that a conventional equilibrium already existed, dismissed "overdramatization" of Soviet force levels and pointed to doubts about the reliability of non-Russian Warsaw Pact troops. They argued for force reductions that did not necessarily result in equality, thus bypassing the long deadlock in negotiations caused by conflicting data on respective force levels. Union spokesmen rejected this circumvention of the data question, and deplored this willingness to undercut NATO's long-standing insistence on parity. Here the opposition was aligned with Genscher, who rejected any unilateral initiative to revive MBFR.[34]

Protracted, at times bitter debate over U.S. proposals in 1977 and 1978 to produce and deploy enhanced radiation or neutron weapons (ERW) in Western Europe brought similar differences to the fore. Reinforcing the objections voiced above all by Bahr—the system's uniquely "immoral" nature, its potential for hastening escalation to nuclear conflict, and its disruptive effect upon arms control—was an underlying SPD concern for the future harmony of Bonn's political relations with the East. Schmidt, however, publicly left his decision open until Washington had formally decided to produce ERW, stipulating that another NATO partner must agree to accept the weapon, and that the alliance should initially try to use it as a bargaining chip in negotiations—Genscher's preferred approach.

Despite some initial reservations about neutron weapons, the Union insisted that if such weapons could enhance NATO deterrence by offsetting massed Soviet armor they were justifiable, or could perhaps be bargaining chips. Thus the party backed Schmidt and his Defense Ministry on their refusal to reject the system out of hand, and in January 1978 the parliamentary group unanimously urged that Bonn request deployment on German soil. When under persistent pressure from his party Schmidt continued to make Bonn's approval conditional, the Union accused him of "caving in" and insisted that he openly embrace the neutron weapon so that Washington would not be seen as forcing it on Germany.

In April President Carter indefinitely deferred production of ERW, partly in the belief that he was sparing Schmidt a major intraparty crisis.[35] The Union blamed Carter's decision on Bonn's conditions, which the party said resulted from Schmidt's "pitiful weakness" in the face of SPD pressure that in turn reflected fear of resisting Moscow's massive propaganda campaign against the weapon. Carter's "fatal decision" also came in for acid comments from Strauss, who blamed him for "bowing to the Red Czar."

In sum, the CDU/CSU, like Bonn defense officials, had wanted a decision based largely on military-security options, in which Ostpolitik considerations played little part. But SPD spokesmen, in what one CDU advisor called a "landmark" case, gave in to "massive Soviet pressure," sacrificing "an element of potential military strength for the sake of political security and detente."[36]

The Union clashed still more bitterly with many Social Democrats over the idea of new medium-range missiles in Western Europe. Here also the opposition stood more fully behind Schmidt's government than did his own party, for Bonn's chancellor had initially broached the issue. Government and opposition leaders alike argued that superpower parity, as ratified in SALT II, "magnified" the imbalance in European-based weapons, thus casting doubt on the credibility of NATO's flexible response strategy. This could create more general doubts about the U.S. commitment to Europe, which Moscow could exploit with nuclear blackmail, actually or perceptually decoupling America from its partners. Soviet deployment of the new, mobile, multiply targeted, medium-range, more accurate SS-20s in ever-greater numbers after 1977 exacerbated the perceived problem of a theater imbalance.[37]

Bahr, Brandt, Wehner, and a large number of their SPD colleagues argued that given Anglo-French systems and U.S. intercontinental missiles assigned to NATO, a more-or-less permanent Eurostrategic equilibrium existed. New missiles were thus in their view both unnecessary and dangerous to detente. Wehner specifically linked the missile issue and Ostpolitik by proposing a moratorium on middle-range systems and a German-German economic confederation. Due largely to such pressure, in December 1979 Schmidt could win at most conditional SPD endorsement of the NATO decision—officially made that month—to deploy intermediate-range nuclear forces (INF) in four years and pursue negotiations in that time to solve the theater imbalance. SPD conditions included toleration of deployment only if (1) all avenues for a negotiated solution had been explored, (2) SALT II had been ratified, and (3) another European state agreed to station the systems as well (nonsingularity).

Given their aforementioned concerns about the theater imbalance as a political and military problem, Union leaders welcomed U.S. willingness to consider new INF deployments and criticized SPD resistance. Party defense spokesmen argued that NATO needed theater weapons of its own "as a general necessity," implying that deployment was vital on security grounds regardless of what might be obtained through negotiations. At least, they argued, stationing must be initiated before any talks began so to ensure a more credible bargaining posture. In any case, the Union gave the arms-control option low priority and assailed the SPD for making willingness to deploy contingent upon exhausting the possibilities of negotiations beforehand. They also called SPD treatment of U.S. SALT II ratification as a prerequisite for possible deployment "a joker" that would be played to block INF modernization.[38] SPD insistence upon "nonsingularity" struck the Union as yet another pretext for undermining the INF plan. Indeed, the party contended that Bonn must make plain to Washington its readiness to deploy *alone* if necessary because as a nonnuclear power the FRG was most affected by the current imbalance. In short, Union politicians accused the SPD of "conditionally" approving the two-track plan only to undermine it and never go through with deployment of INF.[39]

For Union leaders the INF issue showed that security in the SPD view rested more on accommodation than on military balance, and indicated the SPD's susceptibility to Soviet and East German blackmail involving German-German relations. They labeled SPD insistence on arms control and nonsingularity "preemptive concessions" designed to sustain Ostpolitik. There was especially sharp protest in the Union when SPD spokesmen talked of initiating a Bonn–East Berlin arms-control dialogue: it argued that the GDR, as a mere tool of Soviet policy, would use practical and humanitarian issues as leverage for blackmailing Bonn into giving up on INF, thus risking Bonn's vital security interests.

Social Democrats hotly retorted that the Union was ruining hopes for arms control, prematurely and frivolously inviting new nuclear weapons to West Germany, undercutting SALT II with its reservations —which the SPD cited as evidence of national chauvinism and anti-Americanism—and raising the specter of a Bonn-Washington special nuclear relationship (Wehner labeled it an "axis"), as well as fear of a German "finger on the button." They saw all this as evidence of the CDU/CSU's continuing inability to accept Ostpolitik in all of its dimensions, and they labeled CDU/CSU security policy a fight against the Eastern treaties by other means.

During this entire period—the late 1970s—Union leaders led by Marx and Strauss also charged Bonn with doing too little to bolster Western security outside of Europe. While Moscow's global strategy aimed to weaken the West on all fronts and divide the alliance, they argued, the SPD-FDP refused to think in global terms. Union fundamentalists conceded that Bonn's means for affecting world events were limited but declared that the FRG could at least ensure Western rhetorical solidarity and political support for U.S. actions. Such a display of will would thwart Soviet efforts to split the alliance while reassuring the United States that resisting Soviet pressures around the world served common interests. Implicitly, the Union wanted Bonn to push the uncertain, erratic Carter into more decisive action. The Europeans, Strauss declared, must introduce a new Western policy; this could be their last chance to defend their own role as an independent part of the Western community. Led by the Bavarian boss, Union leaders also argued for unilateral steps, such as a China policy that would possibly "again loosen fronts which have become rigid." Development aid, military know-how, even ships could be provided to Peking to exploit the China card and offset Soviet pressure against the West.[40]

Though less strident than in the period from 1969 to 1973, domestic wrangling over Ostpolitik in the late 1970s often appeared to indicate no emerging consensus between government and opposition. Yet the Union was subtly signaling a readiness to make its long-standing positions fit more easily with continuation of a policy based on negotiations. Moreover, precisely by focusing its criticism on left-wing pressure that could ostensibly lead to a dangerous change in official Schmidt-Genscher policy, the Union indicated how much it had itself moved—often reluctantly, even unconsciously—toward accepting the status quo. A period of crisis putting additional strain on Bonn's detente policy and exacerbating divisions within the coalition would confirm the CDU/CSU's gradual, reluctant conversion to Ostpolitik.

7

Crisis and Consensus, 1980–1982

As the 1980s began, it was increasingly evident that domestic debate over Ostpolitik had begun to change. The slowing pace of improvement in relations with the East exposed as many divisions over substantive issues within the SPD-FDP coalition as between the coalition and the opposition. As the SPD left grew disenchanted with Schmidt-Genscher pragmatism, the Union became tacitly reconciled to it. At the outset of the new decade a series of crises—in relations with East Berlin, Moscow, and Washington—would underscore and reinforce both shifts in attitude.

Afghanistan and Ostpolitik

In the winter of 1979–80, the Soviet Union intervened in Afghanistan, prompting a sharp reaction from Washington. Already beset by the hostage taking in Iran, a frustrated Jimmy Carter expanded America's military presence in Southwest Asia, shelved the unratified SALT II treaty, appealed for Western sanctions against the Kremlin, and urged a boycott of the Olympic games in Moscow. The American goal was "to ostracize and condemn the Soviets and to reinforce regional confidence."[1]

Schmidt reacted more cautiously. As the sense of international crisis mounted, he increasingly warned against a repetition of

August 1914; his fear was that belligerence, miscalculation, and overreaction would intensify the crisis and expand it to Europe. Bonn thus commenced a "crisis management" policy to protect detente in Europe, for which it found a partner in Paris: both Schmidt and French President Giscard d'Estaing urged calm and "calculability," cautioned against U.S. overreaction, and pledged their mutual belief in Europe's special responsibility to preserve East-West dialogue.

For its part, Bonn promised specifically to honor existing treaty commitments and continue negotiations. Initially Schmidt and Genscher hoped that various high-level meetings with Soviet-bloc leaders could go off as planned. Even when Moscow cited mounting East-West tension as a reason to postpone them, Bonn officials interpreted the "polite" manner of this announcement as reason for long-term optimism. Schmidt made plain his desire to carry through on planned summits with Brezhnev and Honecker despite the crisis. Routine, working-level talks continued, contributing, as one Bonn cabinet member said, "to the preservation of normal relations in Central Europe." Schmidt declared before the Bundestag that especially in hard times, the dialogue must be maintained and "that applies to a special degree" to Germany.[2]

Crisis management also included Schmidt's effort to restore a U.S.-Soviet dialogue. He urged a diplomatic solution to Afghanistan and proposed ways to keep the superpowers talking about arms control, such as a moratorium on intermediate-range nuclear force (INF) deployment. There was no room in Schmidt's crisis-management strategy for Western military activity in the Mideast or Southwest Asia (although Genscher did talk vaguely of Germany filling the gap if some U.S. forces left Central Europe for other regions). Bonn instead voiced a preference for stabilizing the region through economic aid and also increased its assistance to Turkey.

Most contentious was the push for sanctions against Moscow. Schmidt warned that trying to isolate or punish a superpower was dangerous, and in any case unlikely to alter its behavior. Moreover, he argued that restructuring trade and trade credits would hurt the West, especially the FRG, more than Moscow. He scornfully dismissed U.S. appeals for an Olympic games boycott: "The Russians will laugh."[3]

Schmidt's SPD colleagues endorsed crisis management, but were even more alarmed than the chancellor about perceived U.S. overreaction. Especially after Carter shelved the unratified SALT II treaty, they feared that what seemed to them a peripheral crisis would be used to block arms control and undermine detente—with Europe (and Germany) suffering the most. Many SPD leftists condemned Washington, urged Bonn's withdrawal from the INF plan and pressed Schmidt to lead Europe in rebuking both superpowers. Brandt and Bahr encouraged Bonn more cautiously to join Paris in stressing European interests (Giscard had already broken ranks by flying off to meet Brezhnev in Warsaw), thus distancing Europe from the United States and rescuing detente. They unequivocally opposed sanctions and Washington's proposed Olympic boycott.

But in public and in private Carter was urging Schmidt to withstand pressure and back the United States.[4] Genscher, among others, grew increasingly alarmed by the threat of a trans-Atlantic crisis. Ultimately Bonn's crisis management was modified somewhat in the name of alliance solidarity. Though insisting on its intention to continue dialogue with Moscow, Schmidt's cabinet —after giving the Kremlin a deadline—recommended that West Germany's Olympic committee boycott the Moscow games. Despite Bahr's open encouragement to attend, the athletic group did narrowly vote to stay home. Moreover, although it promised to continue ongoing commerce, Bonn agreed not to undercut U.S. economic sanctions by increasing exports to Moscow in those areas, mainly agricultural and high technology goods, where the United States restricted trade. It also agreed to discuss tighter Western restrictions on "strategic goods" going East, goods on the so-called CoCom list, provided that existing contracts would not be broken.

Polls from January to July showed broad public support for Schmidt's approach, and most of those who criticized it did not prefer a stricter response. Though the public was increasingly suspicious of Soviet designs and pessimistic about the prospects for detente, 70 to 80 percent in several surveys wanted continuation of a detente policy, increased cooperation with Moscow, and a summit meeting between the German leaders. And though the public approved of closer trans-Atlantic ties and greater NATO spending, there was ambivalence and division on economic sanctions and an Olympic boycott.[5]

The Union Response

Union leaders characterized Moscow's intervention as consistent with a long-term, opportunistic, imperialistic strategy for fulfilling historical ambitions and advancing world revolution. Strauss, Kohl, and others said that Soviet boldness had unnerved countries already made vulnerable by centrifugal tendencies, including Turkey and Yugoslavia. More important, Strauss insisted, NATO's "unguarded rear door" was threatened: the Red Army could now seize Persian Gulf oil, severing the West's vital energy lifeline and satisfying its own demand. Many fundamentalists blamed this crisis on a decade of detente, which they said had undercut efforts to preserve global military balance. Some also blamed Bonn's own Eastern agreements as "reinsurance treaties" and appeasement that cleared the way for Soviet expansion outside of Europe.[6]

More important, Union leaders argued that Bonn's crisis-management policy also rested on the false premises of the detente era. Europe, they insisted, could not be an island of serenity and stability when Western security interests were threatened. Detente could never be divisible, and the attempt to make it so endangered Western Europe. Party leaders echoed Kohl's sentiments when he declared that it would be "mistaken, dangerous, even fatal" to act as if Europe were a political niche sheltered from the new storm. German-German dialogue could not continue as if nothing had happened, lest Moscow's "closest vassal"—the GDR—be used as bait to lure Bonn away from its allies.[7]

Above all the Union attacked the coalition for appearing to distance itself from Washington and acting as an "interpreter" to facilitate dialogue between the superpowers. Union spokesmen also urged Schmidt against trying to reactivate the U.S.-Soviet arms-control dialogue through his proposed bilateral INF moratorium and his planned trip to Moscow, which they said would help the Kremlin end its isolation. They faulted Bonn for its resistance to increasing German (and overall European) defense efforts, its hesitance about supporting U.S. military countermeasures in Asia, and its sluggish response to the American call for sanctions.

Union leaders argued that the coalition's attempt to make detente divisible would jeopardize German security. As an "interpreter," even with French assistance, Bonn would fall between stools by distancing itself from Washington. "Our special role is alongside the U.S.," Kohl declared, adding that Germany depended especially heavily on U.S. protection.[8] Above all they faulted Schmidt for scornfully criticizing Carter and for failing to chastise or disavow the SPD left, which they called the "Moscow faction." Bahr's open resistance to U.S. policy, talk of a Bonn-Moscow special relationship, and the left's anti-American tone were—in Union eyes—certain to alienate Washington, conjure up images of Rapallo (the interwar German-Soviet treaty aimed against the West), and spark an isolationist backlash in the United States.

Despite this sharp criticism, Union leaders, including Strauss, showed considerable caution about giving the impression that they would put Bonn's Eastern dialogue at risk. This show of moderation reflected evolving party attitudes, but it also indicated Union desires to neutralize Ostpolitik as a campaign issue. Strauss in particular, who had so often polarized the electorate to win right-wing voters, now—as chancellor candidate—saw good reason to assert his credentials as a statesman.

From the outset, then, Union leaders appealed for a bipartisan West German response. Reformists like von Weizsäcker (recently selected CDU party chief in West Berlin) urged all-party cooperation to ensure that the divided city was not affected by the crisis. He urged West Berlin's SPD mayor to visit Washington and praised him for doing so. Mertes published an open letter to Schmidt, appealing for a sober, bipartisan security policy. Mertes also warned his own party against "rhetorical shows of strength." More significant, though attacking the SPD left, Strauss also urged bipartisan cooperation: "I want no quarrels," he declared, "the situation is far too serious for that." Even in his Ash Wednesday address in "deepest Bavaria," normally an occasion for fiery rhetoric, Strauss appealed for calm.[9]

Government and opposition leaders sat down to discuss FRG policy, the first such gesture since the domestic terrorist wave of the mid-1970s. There was vague, public talk by Schmidt, Genscher, and Strauss of German steps to replace any gaps created by a U.S. decision to shift forces out of the region. Union Bundestag support proved vital for passage of additional German aid to Turkey, which forty SPD delegates opposed. Mertes reiterated Union support for Bonn's official arms-control policy.

Government and opposition also seemed united in the desire to restore detente. All its criticism of Schmidt's crisis management notwithstanding, the Union left the door for East-West dialogue open. Kohl and Albrecht declared that Afghanistan had *not* destroyed the need for detente, merely the illusion that European detente could be totally separated from the reality of global power politics. Mertes reminded his own party that voters would not be interested in what the Union might like to do in this crisis, but what—given the treaties and the balance of power—it *could* do.[10]

Observers were struck by the fact that chancellor candidate Strauss echoed Mertes's claim, stressing that "only a fool with criminal instincts could want to conduct something other than a policy of detente." Continued East-West cooperation, he added, was vital to preserve human contacts, Berlin's security, and overall political calm. What Bonn needed was a "realistic detente"; rather than detente as dogma or an end in itself, there must be a policy that took into account the fact that military factors and events outside of Europe had increased rather than decreased in importance since 1969.[11]

Union leaders insisted that Bonn must reconcile its approach to security and detente in a new overall policy, a "Gesamtpolitik." East-West cooperation need not be abandoned, but must be pursued within the framework of a more realistic concept of global security. Acting together, the party argued, the Western states had to offset Moscow's arms buildup and contain its expansion in the third world. This presupposed European solidarity behind strong global U.S. leadership, and Union leaders expressed relief that Afghanistan had shocked America out of its malaise—what Strauss called its long, post-Vietnam "passion play."[12]

Moreover, the Union insisted upon general support for U.S. efforts to show Moscow that it could not expect business as usual after Afghanistan. This meant backing U.S. appeals for economic sanctions and a boycott of the Olympics; trade and sport must be subordinated to national interests. Such measures might not force Soviet withdrawal, the party conceded, but would demonstrate Western solidarity and persuade Moscow that its actions were not cost free. Bonn should avoid the appearance of being forced into a boycott by U.S. pressure.

Finally, a Gesamtpolitik as outlined by the Union had to forswear unnecessary unilateral diplomacy: Kremlin leaders must be convinced that they could not exploit European desires for detente as a way to divide and weaken the West. Since this would in turn reduce Moscow's scope for blackmail, the party argued, such a Gesamtpolitik would make realistic East-West bargains more, not less, likely.

Articulating the Gesamtpolitik

Plainly this Gesamtpolitik indicated a Union desire to reconcile its pro–U.S. stance and its harsh criticism of the SPD with a display of moderation and commitment to dialogue. Yet party leaders found it difficult to strike the right balance. Some advocated confrontation with the coalition on this issue, others supported bipartisanship, and most opted for one or the other tactic at different times. Adding to the picture of frustrated confusion was a surprising role change, for it was Strauss who consistently went the furthest in attacking the SPD and in appealing for bipartisanship and the need to preserve detente.

When it came to specifics, CDU/CSU leaders were equally unclear, ambivalent, or divided on precisely what their Gesamtpolitik meant. They urged Bonn to meet NATO's target of a 3 percent increase in defense spending but gave no specifics on whence the funds should come. More controversial was their intimation that NATO's security belt should be extended beyond the Tropic of Cancer.[13] Dregger even argued that constitutional limits on FRG use of force beyond German borders did not preclude helping to boost the West's naval presence in the Indian Ocean. "German ships are free to sail anywhere," he observed. But party leaders like von Weizsäcker criticized such talk, and after a brief controversy, Strauss, Wörner, Dregger, and Kohl disavowed any idea of expanding either NATO's formal scope or FRG military activities and merely stessed that the alliance must be seen in a global context.[14]

Moreover, although Union leaders stressed that Bonn could not be an island of detente, they were clearly ambivalent on what this meant for ongoing negotiations. Von Weizsäcker echoed Schmidt's appeal to prevent the crisis from spreading to Europe. Kohl implicitly agreed, as did Strauss, who observed that Bonn must remain "credible and trustworthy" toward its Eastern negotiating partners, as well as its Western friends.¹⁵ To demonstrate interest in smooth relations, CDU officials from Lower Saxony visited the East German trade fair in Leipzig in March (although they did not meet GDR leaders).

Mertes tried to put the best possible face on CDU/CSU ambivalence by arguing for a low-key dialogue. "Especially in crises," he said, contacts and talks were vital, but they could be conducted strictly at a low, technical level. To underscore the point, he canceled his own planned visit to Moscow. But although Mertes's party colleagues urged Schmidt to postpone planned summit meetings with Honecker and Brezhnev, none pressed the chancellor to break those engagements altogether. Von Weizsäcker even encouraged the chancellor to meet Honecker sometime in early 1980.¹⁶

In the middle of the crisis, moreover, Strauss affirmed that as chancellor he would be interested in new accords with the Soviet bloc. The CSU chief also made no secret of his desire to visit Moscow during the year. He described party chief Brezhnev as a "statesman of significance" whom he would willingly meet to discuss the world situation. "I make no moral judgments," the Bavarian said, adding that in occupying Afghanistan Brezhnev had acted properly within the Soviet code of conduct and according to Soviet interests.¹⁷

Strauss did visit Bucharest for well-publicized talks with Romania's boss Ceauşescu. It was the highest-level meeting between a West German official (Bavaria's minister-president) and a Soviet-bloc leader during the early part of 1980. Upon his return, Strauss attributed the freeze in contacts between East and West to Moscow, implying that the Western side still had an active interest in unbroken contact.

During the winter and spring CDU/CSU leaders remained particularly cautious about disturbing Bonn–East Berlin relations. Von Weizsäcker characteristically urged that East Germans should not be made to pay the price for Moscow's use of force. Strauss told a foreign journalist he wanted better ties not to delude himself "but for the sake of humanity and of our common fatherland."¹⁸ And although Union leaders criticized the "lack of real reciprocity" in a new Bonn–East Berlin agreement on traffic, they did not urge delaying it to prevent the appearance of "business as usual."

As the date of Schmidt's summer Moscow meeting approached,

the Union grew more ambivalent. Mertes called the summit a bad idea; Soviet pressure upon Schmidt to modify Western arms-control positions and even the meeting itself could damage Western unity. "We must talk in crises, . . . without any doubt," Mertes hastened to add, but "discreet low-level talks" were better than "spectacular summits." Marx and Dregger also criticized a summit "in the overall context" of Bonn's present policy but supported it on the condition that Schmidt explicitly reaffirm Germany's support of U.S. and NATO policy while in Moscow. Even Dregger reiterated the need for dialogue in crises. Strauss declared that "in principle" such a summit could be useful.[19]

By early summer, however, Bonn-Washington tension over Schmidt's summit had arisen. Jimmy Carter had already made known his reservations about "Helmut's" travel plans; he sent off a note expressing concern that Schmidt's statements urging both sides to "desist from any further [missile] deployments" might be taken as an appeal for a moratorium that Moscow would use to divide the allies. Publication of this warning note led to "an unbelievable meeting" in which Carter described Schmidt as "ranting and raving."[20] Union leaders warned Schmidt against sparking a crisis in relations with Washington, yet did not openly oppose the Moscow summit.

Similarly, although the Union urged solidarity with Washington, it showed no desire to be out front on the question of Western measures against Moscow. Strauss and Kohl alike declared that they would offer concrete proposals once in positions of responsibility, but said it was not the opposition's duty to advance concrete, "unpopular measures."[21] This vagueness persisted throughout 1980.

With the public initially two-to-one against an Olympic boycott, the Union equivocated on this issue too. Only after several weeks' delay did the CDU leadership formally endorse a boycott, and the chancellor candidate hesitated until late February, when public support had increased. Then they backed a boycott fully and attacked the SPD for resisting it.

On economic sanctions, Union ambivalence was marked and more persistent. In general terms, the party urged Schmidt not to leave Washington stranded in the effort to send Moscow a message. In practice, the party urged that German firms not be permitted to undercut U.S. restrictions on wheat and high-technology shipments. It also supported expanding the West's CoCom list of restricted strategic goods. But these steps were already being taken by Schmidt's government. Though criticizing Bonn for not making clear whether it would go further unilaterally and also persuade the European Community (EC) to apply sanctions, the Union offered few specific alternatives.[22] In trade policy too it appealed for greater intra-Western consultation and coordination, but again did not advance concrete proposals. Moreover the party openly opposed a total trade embargo and indeed even echoed Schmidt's hope for future improvements in Eastern trade.

Strauss in particular made little secret of his ambivalence about sanctions. Though condemning Bonn for not fully supporting U.S. measures, he attached numerous conditions to his own advocacy of further economic punishment measures—and this while on a visit to Washington. Moscow's East European allies should not be automatically boycotted, he said; only future and not current German-Soviet contracts should be affected; and no allies, including the United States, should gain a unilateral advantage from German trade restraint. Given the well-known unwillingness of France to apply sanctions, Strauss was implying that Washington must force Paris into line—a nearly impossible task—before achieving Bonn's agreement. He was thus effectively ruling out sanctions.[23]

Indeed, though criticizing the "Bonn-Paris front" against Washington, once even in Giscard's presence, Strauss implied sympathy for the reluctance of European leaders to support U.S. sanctions. Such measures, he agreed, were rarely effective. Moreover, he acknowledged, Bonn and Paris feared that if they boycotted Moscow, they would be laughingstocks if the United States then reversed course—as it had in the neutron-weapons episode. Moreover, he said, being geographically closer to the crisis region, European leaders were naturally reluctant to escalate a crisis. Indeed, by recalling past U.S. failure to consult its allies, Strauss was effectively justifying German and French reserve toward Carter's current punishment measures. More explicitly still, he echoed Schmidt's argument that it was pointless to try threatening a superpower. Though Strauss claimed to be merely paraphrasing Schmidt, Genscher, and Giscard's views, he clearly seemed comfortable making these arguments. His own distrust of the "erratic" Carter rivaled that of Schmidt.[24]

Strauss justified his clear reluctance to back U.S. measures by providing a more precise definition of a credible Gesamtpolitik. He argued that Bonn must manifest "seamless solidarity" with Washington, but this did not necessarily mean endorsing individual policy actions. It was vital to demonstrate that Bonn shared Washington's view of the global situation after Afghanistan and was willing to reorient Western strategy toward Moscow accordingly. Within that broad context specific measures could be examined individually for their usefulness and advisability: some he felt might not merit support, others would. But the essential point lay in a common threat perception and agreement on the need for a joint, global strategy to resist Moscow. This the Union, not the leftward-drifting SPD, could assure.[25]

For their part, CDU leaders pledged to reverse SPD priorities by making defense the centerpiece and detente the supporting leg of a West German foreign policy. As traditional Atlanticists they were less openly critical of U.S. policy. But they too tried to avoid any charge that the Union would jeopardize Ostpolitik and thus remained circumspect on the sanctions issue.

In short, Strauss and other Union leaders hoped to show that their Gesamtpolitik could maintain Western cohesion in the face of Soviet challenges and simultaneously leave room, indeed create room, for "realistic detente" by ensuring that cooperation with the East did not isolate the FRG from its major ally.

> Ostpolitik, the Polish Crisis, and the
> Federal Election

Events later in the year, during the campaign's final stages, further confirmed the Union's preoccupation with neutralizing the Ostpolitik issue through its Gesamtpolitik. Party leaders did warn that if the planned Schmidt-Honecker summit focused on global issues and arms control it would be misused to split Bonn from Washington. They stressed that the meeting must indeed deal with new humanitarian gains and serve the goal of German unity. Despite these qualms, conditions, and additional warnings that Schmidt should not try to gain politically from an election-year summit, the Union stopped far short of opposing the meeting. There was even discussion of a Union politician, namely von Weizsäcker, accompanying Schmidt.

In late August, however, the summit was postponed, clearly because of labor unrest in Poland. Union leaders criticized Schmidt both for his cautious refusal to concede that Poland was the reason for cancellation and for his party's tepid support of the Solidarity trade union. For Kohl, it clearly reflected the "dilemma of detente" that Schmidt could not visit East Berlin because Polish workers were striking; this showed that SPD-FDP Ostpolitik had become more concerned with communist leaders' sensitivities than with the plight of communist subjects. Union leaders urged Bonn to warn Moscow against intervening to crush Solidarity. They also spoke of "suspending" newly extended credits to Poland until it was clear that ordinary workers would benefit from them.[26]

Otherwise, however, the Union remained cautious, so much so that observers spoke of a basic consensus in Bonn about not intensifying the crisis. Strauss and Kohl avoided proposing concrete alternatives for the German response. Strauss warned against repeating the pattern of 1956 and 1968, when the West had given Soviet-bloc dissidents false encouragement. Moreover, the party became ever-more vague in talking about trade credits as a tool for helping Solidarity. In a preelection article Strauss declared that "every reasonable, democratic, peace-loving politician" must work for detente, though it must be clear that East-West relations remained adversarial.[27]

As in the Afghan crisis, this Union approach did not seem to be out of step with public opinion. Polls showed that Germans were concerned about events in Poland but anxious to shield detente from their effects. The public—even a relative majority of Union voters—opposed sanctions as a form of leverage on Solidarity's behalf. Yet despite Union calls for realistic detente, a broad majority (including one of three CDU/CSU identifiers) still believed the SPD was far better able to improve ties with the East.[28]

In this sense, then, though Union assurances of its commitment to dialogue revealed an ongoing evolution of party attitudes toward Ostpolitik, the political rewards never materialized. Partly because many CDU/CSU leaders—including Strauss—balanced their moments of moderation with more familiar, harsh attacks on the SPD and even Schmidt, many voters did not trust this conversion. If anything, Union moderation merely confused CDU/CSU supporters. A series of spring state-level elections showed dropping support for the Union.

Blowing hot and cold plainly also proved inadequate to mobilize voters against a popular chancellor. In fact Strauss's attacks on the SPD—on domestic as well as foreign issues—only benefitted Genscher, who could argue that a vote for the FDP counted as a vote against extremes on the right and left. All of this came on top of deeply rooted anti-Strauss feelings within the CDU and among voters outside Bavaria, and Strauss continued to fall behind in the polls. By midsummer CDU party officials were said to be taking bets on their candidate's margin of defeat and simply hoping that the Union would retain its position as the largest party. Many saw a silver lining: they hoped that if the Bavarian were humiliated it would deflate the CSU and allow the CDU to dominate the opposition.

In October, as expected, Strauss led the Union to its worst performance at the federal level since the early 1950s.[29] With 44.5 percent it remained the largest party, but Schmidt's SPD held steady at 43 percent and the FDP shot up to 10.6, giving the coalition an easy majority.

Gera and the Emerging Ostpolitik Consensus

Shortly after the election Bonn's Ostpolitik faced yet another crisis, and the Union thus faced another test. In mid-October East Berlin again displayed its grasp of one capitalist principle, the price inelasticity of demand in a monopolized market, by doubling its mandatory minimum currency exchange for Westerners crossing into the East. The move was clearly designed to limit human traffic. In a speech in the city of Gera, Erich Honecker linked the fee increase to long-standing SED demands for "normalization": the rate could be reduced if Bonn elevated the permanent representative mission to embassy status, recognized GDR citizenship, accepted the middle of the Elbe as a border, and closed the West German bureau in Salzgitter, which monitored shootings on the border. Despite these "Gera demands," speculation as to Honecker's motives also centered on Soviet-bloc nervousness about Western contacts at a time when Solidarity's emergence threatened communist rule in Poland. It was also assumed that communist leaders wanted to show Bonn that it could not enjoy the fruits of detente while supporting U.S. policy on Afghanistan.

Whatever the cause, it was plain that Central Europe's island of detente, which had survived the Afghanistan tempest, would be hit hard. Schmidt declared the rate rise a severe setback for detente and a violation of the letter and spirit of German-German pledges to facilitate human contacts and political cooperation. Yet though he promised to work "decisively" for a reversal of the decision, Bonn's lack of options was clear to government officials and press observers. Schmidt's cabinet announced a delay in the talks over extending the "swing" credit and expanding cooperation on energy and traffic; the Schmidt-Honecker summit was pushed further back. But reversing these steps was made contingent only upon SED willingness to discuss reducing the exchange requirement. Moreover, no harsher measures were taken in the economic realm. Government officials conceded that retaliation would only hurt ordinary citizens, adding "we should not answer delimitation with delimitation." No existing commitments would be reneged upon. Although Genscher protested the GDR action at the Conference on Security and Cooperation in Europe (CSCE) in Madrid, Bonn's political response remained mild.

Union fundamentalists initially seized upon Bonn's relative helplessness with cries of vindication. They pointed to the irony of SPD-FDP claims during the recent campaign that only Schmidt's coalition could preserve Ostpolitik. Strauss proclaimed the end of SPD-FDP detente, and others labeled the episode a "fiasco," a "scandal" and the receipt for years of unserious West German policy. Schmidt was urged to reject Honecker's Gera demands and rebuff those in his party inclined to accommodate East Berlin. Speaking for the parliamentary group, Olaf von Wrangel called upon the government to raise the issue at the CSCE session in Madrid, delay any summit with Honecker, postpone talks on the swing and reduce, suspend, or renegotiate payments not obliged by treaty.[30]

But aside from the last item, these proposed steps differed little from Bonn's official response. Moreover, although the CSU continued to speak of stiff, specific countermeasures, its CDU colleagues became increasingly cautious. Von Weizsäcker blamed the episode largely on Soviet pressure, argued that both Bonn and East Berlin retained an interest in dialogue—the former's motive being humanitarian, the latter's financial—and thus warned against counter-delimitation. In the Bundesrat, CDU reformist state-level leaders like Gerhard Stoltenberg and Bernhard Vogel explicitly warned against suspending any formally arranged payments to the GDR, however imprudent they may have been originally, or breaking any other current agreements. Like most Union politicians, these state leaders became increasingly vague when suggesting how, short of such steps, "economic leverage" could be used to reverse the hike in the exchange. Most party officials were content to insist vaguely upon the need for "more than verbal protests." Observers attributed this Union caution in part to substantive agreement between government and opposition on the situation's origins and Bonn's limited options. Others said the Union was merely trying to further refurbish its image.[31]

A Union Godesberg?

Both of these factors—substantive agreement with the government and concern about the Union image—prompted the party to renew its appeal for a new bipartisanship in Ostpolitik. Fundamentalists repeated the customary offer to help Schmidt against resistance from SPD leftists in developing a stronger policy. More significant, the CSU's Fritz Zimmermann echoed Mertes's standing appeal to "draw a line [Schlussstrich] under the ten-year long argument over Ostpolitik," saying that the party had no interest in "cheap self-righteousness." CDU state government chiefs Stoltenberg, Albrecht, Vogel, and Lothar Späth of Baden-Württemberg—all reformist oriented—urged bipartisan cooperation to manage the crisis, as did CDU General-Secretary Heiner Geissler. All Union politicians linked these appeals for bipartisanship with calls for both government and opposition "to take stock" of the past and present. Geissler indicated that if the coalition reevaluated its positions, the Union could follow suit. A sober balance was needed.[32]

There was, however, evident internal discord over whether this new bipartisanship and reevaluation should appear to entail an explicit change in Union policy. CDU state leaders declared that their party should be ready for greater dialogue with the East. Späth openly conceded a past lack of Union effort in establishing contacts with the Soviet bloc; this had "aroused the suspicion among voters that the Union did not want to talk with communists and was thus against detente." Albrecht agreed and added that the party had too often allowed itself to be pushed into the nay sayer's corner. Geissler conceded that the party must recognize the successes of Ostpolitik, above all the gains of Helsinki. He and his predecessor Biedenkopf declared that even in light of recent events the Union must go beyond its old slogan of "*pacta sunt servanda.*" The reformist-oriented Rhineland CDU also urged fundamentalists to honor the party's pledge against waging old battles and restating maximal positions.[33]

Such talk aroused immediate press speculation about a major, formal reorientation of CDU/CSU policy, a Union Godesberg. But the CDU reformists had created a misimpression. Their fundamentalist colleagues in the parliamentary group denied that the Union was ready for a Godesberg, "let alone a Canossa." Zimmermann hastily stressed that in calling for an end to the debate and a new cooperative spirit he did not mean to imply a need for reevaluating past Union policy. It was, he said, the SPD that, after ten years of illusion, must reverse course. Recent events showed that the CDU/CSU had been right all along and had no need to change course. Strauss agreed: "Policy can not be put on and off like a shirt." After having "resisted the *Zeitgeist* for a decade," there was "less reason than ever" for the Union to adopt the collapsing SPD-FDP policy.[34]

Mertes, though praising bipartisan cooperation as a national duty, tried to reconcile the party's two views. The Union could meet the SPD halfway, but there would be no adaptation "without contours" to an Ostpolitik that recent events had called into question. Mertes also downplayed suggestions that the Union had too few Eastern contacts, citing its participation in all Bundestag meetings with Soviet and Polish representatives and other multilateral or bilateral fora.[35]

It was Kohl who ultimately clarified the Union's position. He personally presented a statement on behalf of the CDU executive board in late October and followed it up with a major Bundestag speech. The former declaration reiterated appeals for bipartisanship based on the willingness of government and opposition alike to "take stock" but stressed that a new orientation would not mean abandoning basic Union principles or assuming "retroactive responsibility" for SPD-FDP policy. Past CDU/CSU positions may have been poorly understood by voters and thus not accepted, but there would be no change in course "a la Godesberg," said Kohl.[36]

Kohl's 26 November 1980 Bundestag address was as close as the Union would officially come to a "Wehner speech," even if it fell short of the latter's formal embrace of government policy. Kohl's tone was mild. He made the by-now near-obligatory offer to seek common ground between government and opposition. No conditions were attached. He appealed for Ostpolitik based on a broad consensus, consensus about the basic conviction that German unity must be preserved. FDP and even some SPD deputies applauded his statement that tension in Europe should not be compounded by German-German disputes and his expression of sympathy for families divided by the inner-German demarcation line.[37]

More significant, the Union parliamentary chief declared that Bonn must continue negotiating with Soviet-bloc states. A clear basis for business was needed, as well as a cautious policy that could neither be denounced as "intervention" nor misunderstood as "disinterest." He explicitly mentioned the Eastern accords as essential components of that policy: "They must be politically, intensively utilized in the interests of the nation and of peace." Such an Ostpolitik meant making Bonn's own basic positions clear in the context of a pragmatic diplomacy with adversaries.[38]

Some SPD spokesmen claimed to have received the CDU/CSU's "clear signals." Others despaired that Kohl's "few hopeful comments" were drowned out by the old CDU/CSU clichés. They insisted that the CDU/CSU still needed a Godesberg, a reevaluation of its past positions.[39]

Kohl's "new orientation" was modest, cautious, and vague. Its tone was milder than its substance was significant. Like most party leaders and not merely the fundamentalist ones, Kohl's genuine ambivalence about dealing with the Soviet bloc ran too deep for a Godesberg-style about-face. Kohl also feared that party unity could not withstand the pressures of developing a Godesberg program. Openly calling past CDU/CSU positions into question, let alone embracing the premises of SPD-FDP policy, could shatter party unity.

Even though the Strauss election debacle seemed to leave Union fundamentalists discredited and vulnerable, Kohl was conscious of their persistent strength and sensitive to how violently they would oppose a CDU/CSU about-face.

Kohl was certainly aware that many CDU reformists—whose cause he had hitherto championed—felt his own approach, one unduly sensitive to the fundamentalists, would not win over new voters or the FDP. The CDU chief simply considered the preservation of an equilibrium within the Union as a necessary precondition for winning converts. He sensed that a unified CDU/CSU offering a consistent policy was more credible to voters and the FDP than a divided Union sending conflicting signals.

Kohl and Continuity

After 1980, then, Kohl and his CDU associates cautiously but clearly underscored the Union's readiness to take over Ostpolitik without renouncing fundamental Union positions, a characteristic effort to blend at least partly contradictory things. But they sensed that only this approach could be sustained by a majority in the Union.

After Kohl's 1980 Bundestag speech explicitly upholding the Eastern treaties, those accords were mentioned increasingly in party documents, as in its 1981 declaration on peace policy. The gains of Bonn's policy toward the GDR and Poland were more frequently admitted, and the treaties themselves were praised as "constructive initiatives."

Before a CDU conference in early 1981, Kohl declared that a Union-led government would do "everything humanly possible" to ease the conditions of life for East Germans. He said that the Union must be ready to pursue a "regulated coexistence with the GDR." Mertes and others underscored the Union's willingness to use the treaties—"essential components of policy"—intensively in the political effort to help the German nation and preserve peace.[40] Strauss, the CSU, and fundamentalists were far more ambivalent about this pledge of continuity. But they were on the defensive after the 1980 election and less bold in challenging Kohl's strategy, which, after all, still seemed comparatively cautious.

There were also efforts to cooperate with Schmidt's government. Press observers saw "more wrestling than fighting" in Bundestag debates over Deutschlandpolitik, with agreement on policy goals, if not always on ways to achieve them. In closed committee sessions bipartisanship was stronger still. In the words of one staffer, many Union politicians were undergoing a learning experience, and the FDP was increasingly mediating between the CDU/CSU and SPD.[41]

There was a correspondingly greater willingness on the CDU's part to be seen encouraging dialogue with the East on practical problems—despite the international climate and GDR delimitation. Genscher's effort to continue improving relations with Poland won limited praise. Union leaders also said that if conducted properly, Bonn-Moscow dialogue could continue, despite Afghanistan and the fierce missile debate. Thus in principle, despite some reservations, they did not reject plans for a European-Soviet natural-gas pipeline out of hand. Though warning about the danger of energy dependency on Moscow, Union spokesmen were also careful to stress that "contracts are contracts"; a new government would honor this inherited commitment even if (one source said) Soviet troops entered Poland.[42]

Moreover, party leaders approved a visit to Bonn by Leonid Brezhnev late in 1981. They agreed that a summit could help "clarify" where the two countries stood on vital issues. To be sure, the Union warned against allowing Brezhnev to sow dissension in NATO on arms issues and denounced the chancellor's claim to be an "interpreter" for the superpowers. Nonetheless, Strauss labeled Brezhnev a "great statesman" who himself wanted peace, although he necessarily served the Soviet system. Kohl expressed even more emphatic support for the summit and bipartisan Ostpolitik. Strauss's meeting with the Soviet strongman was described by one aide as much like a get-together between old friends; as in 1978 Brezhnev was so engrossed in their *tour d'horizon* that he waved off the Soviet protocol officer who was notifying him of the next guest's arrival.[43]

Union leaders in 1981 also warned Schmidt against his "unseemly overeagerness" in "chasing after" Honecker to arrange a summit and criticized him for hinting that Bonn might link an extension of the swing credit to a reduction of the exchange requirement. Even reformists held that the latter must be reduced unconditionally. They insisted that East Berlin ultimately return to the status quo ante and discuss fundamental issues at any upcoming summit if it expected to receive the benefits of cooperation.

But this Union notion of linkage did not make such negotiations *contingent* upon a prior decrease in the mandatory minimum exchange requirement. While the party did insist that there could be no "expansion of relations and certainly no agreements" until the status quo ante was restored it did not exclude negotiations. Indeed, the Union eventually endorsed the summit, provided that it aimed for concrete results and not merely a show. Reformists even hinted that with regard to the Gera demands "some wishes of the GDR can be fulfilled in reasonable ways."[44]

That the party was willing to practice and not merely pledge continuity became most evident on the state level, where CDU-led governments dealt with the practical details of dialogue. In Lower Saxony, for example, Albrecht's government became increasingly preoccupied with an accord to stop GDR pollution of the Elbe and met with members of the SED central committee at the annual Leipzig trade fair in 1981 to discuss improved relations.

More important still was the May 1981 election of Richard von Weizsäcker as mayor of West Berlin—made possible by a tacit coalition with the local FDP. Given its many special practical problems and arrangements with the GDR, West Berlin was central to Bonn's Deutschlandpolitik. This fact and the divided city's unique, partial autonomy from Bonn made it unavoidable for the federal government to consult closely and formally with the new mayor. A von Weizsäcker appointee began meeting regularly in the Chancellory with a high-level, five-member working group. He was privy to discussions of sensitive material that escaped the purview even of many prominent federal government officials. As one observer put it, henceforth there would effectively be a "Grand Coalition" in the formulation of Bonn's policy toward East Berlin.[45] There were few disputes within the Union about this codetermination of federal policy. Despite initial SPD concerns, CDU/CSU leaders did not exploit their new role to sabotage or hinder German-German relations.

As mayor, von Weizsäcker also effectively began conducting an independent policy of his own toward East Berlin. Numerous practical issues involving the divided city lay within his jurisdiction, such as transit, energy provision, and pollution controls. And as one critic pointed out, "Many questions appear a bit different, very much more concrete, to the Union now that it has acceded to a key role in Berlin.... For the present opposition in the German Bundestag, pure theory has become solid practice. Thus the Union, just like the government, must consider whether one can not arrive at practical regulation of these questions."[46]

The nature of von Weizsäcker's policy further accustomed the Union to the practice of setting aside fundamental issues to make progress on practical ones, a trade-off he had long urged on the party. Even critics credited him with understanding the "dialectic of Deutschlandpolitik," including the necessity of paying for concessions. He now appealed to our "vital interest in a detente that doesn't mean a static freeze, but rather a peaceful improvement." He warned against merely relying on "defensive and delimiting ideological dogma at the expense of further development of concrete themes." Berlin, he added, was the "chosen lobby" for ensuring that "the division . . . is overcome and made more tolerable, so long as it lasts."[47]

The Union and Intracoalition Differences on Detente

As in the late 1970s the Union's cautious signs of adaptation appeared against the backdrop of ever-growing differences over Deutschlandpolitik within the SPD-FDP, differences exacerbated by stalemate in German-German relations and Honecker's Gera demands. Schmidt, his circle of advisors, and Genscher's FDP preferred coolness and caution in dealing with East Berlin. But Brandt, Wehner, Bahr, and the SPD left urged greater sensitivity to East German interests as the way to facilitate dialogue; they were implicitly ready to treat the Gera demands as negotiable. Their pressure on the government to reactivate dialogue and even meet Honecker without preconditions mounted in 1981. The Union argued that in the current international climate and given the Gera demands Bonn could effect progress only by accepting the GDR demands, which would infringe upon the constitution and run counter to established policy. In this sense, the opposition supported the government against prominent Social Democrats (and a few maverick Free Democrats) who pressed Bonn to accommodate GDR demands for recognition of a separate East German citizenship in particular.

Nothing better illustrated this trend than the debate that erupted over comments made by Günter Gaus. Shortly before his planned departure from the post of Bonn's representative in East Berlin, Gaus gave an interview to *Die Zeit*. He said that the FRG's constitution was framed at a time when there was a completely different expectation of when national unity could be achieved. Bonn could thus remain within the broad framework of the constitution but be flexible, perhaps even cease repeating the word "nation," which merely lent credence to SED claims that the "revanchist" FRG refused to accept the GDR's existence. He urged West Germans to modify their attitudes toward the GDR, to stop seeing it only as a police state, to concentrate more on the needs of East German citizens and less on the nature of their government, and to halt the high-profile debates about restoring state unity or even unity of the nation. To speak of cultural unity was better, he added, but it was best to abandon the nation concept altogether.[48]

Naturally the CDU/CSU zeroed in on what seemed to be a break with official policy and a breach within government ranks. It demanded to know for whom Gaus was speaking and urged Schmidt to stand by Bonn's formal rejection of the Gera conditions — which Gaus clearly considered negotiable. Arguing along traditional lines, the party also insisted upon the importance of upholding Bonn's right to pursue state unity, adding that otherwise at some future date communists would exploit the latent sense of nationalism to legitimize their rule in East Berlin. As if on cue, several weeks later Erich Honecker mentioned the prospect of reunification for the first time in years. At an SED conference, the GDR's chief of state spoke approvingly of reunification, provided West Germany became "socialist." Though Honecker's change of tone had many causes, the Union treated it as clear proof that SED leaders were "filling a vacuum" on the national issue.[49]

Schmidt subsequently did reaffirm his government's commitment to national unity in his April state-of-the-nation address. Although he did not use the word "reunification," press observers and the Union alike saw his tribute to the concept of the nation as a disavowal of Gaus's remarks. Moreover, though hinting at some flexibility on the issue, Schmidt pledged to stick by Bonn's traditional view of citizenship "as it is presented in the constitution."

Union leaders claimed credit for "reinforcing" established government policy.[50]

INF and the Domestic Debate over Detente

Beyond the narrow realm of German-German relations, there were intracoalition tensions over detente on another level—especially in the area of arms control—that the Union was able to exploit. A new administration in Washington was urging a firmer Western stance against Soviet third-world activities and Moscow's nuclear-arms buildup: Ronald Reagan aimed to revitalize containment, an endeavor for which he expected allied support. Schmidt's personal relationship with Reagan lacked the bitterness that had poisoned the trans-Atlantic atmosphere when Jimmy Carter was in office. Though wary of the new administration's rhetoric, Schmidt initially hoped that by improving relations with Washington he could persuade Reagan to adopt a detente and arms-control policy reminiscent of the approach taken by Richard Nixon. As Schmidt observed, "we must remain in the position to hold leverage over East and West."[51]

Schmidt's party colleagues, however, wanted Bonn to distance itself completely from what they considered Reagan's adventurism and pursue if necessary a largely unilateral detente policy. Bahr and Brandt deplored even formalistic support (especially by Genscher) for the "rigid U.S. position" on arms control and Washington's "rabid" rhetoric (*Spiegel's* wording). They held that Bonn's stance only confirmed Soviet suspicion that this U.S. administration had no interest in arms control as traditionally conceived, ruining the hopes for future talks. SPD leaders let it be known that they shared both the Soviet suspicions and its concern that "the Eastern treaties would become empty shells, [and] we would be thrown back to the status quo ante" before Ostpolitik.[52] Schmidt, Genscher, and government officials cautiously disavowed this criticism of the United States, further alienating the SPD from the government. The focus of this debate became the INF issue, which began to undermine the Social-Liberal partnership severely in 1981.

Plainly the Union was, in many respects, comfortable with the Reagan administration's policy. Politicians like Kiep and Biedenkopf had long-standing ties to the U.S. establishment, and Mertes,

Wörner, and to some extent Strauss enjoyed a special affiliation with officials who staffed this administration. The Union's semi-official Konrad Adenauer Foundation had facilitated broader contacts on a regular basis at the working level by setting up a Washington bureau in 1976, which became a virtual CDU embassy in the United States. Republican and Union politicians exchanged visits, as did academics and congressional staff assistants. In 1978 the foundation had hosted a visit by Ronald Reagan and arranged a series of meetings for him in Bonn.[53]

These contacts reinforced a broad philosophical compatibility. Union leaders welcomed "the new wind from Washington" and urged Schmidt to join the United States in a new, more sober, realistic emphasis on the restoration of an East-West equilibrium. Such a Gesamtpolitik, they argued, would compel Moscow to accept "binding norms of peaceful partnership" and thus also facilitate Bonn's Ostpolitik. Support for NATO's INF decision would be the first key step in such a policy.[54]

What stood in the way of such a Gesamtpolitik, the Union claimed, was Schmidt's inability to control his own party. CDU/CSU leaders decried the unconditional opposition of many SPD leaders to any new nuclear weapons deployment in the FRG and the delaying tactics of others. They pointed to the pressure the SPD put on Schmidt to press for greater U.S. accommodation of Soviet bargaining offers and condemned sharp SPD criticism of the U.S. position. The Union continually urged Schmidt to distance himself from SPD colleagues who, it said, constantly voiced anti-American sentiments and criticized NATO policy, as well as from the SPD parliamentarians and thousands of party members who attended anti-INF rallies.

Union leaders vocally attacked any signs of SPD willingness to contemplate a German-German arms-control dialogue. Honecker, they argued, would clearly exploit humanitarian issues, blackmailing Bonn into diluting its support for deployment of NATO INF. In Mertes's words, Moscow sought to effect "preventive good behavior" in West Germany.

Occasionally the Union claimed that Schmidt was giving in to SPD pressure to overemphasize detente. It criticized his effort to act as an interpreter between Washington and Moscow and thereby promote an INF compromise. When Schmidt failed to persuade

Ronald Reagan to modify his arms-control offer in mid-1981, Strauss declared, "Thank God . . . he came back empty handed."[55] The Union also condemned the chancellor for allowing the SPD to defer a final decision on INF until 1982.

Generally, however, the Union backed official policy but insisted that Schmidt and Genscher lacked support in the coalition. A top Kohl ally, Frankfurt's mayor, Walter Wallmann, remarked that the distinction between government and opposition was that the former provided "words without a majority," and the Union offered "unity and decisiveness."[56] When it required threats of resignation from Schmidt and Genscher to enforce coalition support for the INF policy, the Union claimed that the opposition now carried government policy. In a major Bundestag vote on the issue in June 1981 the CDU/CSU voted with the government (while a dozen SPD deputies did not) and submitted a resolution on the missile controversy, parts of which were subsequently integrated into the government's statement upon insistence of the FDP.

As nuclear anxiety grew in the FRG during 1981, Union leaders did hope for softening of U.S. policy. In their view, an increasingly nervous West German public had to be reassured that the arms buildup was not out of control lest there be a backlash against NATO and U.S. policy—and against the CDU/CSU itself, slowing the party's political revival. Poll data varied depending on how questions were phrased, but most showed opposition to new U.S. INF and animosity toward the new U.S. administration. A majority of the Union's supporters had reservations about INF and opposed enhanced radiation (neutron) weapons or ERW altogether.[57]

Consequently CDU/CSU politicians, including Strauss, cautioned the United States against official talk of capabilities to wage limited nuclear war in Europe. Wörner and other leading Atlanticists labeled "unfortunate" the U.S. decision to resume production of ERW in 1981, fearing the news would cause a sensory overload among Germans already nervous about INF. Though defending the neutron weapon in principle, Wörner, Marx, Mertes, and von Weizsäcker backed away from any unequivocal commitment to support its deployment in the FRG—a change from 1978. Fearful that public opinion might grow hostile to the United States, they stressed the importance of giving more than a "mere 'no'" to Soviet arms-control proposals.

Along with cautioning Washington to take the new German mood into account, Union leaders attempted to show their own sympathy for genuine nuclear anxiety. Most called antinuclear protesters sincere (if misguided), but condemned what they labeled the hardcore left. The party presented arguments for its own peace policy in a large literature drive, conferences, Bundestag resolutions, and mass public petitions to rival the peace movement's activities. It underscored CDU/CSU support for nuclear and chemical/biological arms control.

Yet in general the Union made plain its firm support for NATO arms policy. In fact it wanted to appear flexible and ready for dialogue precisely to persuade critics that INF was necessary and ethically justifiable. The Union leadership, especially the CSU, felt there need be no debate over or modification of party policy favoring deployment.

Testing the Union Consensus

One year after the Union's worst electoral setback in decades, Kohl's cautious, consensus-building approach to Ostpolitik could be classified a success. Avoiding gambles had meant avoiding mistakes; avoiding controversies had meant avoiding major disputes. Kohl even appeared to have tamed the CSU, and the unprecedented intra-Union harmony was evident at a March 1981 CDU conference that one observer called a "boring success" for Kohl. Another newspaper remarked that "probably only Konrad Adenauer ever stood as undisputed [atop the CDU/CSU] as Kohl."[58]

Most encouraging were the opinion polls. By mid-1981 one quarter of Schmidt's 1980 voters had drifted left to the new ecological Green party, or right—to the Union. Many Germans viewed the SPD's infighting negatively and classified the party as too left-wing and accommodating toward the Soviets. These polls showed increased public confidence in the Union on a range of issues, especially economic policy. But the party also earned praise for assisting the government in forming a bipartisan foreign policy. Polls in 1981 gave the Union a 50 percent approval rating, ranked Kohl higher than ever, and even briefly put him above Schmidt in popularity.[59]

Moreover, with events in Berlin as a precedent, speculation about an imminent Union-FDP coalition in Bonn grew. Union and FDP agreement on security and economic issues was already clear, and the Liberals increasingly distrusted the SPD left for its pressure on Schmidt's government policy and the resulting fall in the coalition's political fortunes. Genscher dropped hints that his party was not bound to the SPD and rewarded Union offers of bipartisanship in foreign policy with remarks defending the opposition from SPD left attacks. By mid-1981, most voters expected a Union-led government within months.[60]

As the *Frankfurter Allgemeine Zeitung* observed, "never has it been so pleasant for the Union to be in opposition."[61] Yet at this stage even many traditional Kohl associates began to worry about complacency, about relying on a "survey majority" created by dissatisfaction with the coalition—a mood that they feared could evaporate rapidly. Moreover, in their view, merely awaiting the coalition's collapse made the Union appear cynically opportunistic. Certain, long-term success, they felt, required making the CDU/CSU into an acceptable partner for the FDP and/or new voting groups, such as young people, who had voted disproportionately for Schmidt in 1980.

These CDU leaders—above all Secretary-General Geissler, his predecessor Biedenkopf, trade unionist Norbert Blüm, Minister-President Späth—almost all reformists with regard to Ostpolitik, urged the Union to encourage more open discussion of major issues and a systematic effort to develop alternative policies. Like Union youth group chairman Matthias Wissman, they urged that the sanctity of party unity not be permitted to create the impression that CDU/CSU policy ignored the concerns of new voters, including younger ones. They could cite the remarks of a British journalist, who called Union gatherings "theaters of conformity" with "well-drilled enthusiasm" and an awe for the leadership reminiscent of East European party gatherings.[62]

Most controversial was the effort spearheaded by Geissler to have Union nuclear arms and detente policy debated more openly. He and others indicated concern that the party not be seen to embrace NATO and Reagan administration policy without reflection and not be heard to discount the growing antinuclear anxiety among West Germans by simply castigating the burgeoning peace movement's naiveté and ties with the far left. To do so, they feared, might discredit the Union in the eyes of many potential voters. Moreover, they worried about the tenuous public support for NATO's nuclear deterrence strategy; Germans needed reassurance that their leaders were conscious of broad concerns about limiting the arms race and would help shape policy accordingly. To this end, these reformists urged a dialogue with antinuclear groups about arms and arms control.[63]

Amidst this debate, the question of a CDU/CSU Godesberg in Ostpolitik resurfaced. As Geissler declared to a Union youth group audience: "We need an opening to the East in our foreign policy. We have not only differences with the Soviets, but also common interests. . . . We must fill the treaties with life. . . . Verbally we have fulfilled our debit in that regard. Now we must act."[64] Biedenkopf agreed, calling for a multidimensional Ostpolitik that included negotiations over common interests; the party, he implied, too often stressed defense. Kiep traveled to Moscow in October, and Geissler used this occasion to press for a formal party commitment to regular consultation with the Kremlin. One U.S. observer sensed an "increasing vagueness" in CDU criticism of Moscow.[65]

These efforts aroused an increasingly tense intraparty debate, especially after an October 1981 antinuclear rally drew several thousand people to Bonn. Kohl, defense spokesman Wörner, and Mertes warned that although the party should discuss the nuclear issue, it must not feed false hopes of a nuclear-free world in the near future. CSU fundamentalists condemned the Union youth group's appeal for discussion and self-criticism as publicity seeking at the expense of party unity on basic questions of war and peace. They continued condemning the peace movement and urged an official investigation of the communist role in antinuclear rallies. As for Ostpolitik, Kohl and Strauss denied the existence of a CDU/CSU deficit in this policy area—the party had no need for an opening to the East.

As the Union approached its 1981 Hamburg conference, Kohl's future suddenly appeared in actual jeopardy to some, as the mounting debate revived doubts about his caliber as a chancellor candidate. Comparing the plights of Schmidt and Kohl, Britain's *Economist* asked, "Which Helmut will they dump first?" German journalists thought Kohl safe only until the next election, adding that his passive policy left the initiative to powerful rivals like finance expert Stoltenberg, who for his part stressed that the selection of the next chancellor candidate was still an open question.[66]

This apparent crisis over party politics and party policy on arms and Ostpolitik was defused at the CDU's November conference in Hamburg. Despite Kohl's preoccupation with unity and his uneasiness at the thought of controversy, he permitted Geissler to invite five hundred young nonmembers, mainly peace activists, for an open forum on nuclear arms and detente. Kohl even opened the conference by proclaiming "we belong to the German peace movement. We all want disarmament and detente." Observers were struck that this ad lib won him more enthusiastic applause, above all from Union youth activists and the guests, than did his caution against neutralism. In his greeting, von Weizsäcker stressed that Germany need not follow every twist and turn in American policy; the view from the United States and the view from Europe were, after all, bound to differ. He, Biedenkopf, and Geissler won enthusiastic applause.[67]

Attention focused primarily on the five hundred young guests, mainly from the peace movement's moderate wing, who approached the microphones and expressed their anxiety about nuclear weapons and irrational politicians with fingers on the button. Some questioned the value of military service, and others wondered openly if the FRG merited defending. Many voiced disappointment in CDU/CSU policy. Some remarks were greeted with applause from party members, primarily from CDU youth activists. Generally the guests were heard out before prominent party politicians responded by repeating or at most rephrasing traditional party policy. Because the guests were not radicals, there was little controversy, and party leaders appeared to be under little pressure.

Despite this orchestrated "dialogue," and even more so because of it, Hamburg was widely seen as a "Triumph and Trump for Kohl" (to quote Die Zeit). The conference had partly satisfied those who called for more openness and discussion of policy. Yet because it took place in a controlled manner and traditional party policy was not openly challenged, CDU (and CSU) fundamentalists were not alienated. Press reaction was generally favorable, and observers were struck by the Union's show of comparative unity.[68]

Hamburg also thus indicated again where the Union consensus lay. There was ever-growing acceptance of the need to demonstrate commitment to continuity in detente policy and Ostpolitik. Given the Hamburg dialogue, observers saw a "tardy, cautious course correction" in Union behavior. Yet Hamburg also showed that there was no majority in the CDU (let alone the overall Union) willing openly to modify traditional party policy or concede past errors. Continuity in the conduct of relations with the East would have to be combined with continuity in asserting traditional Union policy priorities.[69]

Toward the Change in Government

In December 1981 Schmidt traveled to a small East German town for the first FRG-GDR summit on German soil in a decade. Despite an ostentatious show of GDR security forces to prevent any public displays (as in Erfurt during Brandt's 1970 visit), Bonn officials praised the atmosphere as friendly and spoke of a "special relationship" between Honecker and Schmidt. A formal agreement provisionally extended the swing credit in exchange for hints of a reduction in the mandatory exchange and other possible future improvements. But the summit was overshadowed by the declaration of martial law in Poland. Despite the sudden air of crisis, Schmidt did not end his visit early. Instead he expressed regret that martial law had been "necessary" and refused to blame either East Berlin or Moscow for their roles in or support of the crackdown.[70]

The Union, Ostpolitik, and Polish Martial Law

Union leaders echoed and amplified criticisms of Schmidt that were mounting in the German press and abroad.[71] CSU spokesmen were most harsh, though even von Weizsäcker condemned Schmidt for his mild, ambiguous response to martial law. But only Strauss and some fundamentalists specifically condemned Schmidt for not having broken off his GDR visit. Indeed, von Weizsäcker and Späth said precisely the opposite: an abrupt departure from the GDR because of martial law would have destroyed new German-German initiatives and would not have been understood by East Germans. Most CDU leaders who had cautiously supported the summit beforehand focused their attention on the outcome of the meeting itself.

Some called the results meager, largely atmospheric, and based on vague hopes. Von Weizsäcker and his advisors spoke of a thaw and hopes for concrete results in the near future. But more important, all tried to avoid linking Polish martial law and the German-German dialogue; they were noncommittal on how one should affect the other.[72]

Similarly the Union blamed Moscow for the events in Poland and recalled Schmidt's own remarks from 1980 that detente could not survive another Afghanistan. Yet, though insisting that there must necessarily be consequences for East-West relations, the party urged that "existing channels" be used to talk with the Soviet bloc during the crisis.

At the same time, the Union appealed for bipartisanship during the new crisis. It worked out a seven-point resolution with the coalition that won endorsement from all parties when introduced in Parliament. Along with its criticisms of and appeals to Warsaw, the resolution noted that Solidarity had profited from the Helsinki Final Act. Possible sanctions against Warsaw were worked out in a compromise formula, as the CDU/CSU argued for certain measures and the SPD wanted none at all. The resolution thus somewhat vaguely called for the FRG and EC to "leave unresolved" questions of economic aid to Poland as long as the repression continued.

Given its desire—reinforced by SPD pressure—to contain the crisis, Schmidt's government, however, interpreted that formula narrowly. It refused to stop economic aid to Poland, or to consider restrictions on private commercial relations, and it rejected measures of any sort against Moscow as inappropriate. Bonn warned that such sanctions would "intensify" the crisis, and Schmidt cautioned against a "trade war."[73]

Schmidt thereby rebuffed both the Union and Washington, which on 29 December 1981 had enacted a series of sanctions against Warsaw and Moscow, including a ban on U.S. commercial involvement in the massive West European–Soviet gas-pipeline project. Many in the Reagan administration believed this step would "focus and dramatize" the West's reaction—and conveniently compel cancellation of a project that they feared would make Western Europe dependent on Soviet energy and thus subject to Soviet pressure.[74]

America's pressure and Bonn's response began to put a serious strain on bilateral relations. Although other countries, including

France, insisted upon preserving detente and resisted U.S. sanctions, Schmidt's sharp rebuff of U.S. policy focused American anger on Germany. Some U.S. senators began discussing large-scale troop withdrawals as a means of pressure.

Union leaders accused Schmidt of bowing to pressure from the SPD left. They demanded that he clarify Bonn's real position, distance himself from his party, unambiguously condemn martial law, support a joint Western response, and disavow any intimation that Bonn play a mediator's role, which would, they said, isolate the FRG in a no-man's-land. Even von Weizsäcker contended that Schmidt was allowing his party to create "massive doubts" about the FRG's "basic orientation." Other Europeans, including those who opposed U.S. sanctions and including many on the left, were uneasy about Bonn's stance and SPD talk of the German interest in a "stable Eastern Europe."[75]

On the sanction issue itself, CSU spokesmen urged support for U.S. measures and an end to official credits and guarantees so that communist leaders would be shown that they could not expect business as usual. Concerned about preserving the perception of bipartisanship, yet also under CSU pressure, Mertes tried in January to devise a new, joint Bundestag resolution. His version was less ambiguous than the earlier one. It called for suspending (rather than merely "leaving open the issue of") economic aid and credits to Poland and suspending Bonn's participation in the Soviet gas pipeline as long as repression continued. By contrast, the coalition's rival version promised to continue credits and aid "when the necessary conditions are present." This open difference on substance and a bitter parliamentary debate dashed hopes for a bipartisan position.[76]

Yet Mertes's resolution was less than a call for full support of U.S. "punishment" measures, a term he himself forswore. The Union, he said, was not putting General Jaruzelski's Polish regime on trial or punishing it, but seeking a "coordinated human-rights policy." CSU leaders responded by urging the CDU to be less ambiguous and criticized the "Genscherist" Mertes's efforts at a bipartisan policy on Poland; the SPD-FDP would only continue demanding vague resolutions that it could interpret as it chose. But it was clear that most CDU leaders remained warily skeptical of sanctions.

Von Weizsäcker expressed reservations, pointing out that such punishment measures often hurt the wrong people. And even the CSU, when it came to specifics, gave consistent, unambiguous support only to two measures: stopping the flow of high technology to the East, and stopping government guarantees for private bank credits to companies dealing with the Soviet Union. Strauss emphasized that trade with the Soviet bloc was still necessary.

A similar pattern seemed evident in June when the United States stepped up its effort to block the Soviet gas pipeline. Most West European states were dismayed that Washington both embargoed materials to be used in pipeline construction and took legal measures against American firms with European affiliates involved in the project. Genscher reacted critically, yet cautiously, and tried to avoid a trans-Atlantic split on the issue through discussions with Washington. Schmidt, however, lashed out at the U.S. move, and SPD party leaders condemned the Reagan administration even more sharply. Some Chancellory advisors, concerned with holding the party together, urged a final showdown with the United States over this issue. Some observers began labeling this episode the worst trans-Atlantic feud in three decades.[77]

Union leaders underscored their agreement with Genscher. Mertes expressed sympathy for the general aim of U.S. policy and rejected the SPD's harsh criticism. At the same time, however, Union spokesmen called for more effective trans-Atlantic prior consultation and clear alliance decisions and coordination—implicit criticism of the U.S. action, but cautiously voiced. Kohl referred to the embargo as one "cause" of bad trans-Atlantic relations, another of "many mutual misunderstandings," and evaded any commitment to back Washington. An effective policy, he said, required a "flexible response" strategy that would make clear in advance to Moscow and allied states what behavior would affect trade and how.[78]

There was clearly little sympathy in the Union for the embargo and U.S. arguments for it, and Union leaders were ready to show that they did not follow Washington unconditionally. In part this stance reflected traditional conservative suspicion of perceived discriminatory U.S. trade practices toward Europe, but it also showed CDU/CSU determination not to be blamed for jeopardizing relations with the East.

The New Pattern of Union Policy

During early 1982 an equally evident softening occurred in the Union position on German-German relations. Admittedly the party did refuse to adopt Schmidt's characterization of Bonn–East Berlin relations as "good-neighborly." It continued to declare the Gera demands nonnegotiable and urged Schmidt to rebuke certain Social Democrats who wanted those issues on the agenda. Party leaders also argued that Bonn had given too much and received too little in postsummit talks that increased the swing credit without explicitly ensuring a cut in the mandatory minimum exchange requirement. Henceforth, they declared, there must be packages linking all financial transfers, such as the swing, to better human contacts.

But it became ever-more clear that this linkage was not inflexible. The Union stressed merely that Bonn's financial leverage should "not be given up" entirely. Negotiations were less and less tied to explicit preconditions of any sort, though fundamentalists in speeches still occasionally insisted upon having the order to shoot lifted as a precondition for talks. Instead the Union more subtly argued that East Berlin could hardly expect improved commercial ties until it eased restrictions on human contacts—above all the minimum exchange.

Moreover the party began treating the GDR more mildly in other ways. When East Berlin denied visas to two prominent CDU politicians, Kohl merely criticized this as an unfriendly slap coming so quickly after the swing extension and hinted that if Honecker had any interest in smooth relations—and a visit to the FRG—he should not constantly rebuff Bonn's overtures. Peter Lorenz, an advisor to Weizsäcker, cautioned East Berlin against treating so brusquely a party that could soon be in power. The Union and SED, he added, were adversaries but shared a common responsibility for discussing substantive issues, "which requires a reasonable association." The Union expressed little unhappiness that Bonn declined to retaliate in any way. In his capacity as West Berlin's mayor, von Weizsäcker shortly thereafter traveled east for talks on an antipollution policy.[79]

Discreetly, if not secretly, the party in 1982 held an increasing number of talks with GDR officials to discuss how a new Union government would approach Bonn–East Berlin relations. Stoltenberg, Mertes, Kiep, and others met with the SED's spokesman on FRG affairs, Herbert Häber. The GDR publicly expressed its view that the Union was "unofficially" conducting negotiations to see how East Berlin would respond to a new FRG government. GDR press and radio reports indicated uncertainty as to whether these talks or public speeches by fundamentalists truly represented party policy. They posed the rhetorical question of whether a future CDU/CSU government would "continue the treaty policy" or risk all the positive changes made in German-German relations in a decade. East Berlin seemed increasingly resigned to, yet still uncertain about, the prospect of a new negotiating partner in Bonn.[80]

After the Polish crisis Union leaders carefully avoided any suggestion that concern with continuity in Ostpolitik was affecting their view of Bonn's role in the alliance. They still promised to pursue a Gesamtpolitik that gave security interests priority yet in so doing made an active detente possible. This by-now familiar formula underscored the Union's increasingly evident alignment with Genscher against the SPD left. For in the aftermath of the Polish crisis, several leading Social Democrats were implicitly or explicitly contending that Bonn should give arms control and detente precedence over NATO nuclear-deterrence policy. The Union rejected Bahr's East-West "security partnership concept" as tantamount to self-neutralization and argued that SPD schemes for renouncing first use of nuclear arms or creating a nuclear weapon–free zone would—by undermining NATO deterrence and isolating the FRG—have the same effect. SPD delays and compromise proposals on INF were condemned as certain to weaken Soviet incentive for serious negotiating. CDU/CSU spokesmen charged Schmidt with failing to resist or disavow his party's left, thereby weakening NATO and alienating the United States (as well as a French government increasingly uneasy about the SPD's apparent slide toward neutralism).

CDU/CSU leaders presented their party, by contrast, as united in its backing of NATO, unwilling to pressure the United States on arms control, and Washington's only reliable partner. They openly flaunted their close connections with Reagan administration figures; Washington in turn seemed to encourage the Union.[81] CSU leaders especially underscored their support for U.S. policy. Strauss—the original German Gaullist—published an "Atlanticist manifesto" in an American journal, which spoke of trans-Atlantic solidarity, the trans-Atlantic lifeline, and the common destiny of Europe and America.[82]

Their party's credibility as an alliance partner, said many Union leaders, reinforced its ability to ensure continuity in FRG foreign policy—including Ostpolitik. The Union alone could continue the policy Schmidt advocated (but, given his party, could not implement) because it alone had the trust of Bonn's allies that made realistic detente possible. Mertes described the Union as the only source of "reliability and continuity," a government in waiting. Others agreed there would be no 180-degree or even 90-degree shift in East-West policy, but a 15-degree shift—to a position somewhat "less trusting" of communist leaders. The party would provide full support for official alliance policy and even increase defense spending.[83]

Yet by contrast fundamentalists and CSU spokesmen still took great pains to circumscribe continuity. They sought to "correct" the image of growing agreement between the government and the opposition by emphasizing remaining differences over human rights, defense spending, Afghanistan, and sanctions against Moscow. Strauss launched attacks on detente and Ostpolitik, arguing that such policies had not altered the German situation. A Bavarian colleague disavowed CDU/CSU support, help, and cooperation in continuing a detente that had proved "illusory and one-sided." This form of continuity would be like putting a new crew aboard a sinking ship, he added.[84]

Ostpolitik and Coalition Politics

In viewing the areas of bipartisan agreement, the CDU leadership primarily saw a glass half full, the CSU and other fundamentalists a glass half empty. In part this divergence arose from different perspectives on the substance of the policy itself. But it also reflected persistent differences over domestic political strategy. Although opposition leaders happily used foreign policy issues to further divide the disintegrating SPD-FDP coalition, they could not agree on the logical next step. Polls put the Union's approval rating at over 50 percent and showed public expectations of a change of government. But should the Union pursue a coalition with the FDP, or power on its own?

Kohl believed that the time was nearly ripe for realizing his cherished goal of a Christian-Liberal partnership, with himself as chancellor. He sensed that Genscher was preparing to separate his party from a leftward-drifting SPD and link up with the Union (differences within the coalition on economic policy had grown sharper). Thus he confidently urged the CDU/CSU to be patient and prepare for power. It need only demonstrate its commitment to continuity and stability in policy, while underscoring the current coalition's susceptibility to SPD-left pressure and emphasizing CDU/CSU agreement with the FDP.

Not all CDU/CSU leaders were content with a strategy that might effectively make the Union dependent upon the FDP. Strauss and the CSU feared that in a Christian-Liberal coalition coveted cabinet posts (above all the Foreign Ministry) would be reserved for the FDP. Thus there was speculation that Strauss would make himself available as a chancellor candidate if the Union wanted to seek power on its own (either through new elections or by waiting until the next scheduled election, in 1984) and squeeze the FDP out. This reinforced CSU and fundamentalist efforts to downplay the Union's pledge of continuity and its areas of agreement with the FDP. In short, domestic politics reinforced the CSU's wariness of pledging continuity.

Much depended, then, on whether the FDP would indeed switch coalition partners before 1984. By mid-1982 the foreign minister and his advisors were again showing concern that the SPD left threatened to bring Bonn's Ostpolitik into direct conflict with its alliance obligations. Despite his dispute with the opposition over sanctions during the Polish crisis, Genscher increasingly praised the Union for moving toward government policy. Some of his Liberal colleagues agreed with the SPD that the Union still refused to honor the spirit of Ostpolitik, wanted to alter GDR behavior through heavy-handed pressure, had no concern with arms control, and would terminate the gas pipeline. But most FDP leaders shared Genscher's emphasis on areas of bipartisan agreement, an emphasis evident in his speeches after the Polish crisis and again in an article he published in the American journal *Foreign Affairs*, entitled "Toward an Overall Western Strategy." Its prescriptions sounded much more like the Union's Gesamtpolitik than the SPD's East-West security partnership. Many press observers and Social Democrats took this as an effort to justify Genscher's planned break with the SPD and began to speak of an approaching change in coalitions.[85]

Observers did note, however, Genscher's ambivalence. In underscoring the Union's movement toward government policy, the foreign minister was also clearly appealing to the Union to complete its process of adaptation. There were, he said, still "shrill tones" in the opposition. Genscher's policy could be conducted with Kohl and von Weizsäcker, but he was less comfortable with Strauss than he was with Brandt. The foreign minister remained unconvinced that Union fundamentalists were in fact entirely ready to live with continuity in West German foreign policy.

Nonetheless, in September 1982 Genscher and his party leadership (over protest from a small, if prominent, FDP minority) calculated that bolting the coalition would cost the party less long-term support than would remaining with a partner that was seen as drifting out of the FRG's political mainstream. The immediate cause for the decision was an FDP-SPD dispute over budget cuts, which arose from a deeper conflict on social and economic policy. But observers saw foreign policy as one of the decisive underlying factors. Genscher feared that continuity in foreign policy and Bonn's international standing could no longer be preserved from SPD-left pressure to develop a security partnership, negotiate the Gera demands and, most importantly, back out on Bonn's commitment to deploy INF if arms talk failed. He expressed his concerns in a last-minute Bundestag session, where he urged Schmidt's party to endorse unambiguously his concept of West German foreign and security policy and demanded an end to SPD claims that other parties were not committed to peace. As the *Frankfurter Allgemeine Zeitung* observed: "With [Genscher's] accusations, the first and last bond of the coalition between SPD and FDP, with which it had successfully waged three election campaigns against the Union, collapsed: the foreign and security policy of the 'coalition,' that was crowned with the word 'peace policy' by its authors."[86]

In bringing down Schmidt's government, the FDP demonstrated its hope that the Union would be a preferable coalition partner. Genscher's leadership calculated that a CDU/CSU-FDP coalition would gain broad public approval, thus ensuring the Liberals a place in government—and political survival. Implicit in this was an FDP assumption that the commitment to continuity in foreign policy was genuine and sufficiently widespread in the Union. FDP leaders knew that CSU and CDU fundamentalists remained suspicious of the Ostpolitik and would insist upon at least a modest change in tone and emphasis, such as demonstrative insistence that the German question remained open. Yet the FDP did not believe that CDU/CSU emphasis and rhetoric need block or unduly complicate negotiations—especially with Genscher remaining as foreign minister. It counted upon Kohl to prevail over the fundamentalists and thus expected that a Union-led government would help promote businesslike relations with the Soviet bloc, including East Berlin.

Most press observers agreed that continuity in Ostpolitik was certain under a Kohl government; such an approach had become inseparably entwined with CDU/CSU positions on foreign policy and Kohl's strategy for regaining (and maintaining) power. East-bloc reaction to this change in Bonn reflected a similar assumption. GDR media voiced regret that years of Bonn's "generally positive" role in East-West relations were ending. It noted that a Union government would be more Atlanticist in outlook and predicted a downturn in German-German relations—especially if hard-liners prevailed in the new coalition, and especially if Bonn deployed NATO INF. But this statement was not unequivocally negative and predicted no collapse of Bonn–East Berlin ties.[87]

On 1 October 1982 Helmut Kohl was elected chancellor by the Bundestag's first successful constructive vote of confidence (a handful of dissident FDP deputies voted against him), replacing Helmut Schmidt. In his government declaration, he pledged continuity in a way that indicated both how far the Union had adopted to existing policy and the limits of its adaptation: "A modus vivendi with the East has been agreed to. We stand by these treaties, and we will use them as instruments of an active peace policy.... The GDR can rely on us to stand by the obligations we take over.... The cooperation of the German states must be improved in the interests of the Germans and of their neighbors in Europe. We are interested in comprehensive, long-term agreements to the benefit of people and on the basis of existing agreements."[88]

IV

Conclusion

The Union's Ambivalent Adaptation

Throughout thirteen years in opposition the CDU-CSU gave ample reason for believing that it was by and large ready to accept the changing nature of Bonn's relationship with the East. Yet it is not possible to detect a uniform, gradual conversion to, let alone an open embrace of, SPD-FDP Ostpolitik. There was instead merely the accumulation over time of indications, most indirect and tacit, that even die-hard Union fundamentalists would not try to reverse the basic change made after 1969: the establishment of a policy focused primarily on direct negotiations with communist regimes (including the SED) and aimed largely at normalizing relations, expanding interstate cooperation, and thus also softening the effects of Germany's division. Whatever else it may have persistently resisted in SPD-FDP conduct of affairs, the Union clearly acknowledged that it would continue this basic approach. The party had accustomed itself to the practice, instrumentalities, and results of SPD-FDP policy.

Factors Necessitating an Adaptive Ostpolitik

Union adaptation to the operational dimension of Bonn's post-1969 Eastern policy, and thus the promise of continuity once it regained office, was a function of international, societal, and intraparty factors working together. Of these, the first two categories were most important and intra-Union developments ancillary. The underlying international constraints and societal influences that caused Union adaptation were basic and enduring. In one form or another they have shaped West German foreign policy since 1945. These factors were (1) the FRG's particular sensitivity to broader developments in divided Europe, and (2) a political culture still affected by the traumas of the past. The importance of these two factors (as well as a gradual, albeit partial, change in Union structure and leadership) provides further evidence of the constraining effect exerted on West German foreign policy by what Wolfram Hanrieder has called the need for "compatibility and consensus."[1]

International Factors

Most decisive in directly or indirectly shaping CDU/CSU behavior with regard to Ostpolitik/Deutschlandpolitik were the international constraints on West German foreign policy. All such constraints might be said to reflect the same widely shared sensitivity of Bonn's policymakers to the international environment. A desire to erase memories of their nation's pre-1945 history partly explains this responsiveness to external conditions, but more decisive still is the FRG's own evolution. As Karl Kaiser has observed, the Federal Republic was a state created by others' foreign policies before it was a state with its own foreign policy.[2] Although Bonn's international role grew with time, the country's special place within the bloc structure of a divided Europe has always limited its room for maneuver and made West German policymakers particularly sensitive to the larger environment within which they work. Rhetoric notwithstanding, the CDU/CSU came to realize it could not escape this constraint.

Bloc System Consolidation

No single force had greater effect in shaping SPD-FDP Ostpolitik and the Union's eventual adaptation to it than the long, gradual, but seemingly unstoppable consolidation of the bloc system in postwar Europe. As early as the mid-1950s creation of two large military alliances made Europe's division more than provisional. The superpower nuclear stalemate, dramatized by the Berlin and Cuba crises, solidified this bloc division by underscoring the potential risks involved in any attempt to challenge it.

One inevitable victim was the credibility of a West German policy guided mainly by the quest for national reunification, a fact the SPD and FDP accepted well before the CDU/CSU did. To be sure, hope of actually attaining reunification never drove overall Union foreign policy, nor was it even the principal short-term motivation of Union Deutschlandpolitik. But even if the party knew that unity could not and would not be achieved in the foreseeable future, it felt this goal must be upheld and espoused—especially in regard to the Soviet bloc. Union leaders believed that Bonn could not accommodate the East on this issue, even if the Union's own policy of integration into the West in effect helped forestall the actual restoration of unity. If anything, insistence upon keeping the national issue at the center of its Ostpolitik grew more fervent among Union fundamentalists as the likelihood of reunification receded in the 1960s. These conservatives and nationalists fought bitterly to retain the basis of the traditional claim that Bonn was morally, politically, and legally entitled to pursue unity within a state structure. Thus many in the Union believed that Bonn must respect the legal provisionality of Germany's division and remain aloof from the GDR, or at least have no full relations with it. There had to remain grounds on which to challenge, if only implicitly, the GDR's existence and legitimacy.

For this reason in the 1960s and early 1970s a fundamentalist majority cast about for ways to block East-West rapprochement. A more flexible reformist minority urged acceptance of the new realities of world politics but advocated influencing the consolidation of the blocs to prevent a definitive and unacceptable answer to the German question. The reformists felt that Bonn could not and should not thwart systemic developments, but *could* ameliorate the damaging effects on traditional West German Deutschlandpolitik.[3]

But as the bloc system became formally and all but permanently consolidated, the Union found itself in a new position and could no longer resist, downplay, or even reshape broader systemic developments. For by 1972, or at the very latest 1975 and the Helsinki accord, East and West alike had in effect declared Europe's bloc division to be the prerequisite for, rather than a challenge to, stable international relations. To keep reunification at the heart of Union policy toward the East-bloc states was no longer merely problematic, it was untenable. "Keeping the German question open" became a plea rather than a demand. What had already been in substance a defensive policy now had to become defensive in form and rhetoric as well.

Union leaders, above all fundamentalists, were admittedly loath to acknowledge this fact. Most considered it more vital to see only the technically provisional, modus vivendi character of the new Ostpolitik. They emphasized that it was thanks to their own efforts that Brandt's treaties permitted Bonn to keep the national question legally open. Yet the party increasingly felt compelled to shift the focus of its Deutschlandpolitik to one more compatible with the real situation in Europe. As early as the 1972 parliamentary debates Union leaders stopped insisting upon including the term "reunification" in the treaties. Even fundamentalists began to imply that West Germany's rights should be reserved and protected but could not be the sole content of Bonn's policy. In short, the legal dimension of the "open German question" took on an implicitly more formal character. Moreover, party leaders increasingly used the less precise, less provocative notion of self-determination in place of reunification.

Union leaders did not stop insisting that reunification remain a vital goal and that even the right to state unity be asserted. What did decrease was the relative centrality of these arguments in CDU/CSU Deutschlandpolitik, indicating the party's recognition that consolidation of the bloc system entirely undercut the credibility of a policy dominated by the notion of reunification—even if that was mostly rhetoric. In the words of a CDU politician, "De facto progress [in relations with the East] became more important than de jure retreats [in the legal realm]."[4]

Westpolitik

A second international factor is closely related to the first and again indicates how much Union leaders came to appreciate the FRG's special susceptibility to its external environment. As the likelihood of fundamental change in Europe's political structure waned, the Western allies developed an interest in a modus vivendi with Moscow: a new basis for relations that would permit an easing of tensions and above all nuclear-arms control. The allies were no longer willing to let the German question block such a detente, and they increasingly pressured Bonn to find a formula accepting the status quo. Union-led governments until 1969 resisted; Brandt's coalition did not, and his policy won Western endorsement, if less-than-enthusiastic support.

This development also put the Union in a quandary. Given the very circumstances of its creation, its history, its security requirements, and its economic position, the FRG was especially responsive to, indeed dependent upon, its Western allies. Because the Union had developed Bonn's Westpolitik, it above all considered allies vital for German security, respectability, and any hope of eventual unity. The CDU/CSU of all parties could least bear to be isolated from Bonn's neighbors, especially the United States.

For over a decade before 1969 the Union had been split by precisely this issue: how much it could afford to antagonize Bonn's Western partners by refusing to sanction acceptance of the status quo as the point of departure for detente. In the 1960s Union Gaullists sought to restructure the Western alliance to circumvent this problem. Atlanticists felt that the Union must go along with its Western partners to avoid isolation and to lessen the risks of an East-West detente without German input. These same divergences appeared again in the 1969–72 treaty debates. By this time U.S. and West European leaders (again with some ambivalence) implicitly, often explicitly, pressured the Union not to obstruct East-West detente by blocking Brandt's treaties. Years later even moderates like Alois Mertes recalled with annoyance the lectures they received from foreign counterparts on the virtues of detente.

Yet fear of isolation from Washington and Western Europe was decisive in reformist efforts to modify party behavior—from Barzel's decision to let the treaties pass to the general downplaying of German legal positions throughout the 1970s. CDU/CSU fundamentalists resisted American and West European pressure more openly and persistently. Some argued that just as the allies had underestimated Hitler, now they misread the Soviet bloc, and on occasion Union spokesmen whipped up a certain nationalistic resentment against allied interference. Yet even the fundamentalist majority ultimately abstained and permitted passage of the 1972 treaties, at least in part because of desire not to be isolated and not to isolate Bonn. They did later choose to vote against the Helsinki Final Act, but only in a nonbinding Bundestag resolution that would not affect Germany's position on the Conference of Security and Cooperation in Europe (CSCE).

To be sure, fear of isolation from the West never compelled CDU/CSU leaders to embrace SPD-FDP Ostpolitik in its entirety. They stressed, rightly, that many Western leaders harbored deep reservations about the long-term aims and impact of SPD policy. After 1974 they could also credibly claim that many in the West wanted to restrain Bonn's detente rather than encourage it. By 1982 it was the SPD that faced the problem of alienating the United States and France, as both allies' ardor for detente had cooled and their reservations about a unilateral, quasi-neutralistic German detente had increased.

What ultimately affected the Union was not Western enthusiasm for detente, with all its ups and downs, but rather the more permanent readiness of Bonn's allies—especially Paris—to treat the German issue as effectively (if not formally) closed. Almost all Union leaders consulted with their European partners, especially during the early 1970s. It is impossible to hear or read accounts of these sessions without noting the disappointment most felt at the readiness of fellow Europeans to formalize Germany's partition. It was clear to Union leaders that given Western attitudes one central tenet of SPD-FDP Ostpolitik must be accepted: Deutschlandpolitik could not continue to insist upon allied rejection of Europe's status quo. The CDU reformist minority had effectively grasped this before 1969; the fundamentalist majority came to the same conclusion more grudgingly.

Admittedly, Union spokesmen, especially fundamentalists, never wearied of pointing to formal Western declarations backing German unity, as well as to public opinion surveys in allied countries showing support for reunification. Even in the late 1970s such polls indicated that public-opinion majorities in all neighboring states favored German unity.[5] Yet the party sensed that French, British, and U.S. government declarations endorsing reunification were entirely formalistic and all but obligatory under the Germany Treaty.

In day-to-day policy, in the press, in political debates, these states, as well as Italy and the smaller countries, showed no interest in, and even opposition to, German unity. Although some aspects of the SPD-FDP policy made the allies uneasy, the European states —again, most important, France—greeted Ostpolitik as an end to the active promotion of, and lingering prospects for, German state unity.

A reformist like Gradl was candid enough to express what the party as a whole came to acknowledge, albeit often bitterly: despite some formal official support and occasional public sympathy for German unity, the West's reservations about reunification were "too frequent, too hard-necked, and too well-thought through" to disregard. As he added, too many West Europeans recalled German occupation, and even those who did not worried about the predominance of a united Germany within Europe.[6] In short Bonn's need to remain in step with the Western allies—especially France—may not have required permanent CDU/CSU enthusiasm for detente, but it did compel the party to ensure that the national question never again blocked East-West cooperation.

Berlin

Berlin's exposed position was another international factor that ultimately reshaped CDU/CSU foreign policy. The divided city played a major role in SPD-FDP Ostpolitik, which aimed to make Berlin less crisis prone. Initially the Union and, according to polls, most West Berliners were pessimistic about the Four Power pact and its follow-on agreements. They thought these accords permitted too little federal presence in the Western sectors and too many possibilities for GDR harassment of traffic on the access routes. But confidence in the city's future grew throughout the 1970s. By the end of the decade, Berliners—even Union supporters—had become the strongest advocates of dialogue with the East.[7]

CDU/CSU politicians accordingly began to see dialogue as vital to assure Berlin's security. During the Afghanistan crisis, both von Weizsäcker and Strauss cited Berlin as a major reason for continuing talks with the Soviet bloc. After the Union came to power in Berlin in 1981, the party became even more cautious and flexible. As one observer put it at the time, "Many questions appear a bit different, very much more concrete" to the Union. "Pure theory has become solid practice."[8]

In contrast with the SPD, the Union opposition never felt compelled to adopt a new Ostpolitik to enhance the security of the FRG; it relied on NATO deterrence policy for that. But the security of exposed Berlin was another matter, and here the CDU/CSU gradually came to see an arrangement with the Soviet bloc as unavoidable. As Hans-Peter Schwarz observed, the CDU/CSU became "more sensitive to how Berlin is a mortgage upon Bonn's foreign policy."[9]

Berechenbarkeit

West Germany's special sensitivity to its external environment facilitated Union adaptation in yet one other respect. Given the divided nation's exposure and vulnerability, as well as its pre-1945 past, Bonn policymakers have always placed a premium on Berechenbarkeit—best translated as "calculability." That is, they have always strived to avoid radical course changes or Gaullist-style unpredictability and unilateralism.

Berechenbarkeit has created a presumption against any government reneging upon, let alone renouncing, the basic substance of established foreign-policy commitments. In the 1960s the SPD accepted Westpolitik in part for this reason, and after Bonn had made its post-1969 initial opening to the East and codified it in treaty form as well as in practice, the Union itself was confronted with a fait accompli. The GDR had been tacitly recognized, a new relationship established, legal commitments toward the inner-German and Oder-Neisse lines made, commercial patterns expanded, and long-term negotiations on follow-up issues initiated. Brandt-Scheel Ostpolitik had legally and politically committed Bonn to a new relationship with the Soviet bloc that in substance could not be reversed without raising questions about West German Berechenbarkeit.

From a very early date the Union tacitly acknowledged that Brandt's policy could not be completely reversed. Alois Mertes dated this fait accompli from the Brandt-Stoph meeting in 1970 that effectively granted recognition to the GDR. Others cited the Bahr paper or the 1972 ratification vote, still others the court's verdict approving the treaties' constitutionality. By endorsing the

Traffic Treaty and letting the Moscow and Warsaw accords pass, the Union signaled its acceptance of the newly established facts. Strauss's *pacta sunt servanda* policy, even in its most narrow sense—a pledge to honor treaties—reflected a certain minimal acceptance of the overall policy's irreversibility. By the mid-1970s Union politicians increasingly devoted their energies to showing *how* they would conduct relations. Argument over the basis on which those relations were established had ceased to be relevant. Fundamentalist Werner Marx, who in 1973 declared "Time cannot heal all things," conceded ten years later, "Time heals."[10]

Domestic Factors

Union willingness to continue the operation of SPD-FDP Ostpolitik was to some extent also a function of domestic factors in West German foreign policy, diverse factors that in one way or another reflected the desire of West Germans to put the past behind them and find a certain normalcy.

Public Opinion: General

Many journalists and political analysts have concluded that CDU/CSU adaptation to Ostpolitik was largely a response to the new policy's popularity. Yet just as public attitudes on this issue were more complex than widely assumed, so too was the Union's reaction more than a matter of following opinion polls.

In its first few years, 1969–72, Brandt's policy won over West German public opinion.[11] Yet it was precisely during this period that, the reformist minority aside, Union leaders most adamantly opposed negotiations with the East. In retrospect most concede that they took the voters a very unpopular message in the 1972 election campaign; even one third of those Germans who identified with the Union accepted the Brandt-Scheel policy that year. At the time many party leaders assumed that Brandt's "survey majority" could be easily converted. At any rate their objections to the accords seemed weightier than their fear of a voter backlash.

After 1972 public enthusiasm for the Ostpolitik waned somewhat.[12] Rarely after 1973, moreover, were West Germans very optimistic about the further development of relations with the East. In the early 1980s, especially after Afghanistan and GDR delimitation measures, a substantial majority expected relations to worsen. CDU/CSU voters were disproportionately pessimistic in both cases. Moreover, surveys also showed a near-linear increase in support for a "harder" policy toward the East, from roughly 30 percent in the early 1970s to a range of 60 to 70 percent in the mid-1970s.[13]

Union fundamentalists often cited this leveling off in the popularity of SPD-FPD Ostpolitik as vindication of their earlier opposition and justification for even sharper criticism of government policy. Yet although there was a brief intensification of Union criticism in 1973 and 1974, thereafter the party as a whole became increasingly committed to continuity—at a time when public enthusiasm seemed to have leveled off.

The Union stance is not so paradoxical as it might seem. Despite the public's disappointment with the Ostpolitik and its willingness to tolerate a more brusque manner of dealing with the East, the idea of bargaining with Moscow and East Berlin had taken root. Allensbach, the survey institute closest to the Union, pointed out in 1976 that there was no generally negative public assessment of Ostpolitik, only disappointment with developments since the ratification of the major treaties.[14] Allensbach reported similar findings at the high point of East-West tension over Afghanistan: in early 1980, only one in five West Germans thought Ostpolitik had not been worth the effort (a ratio unchanged from seven years earlier)—and this despite *increasing* suspicion of Soviet motives.[15]

What were the reasons for public satisfaction with Ostpolitik? For many Germans, the greater possibilities for travel to the East and reunions with East German family were important. But even the majority that had no comparable personal stake in such human contacts increasingly considered a policy of dialogue to be a reassuring sign of stability and normalcy. A policy aimed at negotiations and contacts, even if it suffered discouraging setbacks, had become widely accepted as tantamount to "normalization." Effectively renouncing West German claims against the status quo was a price most were willing to pay in exchange for such normalization—not merely normalization of relations with all East-bloc states (including the GDR, within limits), but normalization of Bonn's foreign policy. After 1972 the FRG could not be isolated because of past German misdeeds, nor could it be blamed for challenging the

European status quo and thus raising tensions. In effect Bonn's Ostpolitik made the Federal Republic a normal actor in international affairs, a change the public welcomed and would not gladly reverse. In Gebhard Schweigler's words, "West Germans know what they want: a relaxation of tensions, an improvement in their security position, and a normalization of relations (where normal is defined as the state of affairs existing in Western Europe). This is what drives the Ostpolitik."[16]

CDU/CSU politicians came to acknowledge this sentiment. Though they carefully stressed that German desire for normalization and stability should not lead to accommodation of Soviet aims, they argued that dialogue could mitigate tensions; a new peace order might not emerge, but crises could be defused. Consequently a strong sign of CDU/CSU adaptation to public opinion lay in the party's avowed unwillingness to destabilize the GDR (even at the cost of downplaying Bonn's cherished legal positions), its desire not to "uproot the Polish people" (which meant living with the Oder-Neisse line), and its reluctance to punish the Soviet Union (thus the party's ambiguous response to U.S. appeals for sanctions in 1980–82).

Public Opinion: National Consciousness

Public acceptance of the new Ostpolitik, and thus CDU/CSU adaptation, can also be attributed to a gradual change in one important area of the West German political culture: *gesamtdeutsch* consciousness. It has often been argued that time, generational change, resignation, and realism eroded public support for, or confidence in, the possible achievement of reunification, thus undermining the foundations of traditional CDU/CSU Deutschlandpolitik. Consequently, it is said, a new form of gesamtdeutsch consciousness evolved, a feeling of national-cultural togetherness nourished by expanding human contacts. The Union thus felt compelled to continue a policy assuring greater interaction that preserved the "substance of the nation."

Public confidence in the prospect of state unity did indeed decline. Polls in 1967 noted that one in three people believed reunification was possible within the following decade; by 1980 the share of optimists had dwindled to less than one in five (and to an even lower level among the young). Nearly three in four Germans considered partition permanent. Union politicians blamed these statistics on the sense of resignation caused by SPD-FDP Ostpolitik itself, arguing that Bonn's leadership gave the public no reason to hope for reunification. The Union took consolation in the fact that the same surveys showed two thirds to three fourths of all West Germans still viewed reunification favorably, and three out of four wanted to keep the national question open by maintaining unity as a formal, constitutional goal. Yet only about one in one hundred of all West Germans considered reunification the most vital issue of the day.[17]

Yet though the SPD-FDP policy mirrored the public's readiness to put reunification on the back burner, it did not, as promised, create a broadened sense of gesamtdeutsch solidarity through expanded human interaction. Whatever else Ostpolitik may have produced to win public approval, its revitalization of national consciousness was difficult to verify. In his assessment of German attitudes toward foreign policy Schweigler concluded that "while the new Ostpolitik achieved many of its objectives, the prospects for maintaining a sense of national cohesion remain in doubt."[18]

Admittedly, the number of West German visitors to the East rose steadily, which the Union recognized as a positive result of SPD-FDP policy. Similarly, the number of East German pensioners permitted to come West rose from 1 million to 1.5 million during the 1970s.[19] Nonetheless the rate of increase in West-to-East travel struck many as less than expected, and it fell sharply (by one fourth) after the GDR raised its mandatory minimum exchange requirement in 1980. East-to-West travel also remained lower than even the SPD-FDP hoped, and the number of younger nonpensioners permitted to visit the FRG remained miniscule. Clearly East Berlin could still successfully restrict contacts.

Moreover, surveys showed that West German interest in, as well as awareness of, life in the GDR waned. At the end of the 1970s only 25 to 30 percent of West Germans had ever been to the GDR (a mere 5 to 6 percent visited regularly), and more than half of those went solely to visit relatives or friends. Well under half of those polled closely followed events in the GDR, and a majority admitted to being relatively uninterested in East Germany.

Younger West Germans remained disproportionately indifferent to life in the GDR.[20]

Not surprisingly, a majority of those polled said that "Germany" consisted of the FRG alone; less than a third believed "Germany" meant both states, and only one tenth identified Germany as the old imperial territories stretching beyond the Oder-Neisse line. In one poll two thirds posited the existence not merely of two German states, but of two German nations. Nearly one in two young West Germans even described the GDR as a foreign country.[21]

Admittedly, those who regularly visited the GDR were far more likely to see that state as part of Germany. But as noted above, this group amounted to a tiny minority, and a greater feeling of togetherness, let alone a wave of national consciousness, could not evolve from such a low level of interaction. Studies concluded that despite the Ostpolitik, there had been little growth of gesamtdeutsch sentiment. People who visited the GDR in 1980 did so for the same reasons they had in 1970 or 1960—to visit family or friends. Most others, especially the young, remained indifferent.[22]

Union leaders, furthermore, showed little sign that they felt compelled to accommodate a new type of gesamtdeutsch sentiment. Party programs and some reformists like Gradl and von Weizsäcker did speak of the role that human contacts could play in preserving the sense of national unity, keeping the torch of hope burning for eventual self-determination. But this was primarily a rationalization of the party's willingness to accept Ostpolitik, a willingness resting on other grounds.

What *did* affect the Union was the more tangible and concrete form that a German policy aimed at humanitarian measures gave to the national issue. Party leaders came to see that human interaction, whatever its limitations, made the German question real in a way that legal abstractions and political exhortations could not. Fundamentalists might long deride the SPD-FDP for reducing Deutschlandpolitik to a question of "tea with Aunt Minna in East Berlin." Yet though public interest in a policy of practical cooperation and contacts might not constitute an overwhelming wave of gesamtdeutsch sentiment, it was considerably stronger than public enthusiasm for a set of legal formulas. The business of day-to-day relations with the East and the pursuit of measurable improvements, however marginal, gave the national issue a certain concreteness even to those not directly affected.

In short, the Union could not long disregard the fact that in the public's view the process Brandt had begun made cooperation, not eventual reunification, the *sine qua non* of successful Deutschlandpolitik. Since Brandt, a relevant national policy had to adopt the SPD-FDP agenda. It might simultaneously assert the legal and political case for state unity, but its central element had to be the pursuit of improved relations.

In fact, far from engendering a wave of gesamtdeutsch consciousness that carried all—including the Union—before it, SPD-FDP Ostpolitik strengthened a sense of West German assertiveness. As Schweigler argued, "West Germans are increasingly losing their all-German national consciousness and developing a strictly West German one instead."[23] By normalizing relations with the East and giving tangibility to Bonn's dealings with the GDR, Brandt-Scheel policy effectively made FRG foreign policy that of a normal state—no longer isolated by the East or totally dependent on the West, no longer a special case, no longer dedicated to the abstract and the unachievable. That more, not fewer, Germans now equated the FRG with "Germany" was a clear sign that this policy reinforced a new sense of identity. The public was content to have leaders who pursued the aims of an ordinary state. If, for example, the public wanted to perpetuate Bonn's Eastern dialogue in the face of U.S. pressure for a return to containment, this desire reflected not a revived sense of gesamtdeutsch solidarity, but the irritation felt by citizens of an independent state toward a demanding ally.

It took time for the CDU/CSU to adapt to this mood. Barzel's plaintive declaration that "I have no wish to become a Federal-Republican [rather than a German]" could not disguise the fact that, however reluctantly, his party was facing an unavoidable challenge. Even without echoing SPD rhetoric about Bonn's Eastern dialogue as the "emancipation" of West German foreign policy (let alone as Bonn's *force de frappe*), the Union had to treat Ostpolitik as part of West German *raison d'état*. A return to the old Deutschlandpolitik, mortgaging Bonn's foreign relations to the Four Powers and restoring its status as simply the forward base of Western containment, would have seemed a denigration of the Federal Republic's current status.

Coalition Politics

German politics since 1945 has been coalition politics. The success of broad, moderate coalitions has been reinforced by historically grounded hostility to "one-party government," fear of ideological extremes within the SPD and Union, and a preference for normalcy and centrism. In large part it is coalition politics that explains the FDP's survival and its disproportionate influence in federal politics. Neither major party, at least since the mid-1960s, has been able to renounce unconditionally the option of coalition with the Liberals.

Moreover, the FDP was clearly committed to, and identified with, post-1969 Ostpolitik. To be sure, Liberals were for the most part more modest in their expectations, less willing than the SPD to offer concessions impinging upon the open national question, somewhat more traditionally gesamtdeutsch, and opposed to raising doubts about Bonn's Western commitments for the sake of better relations with the East. Yet the FDP was fundamentally dedicated to preserving intact the relationships established since 1969, willing to abandon excess legal baggage on the national issue, and committed to helping improve the East-West atmosphere through arms control. It was, after all, largely to pursue a new Ostpolitik that the FDP joined the SPD in 1969, and Liberals came to embrace the policy in practice. FDP foreign ministers, above all Genscher, treated foreign relations including Ostpolitik as their private domain. Even as SPD-FDP relations crumbled in the early 1980s, the treaties remained a common bond holding the coalition together.

The Union thus faced a difficult political choice that its leaders debated inconclusively for thirteen years: Should the party attempt to regain power without the FDP, and if not, how far should the CDU/CSU go to attract the Liberals? Should it respond to FDP appeals in parliamentary speeches as well as in closed committees for a flexible, bipartisan Ostpolitik?

Most CDU leaders believed the Union had little choice. Some, like Kohl, had long openly desired a nonsocialist, Christian-Liberal majority government. Others lacked Kohl's affinity for the "opportunistic" Liberals, but they considered the FDP an indispensable political partner. State-level CDU branches gained an even greater stake in improving ties with the FDP: first in the Saarland, then in Lower Saxony under Albrecht, and last in Berlin under von Weizsäcker, the CDU worked to forge coalitions with the Liberals.

This slow progress toward a Christian-Liberal federal coalition reinforced any willingness the party had to pledge continuity with regard to Ostpolitik. Most of the key episodes in the Union's conversion, from working out the 1972 Joint Resolution to passing the 1976 Polish accords to Kohl's 1980 parliamentary address, were designed in part to make the Union a more attractive coalition partner.

CSU leaders by no means shared the CDU's tolerant attitude toward the FDP, for the Bavarians feared that their own influence would be diluted within a broad multiparty coalition. Whenever polls gave reason for hope that the Union could win a majority on its own (in 1976, and again in 1981 and 1982), CSU leaders urged CDU colleagues to abandon the FDP-coalition option and refrain from trying to placate the Liberals with concessions on foreign policy. At the same time, however, even the CSU wanted at least to disrupt the Social-Liberal coalition by playing on its internal differences, and to do that it was at times necessary to underscore and broaden the common ground between the Union and the Liberals. Often the real disagreement within the CDU/CSU was not over whether to accommodate the FDP, but over how far it should go in doing so and what terms it should demand. At the very least the need to play coalition politics restrained the party from following a constant, strict fundamentalist line.

Economic Benefits

Major economic interests also influenced CDU/CSU policy. Trade with the East, including the GDR, expanded substantially in the Ostpolitik's early years. Leaders of the major West German industrial associations such as Wolff von Amerongen and Bertoldt Beitz advocated expanding commercial relations. They supported government assistance to promote trade financing and resisted linking the swing credit to East German behavior. It was continually stressed that the well-being of certain major industrial sectors and some 300,000 jobs depended on trade with the Soviet bloc and that several thousand West German firms depended indirectly on the swing credit and the trade it promoted.

Given the Union's substantial ties to West German industry, business influence on the party was certainly to be expected. The CDU/CSU had the largest share of parliamentarians with business backgrounds; private lobbyists generally had easy access to the Union and its auxiliary organizations institutionalized this access in the party's structure; business leaders who joined a party most often joined the Union; and the largest share of both direct and indirect financial contributions from private industries flowed to the CDU/CSU.

Moreover, the Union became more committed to continuity in the late 1970s and 1980s when the stake of German firms had become most substantial. In the early 1970s Union leaders had attacked trade credits to communist countries, calling them "reparations," a burden to taxpayers, even extortion; later in the decade the party called more cautiously for linkage of economic and political issues; eventually it merely said that economic transfers should not be unreciprocal. Consequently many informed observers suspect that "behind closed doors" industry worked very hard to change CDU/CSU policy.[24]

Yet the economic dimension of CDU/CSU adaptation was both less and more than a matter of catering to private firms with a stake in Eastern trade. Angela Stent and Michael Kreile have argued that economic pressures did not really drive the original Ostpolitik. Brandt's opening to the East was based on political grounds, and trade followed the flag; indeed, it was a tool to improve relations. Despite the enthusiasm of some corporate officials, most German industry was tepid—one Union leader used the word "schizophrenic"—about prospects for commercial gain through trade with the East. Some firms warned about competition from East-bloc imports. Kreile points out that SPD finance minister, Karl Schiller, had to plead for more support from industry during the ratification debate. Even as Ostpolitik succeeded in removing many hindrances to trade and commercial relations expanded, West German firms remained sober about the prospects for real gain. Despite the expansion of trade ties, Eastern trade remained a modest proportion of the FRG's overall foreign commerce, roughly 6 to 7 percent of total exports by the early 1980s, including intra-German commerce.[25]

Far from bringing heavy pressure to bear on the Union, moreover, during the ratification debates the business community often downplayed the economic benefits of Eastern trade partly so as not to alienate the Union. Industry contributions to the party showed no drop during the height of the Ostpolitik debate. Party officials, including CDU treasurer Leisler Kiep, admit to having felt no business pressure to assure continuity in relations with the East.[26] One study showed that the German industrial associations concerned with promoting Eastern trade devoted very little energy to winning over the opposition, focusing instead on the executive.[27]

Moreover, although the CDU's business auxiliary came to support trade with the East, its leaders took no active part in the party's Ostpolitik debate, and aside from shadow finance minister, Gerhard Stoltenberg, few CDU/CSU business and industry experts could be counted as important foreign-policy reformists. Indeed their primary concern, discouraging CDU/CSU support for greater trade-union influence over industrial management, led them into a long-standing coalition with archconservative Union fundamentalists.

Nonetheless, improved commercial ties did become one of many facets of Bonn's increasingly "normalized" relations with the East, and the Union grew reluctant to call for steps that might disrupt trade patterns after they were established. By the early 1980s the party was backing down from open calls to punish or pressure the East economically, much to Washington's dismay.

To some extent this growing caution about using economic leverage reflected some quiet encouragement from business and industry involved in trade with the East. But it indicated more general pressures as well, including a bipartisan consensus in Bonn that a state so dependent on trade could not cast doubt on its reliability by restricting commerce for political reasons. Sanctions were seen as unappealing regardless of the target nation. Moreover, the Union's reluctance to restrict Bonn's modest Eastern trade reflected an awareness that certain West German economic sectors (such as machine-tool manufacturers) had become somewhat dependent on export markets in the Soviet bloc. One parliamentary staffer concluded that "industry exercised no pressure on the CDU/CSU, but the party was conscious of commercial interests—especially when the economic situation was bad in the FRG."[28]

Last, as other largely noneconomic factors pushed the Union

The Union's Ambivalent Adaptation | 253

toward accepting Bonn's new Ostpolitik, the party became increasingly aware that trade could be a positive incentive to promote further dialogue without a compromise on legal positions. As Strauss observed in his 1978 speech following Brezhnev's Bonn visit, Moscow's need for trade with the West could be the basis for expanding cooperation. For the Union, trade neither preceded nor followed the flag, but came along with it.

Intraparty Factors

Certain shifts in the Union's internal balance of power and changes in its preferred domestic political strategy during the decade before 1982 also facilitated its adaptation to SPD-FDP Ostpolitik. For the most part, these developments either objectively or subjectively strengthened the hands of those who most strongly believed their party must not try to resist societal and international constraints. Thus these party-internal factors played a supporting role in the overall evolution of Union policy.

Internal Structure

From 1969 to about 1973, the period of the ratification debates, the parliamentary group acted as the decision-making body in opposition, especially with regard to foreign policy. Due to the disproportionate influence of older politicians and the CSU with its bloc vote, the parliamentary group fought Brandt's Ostpolitik. After 1972, however, the parliamentary group was increasingly compelled to share power with the CDU party organization. In part, the parliamentarians suffered from the relative inexperience of their new chief, Karl Carstens. In addition, with the ratification debates largely finished, the Bundestag as an institution returned to its more familiar role: a public forum, rather than a working organ of government. The opposition parliamentary group's role waned with the waning of the Bundestag.

At the same time, the CDU party organization, so long merely an electoral support staff for Union chancellors, was changing.[29] Under Kohl and especially two successive general-secretaries, Kurt Biedenkopf and Heiner Geissler, the CDU actively solicited dues-paying members, developed grass-roots organizations, held open discussions of party policy, and produced comprehensive programmatic statements.

Certain organized interests within the CDU gained somewhat greater influence during the 1970s: the Union youth group, for example, increased its membership by 50 percent and—along with the trade-union wing—resisted party conservatives on a range of issues, including foreign policy. At the same time, Union expellees, concerned over their shrinking numbers and their constituency's greater integration into West German society, formed a new association within the party, but this could not conceal their relative loss of influence. Other conservative groups, such as those active on economic issues, played little role in the foreign-policy debates.[30]

One result was a steady, if by no means completely successful, effort by the CDU to help effect a more adaptive Union Ostpolitik after 1972.[31] Party officials resolved to encourage a shift in public focus away from the Union's electorally unrewarding opposition to Ostpolitik. This was evident in the hammering out of party programs, such as the Mannheim Declaration of 1975 and the Basic Program of 1978: both incorporated cautiously receptive statements about dialogue with the Soviet bloc. Kohl's CDU party conference in Düsseldorf in 1977 tried to go even further in this direction, although the attempt proved abortive. The 1981 Hamburg conference, featuring Geissler's dialogue with the peace movement, attempted to underscore CDU/CSU receptiveness to detente and arms control.

In short, the Union's more flexible stance on Ostpolitik cannot be separated from the effort to regenerate the CDU. After the debacle of 1972, the party organization's growing clout gave reformists a more secure basis of operations. Not coincidentally Biedenkopf and Geissler were among the reformist leadership.

Oppositional Tactics

The way in which the Union conducted itself as an opposition during the 1970s also changed, which further facilitated adaptation to Ostpolitik. From 1969 to 1972 most Union leaders believed that their party was unjustly sentenced to opposition by the "unethical" creation of an illegitimate coalition comprising two smaller rivals, the SPD and the FDP. They thus directed their energies toward harassing the new government and bringing it down. There was relatively little Union interest in competing with the SPD-FDP for the political center by offering a fully developed alternative program.

From 1972 on, however, chastened by its clear electoral setback, the Union gradually grew more reconciled to attracting the FDP and playing the role of a competitive opposition. With regard to Ostpolitik, this meant that spokesmen like Alois Mertes and even fundamentalists increasingly argued that the Union could handle negotiations with East Berlin and Moscow more effectively than the coalition. Generally this meant a mere appeal for "harder bargaining." But in many cases, from the Union's call for more active use of the treaties and the Helsinki Final Act to Strauss's meetings with Soviet-bloc leaders, the opposition showed its determination to beat the SPD-FDP at its own game. Von Weizsäcker typified this tendency in remarking that the SPD-FDP wanted to monopolize Ostpolitik and feared anything *except* Union obstructionism: "But I won't go along," he declared.[32] At times, including his 1978 meeting with Brezhnev, Strauss adopted a similar line. In short, Union leaders knew their party must compete with the government on Ostpolitik or risk irrelevancy. This meant working with the given conditions despite reservations.

Playing the role of a competitive opposition furthered the Union's adaptiveness in another respect. In presenting its alternatives for the conduct of an established policy, the party gradually came to insist that it possessed certain advantages in negotiating with the East. In the Union view the SPD-FDP had taken the risks, made the mistakes, and created a fait accompli—a comprehensive dialogue with the Soviet-bloc states. And the CDU/CSU said the Social-Liberal coalition was thus under pressure, often self-imposed, to prove the policy's wisdom. Many Union leaders came to suspect that because the Union was in their view free from such pressure, it would be taken as a more formidable negotiating partner in East Berlin and Moscow. Similarly, Union leaders came to believe that their party's unquestioned pro-West credentials would enhance its room for maneuver and credibility in the East: there was less risk of a conservative government entering ambitious commitments and being disavowed by its allies. Finally, Union leaders like Strauss convinced themselves—and others—that the communists would prefer bargaining with conservative infidels to dealing with Social Democratic heretics who might seek to dilute Soviet-bloc orthodoxy with Western revisionism.

Similarly, later in the 1970s opposition leaders made a more concerted, credible effort to promote bipartisanship, which had long had strongly positive associations in West German political culture. Although Barzel was unsuccessful in his 1972 attempt to persuade the party to support Brandt's treaties as a display of bipartisanship, Union arguments in support of the Polish accords in 1976 indicated that the party had come to appreciate that even opposition must be seen as constructive. That this Union behavior was surely influenced by electoral considerations only confirms the appeal of the bipartisan ideal. Moreover, after 1977 Mertes made bipartisanship a routine part of Union policy statements, underscoring areas in which there was agreement and areas in which the opposition critically supported Bonn by backing up official interpretations of the treaties. Growing splits within the SPD gave the Union new chances to support Schmidt and Genscher against their SPD critics. In large part because the Union wanted to appear constructive in its opposition role, the party in effect became a codefender of established policy—Strauss during the Afghanistan crisis, for example—while disagreeing with the policy's original premises.

One final aspect of party strategy worked in favor of a more flexible position. By the late 1970s the Union, in particular the CSU, had reintegrated most right-wing voters: the share of votes won by extremist right-wing parties dropped from 4.3 percent in 1969 to .6 percent in 1972, .3 percent in 1976, and .2 percent in 1980. Plainly it was politically less rewarding to maintain a rigidly uncompromising nationalist-fundamentalist position by decade's end. Strauss's efforts to display statesmanlike flexibility on Ostpolitik in the hectic days of 1980 could be explained by his confidence that the Union's right flank was secure.

Individuals

Finally, the extent to which the Union accepted the need for a more adaptive Ostpolitik depended upon several party leaders.

The Union's adaptation, so cautious and modest, closely paralleled Helmut Kohl's political fortunes. Adaptation was slowest in 1973 and 1974, when Kohl had not yet consolidated his power, and it accelerated in 1975 and 1976 and again after the 1980 elections—moments of Kohl's greatest power as opposition leader.

Though he clearly articulated the argument that German self-determination was an objective compatible with democracy, Kohl's own ideas on Ostpolitik remained largely platitudinous. His real contribution to a more adaptive Union policy lay in his political strategy, which was in turn the more-or-less indirect result of his concern with preserving the Union's tenuous unity while moving the party toward power—preferably in coalition with the FDP. For this purpose, he knew the party must neutralize the Ostpolitik as a political issue and limit the political damage created by the Union's skepticism and opposition. A more flexible Union stance on Ostpolitik could split the SPD-FDP coalition and lay the basis for Kohl's cherished aim: a broad nonsocialist majority government. Yet Kohl also knew that no leader could press the party to move more quickly toward adaptation than its fundamentalists could tolerate.

In his effort to preserve an internal Union consensus while identifying with a broader majority in the country, Kohl created an atmosphere in which two policies could coexist in party thinking and rhetoric. Thus as party and parliamentary chairman, he cautioned against sharp rhetoric and nationalistic overtones and urged bipartisanship. More important, by promoting spokesmen like von Weizsäcker and Mertes, Kohl further contributed to a party policy combining CDU/CSU tradition with the new Ostpolitik. Kohl also tried, with modest success, to replace hard-line fundamentalists in the parliamentary group with his own men. Yet Kohl was careful never to press fundamentalists very far, and was particularly sensitive to the CSU's opposition. He rarely pushed for bold, open changes in party policy (the postelection experience of 1977 was the one chastening exception), which disappointed real supporters of a Union Godesberg on Ostpolitik. Kohl aimed, in short, to integrate new people and policies into the Union without upsetting its internal equilibrium.

In blending orthodoxy and reform, Alois Mertes reflected, but in large part also directed, the Union's adaptation to the new Ostpolitik. The ex-diplomat's political career was advanced by his colleague and former boss from Rhineland-Palatinate, Helmut Kohl. Both men, the multilingual foreign-affairs expert and the provincial politician, constantly stressed that Germany's decision for the West was more than a strategic choice; it reflected a commitment to democratic principles and ideals, a form of recompense for the Nazi years. Mertes also believed that asserting the cause of national unity served as a reminder that the Federal Republic's raison d'être was the restoration of freedom on German soil and was necessary to preclude the emergence of a nationalist party on the Union's right.[33] Finally, Mertes argued that given its past Bonn must put faith in and uphold the law. Thus he defended the orthodox Union emphasis on legal positions and on these grounds articulated a compelling case against the Brandt treaties.[34]

At the same time Mertes was flexible. Moral considerations, he warned, had to inform political decisions, but policy choices—including the Union's opposition to the treaties—resulted from a strictly political risk-benefit analysis. Nor could legal rights alone dictate or constitute policy. Mertes was deeply devoted to preventing unnecessary polemics on such critical fundamental issues from polarizing opinion and undermining the consensus for the FRG's foreign policy. He continually tried to emphasize areas of agreement on principle and in day-to-day matters between government and opposition. In the mid-1970s he urged an end to the divisive Ostpolitik debate, an appeal directed at both sides of the political aisle. Because of his unquestioned integrity and sincerity, and his articulate appeal for a balance between Union orthodoxy and Ostpolitik, Mertes became the Union's most important foreign-affairs spokesman. He shaped an image that many in the party were compelled to live up to.

Like Mertes, Richard von Weizsäcker articulated Union orthodoxy in a nonpolemical way and in tones designed to avoid polarization over Ostpolitik. This manner, and the moral convictions that it conveyed, broadened the appeal of Union ideas and won the party a hearing in otherwise-hostile quarters—among the young, in universities, among liberals, among workers. Although the liberal patrician was not a typical CDU politician, he was an asset for the party and thus valued even by colleagues who disagreed with him. Von Weizsäcker's influence was also enhanced by his position as governing mayor of Berlin after 1981. He became the first Union figure after 1969 to exercise power over a political unit that could vitally affect East-West relations and his chosen representative sat in on an innergroup of Bonn officials who helped formulate government policy.

Von Weizsäcker was thus in a position to help shape his party's policy, and there was an audience for his message of adaptation. He was motivated by the fear that domestic polarization over relations with the East would risk the country's hard-won respectability abroad and its social fabric at home. Von Weizsäcker also believed reconciliation with Poland was a moral imperative and desired as well a policy to ease the daily life of Germany and his adopted home, Berlin.

Somewhat paradoxically, Franz Josef Strauss was another individual who furthered the Union's adaptation to Ostpolitik. By the 1970s Strauss's influence was almost entirely independent of his specific title; his influence inhered in his role as the symbol and most effective exponent of fundamentalist conservatism. He was more important for the CSU than its parliamentarians or even the Bavarian government itself, though in several episodes where CSU interests were at stake, Strauss could not take party support for granted.

Yet Strauss was a shrewd tactician; his success in this regard is borne out by the fact that critics could rarely agree on what to label him, except an opportunist. There were times when Strauss, for varied and mixed motives, saw gain for himself or his party in appearing flexible on Ostpolitik: the 1972 effort to devise a Joint Resolution; the declaration of *pacta sunt servanda*; the 1978 Brezhnev visit; the subsequent trips East; and the generally cautious reaction to the Afghanistan crisis in 1980. Strauss wanted to show that he could outdo his rivals, but he also felt called upon to educate his party to think strategically and pragmatically. Conservatives could and must practice *Realpolitik*, he said, because they could deal more openly and confidently with communists than could socialists. However he might distinguish his "realistic detente" from the SPD's "illusory, romantic detente," Strauss was ready to take over the Ostpolitik positions created by others and abandon some of those the Union had long held.

In the cases when he urged pragmatic adaptation of party principles, Strauss generally had enough credibility to bring many Union fundamentalists along with him. He was thus at one and the same time the party's most effective exponent of both fundamentalism and pragmatism. To be sure, however, Strauss's opportunism and his use of nationalistic rhetoric to resist SPD policy made him to some extent a prisoner of those who were averse to compromise. That relationship prevented him from going very far in facilitating an adaptive Ostpolitik.

Overcoming Ambivalence: Factors Permitting Adaptation

It might seem that the CDU/CSU had sufficient reason for reconciling itself completely to the new shape of West German foreign policy almost immediately after 1972. Indeed, the foregoing discussion alone might imply that it did so. Yet the most notable aspect of CDU/CSU adaptation is perhaps not that it occurred, but that it occurred the way it did—so slowly and ambivalently. Despite many reasons for feeling compelled to accept Bonn's new relationship with the East at the time the treaties were ratified, many Union leaders resisted—some conditionally, others unequivocally. Contrary to most predictions, there was no CDU/CSU Godesberg-type declaration, no Wehner-type speech accepting government foreign policy and setting aside many of the party's past positions.

Instead, even after 1972 the party's endorsement of dialogue with the East was in most cases strictly conditional. The Union continued to insist upon harder bargaining, no concessions on the legal provisionality of the national issue, and pressure to improve human-rights conditions. At times critics despaired that Union rhetoric was becoming harsher than it had been during the early 1970s and that the CDU/CSU might even retreat to positions it held before the Grand Coalition. Kohl's difficulty in even modestly modifying the CDU program in 1977 and 1978, for example and his reluctance to push the CDU/CSU's "Godesberg" very far after the 1980 election show the strength of Union resistance. But it was not merely a dominant fundamentalist majority that blocked a Union Godesberg: most party leaders, a minority aside, remained genuinely ambivalent about SPD-FDP Ostpolitik and its implications.

To be sure, partisan animosity partly explains this hesitance and ambivalence; many party leaders, especially fundamentalists, simply remained unwilling to concede that their SPD rivals' "sell-out policy" had succeeded in easing the effects of partition. More decisive, however, was genuine, persistent CDU/CSU concern about the longer-term impact and implications of SPD-FDP Ostpolitik. The party might have compelling reasons to accept the instrumentalities, practices, and immediate consequences of the new policy. But Union orthodoxy with regard to the German question and East-West relations still led the party to a different, skeptical calculation of the policy's longer-term benefits and risks. Cooperation with communist authorities based on acceptance of the status quo might have become unavoidable for all the reasons already mentioned. Yet Union leaders still failed to see such a policy as the route to resolution of the German national issue. The traditional CDU/CSU view of SED aims and motives gave them little faith in the theory that human contacts would truly "overcome" the division: GDR delimitation would be applied to prevent that. Even reformists like von Weizsäcker argued that the SED's interest in delimitation easily outweighed its (financial) stake in cooperation. Union leaders, needless to say, thought little of Bahr's theory that accommodation would help transform the GDR's internal structures. Persistently and nearly unanimously, they maintained that East Berlin would cut off all contacts rather than permit a process of real liberalization that might threaten the SED's power monopoly.

More important, Union leaders feared that SPD-FDP Ostpolitik could put at risk any plan for achieving German unity in self-determination and might jeopardize Bonn's all-important Westpolitik. Perhaps indirectly, perhaps by design, they argued, the effort to promote German-German accommodation would demand ever-more concessions to the SED. East Berlin could lure Bonn with hints of human contacts into meeting all of its demands for status, resources, and recognition. Talk in the SPD about "stabilizing the SED" and "removing its reason for anxiety" generated CDU/CSU concern that Bonn's government might move in this direction.

Union politicians were equally alarmed about efforts to reinforce German-German relations through the construction of a "new European peace structure." They feared that Bonn's effort to propel detente with pressure for arms control and disengagement could weaken the alliance and isolate Bonn from its Western partners.

Last, for years Union leaders had worried that the new Ostpolitik could corrode the FRG's domestic structures. By making the communist regimes fully equal negotiating partners, by downplaying the underlying power-political and ideological sources of East-West tension, SPD-FDP detente proponents were "blurring the fundamental distinctions between East and West." This, it was feared, would erode the long-term resolve of West Germans to defend the FRG's institutions against Soviet blackmail, penetration, and even subversion.

In other words, after 1972 Union politicians—and not merely fundamentalists—remained far more worried about the Ostpolitik's long-term direction than its initial steps. They feared that Bonn's new Eastern relationship, accidentally or by design, could develop a dangerous momentum toward a fundamental change in the orientation of the Federal Republic.

These concerns by themselves made CDU/CSU adaptation slow and incomplete. But they were reinforced in their effect by the party's very structure and policymaking processes. Although it changed in other respects during the opposition years, the Union remained a decentralized party without a single unchallenged leadership position. The Union was divided internally along functional lines with a persistent institutional tension among subgroups —above all the parliamentary group and the party organizations. More important, despite fluctuations in the CSU's fortunes, the Bavarian sister party's compositional and ideological cohesion, separate structure, share of parliamentary seats, and consequent ability to confront the CDU with a unified bloc vote gave it disproportionate influence within the Union—almost a veto power over decisions on the chancellor candidate, campaign platforms, and parliamentary policy. Moreover, no single nominal leader shaped Union policy. Both Barzel and Kohl were almost permanently on probation. Kohl remained CDU chief for a decade largely because he did not force uniformity upon the party's factions.

Incrementalism and a constant quest for consensus thus dominated Union policy formulation. This was not merely a matter of individual styles but an imperative inherent in the Union's structure that mitigated against major changes in established policy or basic positions. Even after the 1980 election, when Strauss and fundamentalists were seemingly discredited, Kohl felt unable to risk Union unity and thus resisted CDU reformist pressure for a Godesberg-style challenge to party orthodoxy.

An essential part of understanding the CDU/CSU's adaptation to SPD-FDP Ostpolitik thus lies in determining what became of this ambivalence. Developments in the decade after 1972 facilitated CDU/CSU adaptation by permitting the party to overcome, or at least live with, its suspicions about the long-term gains and risks of such a policy.

It was primarily the constraints upon West German foreign policy that led the Union to conclude that dealing with the East on the basis of the status quo would not inevitably lead Germany down a special path toward permanent partition, isolation, and neutralism. It became clear to the CDU/CSU that both international and societal factors so restrained FRG policymakers that the Federal Republic was in no great risk of slipping its Western moorings and drifting into neutralist currents—regardless of its Ostpolitik. This in turn helped Union leaders grow confident that day-to-day, operational Ostpolitik could be safely conducted—especially by a Union government.

International Factors

The FRG's special responsiveness to its external environment explains why the Union came to accept that it *had to* adapt to SPD-FDP Ostpolitik. But this same sensitivity also helps explain why the party felt it *could* adapt.

For Union leaders, SPD-FDP Ostpolitik's long-term risks seemed most grave in the late 1960s and early 1970s when, as Anton DePorte observed, "changes were underway which [it seemed to many], in an atmosphere of relaxation of tension, could have profound effects on the European system."[35] U.S. disengagement from Europe or even a superpower joint condominium seemed at least conceivable. With the postwar system's foundations apparently shifting, the Union feared that FRG leaders would be compelled, and in some cases tempted, to let Bonn's own initially modest policy of detente develop greater momentum, resulting in total abandonment of efforts to keep the German question open, German entry into a Kremlin-dominated all-European collective framework, possibly a German-German confederation, and even eventual neutralization. Certainly Bahr's think-pieces envisioning dissolution of the blocs and the SPD left's talk of East-West convergence fed such fears.

Yet it became apparent, especially after the superpower ardor for detente had cooled, that detente was primarily about the postwar European system's stabilization. Bipolarity and bloc division remained fundamentally intact. Indeed, toward decade's end and in the early 1980s many leading Social Democrats began voicing their disillusionment with the sluggish pace of real change. The crises of 1980 through 1982 compelled Schmidt to choose between the aspirations of many in his party and the imperatives of Bonn's alignment with the West. Despite occasional talk of a divisible detente, Bonn ultimately acknowledged the strength of its ties to the West. Given its sensitivity to the status of relations between the blocs, and given its responsiveness to the attitudes of its Western partners, the FRG could not easily pursue a more ambitious set of relations with the East after the early 1970s. Its room for maneuver was still too limited. Only a more modest, pragmatic, businesslike policy was compatible with the bloc system and Bonn's role in it, especially given the new international environment of confrontation after 1972.

For several years, this was precisely the policy followed by Schmidt, but he eventually became caught in the crosspressures generated by the realities of Bonn's geopolitical role and his own party's aspirations and expectations. Because the Union had always operated on the assumption of an essentially adversarial East-West relationship, it was more comfortable with dialogue when the limits upon it were clear, and this made the party more amenable to the idea of dealing with the East. The CDU/CSU thought it was safer to bargain when, in effect, the stakes were lower—when fundamental change (and thus foreign and domestic pressure to compromise on fundamental issues) was not in prospect. Although dialogue based on acceptance of the status quo still disconcerted many in the Union, that dialogue's potentially greater risks were ameliorated by international constraints on West German policy.

In this same paradoxical way, Union adaptation was also facilitated by the specific constraints which the GDR imposed on inner-German relations. The SED could afford neither a level of human contacts that might create challenges to domestic stability in the

GDR nor a degree of German-German political cooperation that might come at the expense of its effort to maintain a distinct identity. The result was persistent restrictions on contacts and legal delimitation that almost permanently circumscribed the scope and momentum of inner-German relations.

Though Union fundamentalists saw GDR delimitation as confirmation of their skepticism and warnings, even they gradually came to recognize that SED measures mitigated against "hazardous" momentum in the inner-German dialogue. Honecker's intransigence on the—for the FRG—constitutionally unacceptable Gera demands effectively limited the *real* inner-German dialogue to an incremental, and thus more realistic, pace. Gone were the broader visions and the public expectations that such visions would be fulfilled.[36]

This helped the Union to conclude that dialogue with East Berlin need not be risky for the FRG. Because the SED could not risk anything resembling systemic change, Bonn need not offer the type of major concession that it would take to encourage such a transformation. Instead a businesslike, pragmatic give-and-take, a true "regulated coexistence" with expanding contacts and a marginal reduction of tensions, could be undertaken—even, or especially, by the Union. The Union was coming to see some scope for affecting GDR external policy through East Germany's growing economic dependence on Bonn. It believed this created an opportunity to encourage SED flexibility not against, but in accordance with, the GDR's own interests. By late in the 1970s even fundamentalists spoke of encouraging realists in East Berlin with offers of economic ties. Rather than trying to soften status and ideological disputes, the Union wanted to circumvent them, and it believed this was the way.

Societal Factors

Domestic factors also effectively circumscribed SPD-FDP Ostpolitik, thus making its potential long-term risks appear less unavoidable in Union eyes.

Public opinion continually endorsed hard bargaining in relations with the East throughout the decade after 1972. As noted above, Union fundamentalists mistakenly overread this sentiment as hostility to dialogue itself. The sentiment instead reflected dissatisfaction with Soviet-bloc obstinance; support for "harder bargaining" or an "energetic policy" was most marked at times of GDR delimitation or East-West crisis, as in 1973 to 1974, 1976, and during the early 1980s. The public had merely grown more cautious and preferred pragmatic incrementalism to a more active policy and accommodation of Soviet and GDR maximal demands.

Gesamtdeutsch tradition also discouraged Social-Liberal policy from developing what the Union considered its maximum-possible momentum. Although the initial popularity of Brandt's approach reflected widespread acknowledgment outside the Union that reunification was unattainable, there were clear limits on any SPD-FDP attempt to accelerate rapprochement by giving up on the goal of unity.

In this regard, respect for the Karlsruhe verdict played a major role. It presented the SPD in particular with a very narrow interpretation of Brandt's treaties, limiting the scope for further negotiation on status issues, such as the GDR's demand that Bonn recognize its separate citizenship. These court constraints occasionally annoyed Bonn officials by limiting their latitude, and they thoroughly frustrated those in the SPD who considered further GDR status demands as well worth negotiating. In private many grumbled about "that damned court opinion."

Union leaders gradually came to recognize that Karlsruhe would indeed limit Ostpolitik, as they had always said it should. Many thus also came to share Gradl's view that a clear, binding definition of the FRG's remaining legal positions in effect made an active dialogue safer by reducing the risks that negotiations would close the national question altogether.[37] In time, Union programs began to state that so long as Karlsruhe's conditions were met, the treaties could be—and should be—"honored both legally and politically," the party's oblique way of endorsing negotiation.

The West German public, moreover, though willing to accept the division as a basis for negotiations, remained lukewarm toward further steps that might in effect "close" the national question altogether. Polls into the early 1980s continued to show two-thirds support for eventual reunification (even though very few considered the objective a realistic one).[38] It was not difficult to explain this ambivalence. Germans naturally wanted a short-term policy of cooperation as well as a long-term policy that to some extent challenged the division and sustained some hope for unity. Steps beyond those taken by Brandt from 1969 to 1973 proved more difficult for the SPD to sell (especially given GDR delimitation). SPD exponents of new concessions began discovering this limitation in the early 1980s, much to their dismay and to the Union's satisfaction. Public support for granting diplomatic recognition to the GDR or for striking from the West German constitution's preamble a commitment to pursue reunification remained modest.

Coalition politics also played a vital role in limiting the momentum of Ostpolitik. For the FDP leaders, Scheel and above all Genscher, accepting the division and dealing with East Berlin was a tolerable price for cooperation and detente. But there was no long-term FDP vision for totally supplanting Bonn's traditional emphasis on the open German question. Genscher, for example, remained gesamtdeutsch, emphasizing holding open the issue and guarding German rights. Liberal leaders were also more cautious than most of the SPD about trying to press Bonn's Western partners too far in the quest for an East-West detente conducive to Ostpolitik—as the INF debate showed. Consequently after 1973 the Liberals continually urged their larger coalition partner to moderate the pace of Ostpolitik. Despite counterpressure from angry SPD colleagues (such as Brandt, Bahr, Wehner, and Gaus), Schmidt, though irritated, often accommodated the FDP.

International and domestic constraints, then, slowed the pace of Bonn's relations with the East bloc after 1973. Had Helmut Schmidt shared his party's enthusiasm for further developing what Willy Brandt labeled "Ostpolitik II," even he would have encountered limits. A more routine, pragmatic, and businesslike policy, entailing fewer new concessions by Bonn, was most compatible with international conditions and had the most solid basis at home. As the CDU/CSU came to acknowledge this, the party was more easily able to live with its concerns about the Eastern dialogue developing what Union leaders considered a self-dynamic dangerous to the FRG's postwar orientations. The status quo was now one the CDU/CSU, Bonn's status quo party, could live with. That had not been the case in 1972.

CDU/CSU Ostpolitik after 1982

When it regained office in 1982 the CDU/CSU was consequently heir to a dual legacy: its own traditional assumptions regarding relations with the East and the German question, as well as the instrumentalities and practices of the SPD-FDP policy that it felt it *must* and safely *could* adopt. Yet this very ambivalence, the very persistence of its concerns, indicates that the CDU/CSU adapted *despite* and not *because* of its attitudes about the German question and East-West relations. Though the Union felt able to accept the policy's operational dimension, it did so with an instinctive caution and wariness that was rooted in a still largely unchanged, traditional system of beliefs. This wary attitude was especially common among fundamentalists.

Thus, the Union never developed a conceptual framework that might have synthesized or reconciled traditional Union assumptions with the new Eastern dialogue. These elements of policy were by no means entirely antithetical, but neither were they automatically compatible. Yet not only did the Union produce no Wehner speech openly embracing the Ostpolitik, it produced no Bahr to synthesize old and new, to reconcile traditional ideals and principles with the pragmatic Realpolitik practices it had adopted.

To be sure, Mertes and von Weizsäcker did attempt a modest synthesis of Union tradition and SPD-FDP innovation. They justified the case for continuity in relations with the East by stressing that humanitarian measures helped to keep the national question open—a goal of Union orthodoxy—and by contending that detente could defuse certain tensions, even if a totally new peace structure remained beyond reach. Their eloquent articulation of these arguments smoothed over the discrepancy between SPD-FDP practice and traditional Union theory but did not eliminate it altogether. More important, the party as a whole did not always echo Mertes's and von Weizsäcker's argumentation. Instead of reconciling SPD-FDP policy and traditional CDU/CSU beliefs, other Union leaders often simply combined them. There was no dialectical synthesis; the two instead came to coexist in an uneasy tension within a dualistic CDU/CSU approach.

A Dualistic Policy

Specifically, by 1982 the Union was determined to stress the modus vivendi character of the treaties while avoiding any challenge to their practical implications and consequences. The Union insisted it would underscore the legal and political openness of the German question and the provisionality of the inner-German border while upholding the Karlsruhe verdict and thus also rejecting all of Honecker's Gera demands. Although few but the expellee leaders were ready to challenge the Oder-Neisse line as Poland's final border—if only for fear of alienating the Western allies—most party leaders described the Warsaw Treaty as not binding on a future German state. Critics dismissed the attitude toward the Warsaw Treaty as fundamentalist demagoguery and a maximal demand, but standing by traditional positions was for most Union leaders the necessary concomitant of a certain flexibility in dealing with the East. They considered this flexibility tolerable precisely because only under a government that remained firm on fundamental issues would pragmatism clearly not be seen at home or abroad as the first step toward closing the national question altogether. For this very reason, Union leaders were ready to permit themselves a degree of latitude—even on certain status issues—that they had long denied the SPD.

Well before 1982 even Union fundamentalists showed their desire to do business with the GDR. Most avoided any appearance of wishing to destabilize the SED, though they would never admit to the aim of intentionally bolstering it. At the same time the party was willing to meet much of East Berlin's desire for Western capital. It would talk about more balanced terms, reciprocity, and even financial leverage against the GDR, but as was clear during the crises of 1980 through 1982, CDU/CSU threats of "economic punishment" were largely meant to inject caution into SED policy. In truth, the Union increasingly saw itself as a bargaining partner that would offer no concessions on fundamental issues but would instead largely circumvent basic questions of status and ideology by treating the inner-German relationship strictly as a business arrangement. In Union eyes this might well entail a certain indirect stabilization of SED rule by helping the East German economy. Though undesirable, such a side effect was considered tolerable because under a CDU/CSU government mindful of the constraints on FRG foreign policy, there was no risk that this was the first step toward full diplomatic recognition or worse.

In a similar fashion, the Union saw its position on human rights as a prerequisite for dialogue with the Soviet bloc. Although some fundamentalists spoke of human rights as a tool for destabilizing the Soviet bloc, even they toned down their rhetoric when in the East, disavowing any intention to bring communist regimes "before a tribunal." In large part their target audience was a domestic one: stressing human rights would underscore the fundamental distinctions between East and West, dispel any illusion that detente had eliminated basic systemic differences and thereby prevent cooperation with the adversary "across ideological lines" from arousing unsafe expectations of convergence or a special German-German relationship.

Above all, the Union was determined to display solidarity with Bonn's Western allies on detente and security. Party leaders believed arms and arms-control policy had to be based first on the traditional requirements of nuclear deterrence—tempered by the need to soothe the anxieties of an uneasy public—and that the European allies must back American global policy to counter Soviet expansion. Yet the Union also increasingly felt that such solidarity would permit it to shelter FRG Eastern policies from the fallout of East-West confrontation. For as the Afghanistan and Polish crises had demonstrated, the Union believed that a credible Gesamtpolitik permitted it to continue dialogue with the East and would even largely obviate U.S. pressure to impose economic sanctions on Soviet-bloc states.

Put differently, the Union counted on restoring harmony with the West by avoiding overt pressure on its allies to make concessions on arms control and by backing U.S. policies, at least rhetorically, on behalf of Western security outside Europe. It believed that this alliance solidarity would allay U.S. and West European (especially French) suspicions about the ultimate aim of overall FRG foreign policy and thereby win allied approval for Bonn's dialogue with the East. Public opinion and East-bloc leaders alike would then see that Bonn's allies had no intention of restraining its Eastern policies. In this view, by giving its partners every reason to trust its Gesamtpolitik, Bonn could in turn win vital latitude and credibility on Ostpolitik.

CDU/CSU leaders were, accordingly, willing to assert a special stake in the Eastern dialogue—albeit without raising the specter of an autonomous detente policy in tension with Western security. Even so fervent an advocate of trans-Atlantic harmony as Manfred Wörner began urging Washington to understand that more was at stake for the Europeans than for the United States in the future development of East-West relations. This assertiveness was increasingly evident among younger CDU politicians, but also among those like Strauss who had historically resisted what they considered discriminatory treatment of the FRG. In underscoring Bonn's stake in detente, they largely avoided any resentful, nationalistic tones or rhetoric about emancipation of German policy. Instead they treated their assertiveness as a logical reflection of FRG raison d'état and felt that their sound Gesamtpolitik permitted them this latitude.

As it prepared to govern, the CDU/CSU was thus hoping that it could "buy" room for maneuver with financial capital, political capital, and rhetoric that—by clearly stressing the irreducible systemic, ideological, legal, and power-political differences between East and West—clarified the inherent limits of cooperation. In this way the Union hoped to prove itself a more serious and calculable, if less accommodating, negotiating partner for the East, as well as a more reliable ally for the West than its rival had been.

Evaluating the Union's Approach

Critics of the Union found valid reasons for faulting this entire effort to combine two policies without reconciling them. It was indeed, as the SPD charged, an ambiguous and expedient combination, a delicate balancing act meant to preserve unity within the party while winning back voters and wooing the FDP. Plainly, the critics said, sustaining this dualistic policy would not always be possible in practice. Like Schmidt and Genscher, whose policy the Union's had increasingly come to resemble, the CDU/CSU once in power was certain to be confronted at many points with the need to make complex choices, set priorities, and ultimately disappoint certain expectations (at home and abroad).

It was also true, as critics maintained, that party leaders never integrated long-standing CDU/CSU theory about East-West relations and the national question on the one hand with its new approach to the practice of relations with the East on the other—and thus never articulated or even evolved a clear set of long-term strategic objectives. The Union accepted the SPD-FDP coalition's means, but never fully came to grips with the question of ends. Where would its dualistic Ostpolitik lead?

To be sure, Union leaders conceded that dialogue could have certain concrete benefits, but fundamentalists in particular could rarely enunciate a broader, guiding vision of the future. They could almost never convincingly show, for example, how the new relationship with the East served the avowed ultimate goal of CDU/CSU foreign policy: unity in free self-determination. At least since Kiesinger's 1966 government declaration, the party had formally conceded that detente in Europe was a vital prerequisite for such an ideal resolution of the German question, and the party agreed as well that human contacts to some extent helped to keep the national issue open. But in the treaty debates and thereafter, the Union manifested deep doubts that true detente was achievable and made clear its conviction that accommodation on the basis of the status quo, though perhaps unavoidable, was more dangerous than desirable for the pursuit of unity. From the standpoint of Union orthodoxy, absent some fundamental and unanticipated change in Soviet-bloc policy, dialogue could not substantively, substantially improve the situation facing divided Germany, but it could create new risks to Bonn's position in the West. In other words, for the Union the road to unity, like the road to security, led first through the West. Consequently the new Eastern relationship's role in achieving traditional long-term CDU/CSU goals was at best ancillary, at worst dangerously counterproductive.

Having emphatically rejected most long-range SPD scenarios without developing one of its own, the Union in effect divorced ends from means. There was no guiding goal, no widely accepted, overarching CDU/CSU rationale for practical measures it was increasingly willing to sanction and continue. Improved relations, negotiations, agreements, trade, summits with the East—all became desirable in Union eyes, but largely as ends in themselves rather than as elements of an integrated long-term policy for resolving the national question and enhancing West German security.

Yet this pragmatic dualism did not, as its critics maintained, necessarily deprive the nascent Union Ostpolitik of all credibility;

indeed, it created some chance of success, at least in the short term. For what characterized the evolving Union policy above all was a sense of limits. Partly because of its very pragmatism, the CDU/CSU approach was by nature highly sensitive to the many basic constraints and influences on West German foreign policy. This gave the party's policy—however apparent its internal contradictions and ambiguities—some hope for success. Even its lack of a clearly articulated long-term goal had advantages. For although the Union was not motivated by an ambitious vision, neither was it bound by the need to justify such a vision. Unlike its SPD rivals the party felt relatively free from self-induced pressure to vindicate Ostpolitik by transforming dialogue with the East into both a solution for the national question and a broad new peace structure for Central Europe.

Instead the CDU/CSU had developed an all-weather Ostpolitik, one well suited to any change in the climate of East-West relations. Given its special sensitivity to the FRG's external environment, the party aimed to promote relations within the context of a structural East-West confrontation; CDU/CSU Ostpolitik would not be rationalized as a policy designed to overcome that confrontation by reunifying Germany or ending all conflict of interest between the blocs. In the words of Strauss, "Detente is for us not the end of the conflict, but a part of the conflict."[39] Accordingly, though superpower harmony would be most welcome, the Union's policy of pragmatic, regulated coexistence would not impel it to launch initiatives—or press its partners—toward cooperation with the East at the risk of intra-alliance discord. Union leaders hoped that this balance between Ostpolitik and Westpolitik would also enhance its credibility in the East; they aimed to encourage Soviet-bloc leaders who, it was occasionally reported, might almost prefer a CDU/CSU government with whom "they would know where they stand," as opposed to a divided SPD that lacked the full confidence of German voters and Bonn's allies.

Its sense of limits also gave the Union approach a certain credibility in East Berlin. The emerging CDU/CSU Ostpolitik promised no basic change in the character of inner-German relations. Its modest agenda and sober expectations seemed to match the mood of the GDR leadership, which, voluntarily or involuntarily, openly conceded the limits of its own flexibility in dealing with Bonn.

Businesslike bargaining rather than an *entente cordiale* altering either state's place in its own alliance would suit both.

Moreover, the evolving Union approach to relations with the East seemed in harmony with the major domestic forces influencing FRG foreign policy. A decade after its position on Ostpolitik had isolated the Union politically, the party was converging back into the mainstream with a policy that increasingly enjoyed the support of a broad political consensus. Its growing commitment to dialogue satisfied the public's desire for continuity and normalcy. Its support for humanitarian cooperation within the context of a policy that avoided talk of further fundamental compromises on the open German question mirrored the ambivalent state of gesamtdeutsch sentiment in the FRG. It was willing to continue dialogue and thus give the national issue tangible form, yet unlike the SPD it showed little explicit readiness to accept the division as permanent. This entire policy also responded to the imperative of coalition politics, as it was increasingly palatable to the FDP. Unlike the SPD, the CDU/CSU was moving toward rather than abandoning Schmidt-Genscher foreign policy, and thus was moving toward a policy that enjoyed relatively broad public and political support.

Further enhancing the potential credibility of CDU/CSU Ostpolitik was its sensitivity to the balance of opinion within the party itself. A CDU/CSU policy was evolving with which reformists and fundamentalists could be generally satisfied, in part because of its dual character and ambiguity. Kohl's preoccupation with party unity had ensured that the party did not move too fast or to a position it could not sustain.

Consensus in Ambiguity

CDU/CSU adaptation to SPD-FDP Ostpolitik both reflected and in part effected a nascent West German consensus on foreign policy. This consensus rested less on shared aspirations or visions than upon a common acceptance of the factors that limit and shape Bonn's conduct of foreign affairs. These constraints compelled the Schmidt-Genscher government to moderate the pace and narrow the scope of Bonn's relationship with the East, which in turn permitted the Union to overcome its ambivalence about taking up the dialogue. The result was a convergence in the policies of government and opposition—a convergence toward a modest, incremental, pragmatic way of dealing with the Soviet bloc.

Yet the very reasons for this consensus on what was necessary and desirable in the daily conduct of Ostpolitik mitigated against a clearly articulated, shared view of where this policy should ultimately lead. Neither government nor opposition inclined toward shaping its policy to fit a long-term prescription for West Germany's future. Above all, both hesitated to rationalize their support for dialogue by treating it as the first step toward a broad change in Bonn's existing relationships with its European neighbors, East or West. For to do so would risk challenging international and societal constraints on West German foreign policy: Bonn's place in the bloc system, its relationship with the West, Berlin's vulnerability, the imperative of calculability, the public desire for normalcy, the need for a tangible Deutschlandpolitik that left open the national issue, and the requirements of coalition politics.

Indeed, the only clear bipartisan consensus on long-term questions by 1982 was that concepts of fundamental change should be separated as much as possible from the conduct of daily policy. On this, the CDU/CSU, the FDP, and most Social Democrats who supported the government could tacitly agree. Only those on the periphery of the Union and the SPD articulated long-term visions. Unregenerate CDU/CSU fundamentalists clung to the hope of eventually resolving Germany's future on traditional Western terms, that is, against the will of Soviet-bloc leaders; the SPD left held out hope for a detente policy that would help dissolve the blocs or perhaps allow the German states to escape the bloc system. But the political mainstream, swollen by the addition of the CDU/CSU, found vagueness on such long-term questions more suitable. Government and opposition alike increasingly spoke of "overcoming" the national division in the course of "overcoming Europe's division." Europeanization of the German question was, as always, a comfortably imprecise and futuristic formula. And because it was contingent upon developments largely beyond Bonn's control, it made a detailed blueprint seem all the more irrelevant. At most, the daily conduct of relations with the Soviet bloc was depicted by government and opposition as a way to keep open the prospect of positive, peaceful change. But the form that change might take was generally left imprecise.

This ambiguity on the part of government and opposition in the late 1970s and early 1980s may merely have obscured lingering divisions over the issue of Germany's future. After all, it is always relatively easy to reach short-term consensus when powerful constraints leave little room for choice; but conflicting visions and ideals will become more apparent when long-term options are at issue. Perhaps a new round of bitter debate about Germany's role in Europe's future was simply deferred, not defused, by the Union's adaptation to a policy of dialogue. Yet it is also likely that the ambiguity regarding the ultimate ends of West German Ostpolitik accurately indicated a simple uncertainty and ambivalence about the future.

Postscript: The Union in Government, 1982–1988

On 7 September 1987 East German Communist party chief Erich Honecker stepped out of a limousine in the forecourt of Bonn's Chancellory and was met by Helmut Kohl, chairman of the CDU/CSU and, for five years, West German head of government. The two men exchanged greetings and stood at attention while a military band played the national anthems of both German states. In the background hung a row of flags, all displaying the black, red, and gold of Germany, but distinguishable in that every-other one had at its center the images of a hammer and compass encircled by a wreath—emblems of the German Democratic Republic.

With seemingly full diplomatic honors, Helmut Kohl thus welcomed to Bonn the leader of a second German state, the existence of which his party had refused to acknowledge for decades. Although the meeting itself accomplished little, it symbolized the all-but-completely normal relations that now existed between the two countries. Moreover, as the chancellor's top advisor told foreign journalists, "Reunification is completely beyond reality."[1]

Little more than one-half year later, Kohl presided over a gathering of CDU party activists in the convention center at Wiesbaden. After months of tumultuous internal debate the delegates approved with little dissent the party's new platform on foreign policy, which stated that "reunification of Germany is the CDU's most pressing goal." As the minister for inner-German affairs told her party, "If the reunification policy were no longer espoused, then the situation in Europe would change, and in the long run the Federal Republic would no longer be able to pose any resistance to the Soviet Union."[2]

These contrasting images illustrate the ambivalent, at times openly contradictory character of CDU/CSU Ostpolitik. For nearly six years, half as much time as its long exile on the opposition benches, the party continued to pursue a dualistic, two-track policy on relations with the East. Few observers were surprised that Kohl's Union once in power continued to deal with Bonn's Soviet-bloc neighbors, but the enthusiasm with which the party did so caught many off guard. At the same time, although it was widely expected that a Union-led coalition would adopt different tones than its predecessor, the stubborn refusal of Union leaders to modify traditional positions or rhetoric on the issues of unity and security was startling.

This mixture was a legacy of the party's past in government and opposition. As one columnist put it, the Union in 1982 had inherited "a dual legacy full of contradictions"—its own traditional policies dating from the days of Konrad Adenauer and the Eastern policies it took over, with great ambivalence, from the SPD-FDP coalition.[3]

Yet Union policy after 1982 was not strictly a product of the past. Much happened after the change of coalitions in 1982 to reinforce the push for a successful, operational policy—more precisely, dialogue with the East-bloc authorities designed to "normalize" relations and soften the human consequences of Germany's national division. In fact it can be asked whether the Union—in tandem with its new coalition partner, Hans-Dietrich Genscher's FDP—began to go well beyond the mere preservation of continuity and toward a more ambitious Eastern policy of its own.

At the same time, many steps in this direction seemed to be taken against the party's will, and some evoked a reaction, stiffening the determination of many fundamentalist party leaders to preserve intact traditional party principles, including the right to seek state unity and the legally provisional character of existing borders. Indeed, many of the same politicians who raced to strike bargains with the GDR and other East-bloc states most adamantly refused to modify traditional party policy questioning the status quo.

Operational Continuity: Dealing with the East

After 1982 Bonn's Eastern diplomacy moved forward in a series of fits and starts. There were periods of routine continuity such as the early months, times of surprising harmony—even progress—exemplified by Franz Josef Strauss's visit to East Germany in 1983, several years of "damage limitation" as Bonn tried to shelter relations with the GDR and other East European states from a colder East-West climate, and then a steady improvement culminating in Honecker's 1987 visit and Kohl's planned trips to both Moscow and East Berlin. Whatever the variations in tempo and direction, there was almost always some form of movement.

Measured by top-level diplomacy, smooth relations with the East ranked high on the priority list of Kohl and his party. Shortly after his election in 1983 the chancellor went to the Soviet Union. Moscow gave him the cold shoulder for the next five years, hosting most other Western leaders first, but in 1988 Kohl finally received an invitation to meet Mikhail Gorbachev in the Kremlin. He also made official trips to Prague and Budapest—and a surprise private journey to the GDR.

Chancellory officials Wolfgang Schäuble and Horst Teltschik represented their chief in East Berlin and Moscow, respectively. Other CDU/CSU cabinet ministers traveled East to discuss issues falling within their own portfolios—Post, Transport, Ecology, and Science and Technology.

A whole host of party officials showed up in East Berlin, including von Weizsäcker (1983), while mayor of West Berlin, and his successor in that post, Eberhard Diepgen (1987), as well as Baden-Württemberg's Lothar Späth and—most significant—Franz Josef Strauss. The Bavarian flew his own plane to Leipzig on several occasions, once to arrange a huge trade credit for the GDR; in late December 1987 he toasted Gorbachev in the Kremlin. President von Weizsäcker and Lothar Späth also visited the Soviet Union in the late 1980s. Parliamentary chief Dregger took delegations to Moscow (1985) and Warsaw (1985).

As for FDP Foreign Minister Genscher, his near-constant travels included official visits to every East-bloc capital but Tirane and an unofficial stop in the GDR. According to one popular quip, "Two planes cross paths—Genscher sits in both."

Despite Bonn's best efforts, no top Soviet leader aside from the foreign minister visited Bonn between 1982 and 1988, but East European party chiefs came, as did a number of East German Politburo members. GDR parliamentary president, Horst Sindermann, accepted the SPD's invitation in 1985, and after considerable wrangling about protocol, was greeted by both Kohl and his West German counterpart, the Bundestag president.

As for a summit between Kohl and Honecker, it was arranged and then deferred on several occasions: the two leaders seemed able to meet only in the general vicinity of a coffin, at the funerals of world leaders. In 1984 Dregger's sarcastic comment downplaying a summit in Bonn—"Our future does not depend on whether Herr Honecker pays us the honor of a visit"—offered a pretext for cancellation, but in fact it was Moscow that restrained the GDR leader from going to the West. Bonn's disappointment at the delay and its embarrassment at Dregger's remarks only underscored how anxious the Kohl government was to host Honecker. To detect any sign of when the SED chief might actually come, Bonn officials dissected every remark Honecker made, from public speeches to a ten-minute chat about machine tools with West German businessmen at the Leipzig Trade Fair.

In high-level and working-level meetings, Kohl's government continued to negotiate on every major topic pursued by the SPD-FDP coalition—and on issues it introduced on its own. Bonn sought agreements with the GDR on, for example, cleansing the River Röde, facilitating postal deliveries, increasing the number of days per year a West German or West Berliner could spend in the East, reducing the mandatory minimum exchange for pensioners and children, limiting the transit of third-world refugees from East Berlin to the West (July 1985), renovating some transit routes (1985), granting city partnerships (1986), formulating general guidelines for cooperation on nuclear reactor safety (1987), and developing a plan permitting West Germans to deposit funds directly into the East German accounts of their relatives. Capping these successes was an accord on cultural relations (1986) and general agreements on ecological and scientific cooperation (1987).

Under existing agreements the GDR permitted an increase in Western visits by East German pensioners to 3.8 million in 1987, involving more than 1.5 million individuals. More significant, the number of travel permits to those under retirement age, which had remained nearly constant from 1973 to 1981, doubled to 60,000 in 1983, remained relatively constant for two more years, and then shot up dramatically to nearly 600,000 in 1986 and 1.2 million in 1987. In sum, during 1987 over 2.5 million East Germans out of a population of 17 million visited the Federal Republic. As minister for inner-German affairs, Dorothee Wilms, declared, "This volume of travel is unprecedented since construction of the Wall."[4]

Youth and sports-group exchanges continued to increase, though more slowly: in 1987 over 60,000 young West Germans spent time in the East, and 4,000 of their East German counterparts came to the FRG. Emigration from the East also rose to over 40,000 in 1984, before settling down to between 10,000 and 25,000 in subsequent years.

There was progress on other fronts. Through 1987 some three dozen city partnerships were arranged, with hundreds more in the proposal stage. Over 90 percent of all East German communities had direct-dial phone connections with the Federal Republic by 1988.

A less widely publicized arrangement—payments for the release of political prisoners in the GDR—also bore fruit, as the number purchased hit a record of 2,500 in 1985.[5] In 1988 Bonn also won freedom for a prominent songwriter and civil rights advocate who had aroused the SED's wrath by exploiting the symbol of martyred Marxist Rosa Luxemburg and her appeal for tolerance of dissent.

Some signs of progress were more unclear. Though at times East Germany appeared to curtail the order to shoot at would-be escapees, an occasional death still occurred at the border. Dismantling of GDR automatic firing devices was followed by erection of more modern, albeit less lethal, detection systems. The accords on sports exchange and cooperative environmental policy remained vague declarations of intent, and East Berlin demanded FRG financing and technology for large-scale efforts to clean up border rivers. When a slightly larger number of GDR tourists started remaining in the West in late 1987, the regime cut the amount of money it customarily gave its citizens visiting the West, and the number of travel permits to be issued in the future appeared in doubt. East Berlin urged Bonn to stop giving East German tourists packets of money and grant the GDR a lump sum instead.

Nonetheless the progress made during the mid-1980s was impressive. One newspaper called it "A Small Miracle for the Germans."[6]

By contrast, Bonn-Moscow ties languished, at least in the Kohl-Genscher government's early years, largely because of Soviet efforts to isolate Bonn and punish it for deploying U.S. missiles in 1983. But accords on consular relations, scientific exchange, and economic cooperation (extending the 1978 agreement between Schmidt and Brezhnev) were signed, and in 1987 the emigration of ethnic Germans from Russia reached its highest level since 1950. Although relations with Poland stagnated during the early 1980s, emigration of ethnic Germans rose from some 27,000 in 1986 to over 48,000 the following year.[7]

The Price of Progress

What price was the Kohl government and the chancellor's party willing to pay for this kind of progress?

For one, the party no longer sought to deny the GDR legitimacy as a negotiating partner. Though adapting to the idea of dialogue while in opposition, the CDU/CSU had steadfastly maintained that Bonn could bargain without enhancing the SED regime's status. Yet after the Union entered government, party leaders abandoned this maxim.

When the president of the GDR Parliament, Sindermann, accepted an invitation from the SPD to a meeting in Bonn, for example, the government was in a quandary: How should Bonn officially treat this visitor from an institution that it said wrongly put the GDR on an equal plane with the Federal Republic, thus legitimizing the SED regime and the nation's partition? After weeks of wrangling, an arcane compromise emerged: Bundestag president Philipp Jenninger would not greet Sindermann in his office (an unwanted elevation of the latter's status) or elsewhere (an insult), but at his official residence.

After Sindermann's visit, moreover, the Union became increasingly flexible on the idea of formal contacts between the two German parliaments. Genscher's FDP had long since endorsed such a dialogue, and Kohl's Chancellory officials, led by Wolfgang Schäuble, intimated their agreement. In 1987 the CDU granted its conditional acceptance. Only the CSU held out, maintaining that legitimizing the GDR Parliament as a legal equivalent of the Bundestag implied that it was an organ guaranteeing self-determination for East Germans. But in 1988 Strauss rebuffed his own party's spokesman and gave parliamentary contact approval, so long as West Berlin's deputies were not discriminated against in any way. After all, he noted, the Bundestag had long-standing ties with such bodies as the Supreme Soviet, which also failed to meet Western democratic standards. Unless it showed flexibility, he noted, the CSU would be isolated on the issue.[8]

In Berlin the CDU demonstrated even greater readiness to abandon its shyness about official contacts. While mayor, von Weizsäcker visited East Berlin without the company of Bonn's permanent representative to the GDR; his successor, Eberhard Diepgen, did likewise in 1988. This effectively did away with Union insistence that Berlin officials stress their city's links with the FRG in dealing with Honecker's regime.

Events marking Berlin's 750th birthday in 1987 likewise raised questions of status. Diepgen urged Honecker to attend an event in West Berlin, pledging that the West German national anthem would not be played, and promising to accommodate—if not give in to—Honecker's insistence upon being treated as a head of state and to find a compromise allaying Honecker's concern about the presence of Kohl and President von Weizsäcker as "domestic" rather than "foreign" guests. Ultimately Moscow, jealous of its occupation rights, dissuaded Honecker from attending. For his part Diepgen wanted to accept an invitation to festivities in East Berlin, arguing that this was a "community" function and thus no infringement upon Four Power status. The Western powers took a dim view of Diepgen's plan, which in any case also fell through.

Preparations for the Honecker visit provoked more debate over protocol: Should substantive discussions take place in the capital or in some more remote place; should Honecker be permitted to meet the federal president in the latter's office or in some convenient castle? Yet by September 1987 Bonn had overcome its status anxiety and welcomed the SED chief as a head of state. A Kohl aide cooly dismissed decades of Union policy by remarking that the "special character" of inner-German relations was more a matter of substance than of external form.[9]

In only one area was the CDU/CSU still unwilling to compromise: though the SPD and FDP had established formal ties with their East German counterparts, the SED and the GDR Liberals, an officially tolerated opposition, the Union would not deal with the East-CDU, calling it another illegitimate tool of the regime. Yet even in this area there were hints of change: some CDU leaders, led by Secretary-General Geissler, stressed the need for contact with *all* social and political groups in the GDR.

In his characteristically blunt fashion, Strauss remarked that status issues should not be "sacred cows."[10] In this spirit of reform the Union sacrificed another tenet of its orthodoxy: the proscription against stabilizing the GDR.

While in opposition the party had disavowed any intention to destabilize the GDR, but it had always held that Bonn's policy should by no means be designed to ease East Berlin's internal problems at the expense of human interaction and human rights. After 1982, however, the Union-led government was always very careful not to let the push for these latter goals become too great a threat to the SED.

When East German tourists flooded the FRG's embassy in Prague seeking emigration visas, Bonn cautiously warned them away. Kohl's minister in the Chancellory, Philipp Jenninger, declared it was not Bonn's policy to depopulate the GDR.[11] Four years later the number of East German tourists who stayed in the West increased from .3 percent to 1.0 percent, and East German church officials complained that the increase in travel from East to West could destabilize the GDR. Bonn rejected their plea to stop offering East Germans citizenship rights in the Federal Republic, yet insisted it was doing nothing to encourage emigration.

Moreover, by the late 1980s Bonn was meeting the SED regime's every financial need through official and commercial transactions. Private visitors from the Federal Republic alone provided the GDR with roughly 1.5 billion marks annually in the 1980s, paid out for the mandatory minimum exchange, visa charges, special taxes in shops for foreigners, and gifts to East German relatives. Yet the Kohl government added much more, expanding its lump-sum payment to cover the user's fees the GDR would otherwise charge West Germans traveling on the transit routes to Berlin (500 million marks annually) and giving out more money to cover the costs of inner-German postal and telephone service: 200 million marks per year, more than double the amount paid until 1982.

Special projects cost the Bonn government additional money: a new highway link between Berlin and Hamburg (largely completed during the Schmidt years, 1 billion marks), renovation and expansion of existing transit routes and bridges (700 million marks), investments in improved rail lines to Berlin (150 million marks). Although many of the most expensive projects came to an end in the late 1980s, one observer noted that "the federal government and the [Berlin] Senate have many [new] wishes, for the fulfillment of which they are ready to pay hard currency."[12]

Bonn also signed trade agreements with East European states and in 1985 agreed to extend the interest-free overdraft or "swing" in trade with the GDR by 25 percent. Strauss pushed for a special trade agreement between the European Community and Hungary.

Most notable, however, was the government's willingness to grant the East bloc credit. No event was more remarkable in this regard than its guarantee of a one-billion-mark credit to the GDR in 1983, set up by Strauss after a surprise flight to meet Honecker in Leipzig. Kohl's Chancellory officials quietly suggested that they had in effect set up the arrangement but allowed Strauss to take credit on the assumption that only a die-hard fundamentalist could get away with making such a sharp U-turn in Union Deutschlandpolitik.

To be sure even Strauss caught fire for this about-face. Dismayed CSU activists sharply attacked him for coddling the GDR. At the 1983 CSU party conference he received only about 80 percent of the votes for reelection as party chairman, which, measured by past standards of near unanimity, amounted to a stinging rebuke. Yet ultimately he prevailed by urging the party to trust his sense of strategy.

From that point on there was no reversing the tide. The old CDU/CSU idea of a "businesslike" dialogue became reality in the fullest sense of the term. Additional credits were extended to the GDR in 1984 (again one billion marks), to Hungary in 1987 (also the round figure of one billion marks) and—most significant—to the Soviet Union in 1988. A group of West German banks granted the Kremlin over two billion dollars (3.5 billion marks) in credit, the largest such East-West deal since the 1982 gas-pipeline controversy.

Regardless of whether the government gave these credits special guarantees or not (in the Soviet case the transaction was purely commercial), it encouraged them, and Union officials could not hide their delight with the deals. If the steady, incremental expansion of trade with the East bloc and the GDR ended in 1985 and commerce actually began to languish, it was not for lack of Western incentives (the real culprit was a drop in world oil prices).

On only one trade issue did the Union show caution, and even there only briefly. As part of the compromise ending the 1982 quarrel over the gas-pipeline project, Bonn had agreed to help review and where necessary tighten the CoCom restrictions on "strategic" goods, or goods deemed by the Western alliance and Japan to have potential military applications. Many Union officials later complained that this list needed to be loosened, and they became less cautious about pressing this case after Strauss, on a visit to the Kremlin in early 1988, and Ronald Reagan at his 1987 summit with Gorbachev, expressed a similar desire to loosen trade restrictions.

The Union conceded that all of Bonn's payments, trade, and credits inevitably helped the GDR and other East-bloc states to stabilize their economies and thus their societies as a whole. The size of the flow of cash and credit underscored the willingness of Union officials to temporize on another of their own guidelines for dealing with the East bloc. Rainer Barzel, briefly minister for inner-German affairs during the government's early days, had promised an end to "money in exchange for promises." But as the CDU/CSU avidly began to purchase progress, it rarely insisted upon a strict quid pro quo: economic benefits were offered with no binding assurances of reciprocity.

No event illustrated this new flexibility more vividly than Strauss's credit. After all, in 1970 Strauss had said "I do not think much of offering the communist world credits and linking to it the belief that one can suddenly get political concessions."[13] As if a surprise flight to Leipzig and a meeting with Honecker were not enough to shatter his carefully cultivated image as a hard-liner, the Bavarian boss proudly claimed credit for arranging the deal even though East Berlin gave no public assurance that it would lead to greater emigration or cancel the East German order to shoot. To shocked observers Strauss proclaimed, "I have become more flexible in my [choice of] means."[14]

To be sure, government officials stressed that the taxpayers had not lost a pfennig on the deal and that in return East Berlin provided "a series of positive signals": increased travel, smoother transit, a reduction in the mandatory minimum exchange for children—in short an end to eight years of stalemate.[15] Yet no such promises appeared in public: the Union-led government had accepted private assurances with no binding effect.

Similarly, Bonn backed a credit to Hungary and encouraged the unguaranteed credits to the Soviet Union (1988) though the communist-bloc states never publicly promised to reciprocate. Except with the 1984 billion-mark credit, any Eastern counter-concessions were left unstated. Barzel's successor as minister for inner-German affairs, Heinrich Windelen—himself a leading fundamentalist expellee—declared, "We have at least in this point backed away from the strict causality of give-and-take."[16]

When rumors of yet another billion-mark credit to the GDR surfaced in 1987, Union officials endorsed the idea. In response to the question of what Bonn would demand for its money, the CSU's Eduard Lintner, Union parliamentary spokesman for Deutschlandpolitik, said, "I have always been against preconditions" (though he added that progress required a give-and-take). One Bonn politician *did* insist that this credit be part of a negotiating package converting "vague declarations of intent" into concrete improvements in inner-German relations—but he was from the SPD.[17]

Equally unabashed was the Kohl government's readiness to forget the Union's long-standing demand for completely unambiguous agreements. Some of Bonn's accords with the East contained the type of vague formulas that the Union in opposition had so often fiercely condemned. To ensure completion of an accord regulating cultural relations with the GDR in 1986, for example, the government settled for a clause that only vaguely designated West Berlin as part of the FRG and another that permitted each state to operate according to its own legal principles. These same formulas had earned sharp criticism from the Union opposition in the 1970s. The conservative *Frankfurter Allgemeine Zeitung* predicted problems arising from this vague wording, noting sardonically that "the government wanted to prove that it can do as well with East Berlin as its predecessor. It has succeeded."[18]

On status and financial questions the Kohl government was clearly willing to satisfy its negotiating partners and receive in return either vague promises or vague formulas. By no means was this always the case, yet plainly the CDU/CSU, including fundamentalists, had little trouble overcoming qualms about copying its predecessor's approach.

Moreover some more assertive CDU leaders were willing to push the new Ostpolitik even when it could lead to a collision with the United States. Although Washington gave the FRG's Eastern policy firm support, there were moments of irritation. In Berlin the CDU desire for dialogue led mayors von Weizsäcker and Diepgen to encroach upon Four Power prerogatives, such as when they made visits to the East. CDU hints that a way might be found around the Gera demands prompted the chief of America's mission in Berlin, John Kornblum, to point out that such issues as the German citizenship question could not be looked at only from a German point of view, as a change in policy had implications for Four Power rights. When U.S. concerns about German-German dialogue mounted von Weizsäcker observed, "Americans can rely on the Germans as partners . . . but only if [they] take Germans as they are [and do] not try to alter the geopolitical and human conditions of life. We West Germans have special responsibilities for the Germans in the East Germany."[19]

So great was the continuity in policy under the CDU/CSU-led government that in 1984 the coalition parties hammered out a joint resolution with the SPD on Deutschlandpolitik. Though such official bipartisanship did not last, there was little concealing the Union's degree of commitment to—and degree of success in—continuing and in fact expanding the dialogue with the East it had inherited.

Sources of CDU/CSU Ostpolitik

Not only did Kohl's party let relations with the East continue to move forward, then, but it put Ostpolitik on full steam and fueled the momentum with sizable lumps of credit. Given its lingering reservations about accepting the status quo—or worse, an unhealthy change in it—why was the party so willing to bargain with, stabilize, and effectively legitimize its Eastern partners?

The International Dimension

Certainly the party had already discovered in opposition that returning to a policy based on rejection of the status quo would be incompatible with the consolidation of Europe's bloc system, contrary to the wishes of its own allies, a sign of dangerous unreliability, and potentially risky for Berlin. Any doubts about these facts of life were dispelled by Italian foreign minister, Guilio Andreotti, who in 1984 provoked controversy among fundamentalists in Bonn by proclaiming, "There are two German states and it should remain two." Austria's chancellor confirmed that Andreotti "expressed more clearly what all think."[20]

Yet to say that its international environment prevented the Union from returning to a policy of challenging the status quo is only to restate the lesson it learned during the years in opposition. What needs explanation is why the party seemed willing to go forward so far and so quickly. Here too international factors played a role.

Shifting winds on the international scene in the early 1980s made it especially prudent for the Union to keep relations with the East on an even keel. The early and mid-1980s saw a return to sharp superpower confrontation and sustained Soviet efforts to split Washington from its NATO allies, above all on the issue of American INF deployments in Europe. Kohl's party stood behind U.S. policy, knowing that this support could cause Moscow to punish Bonn by isolating it diplomatically—especially from East Berlin. To guard against such a freeze in inner-German relations, which might feed domestic pressure not to deploy American missiles and exacerbate anti-U.S., anti-NATO sentiment, the Union became ever-more willing to buy protection for its Eastern relations: better to make financial sacrifices than to be forced into making concessions at the expense of Bonn's good name with the West.

Consequently the party leadership chose to limit the potential damage by extending a substantial trade credit to East Berlin. Heinrich Windelen described the idea this way:

> The situation of the new federal government was not simple. It had from the beginning on clearly given people to understand

its priorities in the stationing question: if we were faced with the decision between inner-German relations and the security of the Federal Republic in the Western alliance, we would decide in favor of the latter. It can be imagined how the opponents of the arms modernization would have exploited it. . . . Through the guarantee [of the credit] the new federal government could signal that it was thoroughly prepared to cooperate with the GDR so long as its security and alliance interests were consistently protected.[21]

Paradoxically this same consideration remained important even after the thaw in superpower relations began after 1985. Almost all Union officials suspected that Mikhail Gorbachev's seductive diplomacy of smiles would offer an opportunity for smoother relations —in Germany as elsewhere—yet such an opportunity could divide the alliance if detente were offered only at the price of compromises on West German security.

Consequently Bonn sought to put its relations with Moscow and East Berlin on a more solid foundation through dialogue and commerce. In 1985 a delegation of party parliamentary leaders journeyed to Moscow in hopes of patching up relations. Though Dregger's group got a frosty reception, it "clearly attached great value to portraying the talks as useful and positive."[22] At the same time, the Union began removing all protocol obstacles to a Honecker visit.

Precisely because it was ambivalent about the fact of progress in European arms control following the Reykjavik summit of 1986, the Union further accelerated its effort to improve relations with the East; it did not want its hard-line security policy to be blamed for derailing detente and crushing hope of more harmonious inner-German relations. Kohl's party (if not the FDP) played a double game: trying to prevent arms control from developing a momentum it considered dangerous to West German security (by leading to removal of all U.S. INF or even all U.S. nuclear missiles from Germany), while welcoming the new East-West detente and the renewed impetus it could give to Ostpolitik.

So even as its leaders stood alone against the zero option and the INF treaty, the Union called for expanded dialogue, granted a new round of credits, prepared for the Honecker visit, and tried to arrange a Kohl-Gorbachev summit. In early 1988 Strauss finally made his long-desired trip to the Soviet Union, where he clinked glasses with Gorbachev in the Kremlin, declared that "the postwar period is over . . . a new era has begun," and basked in the glow of having beaten the chancellor to Moscow.[23]

In other words, precisely because of its ambivalence about East-West arms control, the Union leadership felt it necessary to keep dialogue going with the East (it ultimately gave in on the zero option more because of allied than Eastern pressure). It wanted to show the SED and the Kremlin Bonn's interest in detente and if possible forestall further Eastern pressure for another round of concessions on security and arms control.

In short, CDU/CSU leaders continually tried putting Bonn's relations with the East on a solid foundation through diplomacy, reinforced by credit, thus guarding against Kremlin efforts to isolate Bonn either by outright pressure (as in 1983 and 1984), or by exclusion from the new thaw in East-West relations (after 1985). Fluctuations in the climate of overall East-West relations in the 1980s made it imperative for the CDU/CSU to continue constructing an all-weather Ostpolitik that did not come at the expense of its security or alliance policies. Ironically the Union aroused both allied criticism for doggedly obstructing arms control and some Western suspicions about its undue interest in smooth relations with the East.

Another international development reinforced this pursuit of an active dialogue: the effort of East European regimes, including the GDR, to develop somewhat greater domestic legitimacy in part through expanded political and economic relations with the West. This had long been apparent in Hungary's case, but the 1980s saw a newly assertive, increasingly flexible GDR approach to relations with Bonn. It was Honecker who, at the height of tension over the missile deployment in 1983, pledged his willingness to "limit the damage" to Bonn–East Berlin relations, even if this meant subtly resisting Soviet efforts to isolate the FRG. In 1986 the East German leader virtually opened the floodgates, permitting an unprecedented flow of short-term visitors to the FRG. Despite subsequent second thoughts about permitting too great an increase in human contacts, the SED proved an accommodating partner, at least in contrast to earlier years.

CDU/CSU officials took note of this GDR flexibility, which they attributed to the Honecker regime's awareness that, "A dramatic worsening of the inner-German relationship could not leave economic relations between [the two states] untouched." They suspected that the SED needed Western trade and contacts to establish a "minimal consensus" with its own population based on improved standards of living and travel opportunities, defusing pressure for major internal reform.[24] Inner-German affairs minister Heinrich Windelen conceded: "One can not underestimate the degree of support that [SPD-FDP] policy with its results found in the 1970s in both parts of Germany. Above all with regard to the GDR. Here the inner-German special relationship has developed into a psychological possession of the population, to an expectation, a demand on the regime, which must avoid disappointing it."[25]

After 1985 Gorbachev's program for domestic restructuring opened the way to still-further Soviet bloc involvement in the international economy. Though the GDR leadership resisted Soviet pressures to demonstrate greater openness at home, it, like other East European states, welcomed this new latitude for expanded relations with the West.

Consequently the Union saw greater opportunities to effect some change, if not liberalization, in Eastern Europe. Strauss argued that Bonn's financial relationship with Hungary allowed it to promote a process of change leading to less state control of the economy and even modest steps toward democratization. Dregger hinted that Bonn could indirectly help promote Hungarian style reform in the GDR. One veteran of the antitreaty campaign described graphically how financial inducements could make the GDR dependent —"like an addict."[26]

Certainly the Union's critics could rightly maintain that the party in effect struck it lucky: the winds of change under Gorbachev and East Germany's growing inclination to ease up on, if by no means end, delimitation measures would make any Bonn government's Ostpolitik look good. Yet the point is that in financial and diplomatic terms Kohl's party was already matching this flexibility in part to ensure against an Ostpolitik stalemate that could be used to drive a wedge between Bonn and its allies. Smooth relations with the East—whatever their long-term effect—were seen as a vital way to stabilize the status quo.

The Domestic Dimension

Yet international factors, which had played the decisive role in compelling Union leaders to modify their Ostpolitik during the 1970s, did not generate the major dynamic of the party's new, more ambitious efforts of the 1980s (though they gave a policy of dialogue greater urgency and latitude). In fact the very threat that a stalemate in relations with the East could be used as a wedge between Bonn and its allies only underscores the fact that this policy was increasingly driven by domestic forces that no government could ignore. After 1982 these factors took on considerably greater weight, ensuring that Kohl's government, far from turning the clock back, would set it forward.

Certainly economics played a role, albeit a supporting one. After they were involved in financing East-bloc states, FRG banks had reason to continue promoting growth in those states. Trade with the East remained vital to certain West German industrial sectors; the GDR was as always an important market for machine exports. Moreover, growing East-bloc demand for Western high technology seemed to offer promise of brisk business, and FRG firms wanted to reduce the CoCom restrictions on exports.[27]

Inevitably this influenced CDU/CSU policy. What Kohl's national security advisor, Horst Teltschik, had to say about overall West German trade had a bearing on relations with the Soviet bloc: "The Federal Republic's foreign trade involvements, the fact that every third job is dependent on exports . . . show to what degree foreign policy must bear in mind the foreign trade interests of our country."[28] The party remained as wary as ever of sanctions adversely affecting German exporters. Moreover it sought to expand trade, in part for economic reasons. While in Moscow, for example, both Späth and Strauss promoted trade between their high-tech regions and the Soviet Union, clearly convinced that with the right political climate, lucrative new export markets could be established.

Yet the FRG interest in Eastern and especially inner-German trade continued to be motivated as much by politics as by economics. Although such commerce expanded in the early 1980s, it dropped in 1986 and 1987, and in any case it remained a marginal share of overall West German foreign trade—roughly 6 percent. Even with ever-more help from Western banks, East-bloc states lacked the means to finance a much larger volume of purchases from the FRG through credit or export revenue. Though West German business and finance wanted to spur more commercial interaction, the overall economic rewards were still seen as modest. Indeed for some time it was uncertain whether credit granted to Moscow in 1988 would have to be used for Soviet purchases of FRG goods only or whether it could be used to cover imports from any country.

Inner-German trade gave rise to equally modest expectations. The primary items shipped from the GDR remained textiles, agricultural goods, and refined oil products, none of which were short in the West. In the words of one economic journalist, German-German commerce "seems now to have reached its limits. . . . The explanation [why Bonn remains so committed to it] is simple: the federal government sees in inner-German trade a political instrument. . . . to strengthen the ties between the two parts of Germany." A Chancellory official conceded as much: "The situation can be reduced to following brief formula: the GDR is principally interested in intra-German trade for economic reasons, while the interest of the Federal Republic of Germany derives primarily from political motives."[29]

For plainly the party had better reason than ever to believe that West Germans desired a policy of normalization with the East and specific, tangible steps softening the impact of Germany's division. Even if the euphoria of the early 1970s had long since waned and the hoped-for wave of resurgent gesamtdeutsch sentiment never materialized, practical cooperation with the East was for most West Germans tantamount to the long-sought normalization and the sine qua non of successful Deutschlandpolitik. During the height of East-West tension over NATO missile deployments, three quarters of those polled wanted to protect inner-German and Eastern relations from damage.[30]

After Gorbachev's "new thinking" took tangible form, the public expected Bonn to reciprocate. By 1987 the Soviet leader was more popular among Germans than the U.S. president and fewer Germans believed in the existence of a Soviet threat. As one official put it, "For our politicians here the best bet at every turn of the road is to say they want the [detente] process to continue."[31]

Union leaders knew that downplaying or disregarding detente

could undermine the political consensus for their overall foreign and security policy (a factor contributing to the offer of credit to the GDR in 1983). Moreover they saw some evidence that dialogue and contacts could in some respects sustain gesamtdeutsch consciousness. Even Strauss argued that practical and humanitarian steps to keep alive a sense of national solidarity have "revived the desire for the restoration of the unity of our German fatherland," and he warned the party to avoid creating the impression that it follows such a course "only half-heartedly and would much rather pursue a hard course of gruff delimitation if political conditions in Bonn permitted it."[32]

Moreover, clearly no CDU/CSU leader wanted to hand the Ostpolitik issue back to the SPD if it could be avoided. From 1982 the Union had effectively deprived its rival of any right to claim a monopoly on success in dealing with the East. In 1983 and 1987 this topic had played little role in the elections and the Union preferred it that way. In fact, by contrast to the SPD, whose leaders were distancing themselves from the relatively cautious approach of Helmut Schmidt, the Union appeared as the defender of established policies.

Intracoalition politics and party strategy also dictated a smooth, successful relationship with the East. Genscher and his appointees continued to dominate the Foreign Ministry. Although defense and inner-German affairs were not in his portfolio, Genscher in effect shaped Bonn's relations with Eastern Europe. As his own advisors pointed out, affairs of this region, as well as German-Soviet ties, took up an increasing proportion of his time.

It was plain where the FDP wanted to take its coalition partner. Prior to the 1987 election Genscher stated flatly, "With us there will be no return . . . to the time before the Eastern treaties or the Helsinki Final Act, not in thought, not in action, not in rhetoric."[33] The foreign minister became ever-more ambitious in his goals: especially after the ascent of Gorbachev, he was said to see hope for a broad set of political and military confidence-building measures. He welcomed the new Kremlin leader's emphasis on the shared destiny of European states, symbolized by the image of a "common house." Negotiations and growing interdependence would, in this view, act as a buffer against tension. Advisors hinted that Genscher saw himself fulfilling the role of a modern-day Gustav Stresemann, the Weimar-era foreign minister. (Since historians differ as to whether the latter's goals were reconciliation or revision of the Versailles settlement, this comparison raised more intriguing questions than it answered.) Beyond dispute was the popularity of his foreign policy; Genscher consistently received the highest approval ratings of any West German leader in the late 1980s.

Though Union leaders were frustrated with an FDP monopoly of the cabinet's most important post—no CDU/CSU politician had been foreign minister since 1966—they could not safely challenge their coalition partner. Kohl's party remained as dependent on the FDP as ever; there was never any hope of shaking off this irritating but indispensable partner. The Liberals did undergo a series of setbacks early in the first legislative period after jumping to the Union, actually leading to the Genscher's resignation as party chief. But by 1987 with strong showing in the federal election and a series of state-level victories, they were clearly resurgent, and observers credited Foreign Minister Genscher's popular detente policies.

It was clear the Union would long need the FDP to build a majority. At the state level, the CDU could cling on to its control of lower Saxony under Ernst Albrecht only by maintaining a team with the FDP. Similarly, CDU cabinets in Berlin, Rhineland-Palatinate, and Hesse all rested on Liberal support; any CDU hopes of regaining power in states where it did not control the government also rested upon coalition with the FDP. Only Strauss's CSU and Späth's CDU in Baden-Württemberg seemed able to govern without the FDP. At the federal level, the Union fell from its fine 49 percent showing in 1983 to 44 percent in 1987, while the Liberals jumped from 7 percent to 9 percent.

Given this dependence, the Union had to avoid alienating the FDP on coalition foreign policy. Trying to dissuade disenchanted Union expellees from sharp attacks on the FDP and convince them to keep supporting government policy, Windelen declared, "So long as we have no majority, we need a coalition partner."[34]

The very popularity of Genscher's foreign policy and, eventually, of his party as well led to new strategic calculations that further reinforced the Union's active Ostpolitik. CDU General-Secretary Geissler argued that voters had grown more fickle and no longer felt bound to support one party. He pointed to the existence of two camps or *Lager* in the West German electorate, one composed of center-right voters who gladly voted CDU/CSU or FDP, the other a left-wing bloc of SPD and Green supporters. As he saw it, few people shifted between the two camps: if they switched affiliation it was most often from one party in their own bloc to the other, and as a result of "short-term influences," popular personalities and issues of the day.

For Geissler it seemed evident that the FDP and CDU/CSU were increasingly competing for the same voters, especially those with the weakest partisan ties: the young, women, employees in high-technology or service industries. The moderate tones of Genscher and his promise of stability and harmony in foreign relations appealed to these voters. To restore the CDU's "structural capacity for a majority," Geissler felt it was imperative for the party to compete for these voters by pursuing—among other things—a more "modern" and "progressive" Ostpolitik. Creating any doubts about Union commitment to the "politically binding" effect of the Eastern treaties or to detente as a whole was "grist for the [FDP's] mill."[35]

Changes within the party had an effect as well. CDU activists felt able to challenge the expellees: Herbert Hupka was denied renomination for a parliamentary seat by his constituency party, and Herbert Czaja was initially not reelected to the Baden-Württemberg CDU's executive board. Generational change within the parliamentary leadership reinforced the trend toward a "modern" foreign policy: deputy parliamentary chief, Volker Rühe, and several CDU members of the Foreign Affairs Committee—Karl Lamers, Lutz Stavenhagen, Hans-Peter Repnik, Karl-Heinz Hornhues—were all younger than Kohl and thus more (if not automatically) inclined towards a reformist, "modern" foreign policy. Some gladly referred to themselves as "Genscherists." They could offset fundamentalists, in the Deutschlandpolitik committee, for example.

CDU/CSU politicians moved into high positions in government where they gained a greater personal stake in the successful conduct of relations with the East. Two expellee spokesmen, Windelen and Ottfried Hennig, became minister and state secretary for inner-German affairs. Despite their fundamentalist rhetoric they began to downplay maximal demands upon the GDR and propose ambitious ways of facilitating dialogue with the GDR. It was Windelen who had to warn East Germans seeking emigration permits from the FRG embassy in Prague to return to East Berlin and seek exit visas through normal channels—an arrangement he as an opposition leader would have castigated. Their behavior indicated that even hard-line fundamentalists gained a new perspective after they were entrusted with conducting relations. As one party official with experience under von Weizsäcker in Berlin observed, "Experts come to a man like Windelen and say 'what do we do about [concrete problems]'; it engenders pragmatism." As Windelen himself conceded, "I cannot dispute [the fact that] many have also expected from me more than I can now deliver within the parameters of the given opportunities. But also—or perhaps especially —in this realm, politics is the art of the possible."[36]

A similar pragmatism affected even some of the new majority in Parliament. The CSU's Eduard Lintner, taking his cue from Strauss but also anxious to assert a role for the parliamentary committee under his leadership, promoted bipartisan statements on inner-German relations and contacts with the GDR. He could make light of the Union's earlier "fear of contact," its unwillingness to approve trips by party officials to the East bloc—"We thought they would all come back as communists!"—and contrast that with the party's (even the CSU's) readiness to promote such contacts.

The simple difference between the obligations of opposition and the role of government also shaped Union thinking. Many party leaders conceded that their function was no longer to act as "a watchdog," but to shape policy. Moreover ten years had changed a great deal: as one CSU spokesman said, "The circumstances of 1972 cannot be applied to the circumstances of 1982." Strauss himself reportedly cautioned party members that "We cannot take up where we stopped in 1969."[37]

During its years in government the Union found more than enough reason to go beyond mere continuity and toward an ambitious Ostpolitik, stabilizing (at least financially) and in fact legitimizing its Eastern partners. The policy it had once accepted largely against its own better judgment seemed to have gained a firm place in overall Union foreign policy. Indeed the party leadership began to see more positive aspects to a dialogue that its own orthodoxy said was replete with risk.

The Limits of a Dualistic Policy

Yet there were other elements of CDU/CSU Ostpolitik. Since its days in opposition the party as a whole had agreed that negotiations with the communist bloc should not preclude an effort to keep the national question alive. Even while the Union-led government avidly pursued contacts with the East, indeed went out of its way to win the favor of a visit from Honecker, the party seemed intent upon revitalizing the national issue, whatever the risks that posed to dialogue.

Party leaders argued that it was vital, and should be possible, to follow both tracks. Berlin official and later defense minister, Rupert Scholz, described the party's policy this way: "If Deutschlandpolitik in the final analysis must, in light of the given conditions, be understood as an operational policy to ameliorate the effects of the division, that should still not become [its] exclusive normative task. Deutschlandpolitik should not be turned into its opposite by giving up its real normative positions—reunification, keeping alive the national issue, the duty to seek state reunification of the Germans."[38]

On one hand this meant continuing to insist that the Eastern treaties constituted a modus vivendi, leaving Bonn's traditional legal positions untouched and Honecker's Gera demands unmet. Windelen, for example, emphasized, "We will hold to treaties—as they have been negotiated. That means that we as the FRG consider [the Oder-Neisse line] inviolable"—a minimalist interpretation that implied the 1970 accord would *not* bind a unified Germany. As for the Gera demands, Chancellory minister Schäuble, himself a reformist, observed, "It is clear to both sides [Bonn and East Berlin] that there is no room for movement in the fundamental positions." He went on to stress that a modus vivendi had in effect already been reached on the Gera demands: both sides agreed to disagree.[39]

Legalisms aside, another "new accent" dominated West German policy. An emphasis on the national division became very much a part of political debate at home and diplomatic dialogue abroad. On his first trip to Moscow in 1983 Kohl confronted his hosts with the question of how they would feel about partition of Russia. On his 1987 visit Strauss too reminded the Soviets of the German commitment to unity.

CDU/CSU leaders also encouraged more gesamtdeutsch tones in political debate. Kohl made such phrases as "our German fatherland" respectable again; the term *"Heimat"* became fashionable once more, at least in part due to government rhetoric. Despite sharp criticism from Poland, Kohl in 1984 and 1985 became the first chancellor in two decades to address large expellee rallies. Ottfried Hennig, deputy minister in the Inner-German Affairs Ministry, declared, "East Prussia belongs to Germany." Kohl told one group, "Fatherland: that is not only the Federal Republic of Germany. That is the land in which our culture has grown for centuries."[40] By the end of its first term back in office the party seemed proud to have revived discussion of the national issue.

Along similar lines, the new government—and especially Kohl—encouraged more discussion of German history. Although he did not see this effort as part of his Ostpolitik, the chancellor, supported by a close advisor, Professor Michael Stürmer, had long argued that West Germans needed a natural, healthy nationalism, which required overcoming the legacy of Nazism and honoring the less shameful chapters of German history. He undertook this effort seriously, urging the construction of history museums and monuments to Germany's war dead, and holding Ronald Reagan to his promise to attend a brief ceremony in 1985 at the graves of German soldiers buried at Bitburg.

Nor did CDU/CSU leaders always downplay criticism of Soviet-bloc actions. They continued to highlight Soviet human-rights violations. Strauss accused GDR border guards of murdering a tourist, and Kohl himself compared Gorbachev with Josef Göbbels—both he said were master propagandists—and condemned GDR prisons as "concentration camps." Detente, the party said, should not prohibit "clear speech."

Although some CDU reformists grumbled about this overdone rhetoric, there was broad consensus in the party for traveling along both tracks of its Eastern policy: the operational and the normative. But at points the two tracks crossed, making for a number of collisions and considerable caution—and the appearance of confusion.

After all, the Union had inherited treaties the interpretation of which had at times been disputed by Bonn and its Eastern negotiating partners. Moreover the party clearly still had two different schools of thought on these issues. On the one hand were the reformists, mainly in the Chancellory staff under Schäuble, the CDU party headquarters under Geissler, the Berlin wing under Eberhard Diepgen, the labor wing, and the youth auxiliary (the latter two continually called for a more active policy of dialogue and efforts to awaken popular interest in life in the GDR among a broad cross-section of West Germans).

Yet on the other hand, fundamentalists still dominated the parliamentary group under Dregger, Strauss's CSU, the expellee groups led by Hupka, and certain regional party organizations. Their own declining influence made them increasingly restive.

Among the expellees in particular a siege mentality took hold. In Baden-Württemberg, they polled the parliamentary deputies on the issue of Heimat rights and after the result proved disappointing declared, "We can only give our vote to those who have expressed themselves on this question in our way, with no ifs or buts.... We should not let ourselves be sent away by Union politicians with empty formulas." The Sudeten Germans warned, "Should the CDU plan to disappoint its most loyal voter potential—the expellees and the 'middle-Germans'... it would permanently block its own way back to governmental responsibility after the next federal election."[41]

Moreover, the CSU and many more conservative Christian Democrats continued to argue for an all-out campaign against the Liberals; they contended that placating or imitating the FDP was already costing the Union conservative voters (though of course it was Strauss's own role in arranging the billion-mark credit that caused several archconservative CSU members to break with him and establish their own party). Yet more than politics was involved in this backlash. Though most fundamentalists had learned to live with their ambivalence about the Ostpolitik, their adaptation was in part due to a belief that relations with the East should not and need not prohibit a firm stance on old ground. In the view of some party officials, the Union had accepted the policy of negotiation as the lesser of two evils, but that was not supposed to mean remaining silent on issues of principle. Having lost the battle against granting the GDR status and stabilizing its economy, many fundamentalists drew the line when it came to other issues.

No one discovered this bellicose mood more quickly than those reformists and government officials (often themselves fundamentalists) who overestimated the party's internal consensus and urged not merely progress but expansion and diversification of Bonn's policy. In breaking down existing barriers to improved relations, these reformists were willing to modify—or in von Weizsäcker's words "spring over"—some of the long-sacred party positions. This sparked not only resistance but at times a sharp backlash.

Attention focused on the border question. In his desire to smooth relations with Poland, Alois Mertes tried to allay Polish fears of Union-sponsored revisionism by stressing that the 1937 borders are "a point of departure in talks, not a territorial goal"; all discussion of a future German state's borders was thus "irrelevant." Volker Rühe hoped to put the entire issue to rest, arguing that the 1970 Warsaw Treaty that accepted the Oder-Neisse line had a "politically binding effect" on a united Germany, even if it created no legal obligation.

But the CSU and other fundamentalists joined in criticizing Mertes and in lambasting Rühe's statement as a violation of party policy. Rühe's view, they said, went beyond the party's minimalist position, namely that this clause of the treaty was legally binding only on the FRG, not on a future united Germany. They pointed back to the 1972 Joint Resolution, which they argued classified the Eastern accords as a modus vivendi with no binding effect on a future united Germany. Rühe's phrase remained an item of contention and never found its way into Union policy statements. Kohl declared the controversy—and thus Rühe's idea—unnecessary, but the expellees were not content to let it rest. After Kohl agreed to address its 1985 convention, the Silesian league came up with the slogan "Silesia remains ours"; only after protest from the Chancellory was it changed to read "Silesia remains ours in a Europe of free peoples."

Even fundamentalists like the CSU's Eduard Lintner got into hot water. In 1985 discussions over a joint parliamentary resolution with the FDP and SPD he approved a clause stating that "the German question does not involve the shifting of borders, but removing from borders their dividing character" and "the Parliament confirms that now and for the future, the inviolability of borders and the respect for territorial integrity and the sovereignty of all states within their present borders, moored in the Moscow and Warsaw treaties, [is] a fundamental condition for peace and thus also for Deutschlandpolitik." Fundamentalists heatedly condemned this draft as "illegitimate, unconstitutional, contrary to the treaties" and "likely to have explosive . . . effects"—even though Kohl himself had said as much in the communiqué following a brief meeting with Honecker at the funeral of Soviet leader Chernenko.[42]

As for the GDR's Gera demands for greater status, most CDU reformists and even many fundamentalist officials like Windelen declared them "nonnegotiable," yet worth discussing. Bonn officials spoke of the need for a modus vivendi on the Elbe border. In private, impatient CDU parliamentary staffers referred sarcastically to "old allied maps with thick lines," implying that the river middle could be accepted as the inner-German boundary—assuming allied agreement. Windelen's equally fundamentalist deputy, expellee Ottfried Hennig, declared that the Salzgitter bureau, which monitored shootings on the border, could be closed if the GDR "order to shoot" were lifted. On the last, most important Gera demand, an end to West German extension of citizenship to all who left East Germany, Windelen also hinted at a compromise: though Bonn would never give this practice up, he stated, it could explore what Honecker meant by requesting FRG "respect for GDR" citizenship.[43]

On all of these points most fundamentalists refused to budge: the old maps showed the border "clearly ran on the Elbe's northern bank"; Salzgitter could not be closed until both shooting at the border and political persecution of would-be emigres in the GDR stopped. Thus initiatives for addressing the Gera demands also failed.

In the coalition's second term the fundamentalist backlash took a new tone; for the first time in decades some Union conservatives challenged party leaders to give national unity absolute priority.

In 1988 Windelen's successor as inner-German affairs minister, Dorothee Wilms—not an expellee—declared that Bonn's constitution did not oblige Germans to pursue "a nation state for its own sake" and added that state unity was not "an end in itself" but could occur only when "in an historical process" Europe's division is overcome. She met with harsh attacks from fundamentalists, especially expellees. Every phrase of her speech was "a targeted provocation," said one group of CDU spokesmen, and she had "disqualified herself" as minister for showing such resignation about national unity: "The policy of so-called small steps should not exhaust itself in a policy of small opportunism."[44]

In 1988 Secretary Geissler set up a working group of reformists to write a new party statement on foreign policy. Although the authors considered it merely "the sum of government policy," party fundamentalists bitterly condemned the first draft for containing little more than prescriptions for "managing the division." Critics said it abandoned all ideas for ending the division by pushing them back to the distant future, and even that it "overemphasized" Western ties. Rupert Scholz said the paper failed to distinguish between operative aims that were "politically correct" and normative goals; seeking human contacts and making borders more transparent were, under the current conditions, worthy goals, but could not replace the real objective of state unity, which required treating the border question as unresolved. It was also wrong to describe freedom as the precondition of unity, because unity and self-determination were in essence freedoms.[45]

To avoid a controversy, Geissler's group had to revise the statement. Its initial draft had declared that "the goal of unity is . . . possible to achieve only with the approval and support of [our] neighbors in the West and the East." Because this was interpreted as an Eastern (and Western) right to veto reunification, the clause was altered to "We need . . . the understanding and support of our neighbors." Similarly, the first draft had classified European unity as Bonn's goal, but the revised version stressed German reunification—a term that had vanished from many earlier statements. Last, the initial draft had referred to the Eastern Treaties but neither the letters on unity nor the Joint Resolution of 1972; the second version corrected this omission. A clause in the earlier version pledging Bonn's desire to make borders less divisive was replaced by a promise to work for removal of the inner-German border through peaceful means.[46]

In short, many of the trial balloons designed to test whether the Union would take new directions in its Eastern policies—especially regarding the GDR—were either shot down or simply allowed to drift away. Plainly there were paradoxes and contradictions.

Windelen and Strauss could get away with shows of flexibility that would bring a hailstorm of criticism down upon reformists. Evident also was the gap between official government statements and party policy on the borders, and on inner-German relations: at times the CDU/CSU would not reproduce the phrases of even its chairman, Helmut Kohl, in party-platform statements.

The discussion of history also brought out discord. On the fortieth anniversary of the end of World War II, von Weizsäcker gave a speech in which he acknowledged Germany's responsibility and contended that those who had not known of deportations of Jews had chosen not to find out. His open discussion of guilt contrasted sharply with Kohl's effort to revive a sense of normal nationalism and provoked bitter criticism from some in the Union. At the same time, Professors Andreas Hillgruber and Ernst Nolte took the effort to "cleanse" German history further than Kohl and his advisor Stürmer. Nolte argued that Nazism, including the Holocaust, was in effect a defense against bolshevism and Hillgruber contended that German soldiers were in effect defending their homeland. This prompted sharp condemnation and a politically charged debate among historians.

In effect Kohl had proven unable to control sentiment he himself had promoted and tolerated. It was the chancellor who had refused to push the party or the government toward new positions on the borders or status issues, accepted the invitation to both expellee conferences, and encouraged cultivation of a "healthy historical consciousness." Many critics blamed the resulting confusion on Kohl's leadership style and his preoccupation with party unity: in the Chancellory, as in opposition, he was eager to placate all elements in the party—above all its fundamentalists, including the expellees, to whom he felt indebted.

Moreover, the death of Alois Mertes in 1985 left Kohl almost alone as a major intraparty mediator among Union subgroups. Kohl tried to balance operative and normative policies and worked out convoluted compromise statements, such as this one following a spat over one party leader's definition of detente: "No politician of the CDU/CSU has called for not pursuing a realistic and illusion-free detente policy."[47] Above all he tried to avoid situations that might require him to choose between operative progress and normative consistency—and thus between his party's two schools of thought.

Ostpolitik and Security

Not only did the party cling to traditional positions on the national issue, it remained committed to its traditional concept of security based on the Western alliance. Union leaders were thus ambivalent about the impact of a new, dynamic Eastern policy upon relations with the Western allies, above all the United States. Unlike the SPD, the Union insisted on separating security policy and Ostpolitik as clearly as possible.

For example, though the Union spoke of the "German community of responsibility" for European peace, it did not support Genscher's initiative for a German-German dialogue on security. CDU/CSU leaders argued that this topic must be left at the bloc-to-bloc level—ensuring that Genscher limited any such discussions to issues already covered in multilateral fora, and thus to issues requiring a NATO consensus.

Kohl from the outset stressed that West Germany acted as "Europe's earthquake observatory"; sitting on the major geopolitical fault line, it was sensitive to every shift in East-West relations. As the chancellor pointed out, dialogue between the blocs and especially between U.S. and Soviet leaders created the conditions necessary for Bonn to conduct its own Eastern policy and eased the overall atmosphere of tension in Europe. But the Union did not press Washington very firmly. Kohl's national security advisor, Horst Teltschik, observed that Bonn would use its good relations with Washington to promote superpower dialogue, but only when its relations with its major allies were on a solid basis. In fact polls showed that many Germans thought the Union far too anxious to give its security policy precedence over detente.[48]

After the superpowers found their way back to each other in 1985, Union leaders welcomed the thaw this produced in East-West relations. Yet many grew increasingly concerned about "bilateralism" at the expense of NATO security policy. For them there was such a thing as too much detente. In late 1986 Strauss warned, "We must watch out like hell lest the Americans agree to solutions which do not damage their security but can work out very problematically for us."[49]

Nowhere did this ambivalence show more clearly than in the specific realm of arms control. To be sure, from 1982 onward the

Union had gently urged the United States to find a satisfactory way of promoting weapons reduction, partly in order to perpetuate the overall East-West dialogue. It was Kohl who in 1983 pressed NATO to settle for an "interim solution" in the reduction talks on medium-range missiles, rather than hold out for what seemed to be unachievable: the zero option, or total elimination of U.S. and Soviet INF. Fearful of the impact that U.S. plans for strategic defense might have on East-West relations and arms control, the CDU's Volker Rühe promoted a "cooperative solution" by which both superpowers would agree not to abrogate the 1972 U.S.-Soviet antiballistic treaty. Right up to the eve of the 1986 Reykjavik superpower summit, Kohl was urging Washington not to let strategic defenses block an arms agreement limiting European INF.

Yet when faced with the choice between its security policy and arms reduction with a beneficial impact upon Ostpolitik, the Union chose the former. In 1983 it did not allow Eastern threats of an "ice age" in inner-German relations to keep it from deploying U.S. INF —certainly the most controversial step taken in any policy area by the Kohl government.

More compelling evidence of the Union's priorities came in the tumultuous year of 1987. After pressing the United States to move ahead with arms control and reduce medium-range weapons in Europe, the party leadership reacted with alarm to the actual breakthroughs that led to the Reagan-Gorbachev INF accord. Despite its desire to demonstrate solidarity with Washington on security, the Union worried that U.S. policymakers were showing both a desire to escape the escalatory risks of extended nuclear deterrence and a weariness about their overall commitment to Europe. Despite an enormous amount of pressure from all sides, West and East, the Union leadership—including reformists like Rühe and Schäuble —waged a lonely battle against the INF accord.

Admittedly, the party did ultimately give in and endorse the zero option (and eventual removal of some jointly controlled U.S.-German systems) so that the superpowers could conclude a treaty. The Union submitted in part to avoid blame for disrupting relations with the East. Honecker's visit to Bonn was planned for September 1987, and Kohl had no desire to see the historic meeting cancelled. Genscher had warned the Union that blocking arms control could cause "a deep break between us and our fellow citizens over there [in the GDR]."⁵⁰ Union leaders also had no desire to be isolated from Gorbachev's new, more accommodating Kremlin.

Yet the main reason for the party's backing down did not lie in the desire to shelter Bonn's relations with the East. Convinced that removal of U.S. INF was severely damaging to nuclear deterrence, most Union leaders would have held out against the zero option had not the allies, above all the United States, been determined to proceed. Many also were concerned that opposition to such an arms-control breakthrough could revive the peace movement and undercut the Union's ability to reassure the public that deterrence need not mean a perpetual arms race.⁵¹

Plainly the Union knew progress in arms control would be conducive to further dialogue, including dialogue on the inner-German level. Yet just as clearly most party leaders, including leading reformists like Rühe, gave their traditional security policy precedence—even to the extent of risking isolation from the allies and enormous domestic political criticism.

In sum, the Union still remained bound by what could only be called the Adenauer set of priorities: it wished to negotiate with the Soviet bloc and to keep the national question open, but it largely subordinated both of these goals to its Western and security policies. Just as it had long insisted that reunification must not come at the expense of Bonn's Western ties, so it held that detente should not be allowed to compromise Bonn's position in the Western alliance. Though it wanted the benefits of relaxed tensions between East and West, it feared any potential, fundamental shift in the European status quo promised—or "threatened"—by the sudden, rapid reduction of nuclear arms.

Generally those in the Union who criticized this consensus order of priorities were fundamentalists who wanted greater emphasis on national unity, or reformists supporting more dialogue. But the leadership's very evident lack of interest in basic change at a time when change seemed possible was precisely what produced a new line of dissent.

In 1987 and 1988, for the first time in decades, a genuine streak of national neutralism emerged in the Union. Its clearest manifestation was the proposal of a parliamentary backbencher, Wilhelm

Friedmann. In light of the rapid progress toward U.S.-Soviet arms control in Europe, Friedmann urged Bonn to insist that German unity now be placed on the superpower agenda. As the primary source of East-West tension, he argued, the division should be discussed. Moreover, with the United States apparently reducing its commitment to Europe, it was up to Washington to carry through on its Germany Treaty obligation to press for unity. Pointing to the slow pace of European unity, Friedmann insisted that a "nation state" concept appeared more achievable. A "neutralist" if not entirely "neutral" state could be established, neutralist in that its foreign policy would not be contrary to Soviet security concerns.[52]

Friedmann claimed to have received thousands of letters from CDU/CSU voters approving his initiative, and he aroused support from a small group of CDU conservatives, including former Berlin interior minister, Heinrich Lummer, and sympathy even from the newly appointed defense minister, Rupert Scholz. Most other party leaders hastened to reassure Friedmann's supporters that the Union had not lost sight of reunification, but they nonetheless smothered his proposal: Kohl labeled it nonsense, and leading fundamentalists like Dregger stressed that Moscow would never truly give up on the GDR. Most Union leaders emphasized that no "special German path" was possible, even with the new era of detente; Europe's division must first be overcome and Western security ensured. And above all, any scheme for unity must not sacrifice democracy: "The basic position remains 'Freedom before unity.'"[53]

The sharp discussion Friedmann's thesis provoked showed both the degree to which national goals remained on the minds of many Union politicians and the extent of uncertainty for the CDU/CSU created by the new era of detente ushered in by Mikhail Gorbachev.

Conclusions

What conclusions can be drawn about the long-term aims of Ostpolitik under the CDU/CSU? Did the party that so ambivalently came to accept dialogue with the East come eventually to develop what in opposition it lacked: a vision or at least a strategy for guiding day-to-day relations with the East?

Many of the Union's domestic critics on the left and the right saw its Eastern policies as largely opportunistic. The SPD praised the Union's pursuit of interaction with the GDR and found its success reassuring, but contended that the CDU/CSU was handicapped by its internal divisions and lack of imagination. Social Democrats condemned Kohl for permitting, even encouraging, revanchist sentiments in the Union. They also reminded the CDU/CSU that, given the GDR's limited room for maneuver, a successful relationship with East Berlin had to be part of a broader detente with Moscow; it was no use trying to separate arms control from Ostpolitik.

In fact the very success of the Kohl government in managing inner-German relations had a domino effect on the SPD, pushing its leaders into a series of initiatives that toppled precedents held to even by the Schmidt government. In the early 1980s some prominent Social Democrats suggested revising the FRG constitution's preamble, striking the clause obliging Bonn to pursue unity; many endorsed compromise on all four Gera demands; Bahr proposed giving up on all legal and status issues. Moreover the party as a whole instituted an independent foreign policy, negotiating "treaties" with the SED and Communist parties in Poland and Czechoslovakia: the main focus was on cooperation and arms control.

Press critics agreed that the Union's Eastern policies were improvised. The conservative *Frankfurter Allgemeine Zeitung* labeled CDU/CSU Ostpolitik "populist" or designed strictly to win votes, and "opportunistic" in downplaying the national question and simply taking over the SPD's overly accommodating interpretations of the Eastern accords. The more liberal *Die Zeit* generally agreed that CDU/CSU policy was populist and without a guiding concept, but said it had not gone far enough in dealing with the East.

One seasoned observer summed up Union policy in this critique: "Conceptually there is nothing new [in Union policy]; they are living off of SPD-FDP policy," pursuing a "reasonable course," but with no connection to long-term goals, let alone to reunification.[54]

Yet there were signs of long-term strategy among some Union leaders. Almost all shared the view expressed by Strauss that a policy of dialogue had kept alive national solidarity and "revived the desire for the restoration of the unity of our German fatherland." Thus many foreign observers, both governments and in the press, feared that the emphasis on inner-German dialogue signified a longing for reunification. Foreign Minister Andreotti of Italy warned against "pan-Germanism," adding that Germany should remain divided. A leading American newspaper believed it saw Bonn's policies "leading toward fulfillment of [the Germans'] secret yearning: reunification of the two countries." Others sensed a movement, a drift toward neutralism.[55]

Yet though the party's push for cooperation with the GDR and its emphasis on the open German question lent some credence to these assumptions and suspicions, many such observers simply overlooked the strict limits Bonn was still putting upon its Eastern negotiation. Moreover they tended to see the party's commitment to dialogue and its insistence upon traditional positions as mutually reinforcing when they were actually often in tension. To be sure, both thrusts of Union policy arose from the unresolved German question, but that did not make them compatible parts of a long-term strategy. Those reformists most enthusiastic about the dialogue were often ready to give up on such goals as state unity, and fundamentalists who stressed state unity (with notable exceptions like Strauss) hoped to restrict negotiations.

As for the other dimensions of Ostpolitik, some Union leaders expressed a view similar to that of Foreign Minister Genscher: that the Soviet Union and Eastern Europe should be enmeshed in a web of multilateral and bilateral relationships with the West, interaction that could act as a form of restraint. Von Weizsäcker told his Soviet hosts in 1987, "The more your readiness for international interdependence grows, the greater becomes our Western latitude for cooperation. The goal should not be to win power, but a coexistence that enables us to resolve conflicts politically." At a German-Polish forum in 1987, the CDU's Volker Rühe observed that "for the first time in centuries this theme [what can we do together for Europe] binds Germans and Poles to a 'we,' [and] for the first time there is talk of common action." Inner-German affairs minister, Dorothee Wilms, declared "We want nothing so much as [we want] all of Europe—West, Central and East and we Germans are included in that—to find its way back together.... We in Western Europe can not merely stand by as these people [in Eastern Europe] struggle for a way of life that corresponds to their European nature."[56]

Consequently some observers—again mainly journalists and intellectuals, especially outside Germany—began to explain CDU/CSU Eastern policies as a first step toward reconstruction of a unified Central Europe between the superpowers, a *Mitteleuropa* such as was often discussed in the 1980s at academic conferences. Although this concept had no precise definition (especially as to how the Soviet Union fit in), its main element was said to be a sense of Central European identity.

Yet comments by people like von Weizsäcker and Rühe could not be taken as representative of party thinking, let alone of party planning. The entire thrust of everyday policy for the CDU/CSU was still to prevent, not promote, dissolution of the blocs; the Union's isolation over removal of INF allows no other conclusion. The concept of Mitteleuropa was irrelevant to a party whose leaders were preoccupied on a daily basis with European Community affairs and NATO policy; it remained a topic only on the agenda of writers' conferences and intellectual gatherings.

In short, though the party's domestic critics underestimated the degree to which it did engage in long-term thinking, many foreign observers tended to see strategic designs where there were none.

To be sure CDU/CSU policy *had* developed more than a strictly opportunistic and expedient character. Most party leaders came to believe that dialogue with the East could contribute to the broader change in Europe that they had long known was a prerequisite for any resolution of the national question. Detente kept the current situation fluid and could help create the proper context in which a "European solution" to Germany's future could take place.

Yet few Union leaders were willing to go further in spelling out their vision of Europe's long-term future, in clearing up the ambiguity surrounding that comforting notion of a "European solution" —would it be based upon state unity or "an Austrian solution"; would it involve a fundamental change in the blocs, and if so what kind of change?

Unity within the CDU/CSU simply could not have survived concrete answers to such questions. But beyond mere considerations of party cohesion, the Union's caution reflected its awareness that a vague concept of the future best fit the constraints long imposed upon West German foreign policy. Just as international and domestic forces compelled the party to accept the need for dialogue, so too did these constraints prevent it from taking Ostpolitik as far as might be envisioned by the SPD, the FDP, or some in its own ranks —reformists, traditional fundamentalists, or newly active national-neutralists.

For CDU/CSU leaders, West German policy had gained some latitude through its relationships with the East, but it was by no means so emancipated that Bonn could begin to shape everyday action according to some long-range blueprint for the reconstruction of Europe. A specific strategy for attaining reunification through absorbing the GDR, or for neutralization, or for building a modern-day Mitteleuropa was simply not consistent with the FRG's position in a Europe still dominated by the blocs, one of which guaranteed West German security.

Moreover there was no societal consensus for such a strategy in the Federal Republic. As Gebhard Schweigler has observed, "Most West Germans simply do not support a clearly spelled-out plan that envisions significant changes in the Federal Republic's current foreign policy posture."[57] As Schweigler notes, the FRG's population has largely internalized the external constraints upon West Germany's "room for maneuver." Even though polls often show a majority of the population favoring reunification as well as a neutralized FRG, those aims are rarely taken seriously—even by those espousing them.

Yet what the late 1980s did begin to change in the German equation was the key factor: external constraints. The "new thinking" of Mikhail Gorbachev's Soviet Union and, arguably, the declining U.S. interest in Europe signified by the INF treaty together raised the prospect of a fundamental transformation of the European bloc system, the Western alliance, and conceivably even the old Four Power role in Germany. Should that prospect prove to be the case, it could spark a commensurate change in the societal context of German foreign policy, creating a public interest in new directions heretofore rejected as unrealistic. Whatever the promise and potential of such a tectonic shift in European politics, it would almost certainly shake the very foundations of the Adenauer consensus that has underlain CDU/CSU foreign policy for four decades.

Appendix

CDU/CSU Leadership Factions on Ostpolitik, 1969–1974

Reformists

        Norbert Blüm
        Richard von Weizsäcker
        Johann Baptist Gradl
        Hans Katzer
        Philipp von Bismarck
        Walther Leisler Kiep

Fundamentalists

        Franz Josef Strauss (CSU)
        Baron von und zu Guttenberg (CSU)
        Hans Graf Huyn (CSU)
        Alfred Dregger
        Herbert Hupka
        Herbert Czaja
        Heinrich Windelen
        Manfred Abelein
        Werner Marx

Uncommitted/Mediators

> Helmut Kohl
> Rainer Barzel
> Gerhard Schröder
> Kurt Georg Kiesinger
> Kurt Birrenbach
> Olaf von Wrangel

CDU/CSU Leadership Factions on Ostpolitik, 1974–1982

Reformists

> Heiner Geissler
> Kurt Biedenkopf
> Norbert Blüm
> Johann Baptist Gradl
> Walther Leisler Kiep
> Ernst Albrecht
> Lothar Späth
> Gerhard Stoltenberg
> Walter Wallmann
> Matthias Wissmann
> Peter Lorenz
> Philipp Jenninger
> Richard von Weizsäcker
> Volker Rühe
> Philipp von Bismarck

Fundamentalists

> Franz Josef Strauss (CSU)
> Friedrich Zimmermann (CSU)
> Hans Graf Huyn (CSU)
> Hans Klein (CSU)
> Franz Ludwig von Stauffenberg (CSU)
> Manfred Abelein
> Gerhard Reddemann
> Alfred Dregger
> Herbert Czaja

Herbert Hupka
Heinrich Windelen
Ottfried Hennig
Heinrich Lummer
Jürgen Todenhöfer

Uncommitted/Mediators

Helmut Kohl
Manfred Wörner
Alois Mertes
Olaf von Wrangel
Karl Carstens

CDU/CSU Leadership Factions on Ostpolitik, 1982–

Reformists

Heiner Geissler
Norbert Blüm
Lothar Späth
Gerhard Stoltenberg
Matthias Wissmann
Peter Lorenz
Philipp Jenninger
Volker Rühe
Wolfgang Schäuble
Karl-Heinz Hornhues
Hans-Peter Repnik
Karl Lamers
Lutz Stavenhagen

Fundamentalists

Franz Josef Strauss
Friedrich Zimmermann
Hans Graf Huyn
Hans Klein
Alfred Dregger

Herbert Czaja
Herbert Hupka
Jürgen Todenhöfer

Uncommitted/Mediators

Helmut Kohl
Walter Wallmann
Manfred Wörner
Alois Mertes
Heinrich Windelen
Ottfried Hennig
Eduard Lintner
Dorothee Wilms
Horst Teltschik

Party and Government Positions (1969–1982)

Chancellor

Willy Brandt (SPD), 1969–74
Helmut Schmidt (SPD), 1974–82
Helmut Kohl (CDU), 1982–

Foreign Minister

Walter Scheel (FDP), 1969–74
Hans-Dietrich Genscher (FDP), 1974–

CDU Party Chairman

Kurt Georg Kiesinger, 1969–71
Rainer Barzel, 1971–73
Helmut Kohl, 1973–

CSU Party Chairman

Franz Josef Strauss, 1961–88

CDU/CSU Chancellor Candidate

Kurt Georg Kiesinger, 1969
Rainer Barzel, 1972
Helmut Kohl, 1976
Franz Josef Strauss, 1980
Helmut Kohl, 1983, 1987

CDU/CSU Parliamentary Group Chairman

Rainer Barzel (CDU), 1966–73
Karl Carstens (CDU), 1973–76
Helmut Kohl (CDU), 1976–82
Alfred Dregger (CDU), 1982–

CDU General Secretary

Bruno Heck, 1967–71
Konrad Kraske, 1971–73
Kurt Biedenkopf, 1973–76
Heiner Geissler, 1976–

SPD Chairman

Willy Brandt, 1964–1987
Hans-Jochen Vogel, 1987–

SPD Parliamentary Group Chairman

Herbert Wehner, 1969–1983
Hans-Jochen Vogel, 1983–

SED General Secretary

Walter Ulbricht, 1953–71
Erich Honecker, 1971–

Notes

Introduction

1. Wolfram Hanrieder, "Compatibility and Consensus: A Proposal for the Conceptual Linkage of External and Internal Dimensions of Foreign Policy," in *Comparative Foreign Policy: Theoretical Essays*, ed. Wolfram Hanrieder (New York: David McKay, 1971), 242–64.
2. Gebhard Schweigler, *West German Foreign Policy: The Domestic Setting*, The Washington Papers, vol. 12, no. 106 (New York: Praeger, 1984).
3. The author has drawn upon parliamentary and party conference addresses by Union politicians; CDU/CSU party statements and programs; interviews with several dozen Union politicians or spokesmen, and outside observers, including journalists and academics; daily and weekly newspaper stories dealing with the party and West German affairs; opinion poll data as reported in the press; memoirs and other published writings of CDU/CSU politicians; and journal articles and books related to the topic.

1. Union Ostpolitik from Adenauer to the Grand Coalition

1. Geoffrey Pridham, *Christian Democracy in Western Germany: The CDU/CSU in Government and Opposition* (New York: St. Martin's Press, 1977), 21–34.
2. Arnold Heidenheimer, *Adenauer and the CDU: The Rise of the Leader and the Integration of the Party* (The Hague: Nijhof, 1960).
3. Indeed, Adenauer's policies created a rift between the CDU and leading Protestants like Martin Niemöller. To protect Protestant interests

and identity within the Union, the Evangelical Working Circle (EAK) was formed.
4. Scornfully dismissed as "sacred-heart Bolsheviks" by archconservatives, and as the CDU's "social fig-leaf" by the SPD, the so-called social committees drew support from Catholic trade unionists in the Rhine and Ruhr regions.
5. Hans-Joachim Veen in an interview with the author, 17 May 1984.
6. Dieter Schmidt in an interview with the author, 11 April 1984.
7. The most comprehensive analysis of the CSU is provided by Alf Mintzel, *Die CSU: Anatomie einer konservativen Partei, 1945–1972* (Opladen: Westdeutscher Verlag, 1975); see also, Mintzel, "Conservatism and Christian Democracy in the Federal Republic of Germany," in *Conservative Politics in Western Europe*, ed. Zig-Layton Henry (London: Macmillan, 1982), 143–59.
8. Bavaria's CSU strongly endorsed the spirit of this Westpolitik, if not every detail of its practical implementation. A revived Western Europe, united by the need to defend its Christian and cultural heritage against the communist East, corresponded to the CSU's image of Bavaria. Party leaders saw their region as either a defender of or missionary for traditionalist Christian values, but in either vision, atheistic, totalitarian militaristic Eastern communism was a deadly peril, and Western cooperation against it vital. Mintzel, *Die CSU*.
9. Hans-Peter Schwarz, "Das aussenpolitische Konzept Konrad Adenauers," in *Adenauer Studien-I*, ed. Rudolf Morsey and Konrad Repgen. Kommission für Zeitgeschichte bei der katholischen Akademie in Bayern, ser. B, vol. 10 (Mainz: Matthias Grünewald Verlag, 1971). 71–90.
10. Konrad Adenauer, *Erinnerungen 1953–1955* (Stuttgart: Deutsche Verlags-Anstalt, 1966), 20.
11. Hans-Peter Schwarz, "Adenauer und Russland," in *Im Dienste Deutschlands und des Rechtes: Festschrift für Wilhelm Grewe zum 70. Geburtstag am 16. Oktober 1981*, ed. Friedrich J. Kroneck and Thomas Opperman (Baden-Baden: Nomos, 1981), 373–75; Schwarz, *Adenauer: Der Aufstieg: 1876–1952* (Stuttgart: Deutsche Verlags-Anstalt, 1986), 425–617.
12. Schwarz, *Adenauer*, 708.
13. Since Bismarck's time and the "struggle against the Church," Catholics felt themselves victims of what Adenauer called "the dark side of the German soul"—extreme nationalism.
14. In his later years, for example, Adenauer was said to be perceptibly moved by the flood of refugees, which for him testified to the harsh conditions of life in the GDR. Remarks by Hans-Peter Schwarz and Wilhelm Grewe in Rhöndorfer Gespräche, *Entspannung und Wiedervereinigung: Deutschlandpolitische Vorstellungen Konrad Adanauers 1955–1958* (Stuttgart: Belser Verlag, 1979), 14–57.
15. Franz Josef Strauss, *The Grand Design: A European Solution to Ger-*

man Reunification (London: Weidenfeld and Nicolson, 1965), 81.
16. Adenauer, Erinnerungen 1953–1955, 454.
17. Schwarz, Adenauer, 655–56.
18. Waldemar Besson, Die Aussenpolitik der Bundesrepublik: Erfahrungen und Massstäbe (Frankfurt: Ullstein, 1970), 104.
19. Konrad Adenauer, Errinerungen 1945–1953, (Stuttgart: Deutsche Verlags-Anstalt, 1965), 536.
20. Besson, Aussenpolitik, 115.
21. Schwarz, "Das aussenpolitische Konzept," 90–98; Schwarz, "Adenauer und Russland," 382–89.
22. Adenauer, Erinnerungen 1953–1955, 63, 211.
23. William E. Griffith, The Ostpolitik of the Federal Republic of Germany (Cambridge: MIT Press, 1978), 61–71.
24. Adenauer, Erinnerungen 1953–1955, 217.
25. FRG, Bundesminister für innerdeutsche Beziehungen, Auskünfte zur Deutschlandpolitik (Bonn: Bundesministerium für innerdeutsche Beziehungen), 1983, 20.
26. Arnulf Baring, Im Anfang war Adenauer: Die Entstehung der Kanzlerdemokratie (Munich: Deutscher Taschenbuch Verlag, 1982), 245–47.
27. Adenauer, Erinnerungen 1953–1955, 63–131.
28. Ibid., 269.
29. Ibid., 450.
30. Schwarz, "Adenauer und Russland," 382–87. Adenauer's policy also subtly reminded his allies that if the Western push for rapprochement became too strong, Bonn had options. This was less a Rapallo threat than a sign of his ever-present Potsdam complex.
31. Bonn thus urged its allies to reject the Rapacki and Eden plans. Helga Haftendorn, Abrüstungs- und Entspannungspolitik zwischen Sicherheitsbefriedigung und Friedenssicherung. Zur Aussenpolitik der BRD 1955–1973 (Düsseldorf: Bertelsmann, 1974), 43–55.
32. Angela Stent, From Embargo to Ostpolitik: The Political Economy of West German–Soviet Relations 1955–1980 (Cambridge: Cambridge University Press, 1981), 35–37.
33. The two later variations of this plan, in 1960 and 1962, envisioned Austrianization for a ten-year trial period, after which United Nations–sponsored elections in both German states would decide whether there would be reunification. Depending on the election outcome, Germans could choose to remain in separate states and accept the Oder-Neisse line, though if they chose to reunite Adenauer's proposals insisted that the new Germany not be neutralized.
34. They also say he was in part prompted to launch these trial balloons by the grim plight of East Germans and the tide of refugees from the GDR. One advisor believed that Adenauer was consequently becoming more conscious of his responsibilities as a German statesman, especially since sound instincts told him that any actual reunifica-

tion lay far in the future. Rhöndorfer Gespräche, *Entspannung und Wiedervereinigung*, 35–45.
35. Besson, *Aussenpolitik*, 207.
36. Schwarz's comments in Rhöndorfer Gespräche, *Entspannung und Wiedervereinigung*, 8.
37. Besson, *Aussenpolitik*, 283–89. Indeed, the chancellor was again secretly testing the Soviet willingness to accept his interim solution (Austrianization of the GDR, followed by free elections on the question of reunification) as a substitute for acceptance of the status quo. The Kremlin had less interest than ever, and was content to make Adenauer stand by his increasingly discredited holding policy.
38. Griffith, *Ostpolitik*, 99–101; Besson, *Aussenpolitik*, 283–89.
39. Although Strauss did claim that the nation-state had been proven obsolete and did speak of a common currency and common industrial policy, he spurned the integrationist framework; the European Community was, he said, stumbling on in hopes that a *deus ex machina* might finally force unity upon so many disparate states. A looser, more realistic confederation along the lines of de Gaulle's "Europe of the fatherlands" was required. This model offered hopes of welding Europe into a unit. Strauss, *The Grand Design*, 24–30.
40. Ibid., 15, 21, 32.
41. Ibid., 10, 38.
42. At this point—the early 1960s—he saw German refusal to recognize the territorial status quo as complementary to these aims, though he later flirted with a change on that issue. Erich Eisner, *Das europäische Konzept von Franz Josef Strauss. Die gesamteuropäischen Ordnungsvorstellungen der CSU* (Meisenheim am Glan: Verlag Anton Hain, 1975), 76–133.
43. The 1960s produced a more stable superpower relationship and interest in dialogue, which inevitably had implications for Bonn. See Henry Kissinger, *The Troubled Partnership* (New York: McGraw-Hill, 1965).
44. Since the early 1960s Union governments had also been secretly purchasing the freedom of East German political prisoners, but the efforts remained marginal to avoid too much direct contact with the GDR, which might imply recognition.
45. FRG, Bundesminister für innerdeutsche Beziehungen, *Texte zur Deutschlandpolitik* [hereafter cited as TzDp] (Melsungen: A. Bernecker), ser. 1, vol. 1, 24-25.
46. *Stuttgarter Nachrichten*, 28 February 1987.
47. Eisner, *Das europäische Konzept*, 82–85.

2. The Initial Agreements, 1969–1971

1. This summary description of the SPD's original strategy is the author's own, but it draws in part from William Griffith, *The Ostpolitik of the*

Federal Republic of Germany (Cambridge: MIT Press), 173–224; Günther Schmid, *Entscheidung in Bonn: Die Entstehung der Ost- und Deutschlandpolitik 1969/1970* (Cologne: Verlag Wissenschaft und Politik, 1979), 15–178.

2. An excellent assessment of the SPD-FDP relationship going into the 1970s is provided in Arnulf Baring, *Machtwechsel: Die Ära Brandt-Scheel* (Stuttgart: Deutsche Verlags-Anstalt, 1982), 27–358.
3. Henry Kissinger, *White House Years* (Boston: Little, Brown, 1979), 98, 409–12.
4. Strauss argued that there was no need to "recognize as an internationally legal [and] sovereign state an administrative organization that has in its hands the official apparatus of power if one wants to achieve agreements on technical problems and questions involving the flow of human traffic." Cited in CSU, Landesgruppe, *CSU Correspondenz*, press release 44, 19 March 1970.
5. Richard von Weizsäcker, "Deutsche Ost- und Westpolitik," in *Die CDU in der Opposition: Eine Selbstdarstellung*, ed. Dietrich Rollman (Homburg: Christian Wegner, 1970), 46.
6. Comments on von Weizsäcker by Friedbert Pflüger in an interview with the author, 15 February 1984.
7. For an excellent account of the connections between CDU/CSU intraparty politics and policy debates, see Christian Hacke, *Die Ost- und Deutschlandpolitik der CDU/CSU: Wege und Irrwege der Opposition seit 1969* (Cologne: Verlag Wissenschaft und Politik, 1975).
8. Remarks by Johann Baptist Gradl before the Bundestag, cited in *J. B. Gradl: Stets auf der Suche: Reden, Äuserrungen und Aufsätze zur Deutschlandpolitik*, ed. Christian Hacke (Cologne: Verlag Wissenschaft und Politik, 1979), 292.
9. *Neue Zürcher Zeitung* [hereafter cited as NZZ], 14 January 1970.
10. CDU, *Deutschland Union Dienst* [hereafter cited as CDU, *DUD*], press release 59, 26 March 1970.
11. There were already bitter Union charges that the government had not consulted the opposition. Although the government did thoroughly brief opposition leaders in early 1970, the latter claimed that their views were not taken into account before official decisions were reached. See Schmid, *Entscheidung in Bonn*, 15–96.
12. Rainer Barzel, *Auf den Drahtseil* (Munich: Drümer Knaur, 1978), 102–3; *Deutsche Allgemeine Sonntagsblatt* [hereafter cited as *DAS*], 5 April 1970.
13. FRG, Presse- und Informationsamt der Bundesregierung, *Bulletin* 7430, May 1970, 727.
14. *Süddeutsche Zeitung* [hereafter cited as *SdZ*], 23–24 May 1970.
15. *SdZ*, 25 May 1970.
16. *TzDp*, ser. 1, vol. 5, 189–201.
17. *SdZ*, 19 May 1970; *NZZ*, 19 May 1970.

18. Brandt had already sought to satisfy Soviet conditions for detente by pledging to ratify the Nuclear Non-Proliferation Treaty, and endorsing an all-European security conference—provided that it included the United States.
19. Karl-Theodor Freiherr zu Guttenberg, *Die Neue Ostpolitik: Wege und Irrwege* (Osnabrück: A. Fromm, 1971), 11.
20. *Bayernkurier* [hereafter cited as *BK*], November 1970.
21. *Handelsblatt* [hereafter cited as *HB*], 2 June 1970.
22. *Nürnberger Nachrichten*, 6 June 1970; Schmid, *Entscheidung in Bonn*, 78.
23. FRG, Presse- und Informationsamt der Bundesregierung, *Bulletin*, 12 August 1970.
24. *SdZ*, 10 August 1970.
25. *Le Monde* spoke of a "turning point in European history," and *The Times* (London), 8 August 1970, hailed "a good step forward," and on 4 September 1970, also warned the Union against a "vigorous rearguard action" and "sterile arguments about self-determination." The *New York Times* foresaw a "fruitful new era for Europe," but also worried about "irresponsible, chauvinistic" CDU/CSU attacks on the accord. *New York Times* [hereafter cited as *NYT*], 8 August 1970; 4 September 1970.
26. CSU, Landesgruppe, *CSU Correspondenz*, press release 104, 21 July 1970.
27. Barzel also insisted that proper evaluation of the treaty required Union access to notes taken during Bahr's negotiating session with Gromyko, in order better to judge each side's understanding of terms like "the inviolability of borders."
28. *SdZ*, 8 September 1970.
29. *SdZ*, 17–18 October 1970.
30. *Die Welt* [hereafter cited as *DW*], 31 August 1970.
31. *NYT*, 23 November 1970; *The Times* (London), 23 November 1970. These observers agreed with Brandt that Bonn had given up nothing Germany had not lost long ago.
32. In a mini-crisis in 1969, for example, the GDR again interfered with traffic on the transit routes to protest the convening of an assembly to select the FRG's president.
33. Kissinger, *White House Years*, 406, 531, 832.
34. CDU, *DUD* 38, 25 February 1971.
35. Ibid.
36. Franz Amrehn, "Berlin: Schlüssel zur Vorherrschaft," in *Ostpolitik im Kreuzfeuer*, ed. Hans Graf Huyn (Stuttgart: Seewald Verlag, 1971), 131.
37. *NYT*, 25 August 1971.
38. *SdZ*, 24 August 1971.
39. Ibid., 25 August 1971.

40. For an excellent history of the Four Power agreement see Honoré M. Catudal, Jr., *The Diplomacy of the Quadripartite Agreement on Berlin: A New Era in East-West Relations* (Berlin: Berlin Verlag, 1978).
41. *SdZ*, 30 August 1971.
42. *DW*, 18 December 1971.

3. From the Ratification Debates to Karlsruhe, 1972–1973

1. Georges Pompidou and Henry Kissinger privately expressed fears openly stated by longtime Atlanticists like Dean Acheson, George Ball, Lucius Clay, and John McCloy, as well as some maverick Republican and southern Democratic congressmen in the United States.
2. *Deutsche Zeitung/Christ und Welt* [hereafter cited as *DZ/CW*], 25 February 1972.
3. CSU, Landesgruppe, *CSU Correspondenz*, press release 44, 3 March 1972.
4. *Bayernkurier* [hereafter cited as *BK*], 19 February 1972. Union leaders also blamed "the confused state of opinion" on the SPD's "court press"—leading newspapers that they said put Brandt's policy in a favorable light. The Union had its own media sympathizers, above all the Springer chain of newspapers, which reinforced fundamentalist pressure against the treaties.
5. Given the unhappy experience of "revolving door cabinets" in the 1920s, framers of the FRG constitution stipulated that a government could be brought down on a confidence motion only if a replacement were simultaneously elected.
6. Rainer Barzel, *Auf dem Drahtseil* (Munich: Drümer Knaur, 1978), 140–54; Barzel, *Im Streit und umstritten* (Frankfurt: Ullstein, 1986), 157–68.
7. Kurt Birrenbach, *Meine Sondermissionen: Rückblick auf zwei Jahrzehnte bundesdeutscher Aussenpolitik* (Düsseldorf: Econ Verlag, 1984), 324–96.
8. Barzel, *Im Streit*, 176–83.
9. See an Emnid survey cited in *Stuttgarter Zeitung*, 21 December 1971.
10. See an Allensbach survey cited in *Die Zeit* [hereafter cited as *DZ*], 26 March 1971; *Der Spiegel* [hereafter cited as *DS*], 1 November 1971. Since Allensbach had close ties to the Union, it was difficult to support the argument that these data showing support for Brandt were the result of tendentious questions and analysis.
11. *Handelsblatt* [hereafter cited as *HB*], 11 October 1971.
12. Cited in Günther Patz, *Parlamentarische Kontrolle der Aussenpolitik: Fallstudien zur politischen Bedeutung des Auswaertigen Ausschusses des Deutschen Bundestages*, Studien zum politischen System des Bundesrepublik Deutschland no. 7, ed. Heino Kaack (Meisenhein am

Glan: Anton Hain, 1976), 121. Fearful that Barzel might give in to allied pressure during one of his trips abroad, the CSU surprised him by publishing "alternative treaties," which in effect rejected all the results of Bonn's negotiators.
13. *TzDp*, ser. 1, vol. 10, 279.
14. Ibid., 300.
15. *BK*, 12 February 1972.
16. Bills deemed by the legal affairs committee to fall within the states' areas of competence were subject to an absolute Bundesrat veto, requiring a two-thirds Bundestag majority for an override. But, confusingly, the Union's overall second-chamber majority—which rested on its control of several larger states, each entitled to slightly more seats than smaller states—did not translate into a majority on the legal committee, in which each state had one vote and in which the SPD had a 6 to 5 edge.
17. *Süddeutsche Zeitung* [hereafter cited as *SdZ*], 25 February 1972.
18. *SdZ*, 9 March 1972; *DW*, 10 March 1972.
19. Cited in Patz, *Parlamentarische Kontrolle der Aussenpolitik*, 115.
20. CDU/CSU, Fraktion, press release, 19 April 1972.
21. Further hardening fundamentalist opposition was the leaked publication of notes taken during Bahr's 1970 talks with Gromyko. The contents differed from an abridged version read to two CDU/CSU leaders just weeks earlier as part of Scheel's effort at bipartisan compromise. Moreover, the new version seemed to indicate Bahr's acceptance of Soviet claims that West Berlin constituted a "third entity," that any final peace treaty would merely confirm the terms of the present accord, and that a renunciation of force accord was in effect a border agreement (which merely carried a different label to avoid violating the FRG constitution.)
22. Arnulf Baring, *Machtwechsel: Die Ära Brandt-Scheel* (Stuttgart: Deutsche Verlags-Anstalt, 1982), 410.
23. *DZ/CW*, 12 May 1972.
24. At least one, as it later turned out, had received unauthorized bribes from a government official. Baring, *Machtwechsel*, 420–24.
25. Cited in Patz, *Parlamentarische Kontrolle der Aussenpolitik*, 138.
26. *SdZ*, 10–11 May 1972.
27. Günther Patz has argued that a tacit coalition of SPD hard-liners under Wehner and CSU fundamentalists tried to sink the efforts at bipartisanship arranged by Brandt, Barzel, and Scheel. Patz, *Parlamentarische Kontrolle der Aussenpolitik*, 130–33.
28. Birrenbach, *Meine Sondermissionen*, 413.
29. Barzel, *Auf dem Drahtseil*, 166.
30. Werner Marx in an interview with the author, 20 June 1984.
31. Barzel, *Auf dem Drahtseil*, 162.
32. Birrenbach, *Meine Sondermissionen*, 402–4. Walter Hallstein, one of

the CDU's "grey eminences," made this case for unity particularly well.
33. Barzel, *Auf dem Drahtseil*, 167–70.
34. In accordance with its commitment, the Union's Bundesrat delegation in a final vote permitted the treaties to pass by abstaining. Had it chosen to use its majority to vote against the accords, the Union would have embarassed Brandt: to override such an action by the upper chamber, the Bundestag needed a clear majority (249) of votes, which the coalition lacked by a margin of one seat.
35. The intricate process by which the Brandt government "fell" and new elections were arranged is covered in Baring, *Machtwechsel*, 447–57, 489–91.
36. TzDp, ser. 1, vol. 11, 150–70; SdZ, 17 August 1972.
37. TzDp, ser. 1, vol. 11, 268–73, 285–89.
38. *New York Times* [hereafter cited as NYT], 10 November 1972, lavished praise upon "this spectacular accomplishment," which cleared the way for detente by "banishing illusions." The *Financial Times* [hereafter cited as FT], 9 November 1972, was less enthusiastic: the treaty ended an era of uncertainty because Bonn had settled for "the status-quo-minus" in its quest for unity.
39. BK, 18 November 1972.
40. See Strauss cited in Alf Mintzel, "Die CSU in Bayern," in *Parteiensystem in der Legitimationskrise: Studien und Materialien zur Soziologie der Parteien in der Bundesrepublik Deutschland*, ed. Jürgen Dittberner and Rolf Ebbighausen (Opladen: Westdeutscher Verlag, 1973), 352.
41. Neue Zürcher Zeitung [hereafter cited as NZZ], 15 December 1972.
42. See, for example, an Infas poll cited in DW, 7 February 1973.
43. Alfred Dregger suggested that Western desires for detente might be another example of the same shortsightedness that had led to appeasement of Hitler. SdZ, 18 December 1972.
44. Johann Baptist Gradl, *Stets auf der Suche: Reden, Ausserungen und Aufsätze zur Deutschlandpolitik*, ed. Christian Hacke (Cologne: Verlag Wissenschaft und Politik, 1979), 335.
45. The Union pointed to polls that showed that slightly more West Germans wanted neutrality or closer cooperation with Moscow than close ties with Washington; Germans held a more positive view of Kremlin leaders and aims than in the past. The pro-Brandt *Stern* magazine greeted the passing of both "wild anti-Communism" and a "one-sided American orientation" in the FRG. See the surveys cited in TzDp, ser. 1, vol. 12, 255, and an Allensbach survey cited in *Stern*, 17 May 1973.
46. TzDp, ser. 1, vol. 12, 100–109.
47. NZZ, 12 February 1973.
48. BK, 26 May 1973.
49. The *Times* (London), 15 June 1973; DZ, 1 June 1973. Even a pro-Union newspaper asked why Strauss had proclaimed his readiness to honor this treaty—*pacta sunt servanda*—if he truly believed it uncon-

stitutional. *DZ/CW*, 25 May 1973.
50. *BK*, 19 May 1973; *SdZ*, 24 May 1973.
51. *BK*, 2 June 1973; *Frankfurter Allgemeine Zeitung* [hereafter cited as *FAZ*], 26 May 1973; *BK*, 26 May 1973.
52. *TzDp*, ser. 2, vol. 1, 79–110.
53. Ibid., 94.
54. *BK*, 4 August 1973.
55. CDU, *Deutschland Union Dienst* 144, 1 August 1973. Alois Mertes in an interview with the author, 13 June 1984.

4. Interpolation: Beyond the Eastern Treaties

1. Cited in *Deutschland nach den Verträgen*, 19th Gesamtdeutsch session of the Coburg Convent and the German Sängerschaft, Berlin, January 1974.
2. *Süddeutsche Zeitung* [hereafter cited as *SdZ*], 3–4 June 1973.
3. *Bayernkurier* [hereafter cited as *BK*], 17 February 1973.
4. *Texte zur Deutschlandpolitik* [hereafter cited as *TzDp*], ser. 1, vol. 12, 51.
5. *TzDp*, ser. 2, vol. 1, 430–33.
6. This leaked version was published in *Der Spiegel* and cited in Werner Kaltefleiter, "Winning Without Victory: The 1976 CDU Campaign," in *Germany at the Polls: The Bundestag Election of 1976*, ed. Karl H. Cerny (Washington: American Enterprise Institute, 1978), 119.
7. See for example the speech by Kohl, cited in CDU, press release, 29 November 1974.
8. Helmut Kohl, *Zwischen Ideologie und Pragmatismus: Aspekte und Ansichten zu Grundfragen der Politik* (Stuttgart: Verlag Bonn Aktuell, 1973).
9. Expellee spokesmen, stressing that Karlsruhe upheld the 1937 borders, used the decision to protest the absence from official German pronouncements and publications of reference to Germany in its prewar configuration, such as any government map that showed the Eastern territories as part of Poland.
10. Johann Baptist Gradl, *Stets auf der Suche: Reden, Äusserungen und Aufsätze zur Deutschlandpolitik*, ed. Christian Hacke (Cologne: Verlag Wissenschaft und Politik, 1979), 335.
11. *TzDp*, ser. 1, vol. 12, 334.
12. CSU, *Information zur Deutschlandpolitik*, vol. 8, *Freiheit und Recht für Deutschland und Europa*, documentation from the Deutschlandpolitische Congress of the CDU/CSU, Ingolstadt, 28–29 November 1975, 12.
13. Ibid.
14. The opposition pressed for closer relations with Peking. But while reformists explicitly downplayed Chinapolitik's importance in rela-

tion to ties with the Soviet bloc, Strauss tried to link them. "Ostpolitik," he declared, "should not end at the Moscow [River]." *Frankfurter Allgemeine Zeitung* [hereafter cited as *FAZ*], 2 January 1975. As states bordering the Soviet empire, Germany and China must cooperate, he added, and he welcomed Peking's support for German unity and its attacks on East Berlin. Ibid.; CDU, *DUD* 158, 21 August 1974.
15. *FAZ*, 20 August 1973.
16. *Bonner General Anzeiger*, 20 June 1975.
17. William Griffith, *The Ostpolitik of the Federal Republic of Germany* (Cambridge: MIT Press, 1978), 225.
18. Henry Kissinger, *Years of Upheaval* (Boston: Little, Brown, 1982), 137–51.
19. Löwenthal, *Vom kalten Krieg zur Ostpolitik* (Stuttgart: Seewald Verlag, 1974), 90.
20. Arnulf Baring, *Machtwechsel: Die Ära Brandt-Scheel* (Stuttgart: Deutsche Verlags-Anstalt, 1982), 614–25; *Vorwärts*, 24 January 1974.
21. Wolfgang Wagner, "Ein Modus Vivendi in Deutschland," *Europa Archiv* 1 (1973): 1–6; Josef Joffe, "Westverträge, Ostverträge und die Kontinuität der deutschen Aussenpolitik," *Europa Archiv* 4 (1973): 11–24; Pierre Hassner, "Old Conflict, New Rules," *Orbis* 17 (Fall 1973): 895–911.

5. Finding the Limits of Ostpolitik, 1973–1976

1. Because the official Four Powers agreement was in the four languages of the occupying powers, no one official German version existed—thus the dispute over translations.
2. Cited in *Texte zur Deutschlandpolitik* [hereafter cited as *TzDp*], ser. 1, vol. 12, 328–29.
3. *Augsburger Allgemeine Zeitung*, 22 November 1973; Infas poll cited in FRG, Presse- und Informationsamt der Bundesregierung, press release, 13 March 1974; *Der Tagesspiegel*, 1 March 1974; Allensbach survey cited in *Die Welt* [hereafter cited as *DW*], 28 February 1974.
4. Although they agreed on the wisdom of neutrality, they argued that the United States had a right to expect help from its allies, especially the one for whom it guaranteed Berlin's independence. They condemned Bonn's reluctance to permit American use of NATO bases in the FRG to ferry supplies to Israel and the failure of Bonn and Paris to promote a joint European position in support of U.S. policy. CDU, *DUD*, 6 November 1973; *Bayernkurier* [hereafter cited as *BK*], 3 November 1973.
5. The fact that East Berlin's representative was not greeted by an honor guard and that the federal president wore a suitcoat rather than the customary morning coat did not mollify Union fundamentalists.
6. They also feared that the nuclear-power industry would be deprived

of uranium imports unless Bonn signed. *Frankfurter Allgemeine Zeitung* [hereafter cited as *FAZ*], 9 February 1974.
7. Arnulf Baring, *Machtwechsel: Die Ära Brandt-Scheel* (Stuttgart: Deutsche Verlags-Anstalt, 1982), 722–62. The affair itself had little lasting effect on the Ostpolitik debate. Union fundamentalists called for an investigation, used the episode to attack Brandt for the naiveté they said underlay his entire Eastern policy, and warned against allowing the new GDR mission in Bonn to become a "nest of spies," but none called for closing it, let alone for an end to talks with East Berlin. CDU/CSU, Fraktion, press release, 2 May 1974.
8. As Arnulf Baring observed years later, the decisive shift in FRG foreign policy came in 1974, not 1982. *Die Zeit* [hereafter cited as *DZ*], 15 October 1982.
9. *FAZ*, 31 January 1975.
10. Allensbach cited in *Deutsche Zeitung/Christ und Welt* [hereafter cited as *DZ/CW*], 10 January 1975; *Frankfurter Rundschau*, 17 October 1974.
11. Kissinger, *Years of Upheaval* (Boston: Little, Brown, 1982), 909.
12. TzDp, ser. 2, vol. 2, 439.
13. Some reformists, including above all Kiep and von Weizsäcker, had begun meeting periodically with Soviet and GDR officials, but most party leaders—and all fundamentalists—remained wary of such contacts. In 1975 Kiep came under heavy fire for conferring in a private capacity with officials of the GDR's own CDU, a government-controlled "opposition" party. Kohl was compelled to rebuke him for legitimizing a GDR-front organization, and only certain prominent reformists defended the meeting. *Neue Zürcher Zeitung* [hereafter cited as *NZZ*], 21 January 1975.
14. CDU, *Protokoll: 23. Bundesparteitag der Christlichen Demokratischen Union Deutschlands, Niederschrift*, Mannheim, 23–25 June 1975, 175–76.
15. Wolfgang Pfeiler, an academic, had warned that any policy promoting change within the GDR would be met by delimitation and restrictions on human contacts. This clashed not only with Union orthodoxy, but with Bahr's stated strategy. *FAZ*, 15 November 1975; *Süddeutsche Zeitung* [hereafter cited as *SdZ*], 24 November 1975.
16. CSU, *Information zur Deutschlandpolitik*, vol. 8, *Freiheit und Recht für Deutschland und Europa*, documentation from the Deutschlandpolitische Congress of the CDU/CSU, Ingolstadt, 28–29 November 1975.
17. *FAZ*, 1 December 1975; *SdZ*, 1 December 1975.
18. For months leading up to the conclusion of the accord, the Union encouraged Bonn to stand firm on points affecting Germany. Yet it was skittish about criticizing an East-West agreement still under negotiation and thus continued to praise CSCE in principle as an historic opportunity. Union observers attended the Geneva talks.
19. CSU, *Information zur Deutschlandpolitik*, vol. 6, *Anspruch und Wirk-*

lichkeit, documents about the Conference for Security and Cooperation in Europe (CSCE), Gerhard Baumann [1976].
20. Mertes in *TzDp*, ser. 2, vol. 3, 274.
21. Cited in Christian Hacke, "Parlamentarische Opposition und Entspannungspolitik—Die Position der CDU/CSU zur KSZE," in *Verwaltete Aussenpolitik: Sicherheits- und Entspannungspolitische Prozesse in Bonn*, ed. Helga Haftendorn, Wolf-Dieter Karl, Joachim Krause, and Lothar Wilkar (Cologne: Verlag Wissenschaft und Politik, 1978), 275.
22. *TzDp*, ser. 2, vol. 3, 295.
23. Ibid., 266–76, 417; *FAZ*, 11 August 1975.
24. Press observers criticized the party for treating the detente process as a zero-sum game. For although the West did not achieve all of its goals, it did best Moscow in some respects: CSCE formalized the U.S. tie to European security, confirmed the principle of armed detente, and won Kremlin acceptance of human rights standards in Europe. *DZ*, 1 August 1975; *Kölner Stadt-Anzeiger*, 25 July 1975.
25. Clearly it was also a compromise between Polish demands for restitution to all victims of Nazi concentration camps and forced labor, and Bonn's standing refusal to pay formal war reparations.
26. *SdZ*, 23 December 1974.
27. Union fundamentalists held as well that even payment as indirect as this set a precedent for further demands for "reparations," tacitly accepting the Soviet-bloc claim that the FRG alone, not the GDR or Austria, was guilty of war crimes.
28. A Wickert survey cited in *Kölnische Rundschau*, 5 November 1975. Schmidt's government held that the collapse of this accord would undercut those moderates in Warsaw—Western-oriented Catholics—who wanted rapprochement.
29. Wolfgang Pauly, "Christliche Demokraten und Christlich-Soziale: Untersuchung zum innerparteiliche Bündnisverhalten von CDU und CSU, 1969–1979" (Ph.D. diss., University of Trier, 1981), 241–51.
30. Strauss cited in *SdZ*, 27 October 1975; Bavarian brief in *DW*, 27 October 1975.
31. They argued that, however flawed, the accords were needed to make up for SPD-FDP Ostpolitik's past failure to secure emigration rights and to create a climate of reconciliation in which the problems of ethnic Germans could be settled. *FAZ*, 2 February 1976.
32. *Welt am Sonntag*, 22 February 1976.
33. Two surveys provided diametrically opposed pictures of the public mood, sparking a debate over polling data. See a Wickert poll cited in *SdZ*, 24 February 1976, and an Allensbach poll in *FAZ*, 3 March 1976.
34. Alois Mertes, "Die Union und Polen," in *Union Alternativ*, ed. Gerhard Mayer-Vorfelder and Hubertus Zuber (Stuttgart: Seewald Verlag, 1976), 113–19.
35. *SdZ*, 10 March 1976. He added unilateral declarations as binding

upon Bonn as the 1972 Joint Resolution. These were to meet Union concerns about avoiding a precedent for reparations, improving conditions for Germans in Poland, and expediting their emigration.
36. FAZ, 13 March 1976.
37. Mertes, "Die Union und Polen," 118.
38. Walther Leisler Kiep in an interview with the author, 15 June 1984.
39. DW, 5 February 1976; Kohl cited in NZZ, 4 August 1976; TzDp, ser. 2, vol. 4, 239.
40. Friedbert Pflüger in an interview with the author, 15 February 1984.
41. Allensbach's assessment in DW, 26 February 1976.
42. DW, 25 September 1976.
43. The Times (London), 25 May 1976.
44. Mertes in CDU/CSU, Fraktion, press release, 26 June 1976.
45. CDU, Union in Deutschland 27, "Das versteht die Union unter Entspannung," 1976; SdZ, 24 June 1976.
46. New York Times, 5 October 1976.
47. FAZ, 27 July 1976; von Wrangel cited in FAZ, 21 June 1976.
48. FAZ, 18 August 1976.
49. SdZ, 16 August 1976.
50. Kohl cited in FAZ, 18 August 1976; Frankfurter Rundschau, 20 September 1976.
51. DW, 6 October 1976; Allensbach cited in FAZ, 14 September 1976.
52. The Times (London), 14 September 1976.
53. Stern, 9 September 1976; CDU, Deutschland Union Dienst 48, 30 November 1976.
54. Kehrmann Institute survey cited in Quick, 9 September 1976.

6. The Changing Ostpolitik Debate, 1977–1979

1. Kohl in CDU, Deutschland Union Diest [hereafter cited as DUD] 112, 15 June 1977, 3; Kohl cited in Frankfurter Allgemeine Zeitung [hereafter cited as FAZ], 14 February 1977.
2. CDU, DUD 152, 11 August 1977, 3–4.
3. Süddeutsche Zeitung [hereafter cited as SdZ], 5–6 February 1977.
4. Marx in effect played the role of the CDU's link to the CSU, while Mertes played that role vis-à-vis the FDP. Die Welt [hereafter cited as DW], 1 July 1977; Gradl, Stets auf der Suche, 375.
5. Johann Baptist Gradl, Stets auf der Suche: Reden, Äusserungen und Aufsätze zur Deutschlandpolitik, ed. Christian Hacke (Cologne: Verlag Wissenschaft und Politik, 1979), 375.
6. Die Zeit [hereafter cited as DZ], 11 March 1977. Indeed, the results of the conference were so mixed that one television journalist called it a possible CDU "Godesberg," and a colleague from the same network predicted that it would never be classified as such. Vorwärts, 17 March 1977.

7. Gradl, *Stets auf der Suche*, 375.
8. CSU, Landesgruppe, *Deutschlandpolitisches Grundsatzpapier: Sonderdruck zum 17. Juni* [1978]; Herbert Prauss, "CDU/CSU Aussenpolitik—nichts dazugelernt," *Die Neue Gesellschaft* 25 (May 1978): 404; *Neue Zürcher Zeitung* [hereafter cited as *NZZ*], 21 January 1978.
9. Henning Wegener, "Deutschland in der Welt," *Aus Politik und Zeitgeschichte* (17 February 1979): 45–48.
10. CDU, *Grundsatzprogramm der Christlichen Demokratischen Union Deutschlands* [1978], 51–60.
11. Contending that it would add credence to East German demands for recognition of GDR citizenship and borders, the Union as late as 1979 also opposed a draft tax law that would have given up the traditional classification of all areas within the 1937 borders as "domestic" lands. It settled for an ambiguous compromise that avoided describing the GDR and East Berlin, if not the Eastern territories, as "foreign." *FAZ*, 28 September 1979; 19 October 1979.
12. *DZ*, 11 March 1977; *FAZ*, 22 September 1979.
13. *Texte zur Deutschlandpolitik* [hereafter cited as *TzDp*], ser. 2, vol. 7, 403; ibid., vol. 5, 190.
14. *SdZ*, 25 May 1977; *Bayernkurier* [hereafter cited as *BK*], 25 November 1978.
15. Kohl cited in *TzDp*, ser. 2, vol. 6, 140; Johann Baptist Gradl, "Deutschlandpolitik—permanente Herausforderung," *Deutschland Archiv* 10 (1977): 252–57.
16. *TzDp*, ser. 2, vol. 6, 213–14.
17. Cited in Wilhelm Bruns, "Polemik statt Politik: Die CDU tut sich mit Deutschland schwer," *Die Neue Gesellschaft* (December 1978): 983.
18. *TzDp*, ser. 2, vol. 6, 212–13.
19. Gradl, "Deutschlandpolitik," 255.
20. Radio Free Europe, *Research Reports, Poland*, no. 17, 28 June 1977; *DW*, 28 October 1978.
21. CDU, *DUD* 214, 8 November 1978.
22. *FAZ*, 15 October 1978; *Zycie Warszwy*, 14 June 1980.
23. CDU, *Protokoll: 26. Parteitag der Christlichen Demokratischen Deutschlands*, Ludwigshafen, 23–25 October 1978, 355.
24. *BK*, 24 June 1978; Norbert Schäfer in an interview with the author, 2 April 1984.
25. FRG, Deutscher Bundestag, *Verhandlungen des deutschen Bundestages, Stenographischer Bericht*, 8. Wahlperiode, 90. Sitzung, 11 May 1978, 7085–93. Because Strauss and Kohl had initially praised the new Bonn-Moscow economic accord, many Union leaders felt obliged to vote for its formal ratification. Mertes dissuaded them by stressing that formal ratification, which was unnecessary, would create the impression of a "special relationship." When Schmidt later sought mere Bundestag approval, Mertes then had to persuade the party that

it safely could support the agreement.
26. FAZ, 15 January 1979; DW, 7 August 1979; von Weizsäcker cited in DW, 24 February 1979. As Bavarian minister-president, Strauss also led a huge 200-man delegation—all but three state-level cabinet members and most CSU Bundestag deputies—to Budapest in August 1979. In talks with Hungarian party chief, Janos Kadar, he was again "candid," proving, as he put it, that mutual understanding could profit more from "pragmatism" than from "clumsy attempts at accommodation or simple flattery." He reportedly fished for an invitation to Moscow, and indeed, Soviet press reports began to speak of his "transformation." *Financial Times* [hereafter cited as *FT*], 7 August 1970.
27. FAZ, 19 January 1977; Vorwärts, 28 April 1977.
28. DZ, 10 March 1978.
29. U.S. policymakers condemmed Schmidt not only for his "patronizing" attitude toward Carter but his tendency to be "the one who was most concerned about the Soviet nuclear threat in Europe and the least inclined to agree to any firm response." Zbigniew Brzezinski, *Power and Principle: Memoirs of the National Security Advisor, 1977–1981* (New York: Farrar, Straus & Giroux, 1983), 289–315.
30. SPD, Fraktion, *Sicherheitspolitische Informationstagung der SPD Bundestagsfraktion*, Augsburg, 17 September 1978.
31. Herbert Wehner, "'Deutschland' statt Politik," *Die Neue Gesellschaft* (April 1977): 268–71; FAZ, 27 March 1979.
32. Alfons Pawelczyk, "Die Entspannungspolitik muss als Element der Sicherheitspolitik genauso ernst genommen werden wie die Verteidigungspolitik," in *Koalition auf Entspannungskurs: Beiträge zur Abrüstungspolitik mit einer Dokumentation*, ed. Rolf Seeligen (Munich: Rolf Seeligen, 1979), 25.
33. Schmidt's government and the SPD left did agree in condemning the Union for having no real interest in arms control as a contribution to security or cooperation in Europe. They publicly castigated the opposition's "policy of strength" as certain to escalate the arms race and kill detente. The litmus test of CDU/CSU adherence to the treaties—*pacta sunt servanda*—was its commitment to arms control. Seeligen, ed., *Koalition auf Entspannungskurs*, passim.
34. He also resented Wehner's "invitation" to politicians to help reshape Bonn's arms control diplomacy. SdZ, 15 September 1979.
35. Brzezinski, *Power and Principle*, 301–06.
36. Hans Rühle, "German Security Policy: Position, Problems, Prospects," *International Security Review* 5 (Summer 1980): 194.
37. Government and opposition leaders did differ on the broader implications of SALT II. Schmidt greeted it as a step toward stability and detente. CDU leaders like Mertes, resigned to parity, cautiously voiced a similar view. But most were still implicitly critical of the United States for letting Moscow erode its once-substantial strategic advan-

tage with an unanswered arms buildup, and the CSU was openly scornful.
38. FAZ, 1 February 1979; CDU, DUD 195, 10 October 1979. In any case, the Union argued, Bonn should not act as a "state's witness" in U.S. debates over a treaty that omitted limits on Soviet medium-range weapons and—through a noncircumvention clause and a protocol-restricting cruise-missile development—might deny NATO the chance to match those Soviet systems.
39. CDU/CSU, Fraktion, press release, 22 January 1979.
40. CDU, DUD, no. 64, 4 April 1978. CDU/CSU leaders also charged that SPD relations with the Italian Communist party and SPD rhetoric about a socialist Europe meant that Schmidt would be forced by party ideologues to pursue a European "popular front" and a European community built along on class lines, which would split the West and destroy hopes for real unity.

7. Crisis and Consensus, 1980–1982

1. Zbigniew Brzezinski, *Power and Principles: Memoirs of the National Security Advisor* (New York: Farrar, Straus & Giroux, 1983), 429.
2. *Der Spiegel* [hereafter cited as DS], 7 April 1980; Schmidt cited in FRG, Deutscher Bundestag, Stenographischer Bericht, 8. Wahlperiode, 203. Sitzung, 28 February 1980, 16172.
3. DS, 10 February 1980.
4. Jimmy Carter, *Keeping the Faith: Memoirs of a President* (Toronto: Bantam, 1982), 500.
5. Infas cited in *Frankfurter Rundschau*, 30 July 1980; Emnid in *Die Welt* [hereafter cited as DW], 29 March 1980; Allensbach in *Stern*, 24 January 1980.
6. Graf Huyn in CDU, *Deutschland Union Dienst* [hereafter cited as DUD] 95, 23 May 1980.
7. *Frankfurter Allgemeine Zeitung* [hereafter cited as FAZ], 14 February 1980.
8. FRG, Deutscher Bundestag, *Verhandlungen des deutschen Bundestages*, Stenographischer Bericht, 8, Wahlperiode, 203. Sitzung, 28 February 1980, 16177.
9. Mertes in *Neue Zürcher Zeitung* [hereafter cited as NZZ], 11 January 1980; Strauss cited in FAZ, 21 February 1980. Even newspapers not counted among the Bavarian's admirers praised his "statesmanlike posture" and "sense of proportion." More cynical observers joked that Strauss, like Kaiser Wilhelm, saw "no parties, only Germans."
10. FAZ, 9 January 1980; Mertes cited in NZZ, 11 January 1980.
11. *Die Zeit* [hereafter cited as DZ], 25 January 1980.
12. FAZ, 21 February 1980.
13. Strauss declared that "today we have other security regions," and

Wörner urged reevaluation of NATO's "structures and tasks," adding that its "geographical limitations must be dropped." Comments made at the Security Policy Congress of the CDU, 11–12 January 1980, cited in "Freiheit durch Sicherheit: Sicherheitspolitischer Kongress der CDU am 11. und 12. Januar in Bonn." [1980.]
14. *FAZ*, 29 January 1980.
15. *Bayernkurier* [hereafter cited as *BK*], 1 March 1980.
16. Mertes in CDU, *DUD*, 14 January 1980; von Weizsäcker cited in *FAZ*, 24 January 1980.
17. *Süddeutsche Zeitung* [hereafter cited as *SdZ*], 8 March 1980.
18. von Weizsäcker cited in *SdZ*, 9 April 1980; Strauss in The *Times* (London), 7 May 1980.
19. Mertes in CDU, *DUD* 81, 2 May 1980; Marx and Dregger cited in *Die Welt* [hereafter cited as *DW*], 18 April 1980; Dregger cited in *FAZ*, 18 April 1980.
20. Carter, *Keeping the Faith*, 535–37.
21. *FAZ*, 29 January 1980.
22. Kohl did speak of reducing FRG dependence on Soviet raw materials, and Biedenkopf and Strauss talked of withholding further trade preferences and limiting credit financing of East-bloc ventures, but the party did not formally endorse these ideas. *SdZ*, 18 February 1980.
23. *SdZ*, 15 March 1980; *Handelsblatt* [hereafter cited as *HB*], 24 March 1980.
24. In a jab at the "unpredictable" Carter, Strauss remarked, "I do not need to say that my view of the Soviet Union has changed dramatically in the last few days." Strauss in the Bundestag, cited in CDU pamphlet, "Der sowjetische Überfall auf Afghanistan—die Konsequenzen für die freie Welt," 22.
25. *HB*, 25–26 January 1980.
26. *FAZ*, 29 August 1980.
27. *NZZ*, 22 August 1980; *BK*, 6 September 1980.
28. *FAZ*, 11 September 1980.
29. Neither Afghanistan nor Poland played a major role in the election outcome. *Infas-Report: Wahlen, Bundestagswahl 1980*.
30. CDU/CSU, Fraktion, press release, 10 October 1980; Strauss in CSU, *Correspondenz*, press release 555, 10 October 1980; von Wrangel in CDU, *DUD* 192, 10 October 1980.
31. von Weizsäcker in *DW*, 16 October 1980; Stoltenberg and Vogel cited in *FAZ*, 29 October 1980; *HB*, 17–18 October 1980.
32. Zimmermann cited in *DZ*, 31 October 1980; others cited in *DW*, 30 October 1980.
33. *DS*, 3 November 1980; Rhineland CDU appeal in *Frankfurter Rundschau*, 29 November 1980.
34. Zimmermann cited in *DW*, 3 November 1980; Strauss cited in *DS*, 3 November 1980; *BK*, 15 November 1980.

35. CDU, *DUD* 198, 20 October 1980; CDU, *DUD* 204, 28 October 1980.
36. *SdZ*, 28 October 1980.
37. FRG, Deutscher Bundestag, *Verhandlungen des deutschen Bundestages, Stenographischer Bericht*, 9. Wahlperiode, 6. Sitzung, 26 November 1980, 45–50.
38. Ibid., 47.
39. SPD, press release 803, 28 November 1980; *FAZ*, 30 October 1980.
40. Kohl in CDU, *Union in Deutschland* 8, *29. Bundesparteitag der CDU*, Mannheim, 9–10 March 1981; Mertes cited in *Die Zeit* [hereafter cited as *DZ*], 30 October 1981.
41. Günther Hindrichs in an interview with the author, 2 April 1958.
42. *New York Times* [hereafter cited as *NYT*], 13 October 1981; John Wallach, "What Europe's Leaders are Saying," *Washington Quarterly* 5 (Winter 1982): 35.
43. *NZZ*, 3 December 1981; Norbert Schäfer in an interview with the author, 2 April 1984.
44. Von Weizsäcker's aide Peter Lorenz argued that the practice of taking in the passports of GDR citizens and issuing them new FRG documents before they traveled on to third countries could be ended, assuming these visitors wished to make no use of their right to West German citizenship and planned to return voluntarily to the GDR. *FAZ*, 7 May 1981.
45. Dettmar Cramer, "Kommentare und aktuelle Beiträge," *Deutschland Archiv* 6 (1981): 562–63.
46. Ibid.
47. *DZ*, 2 October 1981.
48. *DZ*, 6 February 1981.
49. CDU, *DUD* 33, 18 February 1981. Leading newspapers agreed. Even the *SdZ*, long a supporter of SPD policy, accused the government of obscuring its long-term goals and its commitment to national unity, adding that "thoroughly justified" Union demands for clarification should not be answered with "platitudes." *SdZ*, 24 February 1981; *SdZ*, 22 July 1981.
50. *FAZ*, 10 April 1981.
51. *DS*, 27 July 1981.
52. Bahr and Brandt in 1981 conducted talks of their own in the East, discussing Soviet offers of regular FRG-GDR consultations (even on nuclear arms), and an economic community—further undercutting the Foreign Ministry and alienating Genscher. *DS*, 15 June 1981.
53. One journalist observed that no German opposition party had ever established "such a close . . . relationship with an American administration," adding that "never before have the American contacts of a party been so systematically prepared." *DZ*, 24 April 1981.
54. CDU, *DUD*, 5 January 1981.
55. *FAZ*, 25 May 1981.

56. CDU, Protokoll: 30. Bundesparteitag der CDU, Niederschrift, Hamburg, 2–5 November 1981.
57. See a Spiegel poll in DS, 2 March 1981, and an Emnid survey in Frankfurter Neue Presse, 26 September 1981.
58. Financial Times [hereafter cited as FT], 11 March 1982; Stuttgarter Zeitung, 11 March 1981. Kohl was overwhelmingly reelected as CDU party leader. Strauss made a guest appearance, tacitly endorsing his rival as both parliamentary chief and even possibly chancellor should the Union form a coalition with the FDP. The Bavarian still had little respect for Kohl but saw him as a necessary counterweight to CDU reformists.
59. FAZ, 4 December 1981.
60. See an Allensbach poll in Capital, September 1981.
61. FAZ, 6 February 1981.
62. CDU, Union in Deutschland 29. Bundesparteitag der CDU, Mannheim, 9–10 March 1981; FT, 11 March 1981.
63. Biedenkopf published an essay in which he warned that there could be no consensus in the long term for any policy that even implied the possible destruction of life on earth. Decisions on such a matter, he added, should not be left in the hands of a few people, including the U.S. president. DZ, 30 October 1981. Kohl, Wörner, Mertes, and even Kiep distanced the party from this "personal opinion," warning that it could be exploited by unilateral disarmers. DW, 2 November 1981.
64. DZ, 2 October 1981.
65. NYT, 6 November 1981.
66. Economist, 7 November 1981; FAZ, 2 October 1981.
67. NYT, 4 November 1981.
68. DZ, 20 November 1981.
69. SdZ, 6 November 1981.
70. DS, 21 December 1981.
71. Even many leftists abroad were "less docile" in reaction to martial law, and found Schmidt's reaction too mild. NYT, 28 December 1981.
72. Strauss cited in FAZ, 14 December 1981; von Weizsäcker and Späth cited in SdZ, 16 December 1981.
73. Wall Street Journal, 29 December 1981.
74. Alexander Haig, Caveat: Realism, Reagan, and Foreign Policy (New York: Macmillan, 1984), 247–58.
75. von Weizsäcker cited in FT, 1 January 1982; Economist, 30 January 1982. Though sharing Bonn's skepticism about sanctions, many Europeans, even in Scandinavia and even on the left, were alarmed that Schmidt and Genscher seemed to show no interest in human rights. Some spoke of Soviet-German harmony at the expense of Polish liberties. A French cartoonist depicted Schmidt polishing Brezhnev's boots, prompting the Economist to warn of latent anti-German impulses.
76. NZZ, 11 January 1982.

77. *SdZ*, 25 June 1982.
78. CDU/CSU, Fraktion, press release, 23 July 1982.
79. Kohl cited in *FAZ*, 21 June 1982; Lorenz cited in *FAZ*, 24 July 1982.
80. *SdZ*, 13 May 1982.
81. During a Strauss visit in the United States, *Spiegel* reported that U.S. Secretary of State Haig denied rumors that he saw Schmidt's political survival as vital to keeping the FRG in NATO, voiced hope for a Union government with which he would have "far fewer problems," and treated Strauss "overtly as a future partner." Cited in the *Boston Globe*, 4 April 1982.
82. Though welcoming stronger U.S. leadership, Strauss showed signs of his Gaullist instincts when he stressed that Europe must not act like nor be treated like a second-class partner and that Washington must neither bear all burdens nor make all decisions alone. Franz Josef Strauss, "Manifesto of a German Atlanticist," *Strategic Review* 10 (Summer 1982): 11–15.
83. Mertes cited in *FAZ*, 19 June 1982; *Boston Globe*, 2 March 1982.
84. *BK*, 15 May 1982.
85. Mertes praised Genscher for moving the government another few steps closer to the Union on essential issues, above all in support for NATO. It was natural, he added, that Genscher put Bonn's Ostpolitik in too favorable a light, but the Union had no desire to reopen that debate and agreed that the treaties had a constructive place in a new Gesamtpolitik. CDU/CSU, Fraktion, press release, 15 September 1982.
86. *FAZ*, 20 September 1982.
87. *FAZ*, 23 September 1982.
88. *Texte zur Deutschlandpolitik*, ser. 3, vol. 1, 10.

8. The Union's Ambivalent Adaptation

1. Wolfram Hanrieder, "Compatibility and Consensus: A Proposal for the Conceptual Linkage of External and Internal Dimensions of Foreign Policy," in *Comparative Foreign Policy: Theoretical Essays*, ed. Wolfram Hanrieder (New York: David McKay), 242–64.
2. Karl Kaiser, *German Foreign Policy in Transition: Bonn between East and West* (London: Oxford University Press, 1968), 1.
3. Many reformists misjudged the rapidity of this consolidation. As late as 1973 Helmut Kohl argued that the international situation was still in flux and criticized Brandt for not winning more assurances that the German question would remain open. Yet even this implied awareness that a policy based on reunification would be discredited by consolidation of the bloc system. *Texte zur Deutschlandpolitik* [hereafter cited as *TzDp*] ser. 1, vol. 12, 105.
4. Wolfgang Dexheimer in an interview with the author, 20 June 1984.
5. *Stuttgarter Nachrichten*, 21 February 1978.

6. CDU, Deutschland Büro, Exil-CDU, Johann Baptist Gradl, "Europa und die deutsche Frage," speech at the Deutschland session of the Exil-CDU, Lübeck-Traveme unde, 2–4 March 1979.
7. *Die Zeit* [hereafter cited as *DZ*], 5 April 1974; *Süddeutsche Zeitung* [hereafter cited as *SdZ*], 29 December 1979.
8. Dettmar Cramer, "Kommentare und aktuelle Beiträge," *Deutschland Archiv* 6 (1981): 562–63.
9. Hans-Peter Schwarz, "What Is Wrong with U.S.–West German Relations?" *SAIS-Review* (Spring 1982): 69.
10. Alois Mertes in an interview with the author, 13 June 1984; Werner Marx in an interview with the author, 20 June 1984.
11. Approval was highest in 1970 during the height of negotiations, leveled off during the protracted Berlin talks, rose again such that Brandt could turn the 1972 election into a referendum on Ostpolitik. Even one in three Union voters approved.
12. By 1976, 58 percent of all voters (87 percent of Union voters) were disappointed with the policy's results; only 40 percent (12 percent of Union supporters) thought it had achieved its goals. Another survey showed 40 percent mildly dissatisfied, 31 percent content and the remainder ambivalent. Kehrmann Institute data in *Quick*, 9 September 1976; Allensbach data in *Münchner Merkur*, 26 February 1976.
13. *Frankfurter Allgemeine Zeitung* [hereafter cited as *FAZ*], 23 December 1980; *FAZ*, 25 October 1976.
14. *Münchner Merkur*, 26 February 1976.
15. Elisabeth Noelle-Neumann and Edgar Piel, *Allensbacher Jahrbuch der Demoskopie 1978–1983* (Munich: Saur, 1983), 637.
16. Gebhard Schweigler, *West German Foreign Policy: The Domestic Setting*, The Washington Papers, vol. 12, no. 106 (New York: Praeger, 1984), 51.
17. *Die Welt* [hereafter cited as *DW*], 13 August 1980.
18. Schweigler, *West German Foreign Policy*, 43.
19. The figure rose from about 1.25 million per year in 1970 to around 3 million in the mid-1970s. Day trips to East Berlin numbered 1.4 million per year. FRG, Press and Information Office of the Federal Republic, *Facts and Figures: A Comparative Study of the Federal Republic of Germany and the German Democratic Republic* (Bonn: Press and Information Office, 1981), 66–74.
20. An Infratest poll cited in *DW*, 26 September 1979; Forschungsgruppe Wahlen data in *Mannheimer Morgen*, 1 October 1979.
21. *DW*, 26 September 1979; *Mannheimer Morgen*, 1 October 1979.
22. Norbert Ropers, "Zwischen Wiedervereinigung, Abgrenzung und Entspannung: Der innerdeutsche Reiseverkehr und die Politik zwischen den beiden deutschen Staaten," in *Europa zwischen Konfrontation und Kooperation: Entspannung für die achtziger Jahre*, ed. Peter Schlotter (Frankfurt: Campus Verlag, 1982), 281–82.

23. Schweigler, *West German Foreign Policy*, 45.
24. Günther Schmid in an interview with the author, 12 April 1984.
25. Angela Stent, *From Embargo to Ostpolitik: The Political Economy of West German–Soviet Relations 1955–1980* (New York: Cambridge University Press, 1981), 173–202; Michael Kreile, *Osthandel und Ostpolitik* (Baden-Baden: Nomos Verlag, 1978), 115–41.
26. Walther Leisler Kiep in an interview with the author, 15 June 1984.
27. Arno Burzig, "Ostpolitik und Osthandel—Das Zusammenwirken von Regierung und Wirtschaftsverbänden in der Ost-West Wirtschaftspolitik," in *Verwaltete Aussenpolitik*, ed. Helga Haftendorn, Wolf-Dieter Karl, Joachim Krauss, and Lothar Wilkar (Cologne: Verlag Wissenschaft und Politik, 1978), 230.
28. Günther Hindrichs in an interview with the author, 2 April 1984.
29. The electoral disaster of 1972 had hit the CDU harder than the CSU, partly because there were more marginal constituencies and floating voters north of Bavaria. This strengthened the claim of CDU leaders who argued that their party needed a broader appeal and a more effective extraparliamentary structure.
30. Wolf Schönbohm, *CDU: Porträt einer Partei* (Munich: Günther Olzog, 1979), 89–137.
31. It was the CDU Presidium that had most consistently backed Barzel's 1972 decision to let the Brandt treaties survive, but the parliamentary group's strong opposition at that stage counted for more.
32. *DW*, 21 June 1980.
33. He recalled as a student in Bonn hearing the SPD's Kurt Schumacher warn that democrats must not leave the potentially volatile national issue to extremists lest the Federal Republic suffer the Weimar Republic's fate.
34. These convictions reflected the influence of the CSU's longtime foreign affairs spokesman, Baron Guttenberg, with whom Mertes had worked and whom he had greatly admired. A picture of the baron remained on Mertes's desk a decade after the Bavarian's death.
35. Anton DePorte, *Europe between the Superpowers: The Enduring Balance* (New Haven: Yale University Press, 1979), 177.
36. "Transformation through rapprochement" thus had to be replaced by more pragmatic expectations and businesslike bargaining. Peter Ludz, "Ostpolitik and the Present State and Future Course of Inner-German Contacts," in *The Political Implications of Soviet Military Power*, ed. Lawrence Whetten (London: Macdonald and Jane's, 1977), 79.
37. Johann Baptist Gradl, "Ausgangsposition, nicht Endstation: Deutschlandpolitik auf der Grundlage der Verträge," *Politik und Kultur* (January/February 1974): 12–15.
38. *DW*, 1 October 1979; *Economist*, 22 August 1981.
39. FRG, Deutscher Bundestag, *Stenographische Bericht*, 8. Wahlperiode, 203. Sitzung, 28 February 1980, 16192.

Postscript

1. *Washington Post*, 6 September 1987.
2. *Frankfurter Allgemeine Zeitung* [hereafter cited as *FAZ*], 13 April 1988; *Die Zeit* [hereafter cited as *DZ*], 17 June 1988.
3. *FAZ*, 6 February 1985.
4. FRG, Bundesministerium für innerdeutsche Beziehungen, *Erfolgreiche Bilanz der Deutschlandpolitik 1987: Erklärung von Dorothee Wilms* (Bonn: Bundesministerium für innerdeutsche Beziehungen), 1988.
5. *Washington Post*, 10 December 1985.
6. *DZ*, 8 January 1988.
7. *FAZ*, 11 January 1988.
8. *FAZ*, 3 March 1988.
9. *FAZ*, 11 August 1988.
10. *Der Spiegel* [hereafter cited as *DS*], 23 March 1987.
11. *FAZ*, 26 March 1984.
12. *DZ*, 17 July 1987.
13. Strauss cited in Deutschland Funk, "Interview der Woche im Deutschland Funk," 11 January 1970.
14. *FAZ*, 28 July 1983.
15. Philipp Jenninger, "Eine Deutsche Bilanz," FRG, Bundespresse- und Informationsamt, *Bulletin* [hereafter *Bulletin*] 83/84 (15 February 1984).
16. *Die Welt* [hereafter cited as *DW*], 19 December 1983.
17. *FAZ*, 28 October 1987.
18. *FAZ*, 17 December 1985.
19. *FAZ*, 21 November 1985; von Weizsäcker in *Newsweek*, 20 August 1984.
20. *FAZ*, 29 September 1984.
21. Heinrich Windelen, "Grundfragen der Deutschlandpolitik der Bundesregierung," *Bulletin* 15 (8 February 1984): 135.
22. *FAZ*, 4 December 1985.
23. *Washington Post*, 17 January 1988.
24. Eduard Lintner, "Zur Lage der amerikanischen-sowjetischen Beziehungen: Rückwirkung auf das innerdeutsche Verhältnis" (Speech at the Konrad Adenauer Stiftung Conference, San Francisco, 17–18 November 1986), 8–9.
25. Windelen, "Grundfragen," *Bulletin*, 135.
26. *FAZ*, 21 August 1987; Dregger in *Neueste Badische Zeitung*, 18 January 1984; Norbert Schäfer in an interview with the author, 2 April 1984.
27. *Hannoversche Allgemeine Zeitung* [hereafter cited as *HAZ*], 22 March 1988.
28. *German Tribune*, 21 April 1985.
29. *HAZ*, 3 March 1988; Johannes Kindler, "The Inter-relationship between 'Deutschlandpolitik' and the Policies of the European Communities (EC)—the Economic Dimension" (Speech at the Konrad Adenauer

Stiftung Conference, San Francisco, 17 November 1986), 3–4.
30. Stephen Szabo, "West German Public Attitudes on Arms Control," in *The Silent Partner: West Germany and Arms Control*, ed. Barry Blechman and Cathleen Fisher (Cambridge, Mass.: Ballinger, 1988), 207.
31. *Washington Post*, 17 January 1988.
32. *FAZ*, 2 March 1988.
33. *FAZ*, 18 March 1986; Genscher at the special FDP party conference, 22 November 1986, FDP, press release, 1986.
34. *DZ*, 2 January 1987.
35. *DS*, 26 January 1987.
36. Friedbert Pflüger in an interview with the author, 15 February 1984; Windelen in *DS*, 24 September 1984.
37. Dieter Schmidt in an interview with the author, 11 April 1984; Strauss in *DS*, 4 January 1988.
38. *FAZ*, 23 March 1988.
39. Windelen in *DS*, 24 September 1984; Schäuble in *DS*, 28 January 1985.
40. Helmut Kohl, "Politik der Verständigung im Interesse des Friedens," *Bulletin* 99 (4 September 1984): 874.
41. *FAZ*, 16 September 1987; *FAZ*, 22 February 1988.
42. *FAZ*, 15 October 1985.
43. Windelen in *DS*, 24 September 1984; Hennig in *FAZ*, 4 January 1986.
44. *FAZ*, 28 January 1988; *FAZ*, 1 February 1988.
45. *FAZ*, 1 March 1988; *FAZ*, 24 March 1988.
46. *FAZ*, 13 April 1988.
47. *DZ*, 6 March 1987.
48. *German Tribune*, 21 April 1985; Szabo, "West German Public Attitudes on Arms Control," 209.
49. *FAZ*, 27 October 1986.
50. *DZ*, 18 May 1987.
51. Clay Clemens, "The CDU/CSU and Arms Control," in *The Silent Partner*, 61–128.
52. *FAZ*, 8 October 1987; *DW*, 18 February 1988.
53. Ibid.; *DW*, 18 February 1988.
54. Dettmar Cramer in an interview with the author, 14 February 1984.
55. *Chicago Tribune*, cited in *Daily Press* [Norfolk, Virginia], 5 April 1987; Christopher Layne, "Deutschland Über Alles," *The New Republic* (28 September 1987): 12–14.
56. von Weizsäcker in *DZ*, 17 July 1987; Rühe in *DZ*, 22 May 1987; Wilms in *DZ*, 8 April 1988.
57. Gebhard Schweigler, *West German Foreign Policy: The Domestic Context*, The Washington Papers, vol. 12, no. 106 (New York: Praeger, 1984), 48.

Selected Bibliography

Primary Sources

Interviews

Baring, Arnulf. Professor, Freie Universität Berlin. Interview, Berlin, 15 February 1984.
Bergsdorff, Wolfgang. Staff, Bundespresse- und Informationsamt. Interview, Bonn, 1 February 1984.
Cramer, Dettmar. Editor, Radio-RIAS. Interview, Berlin, 14 February 1984.
Dexheimer, Wolfgang. Staff, Bundestag. Interview, Bonn, 16 March 1984.
Dobiey, Burckhardt. Staff, Bundestag Member. Interview, Bonn, 30 January 1984.
Görtemaker, Manfred. Instructor, Freie Universität Berlin. Interview, Berlin, 15 February 1984.
Hindrichs, Günther. Staff Director, Bundestag, Innerdeutsche Ausschuss. Interview, Bonn, 2 April 1984.
Hupka, Herbert. Member, Bundestag, CDU. Interview, Bonn, 25 June 1984.
Huyn, Hans Graf Huyn. Member, Bundestag, CSU. Interview, Bonn, 16 March 1984.
Kaack, Hans-Jürgen. Staff, Bundestag, Innerdeutsche Ausschuss. Interview, Bonn, 22 March 1984.
Kaltefleiter, Werner. Professor, Universität Kiel. Interview, Boston, 1982.
Kiep, Walther Leisler. Treasurer, CDU. Interview, Bonn-Plittersdorf, 15 June 1984.
Klein, Hans. Member, Bundestag, CSU. Interview, Bonn, 20 February 1984.
Kupper, Siegfried. Staff, Gesamtdeutsches Institut. Interview, Bonn, 19 January 1984.
Lintner, Eduard. Member, Bundestag, CSU. Interview, Bonn, 19 March 1984.

Marx, Werner. Member, Bundestag, CDU. Interview, Bonn, 20 June 1984.
Merkel, Hans. Staff, Bundestag. Interview, Bonn, March 1984.
Mertes, Alois. State Minister, Auswärtiges Amt. Interview, Bonn, 13 June 1984.
Niclauss, Karl-Heinz. Instructor, Universität Bonn. Interview, Bonn, 22 February 1984.
Pfeiler, Wolfgang. Researcher, Konrad Adenauer Stiftung. Interview, Sankt Augustin, January 1984.
Pflüger, Friedbert. Staff, Governing Mayor of Berlin. Interview, Berlin, 15 February 1984.
Plate, Bernard von. Researcher, Stiftung Wissenschaft und Politik. Interview, Ebenhausen, 10 April 1984.
Pond, Elizabeth. Correspondent, *Christian Science Monitor*. Interview, Bonn, 2 March 1984.
Royen, Christoph. Researcher, Stiftung Wissenschaft und Politik. Interview, Ebenhausen, 10 April 1984.
Rüddenklau, Harald. Staff, Deutsche Gesellschaft für Auswärtige Politik. Interview, Bonn, 10 January 1984.
Rummel, Rheinhardt. Researcher, Stiftung Wissenschaft und Politik. Interview, Ebenhausen, 10 April 1984.
Rupprecht, Wilfried. Staff, FDP, Fraktion. Interview, Bonn, 8 March 1984.
Schäfer, Norbert. Staff, Bundespresse- und Informationsamt. Interview, Bonn, 2 April 1984.
Schmid, Günther. Professor, Universität München. Interview, Munich, 12 April 1984.
Schmidt, Dieter. Staff, Hanns-Seidel Stiftung. Interview, Munich, 11 April 1984.
Schönbohm, Wolf. Staff, CDU. Interview, Bonn, 2 April 1984.
Schwarz, Hans-Peter. Professor, Universität Köln. Interview, Cologne, 9 February 1984.
Sontheimer, Kurt. Professor, Universität München. Interview, Munich, 10 April 1984.
Veen, Hans-Joachim. Director, Social Science Research Institute, Konrad Adenauer Stiftung. Interview, Sankt Augustin, 17 May 1984.
Wrangel, Olaf von. Director, Norddeutsche Rundfunk. Interview, Hamburg, July 1984.

Documents

Documents/Government

FRG. Bundesminister für innerdeutsche Beziehungen. *Auskünfte zur Deutschlandpolitik*. 1983.
FRG. Bundesministerium für innerdeutsche Beziehungen. *Erfolgreiche Bilanz der Deutschlandpolitik 1987: Erklärung von Dorothee Wilms*. 1988.
FRG. Bundesminister für innerdeutsche Beziehungen. *Texte zur Deutsch-*

landpolitik. Melsungen: A. Bernecker, series 1, 1968–73, series 2, 1975–83.
FRG. Deutscher Bundestag. *Verhandlungen des deutschen Bundestages, Stenographischer Bericht.* 8. Wahlperiode [1976–80]; 9. Wahlperiode [1980–83].
FRG. Presse- und Informationsamt der Bundesregierung. *Bulletin.*
FRG. Presse- und Informationsamt der Bundesregierung. *Facts and Figures: A Comparative Study of the Federal Republic of Germany and the German Democratic Republic.* Bonn: Presse- und Informationsamt. 1981.
FRG. Bundeszentrale für Politische Bildung. *Kontrovers: Die Ostpolitik der Bundesrepublik Deutschland 1966–1973.* 1982

Documents/CDU/CSU

CDU. *Deutschland Union Dienst* [1969–82].
CDU. *Grundsatzprogramm der Christlichen Demokratischen Union Deutschlands* [1978].
CDU. "Der sowjetische Überfall auf Afghanistan—die Konsequenzen für die freie Welt." Helmut Kohl, Franz Josef Strauss. Speeches to the Bundestag. [1980].
CDU. "Die deutsche Einheit bleibt unser Auftrag. Reden vor dem Deutschen Bundestag, 17. Juni 1980. Helmut Kohl, Richard von Weizsäcker." Speeches to the Bundestag [1980].
CDU. "Freiheit durch Sicherheit: Sicherheitspolitischer Kongress der CDU am 11. und 12. Januar 1980 in Bonn." Speeches at security policy conference. [1980].
CDU. *Protokoll: 23. Bundesparteitag der Christlichen Demokratischen Union Deutschlands, Niederschrift,* Mannheim, 23–25 June 1975.
CDU. *Protokoll: 26. Bundesparteitag der Christlichen Demokratischen Union Deutschlands, Niederschrift,* Ludwigshafen, 23–25 October 1978.
CDU. *Protokoll: 27. Bundesparteitag der Christlichen Demokratischen Union Deutschlands, Niederschrift,* Kiel, 25–27 March 1979.
CDU. *Protokoll: 28. Bundesparteitag der Christlichen Demokratischen Union Deutschlands, Niederschrift,* Berlin, 19–20 May 1980.
CDU. *Protokoll: 30. Bundesparteitag der Christlichen Demokratischen Union Deutschlands, Niederschrift,* Hamburg, 2–5 November 1981.
CDU. *Union in Deutschland,* 8, 29. *Bundesparteitag der CDU,* Mannheim, 9–10 March 1981.
CDU. *Union in Deutschland* 27, "Das versteht die Union unter Entspannung," 1976.
CDU/CSU. Fraktion, press releases.
CSU. *Information zur Deutschlandpolitik,* vol. 6, *Anspruch und Wirklichkeit,* Dokumente der Konferenz für Sicherheit und Zusammenarbeit in Europa (KSZE), Gerhard Baumann [1976].
CSU. *Information zur Deutschlandpolitik,* vol. 8, *Freiheit und Recht für*

Deutschland und Europa, Dokumentation zum deutschlandpolitischen Kongress der CDU/CSU, Ingolstadt, 28–29 November 1975.
CSU. Landesgruppe, *Correspondenz* [press releases].
CSU. Landesgruppe. *Deutschlandpolitische Grundsatzpapier: Sonderdruck zum 17. Juni* [1978].
Exil-CDU. *An der Einheit Festhalten. Parteitag und Deutschland-Tagung der Exil-CDU*, Fulda, 1981.
Exil-CDU. *Europa und die deutsche Frage. Deutschland-Tagung der Exil-CDU*, Lübeck-Travemuende, 2–4 March 1979.
Exil-CDU. *Ringen um Deutschland. Feststellungen und Forderungen des XII. Exil-Parteitages der Christlich Demokratischen Union der sowjetischen Besatzungszone*, Lübeck, 1–3 July 1972.

Documents/Speeches/Other

Deutschland Funk, "Interview der Woche im Deutschland Funk," 11 January 1970.
Deutschland nach den Verträgen. 19th Gesamtdeutsch session of the Coburg Convent and the German Sängerschaft. Berlin, 1974.
Infas. *Infas-Report: Wahlen, Bundestagswahl 1980*.
Jenninger, Philipp. "Eine Deutsche Bilanz." Speech cited in FRG, Bundespresse- und Informationsamt, *Bulletin* 83–84. 15 February 1984.
Kindler, Johannes. "The Inter-Relationship between 'Deutschlandpolitik' and the Policies of the European Communities (EC)—the Economic Dimension." Speech at the Konrad Adenauer Stiftung Conference, San Francisco. 17–18 November 1986.
Kohl, Helmut. "Politik der Verständigung im Interesse des Friedens." Speech cited in FRG, Presse- und Informationsamt der Bundesregierung 99. 4 September 1984.
Lintner, Eduard. "Zur Lage der amerikanischen-sowjetischen Beziehungen: Rückwirkung auf das innerdeutsche Verhältnis." Speech at the Konrad Adenauer Stiftung Conference, San Francisco. 17–18 November 1986.
Radio Free Europe. *Research Reports*.
SPD. Fraktion. *Informationen* [press releases].
SPD. Fraktion. *Sicherheitspolitische Informationstagung der SPD Bundestags Fraktion*. Augsburg. 17 September 1978.
SPD. Parteivorstand. *Service: Presse, Funk, TV* [press releases].
Windelen, Heinrich. "Grundfragen der Deutschlandpolitik der Bundesregierung." Speech cited in FRG, Bundespresse- und Informationsamt, *Bulletin* 15. 8 February 1984.

Newspapers, Magazines

Augsburger Allgemeine Zeitung
Bayernkurier [BK]

Berliner Rundschau
Bonner General-Anzeiger
Boston Globe
Capital
Deutsche Allgemeine Sonntagsblatt [DAS]
Deutsche Zeitung/Christ und Welt [DZ/CW]
Deutschland Union Dienst [DUD]
Economist
Financial Times [FT]
Frankfurter Allgemeine Zeitung [FAZ]
Frankfurter Neue Presse
Frankfurter Rundschau
German Tribune
Handelsblatt [HB]
Hannoversche Allgemeine Zeitung [HAZ]
Kölner Stadt-Anzeiger
Kölnische Rundschau
Mannheimer Morgen
Münchner Merkur
Neue Zürcher Zeitung [NZZ]
Neueste Badische Zeitung
New York Times [NYT]
Newsweek
Nürnberger Nachrichten
Quick
Der Spiegel [DS]
Stern
Stuttgarter Nachrichten
Stuttgarter Zeitung
Süddeutsche Zeitung [SdZ]
Der Tagesspiegel
Texte zur Deutschlandpolitik [TzDp]
Times (London)
Vorwärts
Washington Post
Washington Quarterly
Die Welt [DW]
Welt am Sonntag
Westdeutsche Allgemeine Zeitung
Die Zeit [DZ]
Zycie Warszway

Secondary Sources

Books, Book Chapters

Books, Book Chapters/General

Baring, Arnulf. *Im Anfang war Adenauer: Die Entstehung der Kanzlerdemokratie*. Munich: Deutscher Taschenbuch Verlag, 1982.
———. *Machtwechsel: Die Ära Brandt-Scheel*. Stuttgart: Deutsche Verlags-Anstalt, 1982.
Besson, Waldemar. *Die Aussenpolitik der Bundesrepublik: Erfahrungen und Massstäbe*. Frankfurt: Ullstein, 1970.
Beyme, Klaus von. "Gewerkschaftliche Politik: Reform aus Solidarität." In *Zum 60. Geburtstag von Heinz O. Vetter*, edited by Ulrich Borsdorff, Hans O. Hemmer, Gerhard Leminsky, and Heinz Markmann, 597–613. Cologne: Bund Verlag, 1977.
Blechman, Barry, and Cathleen Fisher, eds. *The Silent Partner: West Germany and Arms Control*. Cambridge, Mass.: Ballinger, 1988.
Burzig, Arno. "Ostpolitik und Osthandel: Das Zusammenwirken von Regierung und Wirtschaftsverbänden in der Ost-West Wirtschaftspolitik." In *Verwaltete Aussenpolitik: Sicherheits- und Entspannungspolitische Entscheidungsprozesse in Bonn*, edited by Helga Haftendorn, Wolf-Dieter Karl, Joachim Krauss, and Lothar Wilkar, 225–40. Cologne: Verlag Wissenschaft und Politik, 1978.
Brzezinski, Zbigniew. *Power and Principles: Memoirs of the National Security Advisor*. New York: Farrar, Straus & Giroux, 1983.
Carter, Jimmy. *Keeping the Faith: Memoirs of a President*. Toronto: Bantam, 1982.
Catudal, Honoré M. *The Diplomacy of the Quadripartite Agreement on Berlin: A New Era in East-West Politics*. Berlin: Berlin Verlag, 1978.
Cerny, Karl. *Germany at the Polls: The Bundestag Elections of 1976*. Washington, D.C.: The American Enterprise Institute, 1978.
Conradt, David. *The German Polity*. New York: Longman, 1986.
DePorte, Anton. *Europe between the Superpowers: The Enduring Balance*. New Haven, Conn.: Yale University Press, 1979.
Eisner, Erich. *Das europäische Konzept von Franz Josef Strauss. Die gesamteuropäischen Ordungsvorstellungen der CSU*. Meisenheim am Glan: Verlag Anton Hain, 1975.
Griffith, William. *The Ostpolitik of the Federal Republic of Germany*. Cambridge: MIT Press, 1978.
Hacke, Christian. "Parlamentarische Opposition und Entspannungspolitik —Die Position der CDU/CSU zur KSZE." In *Verwaltete Aussenpolitik*, 263–78.
———. *Die Ost- und Deutschlandpolitik der CDU/CSU: Wege und Irrwege der Opposition seit 1969*. Cologne: Verlag Wissenschaft und Politik, 1975.
Haig, Alexander. *Caveat: Realism, Reagan, and Foreign Policy*. New York:

Macmillan, 1984.
Haftendorn, Helga. *Abrüstungs- und Entspannungpolitik zwischen Sicherheitsbefriedigung und Friedensicherung. Zur Aussenpolitik der BRD 1955–1973*. Düsseldorf: Bertelsmann, 1974.
Hanrieder, Wolfram. "Compatibility and Consensus: A Proposal for the Conceptual Linkage of External and Internal Dimensions of Foreign Policy." In *Comparative Foreign Policy: Theoretical Essays*, edited by Wolfram Hanrieder, 242–64. New York: David McKay, 1971.
Heidenheimer, Arnold. *Adenauer and the CDU: The Rise of the Leader and the Integration of the Party*. The Hague: Nijhof, 1960.
Irving, R. E. M. *The Christian Democratic Parties of Western Europe*. London: Allen and Unwin, 1979.
Joffe, Josef. *The Limited Partnership: Europe, the United States and the Burdens of Alliance*. Cambridge, Mass.: Ballinger, 1987.
Joop, Mathias. "Embargo oder Business? Der Osthandel der Bundesrepublik Deutschland und die deutsch-amerikanischen Beziehungen." In *Europa zwischen Konfrontation und Kooperation: Entspannung für die achtziger Jahre*, edited by Peter Schlotter, 193–220. Frankfurt: Campus Verlag, 1982.
Kaiser, Karl. *German Foreign Policy in Transition: Bonn between East and West*. London: Oxford University Press, 1968.
Kelleher, Catherine McArdle. *Germany and the Politics of Nuclear Weapons*. New York: Columbia University Press, 1975.
Kissinger, Henry. *The Troubled Partnership*. New York: McGraw-Hill, 1965.
———. *White House Years*. Boston: Little, Brown, 1979.
———. *Years of Upheaval*. Boston: Little, Brown, 1982.
Kreile, Michael. *Osthandel und Ostpolitik*. Baden-Baden: Nomos Verlag, 1978.
Ludz, Peter. "Ostpolitik and the Present State and Future Course of Inner-German Contacts." In *The Political Implications of Soviet Military Power*, edited by Lawrence Whetten, 65–80. London: Macdonald and Jane's, 1977.
Löwenthal, Richard. *Vom kalten Krieg zur Ostpolitik*. Stuttgart: Seewald Verlag, 1974.
Mintzel, Alf. *Die CSU: Anatomie einer konservativen Partei, 1945–1972*. Opladen: Westdeutscher Verlag, 1975.
———. "Conservatism and Christian Democracy in the Federal Republic of Germany." In *Conservative Politics in Western Europe*, edited by Zig-Layton Henry, 131–59. London: MacMillan, 1982.
———. "Die CSU in Bayern." In *Parteiensystem in der Legitimationskrise: Studien und Materialien zur Soziologie der Parteien in der Bundesrepublik Deutschland*, edited by Jürgen Dittberner and Rolf Ebbighausen, 349–426. Opladen: Westdeutscher Verlag, 1973.
Moreton, Edwina, ed. *Germany between East and West*. Cambridge, England: Cambridge University Press, 1987.

Niclauss, Karlheinz. *Kontroverse Deutschlandpolitik: Die Politische Auseinandersetzung in der Bundesrepublik Deutschland über den Grundlagenvertrag mit der DDR. Dokumente zur Deutschlandpolitik. Beihefte, Band 3*. FRG, Bundesministerium für Innerdeutsche Beziehungen. Frankfurt: Alfred Metzner Verlag, 1977.

Noelle-Neumann, Elisabeth, and Edgar Piel. *Allensbacher Jahrbuch der Demoskopie 1978–1983*. Munich: Saur, 1983.

Patz, Günther. *Parlamentarische Kontrolle der Aussenpolitik: Fallstudien zur politischen Bedeutung des Auswärtigen Ausschusses des Deutschen Bundestages*. Studien zum politischen System der Bundesrepublik Deutschland, no. 7. Edited by Heino Kaack. Meisenheim am Glan: Anton Hain, 1976.

Pridham, Geoffrey. *Christian Democracy in Western Germany: The CDU/CSU in Government and Opposition*. New York: St. Martin's Press, 1977.

Rhöndorfer Gespräche. *Entspannung und Wiedervereinigung: Deutschlandpolitische Vorstellungen Konrad Adenauers 1955–1958*. Stuttgart: Belser Verlag, 1979.

Ropers, Norbert. "Zwischen Wiedervereinigung, Abgrenzung und Entspannung: Der innerdeutsche Reiseverkehr und die Politik zwischen den beiden deutschen Staaten." In *Europa zwischen Konfrontation und Kooperation: Entspannung für die achtziger Jahre*, edited by Peter Schlotter, 265–87. Frankfurt: Campus Verlag, 1982.

Schmid, Günther. *Entscheidung in Bonn: Die Entstehung der Ost- und Deutschlandpolitik 1969/1970*. Cologne: Verlag Wissenschaft und Politik, 1979.

Schwarz, Hans-Peter. *Adenauer: Der Aufstieg 1876–1952*. Stuttgart: Deutsche Verlags-Anstalt, 1986.

———. "Das aussenpolitische Konzept Konrad Adenauers." In *Adenauer Studien-I*, edited by Rudolf Morsey and Konrad Repgen, 71–108. Kommission für Zeitgeschichte bei der katholischen Akademie in Bayern, ser. B, vol. 10. Mainz: Matthias Grünewald Verlag, 1971.

———. "Adenauer und Russland." In *Im Dienste Deutschland und des Rechtes: Festschrift für Wilhelm Grewe zum 70. Geburtstag am 16. Oktober 1981*, edited by Friedrich J. Kroneck and Thomas Oppermann, 365–89. Baden-Baden: Nomos Verlag, 1981.

Schweigler, Gebhard. *West German Foreign Policy: The Domestic Context*. The Washington Papers, vol. 12, no. 106. New York: Praeger, 1984.

Seeligen, Rolf, ed. *Koalition auf Entspannungskurs: Beiträge zur Abrüstungspolitik mit einer Dokumentation*. Munich: Rolf Seeligen, 1979.

Stent, Angela. *From Embargo to Ostpolitik: The Political Economy of West German–Soviet Relations 1955–1980*. New York: Cambridge University Press, 1981.

Tilford, Roger, ed. *The Ostpolitik and Political Change in Germany*. Westmead, England: Saxon House, 1975.

Veen, Hans-Joachim. *Opposition im Bundestag: Ihre Funktionen, institutionellen Handlungsbedingungen und das Verhalten der CDU/CSU Fraktion in der 6. Wahlperiode 1969–1972.* Bonn: Eichholz Verlag, 1976.
Whetten, Lawrence, ed. *The Political Implications of Soviet Military Power.* London: Macdonald and Jane's, 1977.

Books/CDU/CSU

Adenauer, Konrad. *Erinnerungen,* 4 vols. Stuttgart: Deutsche Verlags-Anstalt, 1965–68.
Amrehn, Franz. "Berlin: Schlüssel zur Vorherrschaft." In *Ostpolitik in Kreuzfeuer,* edited by Hans Graf Huyn, 122–43. Stuttgart: Seewald Verlag, 1971.
Barzel, Rainer. *Auf dem Drahtseil.* Munich: Drümer Knaur, 1978.
———. *Im Streit und umstritten.* Frankfurt: Ullstein, 1986.
Biedenkopf, Kurt. *Fortschritt in Freiheit: Umrisse einer politischen Strategie.* Munich: Piper Verlag, 1974.
Birrenbach, Kurt. *Meine Sondermissionen: Rückblick auf zwei Jahrzehnte bundesdeutscher Aussenpolitik.* Düsseldorf: Econ Verlag, 1984.
Brentano, Heinrich von. *Deutschland, Europa und die Welt: Reden zur Deutschen Aussenpolitik,* edited by Professor Dr. Franz Bohm. Bonn: Siegler, 1962.
Dregger, Alfred. *Freiheit in unserer Zeit: Reden und Aufsätze,* edited by Günter Reichart. Munich: Herbig, 1980.
Gradl, Johann Baptist. *Stets auf der Suche: Reden, Äusserungen und Aufsätze zur Deutschlandpolitik,* edited by Christian Hacke. Cologne: Verlag Wissenschaft und Politik, 1979.
Guttenberg, Karl-Theodor Freiherr zu. *Die Neue Ostpolitik: Wege und Irrwege.* Osnabrück: A. Fromm, 1971.
Kiep, Walther Leisler. *A New Challenge for Western Europe: A View from Bonn.* New York: Mason and Lipscomb, 1974.
Kohl, Helmut. *Zwischen Ideologie und Pragmatismus: Aspekte und Ansichten zu Grundfragen der Politik.* Stuttgart: Verlag Bonn Aktuell, 1973.
Mertes, Alois. "Die Union und Polen." In *Union Alternativ,* edited by Gerhard Mayer-Vorfelder and Hubertus Zuber, 113–19. Stuttgart: Seewald Verlag, 1976.
Rollman, Dietrich, ed. *Die CDU in der Opposition: Eine Selbstdarstellung.* Hamburg: Christian Wegner, 1970.
Strauss, Franz Josef. *The Grand Design: A European Solution to German Reunification.* London: Weidenfeld and Nicolson, 1965.
Weizsäcker, Richard von. "Deutsche Ost- und Westpolitik." In *Die CDU in der Opposition: Eine Selbstdarstellung,* edited by Dietrich Rollman, 35–46. Homburg: Christian Wegner, 1970.

Journal Articles

Journal Articles/General

Bender, Peter. "Deutsch-Polnische Beziehungen—Ein Stück Gesamteuropa." *Deutschland Archiv* 11 (December 1978): 1280–83.
Buchheim, Hans. "Freiheit als Staatsprinzip: Die Deutschlandfrage und die Ostpolitik." *Die Politische Meinung* 17 (March/April 1972): 5–20.
Cramer, Dettmar. "Die deutsche Frage bleibt offen." *Europäische Rundschau* 7 (1979): 27–35.
———. "Kommentare und aktuelle Beiträge." *Deutschland Archiv* 6 (1981): 562–63.
———. "Kommentare und aktuelle Beiträge." *Deutschland Archiv* 14 (June 1981): 562–63.
Hacke, Christian. "Soll und Haben des Grundlagenvertrages." *Deutschland Archiv* 15 (December 1982): 1282–1304.
Hahn, Walter. "West Germany's Ostpolitik: The Grand Design of Egon Bahr." *Orbis* 16 (Winter 1973): 859–80.
Hassner, Pierre. "Europe: Old Conflicts, New Rules." *Orbis* 17 (Fall 1973): 895–911.
Joffe, Josef. "Westverträge, Ostverträge und die Kontinuität der deutschen Aussenpolitik." *Europa Archiv* 4 (1973): 11–24.
Noelle-Neumann, Elisabeth. "In West Germany, Conservative Mood Isn't Helping the Conservative Candidate." *Public Opinion* (August/September 1980): 41–45.
Pridham, Geoffrey. "The CDU/CSU Opposition in West Germany 1969–1972: A Party in Search of an Organization." *Parliamentary Affairs* 26 (Spring 1973): 201–17.
Schwarz, Hans-Peter. "What Is Wrong with US–West German Relations?" *SAIS-Review* (Spring 1982): 53–70.
Wagner, Wolfgang. "Ein Modus Vivendi für Deutschland." *Europa Archiv* 1 (1973): 1–6.
Wallach, John. "What Europe's Leaders Are Saying." *Washington Quarterly* 5 (Winter 1982): 33–46.
Wegener, Henning. "Deutschland in der Welt." *Aus Politik und Zeitgeschichte* (17 February 1979): 45–48.
Yost, David. S., and Glad, Thomas C. "West German Party Politics and Theater Nuclear Modernization Since 1977." *Armed Forces and Society* (Summer 1982): 525–60.

Journals/CDU/CSU

Gradl, Johann Baptist. "Ausgangsposition, nicht Endstation: Deutschlandpolitik auf der Grundlage der Verträge." *Politik und Kultur* 1 (January/February 1974): 13–23.
———. "Deutschlandpolitik—permanente Herausforderung." *Deutsch-

land Archiv 10 (1977): 252–57.
———. "Nation auf dem Prüfstand." *Politik und Kultur* 4 (May/June 1977): 23–30.
Lummer, Heinrich. "Die Vorteile des Ostens aus Handel und Verträgen." *Politik und Kultur* 4 (March/April 1977): 37–50.
Mertes, Alois. "Wie offen ist die deutsche Frage?" *Politik und Kultur* 9 (July/August 1982): 3–21.
———. "Wie relevant ist die deutsche Frage?" *Politik und Kultur* 7 (March/April 1980): 17–30.
———. "Neue Wind aus Washington: die deutsche Aussenpolitik unter der Ägide Reagan." *Die Politische Meinung* 26 (May/June 1981): 14–21.
———. "Hinter Honeckers Forderungen steht Moskau." *Deutschland Archiv* 14 (1981): 374–77.
Rühle, Hans. "German Security Policy: Position, Problems, Prospects." *International Security Review* 5 (Summer 1980): 194.
Strauss, Franz Josef. "Manifesto of a German Atlanticist." *Strategic Review* 10 (Summer 1982): 11–15.
Weizsäcker, Richard Freiherr von. "Deutsche Frage im internationalen Zusammenhang." *Politik und Kultur* 4 (May/June 1977): 11–30
Wrangel, Olaf von. "Verpflichtungen der Bundesrepublik Deutschland." *Politik und Kultur* 1 (January/February 1974): 31–36.

Journals/SPD

Bruns, Wilhelm. "Polemik statt Politik: Die CDU tut sich mit Deutschland schwer." *Die Neue Gesellschaft* 25 (December 1978): 980–83.
Mosdorf, Siegmar. "CDU—Ludwigshafen war kein Godesberg." *Die Neue Gesellschaft* 26 (March 1979): 203–7.
Prauss, Herbert. "CDU/CSU Aussenpolitik—nichts dazugelernt." *Die Neue Gesellschaft* 25 (May 1978): 402–6.
Wehner, Herbert. "'Deutschland' statt Politik." *Die Neue Gesellschaft* 24 (April 1977): 268–71.

Other Materials

Dissertations

Pauly, Wolfgang. "Christliche Demokraten und Christlich Soziale: Untersuchung zum innenpolitischen Bündnisverhalten von CDU und CSU, 1969–1979." Ph.D. dissertation, University of Trier, 1981.
Smith, David Brent. "The Opposition to Ostpolitik: Foreign Policy as an Issue in West German Politics, 1969–72." Ph.D. dissertation, Harvard University, 1977.

Index

Abelein, Manfred, 179, 180
ABM Treaty (Anti-ballistic treaty of 1972), 307
Adenauer, Konrad, 6, 14–16, 60–61, 321 n.14; and the "chancellor democracy," 14; consensus shaken, 313; distrust of Soviets, 34; early policy, 30; "holding policy," 32, 34–39, 40; legacy in CDU/CSU Ostpolitik, 278; longevity of, 17; Moscow initiatives, 35–36, 38; and partition/reunification, 25, 39; resignation, 41; and Union Ostpolitik, 13–41; and war prisoners' release, 36; Westpolitik of, 18, 24, 55, 322 n.30
Konrad Adenauer Foundation, 216
Afghanistan crisis, 193–203, 228; and Berlin, 241; bipartisan response, 197; "crisis management" policy, 194, 196; economic sanctions, 195; strategic implications, 196
Ahlen program, 13
Albrecht, Ernst, 163, 183, 250

Allensbach institute, 147, 152, 244
All-European Conference on Security and Cooperation in Europe (CSCE). See CSCE
America. See United States
Amerongen, Wolff von, 250
Amrehn, Franz, 85
Andreotti, Guilio: on German partition, 289; and "pan-Germanism," 310
Arms control: and German security, 306–307. See also Detente
Arnold, Karl, 13
"Atlanticism," 41–47, 135, 239
Auseinandersetzung, 140
"Austrianization" solution, 39, 61, 312, 322 n.33

Bahr, Egon, 55, 56; and bloc system, 264; criticism of, 73–74, 85–86; and East-West partnership, 58, 227; and Eastern treaties, 98; and FRG-GDR travel treaty, 107; and "money for promises," 286; Moscow negotiations, 74, 327 n.21; Moscow

treaty, 76; Ostpolitik, 114–115; and renunciation-of-force accord, 71
Bahr-Gromyko working paper, 74, 75, 76; Union attack on, 76
Baring, Arnulf, 33
Barzel, Rainer, 47, 66, 68, 77, 107, 153; and the Basic Treaty, 113; and Berlin accords, 87; and bipartisanship, 256; gesamtdeutsch sentiments of, 248; and Joint Resolution, 105; and Moscow treaty, 78; negotiations with Soviets, 103; and no-confidence vote (April 1972), 100–101; Ostpolitik strategy, 93; and Pompidou, 99; resignation, 117; self-determination strategy, 138; and Social-Liberal Ostpolitik, 79; *So Nicht* strategy, 91–94
Basic Treaty, 176; CDU/Bavarian legal challenge, 119; and CDU/CSU orthodoxy, 110; court battle, 116; and German unity, 113; judicial interpretations of, 118, 119–121; Karlsruhe ruling, 118–123; main points, 107; ratification of, 137; Union criticisms, 111
Basket III, 158, 178
Bavaria, 22
Bayerncourier, 73, 108, 326 n.4
Beitz, Bertoldt, 250
Berechenbarkeit, 242–243
Berlin: and CDU/CSU foreign policy, 85, 241–242; and Four Power status, 41; ties to GDR, 131
Berlin accords (1971): acceptance, 88; contents, 87–88; ratification, 98; violations, 146
Berlin crisis (1958), 39, 237
Berlin wall (1961), 41, 56; as symbol, 83, 177
Besson, Waldemar, 27, 39
Biedenkopf, Kurt, 135, 141, 155, 173, 219
Bilateralism: and German security, 306–307
Bipartisanship, 256
Bismarck, Otto von, 3
Bismarck, Philipp von, 181
Bismarckian empire (of 1871), 22; return to, 61, 112
Bloc system. See European bloc system
Blüm, Norbert, 219
Bonn: and the status quo, 2. See also FRG
Bonn-Moscow accord on economic cooperation, 183, 334 n.25
Bonn-Moscow relations: economic basis of, 183; trade, 182
Bonn-Paris reconciliation treaty, 41
Bonn-Prague treaty, 150
Bonn-Warsaw talks, 72
Bonn-Warsaw treaty (1970), 181–184
Brandt, Willy, 2, 55, 56, 58, 64, 67; address to parliament (October 1969), 67; Bundestag margin, 89, 91, 98; and CDU/CSU, 5; as chancellor, 55–88; his coalition, 239; as foreign minister, 47; Ostpolitik concept, 55–60, 82, 142; popularity, 106; resignation, 151; and reunification, 5; and the Soviet bloc, 1–2; and the status quo, 2, 51; his "20 points," 70; Union opposition, 74; and Warsaw treaty, 80, 161; and Western European solidarity, 73–74
Brandt-Scheel Ostpolitik, 242; and German identity, 248; last phases, 145–147; and West German public opinion, 243
Brandt-Stoph meeting (1970), 242
Brezhnev, Leonid, 99; Bonn visit

358 | Index

(1978), 182–183; Bonn visit (1981), 211
Brezhnev Doctrine, 50, 59, 158
Bundesrat: review of treaties, 97
Bundestag: deadlocked, 101

Carstens, Karl, 118, 132; as CDU party chief, 253; and the FDP, 133
Carter, Jimmy, 335 n.29, 337 n.24; and Afghanistan crisis, 193–203; and 1980 Moscow summit, 201; Olympic games boycott, 194; and Helmut Schmidt, 186, 189
Catholic party (pre-1933), 16
Catholics, 321 n.13; and the CSU, 18–20; and division, 20; and German nationalism, 22; and the status quo, 46–47; trade unions, 321 n.4
CDU (Christian Democratic Union): dialogue with East, 211; elections of 1976, 160; Geissler strategy, 297; and Helsinki agreements, 162; origins of, 15–16; regeneration and flexibility, 254; trade union wing, 66
CDU/CSU (Christian Democratic Union/Christian Social Union), 1; acceptance of status quo, 192; adaptation to Ostpolitik, 8; adaptation to Social-Liberal Ostpolitik, 141; "all-weather Ostpolitik," 273; ambivalence to SPD-FDP Ostpolitik, 260–263; anti-Brandt strategies, 74; anticommunism of, 25; Basic Program (1978), 254; and Basic Treaty, 118; and Berlin question, 83; and Bonn-Warsaw talks, 72; and coalition of 1982, 8; differences over detente, 184–185; differences over Westpolitik, 185–192; divisions within, 45; in East-West equation, 88; election victory (1976), 171; expellees within, 39, 62, 296, 329 n.9; foreign policy origins, 13–51; "holding policy" of, 28–39; Moscow treaty reactions, 77; and Oder-Neisse line, 73; opposition to CSCE, 160; as opposition party, 55, 235, 254–256; opposition to Warsaw treaty, 81; and Ostpolitik/Deutschlandpolitik, 236, 238, 248; "policy of strength," 29; and the Polish accords, 149–166; in power (1982–1988), 277–313; Republican party (U.S.) ties, 216; resistance to American pipeline embargo, 225; and reunification, 21, 24, 25–30, 61; rifts within, 250; and self-determination, 26; and *So Nicht* strategy, 91–97; threatened rifts, 118, 162; and waning support, 205; and "Weimar-style rhetoric," 133
CDU/CSU Adaptive Ostpolitik, 260–268; adaptation to Berman question, 267; bilateralism, 306; and bloc system, 236–238; and detente, 264; domestic factors, 243–252; economic factors, 253–256; individuals, 256–260; international factors, 236, 263–267; intraparty factors, 253–256; and Helmut Kohl, 257–258; main factors, 236; and Alois Mertes, 257–259; necessitating factors, 235–260; and status quo, 267; summarized, 309–313; symptoms of, 245; and Richard von Weizsäcker, 258–259
CDU/CSU-FDP coalition, 230–231, 249–250; GDR reaction, 231; and Hans-Dietrich Genscher, 278
CDU/CSU "fundamentalists,"

62–64, 147
CDU/CSU "Godesberg" (reevaluation), 209, 220
CDU/CSU orthodoxy, 78; and adaptation, 141; against all-European conference, 129; and Basic Treaty, 110; and communist behavior, 165; defenders of, 81; on Ostpolitik/Deutschlandpolitik, 60–61
CDU/CSU Ostpolitik: continuity versus correction, 228; and European status quo, 261, 264; "Godesberg" (reevaluation), 220; popular misgivings, 147; public opinion, 243–248
CDU/CSU Ostpolitik (after 1982), 268–276, 277, 278; Adenauer legacy, 278, credibility inside GDR, 273–274; criticisms of, 272–274; and detente, 290, 306; detente misgivings, 272; discord, 305; domestic factors, 293; dualism of, 268–271, 300–301; dualistic problems, 299–313; evolving consensus, 274, 276; and Foreign Minister Genscher, 296; foreign trade, 293–294; fundamentalist backlash, 301–305; and GDR Liberals, 284; Gesamtpolitik of, 271; human rights position, 270; as independent foreign policy, 310; and Karlsruhe verdict, 269; negotiated topics with GDR, 280–281; operational continuity, 279–298; "operative progress versus normative consistency," 305–306; "populism" of, 310; pragmatism, 273; rationale behind, 289–298; and recognition of GDR, 269–270; revival of "Heimat," 300; security concerns, 306–309; security policy, 308; sources of, 288; and the SPD, 295; "two-track policy," 300; and Warsaw Treaty, 269; and Western allies, 270–271
CDU/CSU reformists, 64–66, 78, 107, 131, 134; and German question, 138, 237
CDU/CSU and SPD-FDP Ostpolitik, 235
CDU reformists: and Gotesberg strategy, 210
Chancery spy case (1974), 151, 331 n.7
China, 56
Chinapolitik, 191, 329 n.14
Christian Democratic Union/Christian Social Union. *See* CDU/CSU
Christian Democrats, 45; origins of, 13
Christian-Liberal coalition, 66
Christian-Liberal federal coalition, 250
Christian "third way," 13, and Helmut Kohl, 135
CoCom export restrictions, 286, 293
Constitution of 1949, 32
CSCE (All-European Conference on Security and Cooperation in Europe), 129, 141, 145, 178, 240; Albanian resistance to, 160; and detente, 155–156; Soviet persistence, 158; Union cynicism, 160, 332 n.24
CSU (Christian Social Union): and Afghan containment policy, 200; anti-Liberal backlash, 301; and Bavaria, 16–17; and Bavarian electorate, 173; nonrecognition of GDR, 283; origins of, 16; Sonthofen conference, 133
Cuban crisis, 237
Cultural unity, 62, 111
Czechoslovakia: normalizing rela-

tions with, 149; Soviet invasion of (1968), 50

DDR. *See* GDR
de Gaulle, Charles, 40, 42, 43; and German unity, 41, 49
Der Spiegel, 147
Detente, 37, 38; and Afghanistan crisis, 198; American concerns over, 153; dangers of, 144, 228; inevitability of, 44; multilateral approaches, 143; perceived risks, 139, 154, 155; as prerequisite for reunification, 48; as prerequisite for "European solution," 312; and Social-Liberal coalition, 73; and West German public opinion, 129
Deutschlandpolitik: adaptations, 176–180; continuity of, 123; failure of, 41; and human rights principles, 178; joint resolution on (1984), 288; and normalization, 294; and reunification, 299; and Rhineland CDU conference, 155
Diepgen, Eberhard, 279; East Berlin visit, 283; and Honecker invitation, 282
Die Zeit, 119, 147, 310
Dregger, Alfred, 279: on Bonn summit, 280
Dubček, Alexander, 59
Dusseldorf CDU forum, 175

East Berlin, 87; communist regime, 56; visiting relatives, 56
Eastern accord (1972), 106
Eastern bloc: CDU/CSU's hostility toward, 1, 130; conditions in, 140, 321 n.14; financial credits to, 285–287; and FRG banks, 293; FRG trade with, 285, 286; hegemony, 59; and human rights standard, 165; "normalized" relations with, 143, 252; repression, 139; resistance to detente, 49; trade with, 45–46, 293–294
Eastern treaties, 2, 55–88, 174; and Egon Bahr, 98; debates, 239, 253, 272; as interpreted by Karlsruhe, 185; ratification, 106; and Union fundamentalists, 89–92; upheld by Kohl, 210
East German refugees, 22
East Germany. *See* German Democratic Republic
East-West equilibrium, 216
East-West troop reduction talks, 188
Elbe River border, 137, 138
Elections: of 1969, 55; of 1972, 106; of 1976, 166–171; of 1980, 205
Erfurt summit (1970), 68, 71; Union criticism of, 69
Erhard, Ludwig, 14–15, 17, 18, 41, 46; defeat of, 47
ERW (Neutron "bomb" weapons): FRG acceptance of, 188; resumed U.S. production of, 217
Ethnic Germans, 23, 38; and a bilateral commission, 164; emigration of, 282; and Helsinki summit, 160, 161; under Polish administration, 72; in the Soviet Union, 153
European bloc system, 264; as CDU/CSU policy, 312 and the status quo, 289; and West German security, 313
European Community (EC), 152
"European peace structure": Union alarm over, 261
European security conference, 58; desired by Moscow, 82
European-Soviet natural gas pipeline, 211
European status quo, 31, 34, 50, 51, 72, 239; allied acceptance of,

240; and CDU/CSU Ostpolitik, 261; and normalization, 244; and Soviet hegemony, 76
European unity, 19; and German reunification, 27; Soviet hostility toward, 99
Eurostrategic equilibrium, 189
Expellees, 16; and the NPD, 63; and Poland, 80, 181; prevalence of, 24; protest rallies, 70; Sudetens, 150; and the Union, 101

Falin, Valentin, 102
FDP (Free Democratic party), 57, 99, 249; Union dependency on, 296
FDP-SPD coalition split, 230; setbacks, 296
Federal Republic of Germany. See FRG
Financial credits: to East Berlin, 289; to Eastern bloc, 285–286, 287; to the GDR, 285
"Finlandization," specter, 140, 188
Foreign policy (FRG): continuity of, 2
Four Power Accord (1971), 145; and West Berlin, 145–146
Four Power authority, 30, 138; documents of, 137; as provisional treaty, 31; solution to German question, 35, 44, 80
Four Power Berlin accord (1971), 86, 89
Four Power talks: and the Moscow treaty, 76
Franco-German entente, 40
Frankfurter Allgemeine Zeitung (FAZ), 156, 178, 181, 287–288
Free Democrats, 14, 58
French entente, 20
FRG (Federal Republic of Germany), 47; aid to Turkey, 197; coalition politics, 249–250; constitution of 1949, 32; domestic structures, 262; external constraints, 313; foreign policy of, 2, 9; identity with prewar Empire, 121; in the NATO alliance, 40, 115; origins, 14; Salzgitter bureau, 205; UN membership, 115, 117; and Western allies, 239
FRG-GDR contacts, 106; and joint UN membership, 115; as threat to GDR regime, 130
FRG-GDR travel treaty, 107
FRG Ostpolitik, 58; and Rainer Barzel, 66; and French detente policy, 58
Friedmann, Wilhelm, 308–309

Gaulism, 41–47
Gaus, Günter, 214
GDR (German Democratic Republic): communist insecurities, 184; de facto recognition of, 67, 242; delimitations, 266; dissidents, 177; escapees, 147, 148; financial credits to, 285; financial leverage against, 269; foreign policy, 2; and FRG constitution, 140; and human rights, 176; international status achieved, 130; isolation of, 45, 50, 130; more flexible policy toward, 46; nonrecognition of, 35, 43; peace initiatives, 33; popular interest in, 301; practical agreements with, 49; public support for, 267; recognition, 49, 51, 57, 70, 75; repressive character of, 47, 114, 117; reunification sentiment, 185; right of self-determination, 32; as seen by West Germans, 246–247; and Sindermann's Bonn visit, 282; "sovereign equality" of, 111; and the Soviet bloc, 28; and Soviet pressure, 57, 68, 207, 283, 291; and

362 | Index

Soviet pressure for openness, 292; as Soviet puppet, 190; traffic with, 106; and West German youth, 247
GDR currency exchange increase, 205; protested at CSCE, 206
GDR-FRG accords (1973–1974), 149–151
Geissler, Heinier, 207, 296; foreign policy statement of 1988, 304
Genscher, Hans-Dietrich, 108, 143, 146, 151, 163; in foreign affairs, 229–230; and German question, 267; and German/Polish emigres, 164; and Gorbachev, 295–296; Ostpolitik ambitions (after 1982), 278–279; and relations with the East, 295; and Union Ostpolitik, 229
"Genscherists," 297
Gera demands, 205, 299; and failed initiatives, 303; Honecker's intransigence, 265
German Atlanticism, 43
German Gaullists, 43, 44–47, 51
German-German relations, 143, 280–281; border incidents, 168; city partnerships, 281; dialogue, 265; trade relations, 175, 179; trade sanctions, 168–169; travel, 246; visitation increases, 281–282, 341 n.19
German nationalism: and Catholic Rhinelanders, 22
German partition, 20, 56
German-Polish forum of 1987, 311
"German question." See Reunification
German unity, 61; Social-Liberal method, 59
Germany treaty (1952–1954), 33, 34, 36, 67, 77
Gesamtdeutschland, 35; defined, 32; and the GDR constitution, 146; neutralized, 31

Gesamtdeutsch sentiment, 22, 23, 24, 245, 334 n.11; of north Germans, 62; versus legalistic formulas, 247
Gesamtpolitik: after Afganistan, 198; articulation of, 199–203
Gierek, Edward, 160
Giscard d'Estaing, Valéry, 152; and Afghanistan crisis, 194
Gorbachev, Mikhail, 279; changes under, 292, 313; diplomacy of, 290–291; and hopes for unity, 309; "new thinking" of, 294; popularity of, 294–295
Gradl, Johann Baptist, 22, 67, 107, 138, 139; on GDR leadership, 180; as Protestant spokesman, 64; and reunification, 241; and shift in Union Ostpolitik, 180–181
Grand Coalition, 48, 61; "detente offensive," 49
Griffith, William, 30, 142
Gromyko, Andrei, 73
Guttenberg, Baron Karl Theodor zu, 70, 72–73, 86

Hallstein, Walter, 35
Hallstein Doctrine, 35, 36, 45, 50; abandonment of, 57
Hamburg conference: and continuity, 222; as triumph for Kohl, 221
Hanrieder, Wolfram, 6–7
"Heimat," 23, 24; and expellees, 301; revival of, 300
Helsinki Final Act, 157, 158, 165, 166; and European bloc system, 237–238; fundamentalist opposition, 240; and Solidarity trade union, 223; as tool used by CDU/CSU, 255
Helsinki summit, 156, 160
Hennig, Ottfried, 297
Hillgruber, Andreas, 305

Hitler, Adolf, 14, 23, 70
Holding policy, 32, 33, 38
Honecker, Erich, 95, 180; Bonn visit of 1987, 277, 283; discusses reunification, 214; Gera demands speech, 205; and visitation increase of 1986, 291
Hungarian reform, 292
Hupka, Herbert, 89, 297; abandonment of Brandt coalition, 98

INF (intermediate-range nuclear forces): deployment, 189–190; and detente debate, 215–218; moratorium on, 194, 196; negative polls, 217; and nuclear anxiety, 217; SPD conditions, 190
INF Accord, 307
Inter-German relations accord, 96; agreement(s), 49; dialogue, 67–71; trade, 293–294; travel, 246, 291–294
International Red Cross, 160
Italian Communist party, 49

Jenninger, Philipp, 284
Joint Resolution (1972), 105, 137, 138, 250

Kaiser, Jakob, 13
Karlsruhe decision, 138, 148, 185; as limit to Ostpolitik, 266
Kassel summit (of 1970), 69, 71; "20 points," 70
Kennedy, John F., 42
Khrushchev, Nikita, 46; and Berlin crisis (1958), 39
Kiep, Walther Leisler, 109, 159, 164; and business pressure on CDU, 252; as reformist, 155–156
Kiesinger, Kurt Georg, 47, 51, 63; commitment to detente, 48; opposition to Moscow treaty, 78
Kissinger, Henry, 58, 149; and Berlin settlement, 82; and Helsinki accords, 156; and Schmidt/Genscher, 153
Kohl, Helmut, 2, 64, 66, 78; and Basic Treaty, 115; and Berlin accords, 87; Bundestag address (November 1980), 209; as candidate (1976), 154; and CDU statement of October 1980, 208, 209; Christian-Liberal partnership, 229; and detente, 140; election as chancellor, 231; foreign policy, 2; formative politics, 134–135; government of, 2; and Hamburg conference (1981), 220–222; and Helsinki summit, 161; Moscow visit of 1983, 299; Moscow visit of 1988, 279; and Oder-Neisse line, 79; pledge of continuity, 210; and the Polish accords, 149–167; in power, 134–136; pro-Americanism of, 135; and reunification, 299–300; and Reykjavik summit, 307; role in CDU/CSU adaptiveness, 257–259; security of CDU/CSU leadership, 218; and Union Ostpolitik, 175; and the zero option, 307
Kohl-Gorbachev summit, 290
Kornblum, John, 288
Kreile, Michael, 251
Kreisky, Bruno, 148

Lemmer, Ernst, 13
Lintner, Eduard, 287, 298, 302
Lorenz, Peter, 226
Löwenthal, Richard, 142
Lower Saxony, 163, 250
Ludwigshafen conference, 176
Luxemburg, Rosa, 281

Mannheim Declaration, 155, 254
Marx, Werner, 99, 101, 243
Mauriac, François, 27
MBFR (Mutual and Balanced Force

Reduction), 145
Mertes, Alois, 158, 163, 174, 239; death of, 305; flexibility of, 258; and Ostpolitik synthesis, 268; and Polish diplomacy, 302
"Mitteldeutschland," 176
Mitteleuropa concept, 311–312
Moscow treaty, 76–79; American reaction, 76; Chinese reaction, 76; and the press, 76, 77, 78
Moscow-Warsaw talks: secrecy of, 73
Munich agreements (1938), 149
Mutual and Balanced Force Reduction (MBFR) Negotiations, 129, 140, 141, 174

NATO (North Atlantic Treaty Organization), 34; and Afghanistan crisis, 196, 199; and "bilateralism," 306; and Brandt government, 115; CDU/CSU support, 218; deterrence policy, 242; and INF deployment, 189–190, 289; and INF talks, 307; isolation of, 58; and nuclear arms, 37; nuclear deterrence strategy, 220; and Ostpolitik, 150; public opinion of, 220; supported by CDU/CSU, 227–228; undermined by SPD, 227
Nazism: legacy of, 13; and racism, 22
Nazi war crimes, 130, 132; in Czechoslovakia, 150
NDP (National Democratic party), 63
Negotiations: with the GDR, 68–70, 129; with Moscow and Poland, 71–74
Neo-Nazis: and reunification sentiment, 21
Neutralist forces, 60; in West Germany, 63, 330 n.4
Neutralization, 111, 114
Nixon, Richard, 58, 85; and Berlin settlement, 82, 98; policy on detente, 215
Nixon-Kissinger detente policy, 57
Nolte, Ernst, 305
NPT (Nuclear Non-Proliferation Treaty), 150, 325 n.18

Oder-Neisse line, 23, 31, 32; acceptance of, 47, 49, 64, 71; permanence of, 182, 245, 302; and Union reformists, 79
Olympic games boycott, 193, 194, 201
"Orders to shoot" policy, 68, 168, 226, 281, 287
Ostpolitik: and Afghanistan crisis, 193–203; bipartisanship, 256; CDU/CSU adaptation to, 7, 132–136; dangers of, 145–171; defined, 3; of Schroder, 46; and the SPD-FDP, 2; and the Sudetenland, 149–150; and trade, 4; Union attacks on, 148; Union interests in, 8; and Western observers, 8; and Westpolitik, 141

Pacta sunt servanda principle, 115, 127, 129, 208, 243
Palme, Olof, 148
Partition, 5, 153; management of, 304; provisionality of, 237
Poland: administration of Oder-Neisse line, 31; administration of Silesia, 23; "consensus" policy and, 80; ethnic Germans, 160, 181; and expellees, 72; and German reunification, 181; Jaruzelski regime, 224; labor unrest, 204; rapprochement with, 132; treaty protocol of 1970, 160; and Union Ostpolitik, 182; West German trade with, 45
"Policy of strength": and reunification, 38
Polish emigration protocol, 160;

ratification, 162
Polish-German package, 160–166; as "blackmail," 161
Polish martial law crackdown (1981), 222; Moscow blamed by Union, 223; suspension of German aid, 224
Polish reconciliation, 63, 65, 71–72, 161–163
Polish Solidarity crisis, 203–205
Polish treaty, 79–81
Pomerania, 23
Pompidou, Georges, 92
Potsdam accord (1945), 19, 36, 78; effect on European configuration, 37
"Potsdam complex," 24, 31, 33
Protestants: and atonement for war crimes, 132; church leaders, 163; laity, 132; in the north, 22; and Prussian militarism, 20

Rapallo treaty, 197
Reagan, Ronald, 215; distrusted by Germans, 216; and 1987 summit, 286; and Schmidt, 215
Reagan administration, 219
Realpolitik, 42
Rearmament, 32, 33
Reunification, 8, 33, 247, 313; and allied public opinion, 240; allied reservations, 241; and the balance of power, 28; and the Basic Treaty, 112, 113; and CDU activists, 277; CDU/CSU emphasis, 178; as closed topic, 240; deferred, 276; and detente, 48; and Deutschlandpolitik, 299; discouraged by SPD-FDP, 246; through European unity, 27; and the Four Powers, 132; and Geissler policy, 304; and *gesamtdeutsch*, 245; after 1982, 275; in opinion polls, 266; and Poland, 181; and Polish misgivings, 302; and rapprochement, 40; revived by Union, 308–309; and self-determination, 238; sentiment for in the GDR, 185; and the Soviets, 28–30; and Soviet Union, 48; and SPD-FDP, 237; versus cooperation, 248
Reunification-of-force accord, 71
Reykjavik summit of 1986, 290, 307; and inner-German relations, 290–291
Rhineland district, 20
Rhineland-Palatinate, 64, 98
"Rollback policy," 29, 37
"Room for maneuver," 313
Rühe, Volker: and "cooperative solution," 307; and German-Polish solidarity, 311
Rumania: formal diplomacy with, 48

Saarland, 163
Salt II (Strategic Arms Limitation Treaty), 189, 190
Schäuble, Wolfgang, 279, 299
Scheel, Walter, 57–58, 74, 151; improvements to Moscow treaty, 76, 78; letter on German unity, 95, 99
Schiller, Karl, 251
Schmidt, Helmut: and Afghanistan crisis, 194; and Jimmy Carter, 186, 335 n.29; and Jimmy Carter meeting, 201; and Giscard d'Estaing, 186; and military equilibrium, 187–188; and "protective fire" controversy, 170; rejection of Polish sanctions, 223; and status quo, 264; Westpolitik, 151
Schmidt-Honecker Moscow summit (1980), 200–201; and Jimmy Carter, 201; postponed, 204, 206; and Washington-Bonn rift, 203
Schmidt-Honecker summit (1981),

222
Scholz, Rupert, 299
Schröder, Gerhard, 41, 50, 66, 68, 74; hard-line position, 90; Ostpolitik of, 47, 159; and policy of movement, 41–47
Schumacher, Kurt, 14
Schwarz, Hans-Peter, 25, 29, 40
Schweigler, Gebhard, 6–7, 246, 248; definition of normalization, 245; on public view of status quo, 313
SED (East German Communist party) 56; insecurity of, 114, 143–144, 168–169
Silesia, 23
Sindermann, Horst, 280; and SPD invitation, 282
Sino-American rapprochement, 86
Social Democratic–Free Democratic coalition. See SPD-FDP
Social-Liberal coalition: and Berlin problem, 82; Union criticisms of, 73–74
Social-Liberal Ostpolitik, 59, 64, 66, 67–71; and American interference, 91–92; and Berlin, 84; foreign manipulation of, 110; popularity of, 69; under attack, 70, 73
Solidarity trade union, 204; and martial law, 222; as threat to communist rule, 206
So Nicht strategy, 91–94
Sonthofen conference, 133
Soviet bloc. See Eastern bloc
Soviet gas pipeline, 222; American pressure against, 222, 223; American sanctions against, 225; and CSU policy, 224
Soviet hegemony, 76, 128; Strauss and, 133; and Union fundamentalists, 157
Soviet Union: arms buildup, 114; and CDU/CSU, 92; and detente, 37, 56; expansionism, 141; and German unification, 20, 48; as "guarantor" of status quo, 75; hegemony, 59, 62; isolation of GDR, 291; manipulation/coercion, 114, 129–130; and Sino-American rapprochement, 86; Stalin leadership, 37; Union's distrust of, 60, 129
Späth, Lothar, 207–208, 219, 279
SPD (Social Democratic party), 6, 47–48, 57, 73, 249; and Afghanistan crisis, 194–195, 199; anti-Soviet sentiments of, 25; Chancellory study leak, 170; and East Berlin, 310; and East-West detente, 65; "inter-German peace order," 184; and Kohl government, 310; and nuclear disarmament, 187; Ostpolitik after 1982, 295; pressure for German-German dialogue, 213; and reunification, 21, 23, 56; and Soviet pressure, 189; and the status quo, 56; and Westpolitik, 242; youth wing, 148
SPD-FDP (1969) alliance, 249
SPD-FDP (Social Democratic–Free Democratic) coalition, 1, 239; bloc system consolidation, 236; foreign policy of, 8; and national reunification, 237; in popularity polls, 74; united by treaties, 249
SPD-FDP Ostpolitik, 62, 139; and bipartisan agreement, 228; criticized by Kohl, 204; dialogue with East bloc, 255; embraced by Union, 240, 243; intra-coalition stresses, 229; irreversibility of, 127–128; legacy of, 292; monopoly of, 255; "Ostpolitik II," 267; public opinion, 74, 244; and sense of resignation, 246; and the status quo, 240; Union characterizations of,

111; and West German assertiveness, 248
Spiegel affair, 43
SS-20's (Soviet intermediate-range nuclear missiles), 189
Stalin, Joseph, 34
Status quo. *See* European status quo
Stauffenberg, Claus von, 127
Stent, Angela, 251
Stoltenberg, Gerhard, 207
Stoph, Willi, 49, 68, 71
Strauss, Franz Josef, 38, 41, 49, 63, 68; and Afghan invasion, 200; agreement on continuity, 208; "Atlanticist" manifesto, 228; and Basic Treaty, 116; and Basic Treaty ruling, 119; in *Bayernkurier*, 118; in bipartisan talks, 102; and "Bonn-Paris front" against Washington, 202; against Brandt, 68; Brezhnev meeting, 182; and Jimmy Carter, 337 n.24; and credits to GDR, 285, 287; and CSU separation, 173; and a European state, 43; against Four Power accord, 86; "Gaulist" policy of, 43, 323 n.39; GDR recognition, 324 n.4; GDR visit of 1983, 279; and gesamtdeutsch, 42, 49; Gesamtpolitic defined, 203; and Grand Design, 42; as "hard-liner," 131; and Helsinki agreements, 162; and human rights, 140; Hungarian visit (1979), 335 n.26; and Joint Resolution, 104; Moscow visit of 1988, 286; and NATO, 336 n.13; Ostpolitik, 183; and *pacta sunt servanda* policy, 243; role in adaptive Ostpolitik, 259–260; and *So Nicht* strategy, 94–95; and trade sanctions, 202
Stresemann, Gustav, 295–296
Stürmer, Michael, 300

Supreme Court (at Karlsruhe): and foreign policy, 97. *See also* Karlsruhe decision
"Swing" credits, 206; linked to exchange rate, 211; and trade, 250

Teltschik, Horst, 279; on trade, 293
Times of London, 119
Trade unions, 65, 130
Trading patterns, 4
Trading policies: with Eastern bloc, 44–46
Traffic treaty, 243
Treaty debates (1969–1972), 239

Ulbricht, Walter, 56, 59; compared with Hitler, 70; ousted by Moscow, 86
Unification. *See* Reunification
Unified European State, 42
Union Deutschlandpolitik, 24, 27, 29; and the German question, 238
Union fundamentalists, 139, 147–148, 332 n.27; and Basic Treaty, 114; and citizenship question, 138; and the Eastern treaties, 90; election successes, 154; fears of detente, 154; and the German question, 238; and leftist radicals, 96–97; after 1973, 127–130; and party Ostpolitik, 176; resigned to GDR, 129; and Soviet hegemonialism, 157; and SPD-FDP Ostpolitik, 140
Union Gaullist faction, 63, 239
Union Gesamtpolitik: Afghanistan response, 198–203; and Hans Genscher, 230
Union "Godesberg," 207
Union orthodoxy: and the Eastern bloc, 166; and Helmut Kohl, 136; and negotiation strategy, 139; and Polish treaty, 164; and pub-

lic fundamentalism, 176–177; and Schmidt's Ostpolitik, 185; Soviet concern over, 167

Union Ostpolitik, 66; acceptance of SPD-FDP policies, 177; ambivalence of, 136; arms policy crisis, 221; and Berlin, 242; bipartisanship, 209; and Eastern contacts, 208; and Hans-Dietrich Genscher, 229; and Johann Gradl, 180; Hamburg conference (1981), 220; and human rights, 64; and INF deployment, 216; juridical claims of, 61–62, 67, 129; and Helmut Kohl, 175; and NATO deterrence, 242; and nuclear protesters, 218; in opposition, 127; and Poland, 182; toward Poland and USSR, 181–184; private talks with SED, 226; and Reagan administration, 215–218; shifts in emphasis, 178; softening toward GDR, 226; strategy debates, 89–97; and youth groups, 219, 220

Union reformists: and Basic Treaty, 113, 114; and the Oder-Neisse line, 79; perceptions of detente, 131–132

Union Westpolitik, 238–241; objectives, 24, 27

United States, 8; and allies' interests, 37; and CDU/CSU ties, 239; conflict over Ostpolitik, 288; and European disengagement, 263; as Europe's "guarantor," 18–19, 186; and FRG Ostpolitik, 76; and German neutrality, 328 n.45; and Moscow/Warsaw sanctions, 223; and neutron weapons (ERW) deployment, 188–199; "new look" nuclear strategy, 38; nuclear monopoly of, 37; nuclear relationship with FRG, 191; post-Vietnam malaise, 198;

pressure on Union, 239; reaction to Moscow treaty, 76; Union assertiveness toward, 271

U.S.-Soviet relations: Afghanistan crisis, 198–203; tensions (of 1973–1974), 131

Vienna Diplomatic convention, 138
Vogel, Bernhard, 207

Wallmann, Walter, 217
Wehner, Herbert, 55, 73, 103, 143; on Deutschlandpolitik, 187; fundamentalists' condemnation of, 148; and GDR insecurities, 146
Weimar era, 22; revanchism, 74
Weizsäcker, Ernst von, 65
Weizsäcker, Richard von, 65, 74, 78; on American trade sanctions, 225; and the Eastern treaties, 90; and German guilt, 305; and German unity, 107; and liberal coalitions, 250; mayor of West Berlin, 212; and the Oder-Neisse line, 79; and Ostpolitik synthesis, 268; self-determination strategy, 138; and Union Westpolitik, 213
West Berlin, 46, 82–85; crisis (1961), 82; and detente, 83; as part of FGR, 84; Soviet consulate in, 86; as "third state," 87
Western occupation authority, 32
West Germany: foreign policy of, 6; split electorate, 297. See also FRG
Westpolitik: of Adenauer, 19; and isolation fears, 239; and Ostpolitik, 141, 321 n.8
Wilms, Dorothee, 281, 303
Windelen, Heinrich, 287, 292, 296; on East Berlin trade credit, 289–290; minister for inner-

German affairs, 297–298
Wissman, Matthias, 219
Wörner, 216, 217
Wrangel, Olaf von, 159, 168, 206

Yugoslavia: formal diplomacy with, 48

Zero-option clause, 291, 307
Zimmermann, Fritz, 207

Clay Clemens is assistant professor of government at the College of William and Mary.